Sideways Selves

Latinx: The Future Is Now

A series edited by Lorgia García-Peña and Nicole Guidotti-Hernández

Books in the series

Sideways Selves

Travesti and Jotería Struggles
Across the Américas

PJ DIPIETRO

University of Texas Press ❦ *Austin*

Portions of chapter 1 are drawn from Pedro Jose Javier DiPietro, "Decolonizing Travesti Space in Buenos Aires: Race, Sexuality, and Sideways Relationality," *Gender, Place and Culture* 23, no. 5 (2015): 677–693. https://doi.org/10.1080/09663 69X.2015.1058756.

Portions of the section in chapter 2 titled "Realism, Embodiment, and Ontological Pluralism" were originally published in "'I Look Too Good Not to Be Seen': Multiple Meaning Realism and Sociosomatics," in *Trans Philosophy*, edited by Perry Zurn, Andrea J. Pitts, Talia Mae Bettcher, and PJ DiPietro (University of Minnesota Press, 2024, 99–120). Copyright 2024 by the Regents of the University of Minnesota. Used by permission.

Portions of chapter 4 were first published in "Hallucinating Knowing: (Extra) ordinary Consciousness, More-Than-Human Perception, and Other Decolonizing *Remedios* within Latina and Xicana Feminist Theories," in *Theories of the Flesh: Latinx and Latin American Feminisms, Transformation, and Resistance*, edited by Andrea J. Pitts, Mariana Ortega, and José M. Medina (Oxford University Press, 2020, 220–236). https://doi.org/10.1093/oso/9780190062965.003.0014.

Library of Congress Cataloging-in-Publication Data

Names: DiPietro, PJ, author.
Title: Sideways selves : travesti and jotería struggles across the Américas / PJ DiPietro.
Description: First edition. | Austin : University of Texas Press, 2025. | Series: Latinx: the future is now | Includes bibliographical references and index.
Identifiers: LCCN 2024047392 (print) | LCCN 2024047393 (ebook)
   ISBN 978-1-4773-3176-7 (hardcover)
   ISBN 978-1-4773-3177-4 (paperback)
   ISBN 978-1-4773-3178-1 (pdf)
   ISBN 978-1-4773-3179-8 (epub)
Subjects: LCSH: Gender nonconformity—Argentina—Buenos Aires. | Indigenous peoples—Argentina—Buenos Aires. | Black people—Argentina—Buenos Aires. | Sexual minorities—Argentina—Buenos Aires. | Gender nonconformity— California—San Francisco Bay. | Indians of Mexico—California—San Francisco Bay. | Nahuas—California—San Francisco Bay. | Indians of Central America— California—San Francisco Bay. | Quiché Indians—California—San Francisco Bay. | Black people—California—San Francisco Bay. | Sexual minorities— California—San Francisco Bay. | Marginality, Social. | Oppression (Psychology) | Intersectionality (Sociology)
Classification: LCC HQ73.8 .D57 2025 (print) | LCC HQ73.8 (ebook) | DDC 306.76/8097946—dc23/eng/20250203
LC record available at https://lccn.loc.gov/2024047392
LC ebook record available at https://lccn.loc.gov/2024047393

doi:10.7560/331767

To those who are no longer here because we didn't yet know how to be there. Your lives have not been forgotten.

Contents

Sideways Selves

Introduction

A paradigmatic shift informs my engagement with the mysteries of embodied differences. Capitalist expansion worldwide introduced the human/nonhuman distinction over five hundred years ago. This distinction classifies and regulates various bodily projects. Colonized communities were reduced to beasts and had their spiritual understanding of nature destroyed and their bodies rendered genderless. At the turn of this millennium, resistant responses to this colonial organization of life endure. I place myself within a radical social of racialized gender nonconforming communities. From within these margins, I learn to witness subaltern, Indigenous, and Afro-diasporic systems of knowledge, for they underwrite dissenting, perhaps decolonizing, spatial practices, bodily habits, and cultural artifacts. Together, these systems give rise to dissenting sideways selves.

Sideways Selves: Travesti and Jotería Struggles Across the Américas examines two populations linked to the colonial history of the Afro-Latinx, Latinx, and Latin Americas, critically comparing networks of racialized Indigenous *travestis* from the Andes to networks of queer and trans Afro-Latinx and Latinx performers from the San Francisco Bay Area. This comparison builds on their shared condition as exiles into the social space of displacement, from the Aymara Andean context to Buenos Aires and from K'iche' and Nahua regions to California. The main goal of *Sideways Selves* is to weave together Latin American travesti/trans theorizing and *jotería* studies.[1] Both are sites of knowledge and practice that, emerging from within gender nonconforming communities, seek to (1) identify the colonial roots of domination and control over gender; (2) explain the link between domination, control, and global as well as national forms of LGBTQ+ inclusion; and (3) query anti-colonial and decolonial alternatives to those colonial forms of domination, control, and inclusion.

1

Each chapter centers ways of living, knowing, and feeling against but also beyond the legacy of colonial gender: *transversalidad, nostredad* or *weness*, shape-shifting "genders," *loísmo*, hallucinating knowing, and jotería poetics. Combined, they illuminate nonconforming bodily projects that I call *sideways selves*. In pursuing their material manifestation, I cultivate accountability as co-interlocutor and critical listener. Within communities of practice and resistance, I theorize the role that sideways selves play in (1) the emergence of anti-capitalist and anti-colonial geographies, (2) the recalibration of the body's impressible responsiveness as it decenters the coloniality of transgender, and (3) the regeneration of Native, Indigenous, and Afro-diasporic systems of knowledge as they underwrite sacred and decolonizing bodily projects.

The voices that I project throughout this sideways journey owe their texture to the radical social body of travesti activists and sex workers, as well as jotería, queer, nonbinary, and trans people of color, especially Afro-Latinx and Latinx. I engage the ways that these marginalized communities and individuals experience and understand systems of power, among them dispossession, precarity, and necropolitics, and how they think and theorize about them while envisioning and practicing resistance to multiple oppressions. Above all, I remain in awe of their resourcefulness as they face, counter, and turn away from globally interconnected heterosexualism, homonationalism, and transnormativity.

Sideways selves examine the traces of colonialism and racialization within their communities. They explore and reflect on the sociosomatic endeavor of crafting bodies that deflate, decenter, and reject the coloniality of transgender. In so doing, they foreground resistant responses to former and current forms of violence, including physical, social, spatial, and epistemic violence. Because colonial power and its modern and nationalist expressions often treat sideways selves as aberrant, perverse, and stagnant in evolutionary time, sideways selves decode and deflect the varying configurations of the genre of the human. They pursue, sometimes erratically and at other times relentlessly, a novel version of materialism. They seek to bring about community, not of the same gender or sexual identity, or other fragments of sameness, but rather of plurality, multiplicity, and variability. Sideways selves activate realities where an individual is not the center. They point beyond an ableist fiction of self-realization and self-definition and, instead, foreground traces of nostredad, *weness*, transversalidad, and jotería in the palimpsest of subaltern, Indigenous, and Afro-diasporic systems of knowledge and lifeways.

Sideways selves envision a politics of transversalidad and *weness*, which serves as a lens for understanding and engaging with the impact of racializing global capitalism. This transversal approach fosters a reconfiguration of knowledge about realities and embodiments in transition. Facing dispossession, they give rise to multiple against-the-grain subjectivities, where "collateral" reflects both a sideways orientation toward those beside us and the cooperation that sustains it.

Working and co-learning with sideways selves, I draw on critical methodologies that challenge the theory/practice divide. Kindred to the late María Lugones's rendering of praxical thinking, sideways selves refashion an ethics of mutual care. They intervene in the disputes about what it means to know, who gets to know what about whom, and for what purpose knowledge is produced. Centering justice, I attempt an engagement *with* intercultural, transnational, intersectional, anti-racist, and activist scholarship methods. Through this critical stance, I contend with settler logics and histories, working across autoethnography, discourse analysis, linguistics, human geography, and philosophy.

Creating space for co-interlocution across Latin American travesti/trans theorizing and jotería studies, I work on unpacking political, epistemic, and experiential practices through which sideways selves foster dissident competence against and beyond white-centered projects of hetero-, homo-, and transnormative exigencies. The chapters gravitate toward five of their paradigmatic contributions. Chapter 1 pursues the study of transversalidad within travesti intellectual activism, and its resonances with the notion of nostredad or *we*ness within jotería collectives. Sideways selves emerge as a hemispheric way of living, knowing, and enacting noncomforming bodily projects underwritten by transversalidad and nostredad. In chapter 2, I develop two theoreticopractical methods of inquiry. I examine philosophical reflections about the *matter* of nonconforming embodiments, witnessing the sociosomatic responsiveness of sideways selves and their labor against eugenicist, white supremacist, deadening, and carceral LGBTQ+ geographies. Through this act of witnessing and interpreting, I outline the *coloniality of transgender* framework with the purpose of giving uptake to what I call "genders" (in quotation marks, in lower case, and in plural), an enigmatic and decolonial sociosomatic formation whose impressible habits point beyond the nuclear family and its colonizing legacy. Sideways selves are theoretically, experientially, and politically intertwined with "genders."

A vibrant repository of technologies to de-stress and deflate *gendered* realities occupies the main concerns of chapter 3. I follow these technologies within Andean and Mesoamerican Catholicism as well as in the

Spanish of Andean and Mesoamerican speakers. They show that the practice of *unlistening to Gender* reveals sacred and Indigenous arrangements of life-germination. This bud of germination lies at the heart of sideways selves and their bodily projects. Chapter 4 focuses on Afro-Latinx and Latinx narratives and performance arts as they foreground *hallucinating knowing*. Diving into the twilight terrain of trauma and decolonization, performance work transforms secularizing, heterosexualizing, and debilitating genres of the human into actionable hallucinations that heal and repair the soul, body, mind of sideways selves. Finally, chapter 5 explores jotería poetics as a diasporic and hemispheric method of perception and communication aimed at fostering coalitional politics. Jotería is often defined as an identity category for individuals of Chicana/o or Mexicana/o heritage involved in dissenting gender and sexuality practices. Michael Hames-García (2014, 139) argues that it transcends identity, for jotería entails both a social process and cultural practice. It extends beyond Eurocentric terms like *queer* or *gay*. By engaging Maya Chinchilla's poetry, chapter 5 resonates with jotería's sensorium for discerning and enacting creative practices. In this sensorium, I examine the significance of collective affects for intergenerational struggles about revolution, solidarity, and language. Chinchilla's poetry and spoken word highlight diasporic sound, dissonance, and resonance and their connections to not only Central America's volcanoes but also Abya Yala's hemispheric epicenters.

In the afterword, I ask that you witness an intimate gathering. I write a letter to my late Mom and Dad. This letter seeks to have us dwell in that enigmatic and often mysterious site of sacred and ancestral residence. What feels like kindred affects to the reader, my parents and I only earned by loving each other well. I cannot assume too much about the orientations and longings that Mom and Dad would cultivate were they still on this Earth. However, as I mention in the afterword, I have taken their lives seriously, witnessing over decades the dazzling flight of their own hummingbird-like wingbeats. You may choose to encounter this offering that we call *book* by beginning with its tail, with the afterword. You shall learn that their kinship, not blood quantum, provides inspiration for the acts of creation that *Sideways Selves* required. I shall be grateful to you for repositioning and adjusting these acts whenever necessary, for being gentle with and forgiving of my shortcomings, and for witnessing, joining in, and encountering, hopefully with astonishment, the twilight, hallucination, and portal that sideways selves promise to us.

CHAPTER 1

Sideways Selves, *Realidades Atravesadas*

Hemispheric Exiles

In December 2002, Buenos Aires passed a civil union bill, signaling its emergence as one of the leading destinations for global and affluent gay travelers. Meanwhile, various cultural industries portrayed Jujuy and Salta, the country's northernmost states, as getaways to an untouched and Indigenous past. Such global marketing strategies targeting the LGBTQ+ community intertwine narratives of sexuality, gender, and race, often juxtaposing representations of gayness and Indigeneity. These narratives also explore how peoples, identities, and communities, including those structured by racist, ableist, and heterocissexist discrimination, partake in mapping operations. In discerning these operations, I examine these narratives and their shaping of homonormative and transnormative histories, spaces, and conflicts. By enacting a decolonial shift, I contend with mapping operations by focusing on the significance that embodiments have in both solidifying and contesting the colonial underpinnings of LGBTQA+ cultures.[1]

In the last twenty years, *travesti*, trans, and other gender nonconforming populations have gained more visibility within the country's LGBTQ+ community. Yet, they still occupy a marginal place in a burgeoning geography of ornamental inclusion. Moreover, a large swatch of the travesti population in the city of Buenos Aires hails from the states of Jujuy and Salta, the Andean and peripheral northwest. Spatial marginalization shapes the lives of self-identified travesti people and many others who signify their subjectivities in opposition to norms about not only heterosexuality but also homosexuality and transgenderism. What these

5

marginalized subjectivities have in common is their condition as exiles. They are displaced peoples from the Andean and subtropical contexts of the northwest to Buenos Aires. Structural inequalities follow them across this journey of displacement, survival, and, many times, political awareness. This outsider condition, which manifests in claims to socioeconomic integration, challenges available signifiers of modern sexual identity. Indeed, these individuals' marginalization as internal exiles stands in contrast to the prevailing tolerance-driven trends within neoliberal arenas concerning LGBTQ+ identities.[2]

By actively listening to this outsider condition, I seek to unpack political and epistemic practices among a racially marginalized travesti population in the city of Buenos Aires. They enact dissident competence against and beyond white-centered projects of hetero-, homo-, and transnormative exigencies. Three discussions contribute to my analysis: (1) transnational reflexivity and its shaping of white-centered projects of homo- and transnormativity, (2) the racialization of travesti individuals as nonwhite by the Latin American nation-state, and (3) the notion of *sideways relationality*, which is a neologism that I introduce to interpret the ways that travesti collectives recalibrate identities and knowledge through a decolonial stance. Moreover, adopting a critical, transnational, and decolonial stance allows me to highlight the foundations of Latin American travesti theorizing and its hemispheric affinity with jotería studies. The latter, rooted in that elusive geography that we call the United States, has established lineages of intersectional and transnational reflection that rigorously examine nonnormative practices and experiences. This labor grounds the decolonizing feminist praxis of Xicana/o/x as well as Afro-Latina/o/x/e and Latina/o/x/e individuals and collectives alike.[3]

Hemispheric resonance between travesti and jotería modes of being illuminates crucial nonconforming bodily projects. In the nonconforming domain of flesh, travesti and jotería projects foreground Indigenous and Native ways of knowing and living. Often othered and excluded, Aymara, Quechua, Kichwa, Maya K'iche', Nahua, and Afro-diasporic lifeways persist, as this chapter shows, in their underwriting of sideways selves. It is their underwriting of travesti and jotería identity and selfhood that leads my engagement with the social production of bodily projects. Tracking the ways that they point beyond colonial legacies, I shall approach these bodily projects with a hemispheric scope, which seeks to chart both broad and localized linkages across the continent.

Mapping Others

In June 2008, four large-scale vinyl panels promoting my native state of Jujuy dressed the famous Avenida 9 de Julio of the city of Buenos Aires (CABA from now on). This avenue is the centerfold of CABA's cosmopolitan landscape. The marketing campaign launched by Jujuy's secretary of tourism underscores the appeal of the state as a travel destination. The panels highlight its four tourism circuits, which represent major focal points targeting both domestic and international visitors. Since the turn of the millennium, state agencies have promoted Jujuy as an ecological sanctuary for its combination of high-altitude plateau, valley, mountain, and jungle. Hailing from Jujuy myself, I reflect on the monumentality of the display. I point out the distance that tourism's marketing delineates between cosmopolitan areas such as Buenos Aires and the Andean northwest. While CABA positions itself as a gay-friendly destination, Jujuy markets itself as a haven for biodiversity and ancient Indigenous culture.

I came of age in Jujuy during the 1990s, a period in which racial, class, and gender politics in the region shaped my subjectivity. These dynamics propelled me into a whitened network of lesbian and gay individuals who share middle-class aspirations. Through my political work with travesti collectives, I learned that their subjectivities don't resonate with either racial whitening or middle-class aspirations. Instead, I came to understand that the term *travesti* signifies both a personal act of self-definition and the collective struggle to embody social resistance. I locate myself within these negotiations. However, I remain mindful of the stark differences related to bodily autonomy that are specific to travesti social formation. Given these particularities, I prefer to keep the term *travesti* in its original Spanish form, even when referring to the plural noun *travestis*.

The modernizing boundary between flatlands, where Buenos Aires is located, and the Andean northwest continues the legacy of colonialism under the civilization/barbarism divide.[4] Within this legacy, CABA figures prominently as the beacon of future liberation from homo- and queerphobia. I have shared many a conversation with friends, acquaintances, and activists who identify as lesbian or gay and for whom CABA represents a land of freedom to aspire to but not quite ever reach. Getting closer to networks of travestis who come from the northwest continues to teach me, instead, that the transition from the Andes to CABA remains quite perilous. With mainstream culture often glossing Jujuy as *indian* and *primitive*, a eugenicist project of nation-building undermines the promise of a cosmopolitan future. Tourism marketing in the age of social media and globe-trotting sharpens the parochial lure of the Andean northwest and the worldly flavor of Buenos Aires. These representations of space are at play in broader neoliberal configurations of difference worldwide. Thus, exploring these contradictions surveys spatiotemporal domains of homonormative and transnormative citizenship and its hemispheric ties to colonial power.

Various scholars and activists examine the collusion between nationalist and imperial projects of racial othering with the depoliticization of nonnormative sexual culture through domesticity and consumption (Puar 2007, 38–39; Duggan 2003; Sabsay 2011; J. Muñoz 1999; Bacchetta and Haritaworn 2011; and Bacchetta, El-Tayeb, and Haritaworn 2018). Jasbir Puar argues that homonationalism documents "the process of discerning" perverse figures of racial and sexual others and their power to rehabilitate conforming gays and queer subjects (2007, 38). My analysis of homonormativity and transnormativity seeks to explain the polycentric nature of globalizing norms about embodiment under colonialism's legacy. From within a radical social, I seek to chart nationalism's dominant reflexivities and the ways that they circulate across LGBTQA+ arenas. Among these arenas, this chapter investigates the increasing alignment of nationalism and transgender bodily projects. There are outsider positions across these arenas, such as Latin American travesti theorizing and jotería studies. They both grapple with narratives of ethnic, racial, and gender othering while contesting nation-state-building practices.

Marginal in the geography of homo- and transnationalism, travesti collectives perform an epistemic and political shift. They expose heteronormativity and heterosexualism but also the dehumanizing features of transgender bodily projects. According to travestis' stance as displaced peoples, heterosexualism and homo- and transnationalism engineer processes in which whiteness regulates bodies, desires, and citizenship status (Collins 2004; Ferguson 2004; Ward and B. Schneider, 2009). María Lugones offers a similar argument by expanding on the colonial roots of heterosexualist exigencies (2007). Her *coloniality of gender* framework goes beyond linking whiteness to capitalist arrangements about sexual reproduction. It underscores that the material oppression of colonial subjects—enslaved populations and indentured servants—relied on their cognitive, bodily, and cultural reduction to the condition of nonhumans. As we shall see, travestis' political dispositions tap into long-standing repositories, which they cultivate from within experiences of nonhuman liminality.[5]

Lugones's work also makes room to examine resistant and collective bodily projects. I join her work by contesting the pitfalls of white-stream feminist, trans, and queer studies.[6] Defying political and experiential invisibility, travesti reflexivity illuminates a labor that, I shall argue, offers novel antidotes against homo- and transnormative inclusion. In the analysis of post-oppositional bodily projects that follows, I submit that Latin American travesti theorizing and jotería studies contribute to vibrant genealogies of epistemic and political demarginalization, such as women of color feminism (Dotson 2014; Sealey 2020), queer of color critique (Johnson and Henderson 2005; Miranda 2002; Hames-García and Martinez 2011; La Fountain–Stokes 2014), and Abya Yala's feminism in Latin America and the Caribbean (Curiel 2007; Gargallo 2013; Viveros Vigoya 2016; Bidaseca 2018a; Zambrana 2021).

Homonormative Counterpublics and Oppositional Space

Reflexivity involves circulation of social asymmetries through discourse. As Michael Warner observes, this circulation calls publics into existence through "infinite axes of citation and characterization" (2005, 91). Publics entail communicative competence in not only acknowledging an almost anonymous quality of a particular public but also anticipating its potential for self-awareness. Social subjects acquire this competence by partaking in cross-citation and decoding, identifying with, anticipating, and altering meaning. Ongoing contestation mediates circuit-like relations between reflexivity and subjectivity. Contestation underwrites processes of self- and collective examination (Domingues 1995; Giddens 1991; Brooks 2005). Through asymmetrical literacies of self-reflection, we become constituents of the public sphere and its antagonisms. Reflexivity is thereby entrenched in the mutual determination of power axes and their shaping of race, gender, sexuality, disability, class, and property relations.

Public reflexivity takes place within the domain of the ruling gaze. Counterpublics, instead, are shaped within parallel arenas wherein subordinated groups access oppositional interpretations of their identities and aspirations (Mansbridge 1996; Fraser 1997; Price 2012; Jones 2020). Like the LGBTQA+ movements that strategically utilize these arenas to circulate counterdiscourse, alternative publics contest the conditions under which the mainstream denies authority, credibility, and circulation to nondominant reflexivity (Felski 1989; Friedman 2017). As theorists of resistance highlight, appealing to dominant reflexivity can limit the potency of counterpublic force (Kelley 1992; Lugones 2000; Scott 1990). That is, when counterpublics approach the mainstream, they bind their negotiations to the ruling mode of communication that dominates *onstage*. Through this public-facing orientation, counterpublics appeal to transcripts in which ruling publics deliver performances of mastery for the impression they seek to make on subordinates (Scott 1990, 49).

Consider the restrictions that LGBTQ+ counterpublics encounter when they communicate with ruling publics through tourism campaigns. Targeting global gay markets, these campaigns operate onstage and, as expected, offer channels for LGBTQ+ counterpublics to contest pathologizing reflexivity. A conservative and biologicist medical establishment is a ruling public. It primarily seeks to make an impression on the wider mainstream. LGBTQ+ tourism instead extends the public sphere to historically marginalized reflexivity. As they challenge, for example, the medical establishment, LGBTQ+ counterpublics must engage mainstream criteria about credibility and legitimacy. Given the history of medicalization, counterpublic discourse seeks to depathologize LGBTQ+ identities and experiences.

There are additional forms of subordinate discourse, including those that remain offstage within "sequestered social sites" (Scott 1990, 20). They provide "hidden transcripts," which oppose both onstage reflexivity and other areas of consent where publics and counterpublics meet (Scott 1990, 183–201). Hidden transcripts mobilize dissent below the public competence displayed onstage. Dissent is a way of rehearsing resistant and oppositional counterstrikes. As I witness radical bodily projects among travesti and jotería collectives, I trace our dissenting gestures toward tolerance-driven mainstream publics, on one end, and toward homo- and transnormative counterpublics, on the other.

Joshua Price adds nuance to our account of counterpublics and the outlets that they open for marginalized individuals and collectives. Price intervenes as a "critical listener" in transdisciplinary and nondisciplinary collaborations alongside marginalized groups, such as cisgender women who practice sex work, and currently and formerly incarcerated individuals (2012, 2015). Critical listening allows him to recognize "speech at the margins" and its use of various rhetorical orientations (2012, 65). Counterpublics, he argues, operate as strategies of communication, expressing differing degrees of autonomy and purpose. Typically, they give uptake to claims put forth by marginal subjects based on (1) either *commonality* of experience, identity, or politics (2012, 67–68) or (2) *difference among their differences* (68). Furthermore, Price's critical listening unveils a paradox within counterpublicity: it both validates and constrains resistant reflexivity and counterhegemonic rehearsal. To notice and gain fluency in the value of difference among differences, subaltern collectives may employ strategies, tactics, and other arts of offstage rather than counterpublic reflexivity.

As a non-Dalit feminist scholar and activist, Himika Bhattacharya facilitates, performs, and partakes in storytelling among Dalit and non-Dalit women from the Adivasi community of Lahaul, India (2017). Her critical listening and witnessing practices center women's lives through oral and textual histories as they narrate love against and despite compound realities of tribe, caste, and violence (11, 15, 36). Bhattacharya also captures the ways of being, doing, and knowing that point beyond the public/counterpublic dynamic. As co-interlocutors, Dalit and non-Dalit women from the Adivasi community, together with Bhattacharya, perform theory against "colonialist ideologies behind knowledge production practices" (11). These ideologies often create an expectation for counterpublics to become legible to the post-colonial mainstream.

Among other narratives against caste and its violence, Bhattacharya tells the story of Kavita, who wavers as she considers the thorny possibility of breaking her silence about sexual violence, which she experienced firsthand (2017, 80–81). Kavita encountered caste domination in the most brutal way, rape, at the hands of a caste-privileged priest.[7] As she wavers, she remembers to negotiate degrees of agentic intentions. A will to remember, Bhattacharya argues, sustains Kavita's resistance against various social forms of silencing and distortion: institutional and state-sanctioned backlash, uncertainty about her community's response, and fear of the consequences for her daughters, to name just a few. Kavita and Bhattacharya enact storied lives, engaging co-interlocution, rejecting an ethnographic gaze, and reaching way beyond self/other and mainstream/counterpublic dyads. Their praxes of critical listening, co-interlocution in storytelling, and faithful witnessing advance effervescent insights that fall beneath the counterpublic appeals to intelligibility.

Introducing sideways selves as ways of being and knowing, I draw out insights from both travesti and jotería collectives. Sideways selves orientate resistance beyond counterhegemony and opposition. In that sense, they point to post-oppositional meaning-making and practices. They craft unprecedented and liminal standpoints that counterpublics cannot fully account for. I turn to Susy Shock's performance work to exemplify this shift in post-oppositional orientations.

Shock's family hails from peri-urban realities in Tucumán, another northwestern state in Argentina. She is currently a resident of CABA. In her *Poemario Trans Pirado* (2011), the artist rejects the idea that *trans* or *travesti* should only be defined as a personal attribute. She opposes the idea that travesti is a quality inherently attached to a person. Shock enacts ways of collectively intervening in the formation of a travesti stance. A case in point is one of her performances at Casa Brandon, a "queer" culture club in CABA's Villa Crespo quarter. Shock repurposes the staircase within Casa Brandon's performance venue, ingeniously connecting the ground floor with the area designated for the seated audience at the rear of the room. Positioned opposite the stage, Shock urges attendees to join in a collective act of singing as a prelude to her captivating burlesque performance. Her emphasis lies in the power of harmonizing, fostering a sense of dispersed unity among the audience. She asserts that within the shared experience of singing, every voice finds its place and no one feels out of tune. Her love for harmonizing embraces individual nuances in each participant's vocal texture, emphasizing the distinctive qualities that make each voice unique. Yet, it is important to acknowledge that in harmonizing lies the opportunity for each voice to show new dimensions.

Shock's style has an outward oppositional orientation. She doesn't take queerness for granted, nor does she assume that it lives in the counterpublic force of shared oppression. If the audience stays close to her dissenting style, they get sucked in by the show's chronicling genre. Themes, characters, and choreographies foreground sensual appeals to multiplicity, of differences among differences. Susy's burlesque encounters Casa Brandon at the outskirts of its own sense of queer culture. In an interview with *Soy* (Tauil 2009), she helps us think about multiplicity of nonconforming and oppositional meaning by turning to the visual of a hummingbird. She likens this acrobatic bird to her state of germination or stasis. Her hummingbird grows breasts, expressing that nonnormative metamorphosis belongs to both human and nonhuman embodiments. Rather than aligning herself with the medicalized concept of transitioning, she metaphorically takes flight, her wings beating at astonishing speed. The bird's winged pace reshapes perception, leading us to question what can and cannot be sensed about the material world.[8] The motion of hummingbirds' wings illustrates the fluidity of matter, constantly shifting between states of passivity and activity. It seems to hang in the air, defying gravity's pull as it hovers, alluding to an ongoing journey of transformation.

Susy seems to graph the hummingbird into existence by calling attention to its flapping wings. Hummingbirds' wingbeat is dazzling and iridescent. Because they reach up to seventy wing flaps per second, hummingbirds create an identifiable humming sound but also an illusion of stasis. Their hovering flight mode makes them look suspended in air. Susy's hummingbird delivers visual dissemblance, making something pass for another, which can be seen as an emphasis on the idea that meanings often contain underlying, oppositional forces, even if they remain concealed or less apparent. There is no doubt that in the twenty-first century, trans encounters its counterpublic interlocutors, but, in the graph of the hummingbird who sweats and grows breasts, Susy seeks a differential, post-oppositional, attention. She steers our attention to embodiment and its brooding stasis. It is in the praxis of differential attention that critical listening, co-interlocution, storytelling, and faithful witnessing arise as decolonizing modes of knowledge production.[9]

Susy more pointedly gestures beyond counterpublic dissent with the title of the performance, *Poemario Trans Pirado*. A *poemario* consists of a collection of poems or expressions that encode forms provoking our senses. The term *trans* indicates the rise of critical awareness about bodies that challenge a biologically determined two-sex model.[10] *Pirado* is a word with caló roots originating with the verb *pirar* or *pirarse*, which means "to flee" or "run away." *Pirado* also stands for a state of mental distress or insanity, working within the semantic field of those who flee ordinary consciousness. The juxtaposition of both words, *trans* and *pirado*, underscores the marginal place that post-oppositional bodily projects occupy. They are not easily legible within sexual dimorphism. Counterpublics allow for such critique of mainstream discourse. In addition to this counterpublic signifying level, the juxtaposed words may mobilize hidden meanings and practices, such as the homonym *transpirado*. The verb for sweating in Spanish is *transpirar*. An audience fluent in hidden transcripts could pick up on the quirky play expressed in both words, *trans* and *pirar*. In its participle form, *transpirado* signals the stasis of metamorphosis, a stationary withdrawing or recoiling, a dormant peak right after the eruption of physical or psychological intensity. For its several meanings, *transpirado* hints at the laborious yet covert process of creation that Susy's performance documents. Crafting a new form as her dwelling remits precisely to the bewildering and mysterious experience of poetry as creation. By qualifying her poemario as transpirado, Susy calls attention to at least two types of bodily provocations: a body that labors its form to the point of great energetic release, and a body whose energetic release modifies matter to the point that it flees its current form.

Shock's poemario participates in the unmooring of matter from human form. Her poemario trespasses on counterpublic meaning about materialism and nonconformity. She breaks down the border between animal and nonanimal bodies by acknowledging that hummingbirds breed transing realities. In addition to hummingbirds, she also declares "loving butterflies" as dwelling sites for trans matter (2011). Birds and insects, I posit, punctuate nonconforming metamorphosis as more than a distinctively human experience. In fact, as philosopher Cynthia Willett (2014) argues, biosocial meaning and engagement establish various relationships of cooperation, symbiosis, and even animosity across a range of species (133–134). All three modalities of coupling across species give rise to material, social, affective, and emotional ties, out of which novel dissident embodiments arise. Moreover, Willett suggests that "gut-or brain-based affects and emotions [. . .] open creatures from the inside out to layers of sense in the world and of the world" (134). Shock's imaginary about bodily matter parallels Willett's undertaking. She foregrounds how interdependence, human and nonhuman animal agency, and intertwined fate codetermine the ways *we* coinhabit both the lived environment and our own bodily projects. In the analysis of travestis' practices that follows, travestis too call upon connectivity in its most material manifestation, both spatial and temporal, at once realist and constructivist, and often resonating with human and more-than-human forms.

Commodifying racial Others/Cleansing gender Others

Henri Lefebvre's work places the body, and its habitat, at the center of material production. A triadic concept of space, which comprises the conceived, perceived, and lived dimensions, unveils its social origins (1991). A half-hour drive from Buenos Aires's Ezeiza International Airport to Barrio Norte sheds light on each of these coexisting spatial folds. First, dominant representations of the northwest and Buenos Aires exemplify how experts conceive space. Second, intricate movements of labor and finance within a global city illuminate the dimension of perceived space. Additionally, myriad narratives and experiences woven by the city's inhabitants exemplify the lived realm of social practice.[11]

The specificity of travestis' spatial practice harbors an unprecedented politics of knowing. Undoubtedly it builds on the spatial analytics of gay and lesbian studies and queer studies. Yet, it also spearheads the critique of this analytics, contributing to the development of trans geographies and, thusly, crossing methodological boundaries imposed by binaries such as hetero/homo, gay/queer, and sex/gender (Browne, Nash, and Hines 2010). In travesti spatial theorizing, we shall find contingent configurations that foreground inquiries about relational embodiments and their sociohistorical, temporal formation. Systemic violence inflicted upon travesti individuals undergirds their commitment to an ongoing theorizing of spatial practices. Primarily, it leads them to take stock of their precarious condition vis-à-vis the human and nonhuman divide, and the ways it bears on contemporary accounts of homo- and transnormative geographies.[12]

Travesti collectives express dissent toward mapping operations of gender and race in Argentina. Specifically, the class, gender, and racial processes that shape travestis' living conditions acquire salience for a differential understanding of their practices—among others, streetwalking and housing habits, migration patterns, and political mobilizations. In these practices, I analyze the spatial form of travestis' offstage reflexivity at the outer edge of both public and counterpublic spheres. Travestis' spatial alterity provides, as we shall see, insightful commentary on colonialism and the bodily regime that it imposed through the human/nonhuman divide.

Argentina has undergone gentrification and tourism-oriented commodification for the past three decades. In March 2022, while the country barely began to manage COVID-19 transmission numbers, the Ministry of Tourism and Sports reported a record rebound of international visitors.[13] Reaching only 47 percent of the pre-pandemic volume of visitors, the March report showed a definite upward trend, from 18.3 percent in January to almost triple that by the beginning of March. Tourism and the sprouting of Airbnb rentals are deeply stratifying the real estate market. The sharing economy benefits gay-only and gay-friendly accommodations, and it increases the capacity of local hosts to access international visitors and their bank accounts. Before the arrival of Airbnb in 2011, Lugar Gay of Buenos Aires took off as a locally owned bed-and-breakfast, whose main purpose was catering to travelers who sought accommodations for "gay men."[14]

In the first decade of the millennium, mainstream and counterpublic reflexivity about tourism and gentrification begin to showcase sexual identity, and its gender nonconforming subjectivities, as a salient marker of Argentine otherness.[15] The country also becomes the first in Latin America to pass federal legislation sanctioning same-sex marriage, in 2010. Not only does the LGBT movement claim it as a major legal victory with international and regional repercussions but so do state agencies and the private service sector (Antoniucci 2016, 30). In the case of the latter, they herald this legal landmark's entrance into the service and entertainment economies. Simultaneously, the country sees increased visibility for celebrities and entertainers who identify as gay, lesbian, trans, travesti, and genderqueer.[16] The street panels advertising Jujuy to international visitors who tour Buenos Aires disseminate reflexivity about minoritized difference; so are tango schools vying for a segment of the gay and lesbian market (Linthicum 2013).[17] They recuperate foreign and domestic tourists into novel narratives of nationalism—biodiversity and tango—while normalizing gay and queer subjects. I submit that this grammar rehabilitates nonconforming subjectivities, employing two interrelated strategies: *cleansing* the history of racialization in the major gayscape of Argentina, its capital district, goes hand in hand with *stressing* racial and ethnic diversity at the northwestern border of the country.

On one end, state-run programs, international cooperation projects, and private investment conglomerates participate in the commodification of the northwest. Jujuy is not only the northernmost state in Argentina, sharing borders with Bolivia and Chile, but also the one with the largest Kolla Indigenous population. This ethnoracial group has a pre-Hispanic history mostly linked to its Quebrada (the Gorge) and Puna regions.[18] Since the Quebrada was designated a UNESCO World Heritage protected site in 2003, Jujuy has experienced an influx of approximately 300,000 visitors annually. However, it's important to note that, back then, Argentina was still recovering from the economic crisis of 2001, which meant that the province had not yet developed the necessary hospitality infrastructure to accommodate an unprecedented surge in visitors. The growing mobilities that tourism attracts, much more so when they flock toward peri-urban and rural areas, also create precarious conditions for Indigenous communities, which in turn are worsened by ecotourism (Guyot 2011).[19] Hospitality businesses find legal loopholes to transform the real estate market against the interest of the Gorge's original inhabitants (Guyot 2011). In this context, Indigeneity as a growing polity continues to raise claims against corporate development. In so doing, Kolla communities engage in "ethnicization," or the process of Indigenous empowerment amid environmental conflicts (Guyot 2011; Mollet 2006). Fast-forward to 2022, under COVID-19 restricted mobility, and Jujuy boasts a whopping 226,588 stays within the first two weeks of January alone.[20] The Gorge went from recording 300,000 visitors per year in 2013 to reaching 75.5 percent of that total in just two weeks nine years later.

On the other end, we find the portrayal of Buenos Aires as gay-friendly, which includes in outlets with impressive worldwide readerships, such as the *New York Times* (*NYT*), *The Advocate*, and *Out Magazine*. The latter two promote themselves as leading sources of gay news in the world. According to *The Advocate*, the city unfolds as a "new bastion of gay friendliness" (Nguyen 2007). Under the title "In Macho Argentina, a New Beacon for Gay Tourists" (Barrionuevo 2007), the *NYT* narrates the gradual assimilation of gender diversity into that city in part due to social mores loosening up in the postdictatorship period after 1983.[21] Not without difficulty, the newspaper holds "sexy tango" dancing, antiquing, shopping, and dining together with bites of political activism, "strapping meat-eater [macho]" men, and gay-only sports and clubs.

Out Traveler, the travel branch of *Out Magazine*, gave Buenos Aires an excellent rating in four out of six markers of desirability for gay destinations in 2004. It described the "sophistication" of the city's gay life and its ability to compete with the Parisian aesthetic (Luongo 2004). Moreover, by citing its links to European culture, Nguyen's (2007) journal entry on *The Advocate Online* paints Buenos Aires as a destination "[where] the buildings lining the corridors are a mixture of old-world Spanish and Italian architecture with a little bit of New Jersey sprinkled here and there." Bryan Van Gorder (2014), also on *Out Traveler*, connects the turn of the millennium to its next decade. The article showcases the journey of a multinational gay and lesbian group of four to the northwestern states of Jujuy and Salta prior to the group's failed trip to Buenos Aires's Pride Parade (La Marcha). The homonormative narrative goes on through the rehabilitation of the northwest and its ecological beauty for lesbian and gay consumption. The scenario of foreign travelers driven by the familiar clout of gay businesses confirms the reach of queer behavior. Consuming ecodiversity folds queer subjects into hiking trips, visits to ruins, camelid sightings, and locally sourced vegetable markets.

Counterpublics across the *NYT*, *The Advocate*, and *Out Magazine* anchor the global appeal of gay Buenos Aires to European sophistication. State and private investments in the tourism industry bind Jujuy and Salta for their attachment to Indigeneity and "primitive" biodiversity. Inclusion of this Andean sanctuary in lesbian and gay travelogues validates counterpublic sensibilities, such as gay-only bars and stays. More specifically, these sensibilities are based on sameness rather than difference. Through homonational orientation, lesbian and gay counterpublics partake in commodifying Kolla Indigeneity and cleansing race out of the metropolitan gayscape. Indeed, both publics and counterpublics collude in normalizing racial and gender cartographies for sameness.

The travesti population whose social formation I examine hails precisely from this geopolitical landscape. Their displacement into metropolitan sex work circuits, such as Buenos Aires, underscores geographies of exclusion, child abuse, job precarity, and lack of educational opportunities. This map retrofits long-standing eugenicist strategies of *criollaje*, or racial mixing.[22] Marisa Miranda distinguishes between Anglo and Latin eugenics primarily due to their differing approaches. Anglo eugenics tends to rigidify biological diversity by relying on racial classifications, whereas Latin eugenics encapsulates the dynamic influence of environmental factors within the concept of pathological deviation (2018, 34).[23] Argentinean eugenics evolved through two distinct periods, the first spanning most of the early twentieth century until 1945, corresponding with the fall of the Nazi genocidal enterprise, and the second covering the immediate years after the end of World War II until the mid-1970s.[24] The first period legitimizes the connivance of science and faith, or doctors and priests, as prime sources of sociological and criminological rationales. The latter approach more effectively justifies the archetype of the nuclear family and its association with the state's regulation of moral authority. In my subsequent exploration of Buenos Aires's *lunfardo* world at the turn of the century, I delve into the earlier era of Argentina's eugenics. However, late twentieth-century eugenics carries on today in the precarious childhood faced by gender nonconforming individuals from the country's popular sectors.

La Sociedad Argentina de Eugenesia, since its inception in 1945, has established two interconnected fronts for the pursuit of the nuclear family. It embraces Catholic-infused dogmas through a pronatalist front, which was supposed to "enhance the race through the promotion of maternal and childcare" (Beccalossi 2017, 305).[25] At the same time, it disseminates psychopathologies meant to elicit apt behavior from the marital couple (Miranda 2018, 37). Eugenics, as a state-supported science, combines religious appeal with population control. Homosexuality, under the figures of *invertidos*, *manflores*, and *tribadistas*, becomes eugenics' favorite means of instruction over the lumpen and underemployed segments of society. The welfare of the nation-state, or so eugenicists argue, relies on the domestication of threatening, and panic-producing, expressions of gender nonconformity.

The cartography for racial and gender sameness at the onset of this millennium more effectively deploys the nuclear family as a national project about sensibility. It seeks to recruit LGBTQ+ counterpublics into the tender, softer, more vanilla attachments of global, tolerance-seeking, gay reflexivity. This time around, *global gay unity* opens its arms to third-world Euro-American *civilization*. Homonational reflexivity on a global scale pulls the Euro-American element in Argentina's *crisol de razas* to cleanse the country's domestic history, resembling the long-standing but always current assertion that the country has de-Hispanicized within the nation's marital pot. Even LGBTQ+ counterpublics invest in the idea that Europeanization successfully melts racial hierarchies away. This shifting representation of space and time transfers the salience of race to the northwest. Albeit a banner of racial otherness, the Andean region accrues a worldly appeal through the approaching reflexivity of homonormative consumption. As the gender politics described next demonstrates, eugenic texts are the backbone of a long-standing anti-Black and anti-Indigenous cartography.

Melting Race in the Eugenic Pot

Prior to the consolidation of the Argentine state, colonial structures shaped a pervasive environment where *peninsulares* (Spaniards) and their descendants accumulated land, wealth, and prestige. This extractivist model relied on placing *casta* populations, mainly Indigenous, Amerindians, and African descendants, at the lower tiers of a highly stratified colonial society. The casta system coded a complex process of white supremacist values, validating colorism as an expression of virulent hostility toward non-Europeans, but, especially, enslaved, formerly enslaved, Indigenous, and Afro-Indigenous people.

In fact, Argentina's national project has long utilized vanishment as a trope to justify perverse operations of muting, silencing, and erasing against Afro-descendant and Black diasporic populations. Sutton, for example, notes that genocidal rationales equally targeted Indigeneity and Blackness (2008, 107).[26] Military expeditions displaced and decimated Indigenous populations through direct violence and forced labor (Sutton 2008, 107; Gott 2007, 276). Intimidation of the Black population played a key role in its disenfranchisement, adding to the notion that by the late nineteenth century, Afro-descendants had been "killed in wars and by disease" (Sutton 2008, 108; Salessi 1995, 80–81). Despite multiple efforts, and as it will be explained later, Black and Amerindian subjectivities survived white-centered projects of nation-building (Briones 1998). They took advantage of conditions created by social, cultural, and ethnic admixture (Cabeza de Baca et al. 2020). At times, they were even pushed to utilize ingenious ways of "hiding in plain sight" (Edwards 2020).

Erika Edwards (2020) demonstrates that ingenious strategies developed alongside shifting state efforts. Promoting education, employment, marriage, property access, and political enfranchisement, state efforts revealed deep-seated anxieties about the supremacist role of whiteness. Edwards focuses on Black women in the state of Córdoba who responded to such efforts in oblique fashion, often camouflaging resistance as steps toward the amelioration of their own social station. Her study shows that imposed sexual exchanges across racial groups enabled members of Afro-descendant communities to establish intimacy and cohabitation with members of the enslaver class (50–51).[27] Moreover, in the period following abolition, intermarriage adopted various social forms, at once safeguarding and challenging the privileged status of white Argentines (Healy 2006, 115).

Within the context described thus far, mestizaje should be understood as an influential yet failed rhetorical and political device. As claimed by Nicole Guidotti Hernández (2011, 235–236), narratives of racial harmony across Latin American countries romanticize the pain, suffering, and loss that settler projects generate. The narrative of eugenics, rooted in positivist development, is characterized by precisely a neocolonial treatment of Indigenous and Black populations. Argentina first sought to extinguish Native lifeways, only to later dress them with the costume of criollo subjectivity. Criollaje functioned as whitening processes of social formation that relationally, and simultaneously, disintegrated Indigenous sovereignty while reimagining racial mixing as inherently Native (Briones 2002; Guano 2003; Salessi 1995; Schneider 2004). Modernization advocates of the nineteenth century considered that mixing Indio, Zambo, and Mulato with Spanish racial strains would result in a homogeneous pack whose only viable future lay in uplifting the values of European civilization (Bunge 1932; Sarmiento 2004; Pierce 2019).[28] Since then, the whitening effect expected from melting-pot rules has become a cornerstone of state politics (Monkevicius 2013).

The colonial distinction between civilized humans (Europeans) and childlike quasi humans (the colonized) lays the foundation for the modernizing neutralization of racial, specifically Indigenous and Black, differences. Disciplining national citizens entails the schooling of bodily projects. Criollaje steers the nation's body toward unity through both the coupling of healthy husbands and wives and the engineering of a new genetic pool (Wagley 1965).[29] Toward the end of the nineteenth century, state technocrats understood that Argentina occupied an uneasy position within Darwinian global dynamics (Dalton 2022, 131; Knight 2022, 165–166). The state faced the challenge of administering a vast territory with scarce population.[30] With the decline of Hispanic Europe, the eugenicist civilizing project in Argentina demands de-Hispanization as its route toward true Enlightenment (Quijano 2000; Sarmiento 2004; Knight 2022). The influx of European immigration, however, would add stress to the labor market without delivering on its modernizing promise.

In the face of the migratory waves Argentina receives between 1884 and 1915, state technocrats experiment with novel positivist taxonomies. They fold racial anxieties into the classification of gender Others, of non-conforming bodily and behavioral projects. Through this process, eugenicist technocracies seek to civilize the insides of the nation and cleanse its racial pool. Jorge Salessi's (1995) work examines this milestone period, uncovering the discursive production of the Argentinean national alongside the emergence of positivist medicolegal categories, such as "uranist," "pederast," "invert," and "third sex."[31] His scholarship identifies a lingering preoccupation with the nation's hygiene and the technocratic resolve to safeguard it. Through an offensive consisting of psychiatric journals, school curricula, criminology manuals, and literary narratives, the nation's ruling publics disseminate homosexual and queer panic. In so doing, they carve out good behavior, which they model after the values of the patrician family, including heterosexist reproduction, an ethics of capitalist exploitation, and obedience toward latifundia-based powers.

Sexual-panic figures sprout during this time, opening assimilation routes for key segments of the migrant population (Bergero 2008, 341–343).[32] They warn against dangerous "fluids" among African, Indigenous, and mestizo peoples. The lunfardo underworld of *milongas* rises to the station of state matter, for it harbors an unruly, deviant, and infection-ridden ethos of tango: petit theft schemes, cabaret performances, brothels, single entrepreneurial women, and flamboyant pimps.[33] Not unlike the cleansing of Buenos Aires's gayscape today, the nation at the dawn of the twentieth century declares the lunfardo world incompetent for eugenicist projects.

The Cartographic Gap: Between racial and gender Others

Despite the global obsession with racialized sexualities, LGBTQ+ international media do not mention travestis who work in *la zona roja* (the red, or vice, zone) located in the Palermo district of Buenos Aires.[34] Travesti communities and networks have a long-standing history in this area. In fact, CABA modifies its Code of Urban Public Behavior to legalize sex work in the late 1990s. Shortly thereafter, it recriminalizes this practice.

Travestis, then, organized and gained recognition by protesting this legal abuse. They sought to assert their rights before the state to both work in general and do that work in public spaces. They mobilized in the year 2008 and brought their claims to a multiagency board whose main goal is to regulate the use of a public park known as Los Bosques de Palermo. They pushed contradictions among political parties and civil society organizations, both already entrenched in the fight over the public definition of access and safety.

The process described above allows travesti sex workers to redefine their media visibility more effectively. No longer are they reduced to headlining crime sections. The zona roja begins to emerge as the twilight urban space where vice and the rights of travesti sex workers coexist. The 2008 mobilization ends with the city agreeing to make Los Bosques more accessible for travestis' sex work. This shift in policy resulted in the city installing portable toilets, providing free access to condoms, and setting up more garbage containers to dispose of them. In the first two decades of the millennium, the strip where solicitation takes place moves from El Rosedal to the green areas closest to Lago Las Regatas, both within the same park. Los Bosques is such a landmark for the politicization of travesti identities that, in October 2018, when CABA hosts the Youth Olympic Games, the city must consult with approximately three hundred travesti sex workers before temporarily moving the solicitation strip three to four hundred feet west of Lago Las Regatas.

Media reports continue to bet on CABA's international appeal, and yet, despite the city's commitment to LGBTQ+ rights, they often downplay the salient presence of travesti collectives. Counterpublic reflexivity either relegates or distorts travestis' struggles, often sidelining their role in taking back the street from decency-oriented projects.[35] I submit that this oversight ensues from a *cartographic gap*, an interlocking of race, gender, class, and sexuality that, in the words of feminist science scholar Evelynn Hammonds (1994), resembles a black hole in the representation of space. *Black hole* refers to an astrophysical phenomenon that allows students of the universe to make sense of the gravitational collapse of stars according to their size, mass, and speed. When a stellar core collapses, it creates extreme gravity, eventually curving space in its vicinity. This gravitational pull may even trap light, hence the name *black hole*, within the collapsing stellar radius. In other words, this phenomenon bends matter. To the scientist's eye, the black hole's surrounding behavior is key. Without paying attention to or understanding what surrounds the black hole, neither its activity nor its place can be engaged.

Hammonds creates this epistemic metaphor as an incisive critique of distortion, silencing, and erasure. She reconstructs the textual and methodological shifts through which white-stream queer and feminist studies distort and disappear "black female queer sexualities" (2004, 304). In a way, the universalizing gloss of sex and gender manifests in the shrinking of the category "black female queer." Hammonds clarifies the stakes within a project such as queer studies, since it often remains oblivious to the additive, depoliticizing bent that it gives to intersectional analysis. Anti-capitalist feminist thinkers and activists, such as the members of the Combahee River Collective (2018 [1977]), Cathy Cohen (2001), Anna Carastathis (2016), and Maria Lugones (2003a), also reflect on the categorial void that white-stream feminist and queer frameworks create through an ornamental account and application of intersectional analysis. Furthermore, Hammonds undertakes the audacious task of discussing Black women's political strategy of dissemblance, of countering both the glossing of Blackness as inappropriately gendered and its contingent morphing over time into cultural feature. By calling this task audacious, I mean to signal the artfulness of Hammonds's idiolect at the crossroads of science studies and interdisciplinary humanities. She certainly covers delicate terrain, as the black hole metaphor unpacks both the invisibility of Black female queer sexualities and their existence inside and without the logic of the void.

The black hole metaphor seeks to highlight the mutually implicated dynamics of oppressive structures, such as gender subordination and white supremacy. It outlines the process of social formation of this void by centering Black female queer sexualities and asking what gender, sexuality, and race can and cannot tell about (in)visibility. The thorough reduction of gender, sexuality, and race as if they were separable underwrites the epistemic pressure that white-stream feminist and queer thinking puts on Black female queer sexualities. From within the curvature of the body-social, of the materiality of flesh and Blackness, undoing the void demands an equally curved, or refracted, analytics of power. Black female queer sexualities, as do black holes, designate an (in)visible (im)possibility, a site of disintegrating collapse whose own relational place in the geometry of power defies annihilation. Deciphering black holes, journeying through their bending gravitational force, we must first locate the practices that mute Black female queer sexualities, including the practice of naming as muting.[36]

The late Argentinean travesti activist Lohana Berkins insightfully contributes to theorizing the void by employing the notion of "realidades cloacales," which I translate as "shitholes" or "sewer realities." She turns to this idea of shitholes to make sense of the void that travestis' embodiments occupy in the reflexivities of the nation-state. By also focusing on multiple systems of power, and the ways they bear on encasing travesti visibility and yet banishing its everyday, political, existence, Berkins contributes to advancing a geometry of feminist analysis. Her geometry is intersectional first and, as we shall see later, anti-colonial always. Travesti theorizing of intersectionality offers kindred company to Hammonds's anti-racist geometry of feminist and queer thinking. Travesti activists and writers, among them, Berkins, Marlene Wayar, and Florencia Guimaraes, speak of the social space of sex work as the imaginary and material site of necropolitics.[37] Guimaraes (2021) examines the condition of travestis who, as social exiles, find themselves forced into the streets at a very early age. The exercise of sexual and reproductive rights, she argues, is an illusion for children and teenagers who, while being trafficked into prostitution, remain outside schools' classrooms. In fact, they are excluded from schools, where since the year 2010 the state has promised but never quite delivers public and integral sex education.[38] Wayar (2018a) reminds readers of *Tiempo Argentino* that state and public reflexivity about LGBTQ+ civil rights typically denies personhood to members of this marginalized community, much more so if they do not meet the decency standards of the putative liberal subject.[39] Wayar mentions that before her passing, Berkins began to illustrate this marginalization with the metaphor of "realidades cloacales." Berkins argues that mainstream and minoritized counterpublics banish travestis' realities from view. They fit neither domestic nor normative standards of consumption and success among entrepreneurial neoliberal subjects.

Similarly to the black hole metaphor, sewage remits to geometries of exile, expulsion, void, clogging, flushing, and debris. Excrement materializes the motility of the body-social and its bowels. It transfers the body-social into a process that breaks down and disintegrates what sustains organic existence. The reality of solicitation, according to Guimaraes, links "sexual acts not to pleasure but economic survival within a minefield where minors encounter adults who are seeking access to travestis' bodies and sexual energies" (2021, 51). After the trick is done with, clients send their own infatuation with travestis down the sewage pipe.[40] Often, this act of self-denial culminates in the violent expulsion of travesti embodiments into the underground of trash and debris. Wayar further extends this metaphor to encapsulate the underlying processes of dispossession and forced expulsion experienced by fellow travestis, whose life expectancy remains tragically low, ranging between thirty-two and thirty-five years throughout Spanish-speaking Latin America. Guimaraes reminds us of the *travesticidio* (murder) of Evelyn Rojas, whose body was discovered precisely at the terminus of a sewage pipe in the city of Posadas, located in Argentina's northeast (2021, 51).

What surrounds the outlet of a sewage pipe is the very condition of precarity and dispossession that travestis cannot escape. Akin to the politics of black holes, the formulation of *sewage realities* as a geometry of power aligns travesti consciousness with critiques and subversions of the state's designs of life and death. As they barely cling to the abstract possibility of accessing healthcare, a living wage, and bodily integrity, travestis confront the twinned cartographies of black holes and sewer realities.

Latin American travesti theorizing in the twenty-first century exposes the contours of racialization and queerness. Assembling gaps, holes, and outlet pipes, these discursive fields seem to be separate and yet bound by the obliteration, muting, and expulsion of travestis. This discursive orientation, which averts the racializing histories of embodiments, permeates white-stream feminist and queer scholarship.[41] Theoretical and political dissent resonates across the analytic arc offered by black holes and sewer realities. They address affinities through the politics of mutual implication.

When I speak of affinities, I refer to examining geopolitical implications between Black female queer sexualities, travestis, and other Latinx and Afro-Latinx projects of nonnormative embodiments. My position here owes to the cross-hemispheric and transatlantic labor that M. Jacqui Alexander (2005b) and Gloria Wekker (2006) perform, specifically because they build cross-generational and cross-cultural bridges of feminist translation. They teach us how to make sense of each other's flesh, how to live side by side in a world that remains hostile to our coming together in a coalitional vein. As critical listener, co-interlocutor, and faithful witness over this bridge and crossing, I seek the political and epistemic company of US third-world women of color feminism and US-based queer of color critique (Sandoval 2000; Moraga and Anzaldúa [1981] 2022; Lorde 1984; Johnson and Henderson 2005; Decena 2011; Hames-García and Martinez 2011; Galarte 2021); multicultural, intercultural, and autonomous feminisms in Latin America and the Caribbean (Carneiro 2005; Espinosa Miñoso 2009; Tzul Tzul 2018); and jotería studies (Alvarez 2014, 2016; Calvo-Quirós 2014; Cantú 2009; Hames-García 2014; Revilla and Santillana 2014). These "pedagogies of crossing," as Alexander names them, extend, expand on, and further the project of intersectional work, of making political, representational, and carnal sense of what can and cannot be seen or sensed about multiple oppressions.

Most importantly, shithole pedagogies rethink and reimagine gender, sexuality, race, and embodiment decolonially (Lugones 2007), questioning the ways in which historical contingences may be overlooked when intersectional research takes for granted the hegemonic scripts of gender, racial, sexuality, disability, caste, and class formations. Decolonizing genealogies work with intersectionality not as the mere addition of axes of power for the representation of the "ethnographic subject" of research (Smith 2011) but rather as the contingent refraction of social ties among and through these axes (see also Silva and Ornat 2014).

Critically listening to travesti reflexivity incites a recalibration of feminist analyses of multiple oppressions. It reveals that the cartographic gap described thus far ensues from the geometries of travesti social formation. I explain these geometries through a three-pronged analysis. First, I follow travestis' framing of identity as oppositional multiplicity, in contrast to mainstream approaches that privilege sexual modern identity as stand-alone kind. Second, I discuss the ways that travestis reject homo- and transnormative projects of neoliberal regulation. Finally, I recognize and describe their anti-colonial standpoint on gender formation, which stems from travestis' racial and geographical locations. Each condition deserves thorough engagement to illustrate the ways in which it decenters cartographies of holes, gaps, and sewage lines.

Transversalidad, a Sideways Framing of Travesti Identities and Embodiments

Reflexivity about their own condition allows travestis to theorize collective agency. This process contends with and negotiates histories of displacement and sex work, recording strategies and tactics of visibility postdictatorship. It also illuminates their commitment to building community against a background of transphobia, competition as sex workers, and lack of access to state-sponsored services and resources. Their reflexivity interweaves multiple identifications and positionings in which class, gender, and nationality gain great salience. Due to the legacy of melting-pot politics, racialization and ethnicity signify unevenly by what cannot be named in those terms (Occhipinti 2003, 171). What I call *travesti reflexivity* is one among many other weaves of collective reexamination. It stems from practice and behavior stretching across the social. Even when I take part in ongoing dialogues with travesti activists, acquaintances, and friends, my engagement with their reflexivity ensues from the plurality of their views, marked predominantly by marginalization, and from recognizing the epistemic privilege that they claim as marginal to homo- and transnormative inclusion.

The late Lohana Berkins partakes in this collective reflexivity with a broad understanding of oppressions and their simultaneous and multiple nature. A native of the state of Salta in the Argentinean northwest, she was a leading figure in feminist, queer, trans, and travesti activism across the region. She received the 2003 Felipa de Souza Award for her persistent fight for sexual and human rights.[42] In *La gesta del nombre propio* (2006), she presents research conducted by transgender and travesti organizations, focusing on the sociopolitical issues that this community faced in the State of Buenos Aires. This publication examines the disenfranchisement of the travesti population, specifically among its members who engage in sex work as their main means of income. When I refer to epistemic privilege, I follow Berkins's claim about cognitive and reflexive processes that collective marginality sparks. She states that "knowledge is constructed based on dialogues among people who are situated quite differently across the social fabric, and the richness of this collective production stems from the contributions of different perspectives about social relations and their consequences" (7). In one of our conversations, Lohana reminds us that *identidad travesti* is not an individual characteristic or attribute. Rather, she understands that marginalized minorities carve a social, political, and bodily space that they call *travesti*. Furthermore, she insists on paying attention to travestis' sideways or transversal[43] mode of relationality, which delivers a pivotal critique of the cartographic gap so far described:

> In the construction of self-affirmation, sometimes what gets lost is something that is very important to me; that is, the *transversalidad* (transversality) of what I am. Today, to tell you that I can stand in front of people and say, "I am travesti," and well, maybe, at best, they will clap for me. Because being travesti is no longer shocking to anyone. You know? Now, if I take that, if I begin to talk about the transversality of being travesti; then, travestis, we are poor. [. . .] We don't have access to education, [. . .] healthcare, [or] housing, [or] dignified work; we are murdered. What I am saying [is that] I take that transversality and I put it out for discussion, for contestation, with picketers. [. . .] Or, also, I stand by human rights activists, with the human rights flag, in the name of thirty thousand of the disappeared

[in the last dictatorship, 1976–1983], among them many lesbians, *maricones*, and travestis. You get what I'm saying? (Interview, Buenos Aires, April 28, 2003)[44]

Berkins critiques homonationalism and its pull toward the privatization of nonnormative embodiments. Her politics of eroticism does not lie with unsettling normative sexual-object choice. Instead, it involves traversing the social fabric by summoning critical and oppositional consciousness. Under this summoning act, travestis deploy transversalidad, availing themselves of myriad forms of wisdom and forward-looking politics. Being travesti, as Berkins puts it, performs an offstage and complex cultural labor against the often insulating, mainstream-facing politics of LGBTQI+ counterpublics.[45] Coming out enacts but *a* site of public dispute for Berkins, since she is not after the applause that rehabilitates minoritized gender or sexual identities. She remains mindful of what Dominican American scholar Carlos Decena recognizes as contemporary confessional standards that govern discourse on modern sexuality (2011). Discussing Latinx subjectivities in the diaspora, Decena critically listens to muffled and tacit voices among nonnormative subjects who negotiate affective and material recognition within familial and intimate constellations. Undoubtedly, travesti sex workers also adapt to diasporic contexts and forced migrations. They navigate displacement and diaspora at the outer edge of the Argentine nation, from rural locales to urban cityscapes, and from vilified domains of "primitive" and disabled Indigeneities to environments of urban politicization.

Berkins considers simultaneous and compound oppressions sites of theoretical reflection. She acknowledges, for example, an interlocking of multiple power axes ("poor [. . .] we don't have access to education [. . .] healthcare"). But through this reflection, she also organically makes sense of intersectionality. Implying more than a metaphor, she conveys that intersectionality performs a displacement, recalibrating social energies at the transfer points between public and private spheres. Intersecting unveils the regulating fiction of individual insulation as travestis cultivate practical consciousness at the outskirt of debilitating, compounding oppressions. As a paradox of sorts, travestis develop coalitional fluency when they tap into different social struggles (human rights and disabled activists, picketers, cisgender women sex workers, among others) to recognize and commit to their mutual implication across histories of dissidence.[46]

Rejecting Homo- and Transnormative Assimilation

Neoliberal integration of marginalized genders and sexualities works through homonormative and transnormative commodification. Travestis turn away from enticing routes leading into integration and assimilation. They trespass on public and counterpublic territories. Increasing privatization of state responsibilities under neoliberal regimes sends travestis, and, more generally, sex workers, to an underground labor market.[47] Roderick Ferguson examines capital's normalizing anxieties about proper productivity and deviant nonreproductive sexualities (2004). Ferguson reveals the significant influence of scientific racism in shaping the American sociological canon, particularly in how it portrays sexual differences and contributes to the pathologization of Black cultures. Sex work, he argues, entails material estrangement for capital's working class. Antithetical to the heteropatriarchal order, selling sex threatens contractual restrictions upheld by the nuclear family. Proletarians must be shown the degree of racial ambiguity that lies with nonreproductive and nonnormative genders and sexualities. Travestis in Latin America mobilize various and at times contradictory agendas toward sex work. Yet they share an anti-capitalist critique of the racial and national anxieties underlying the vexing link between autonomy and gender nonconformity. In that sense, they also defy sociological investment in correcting sex work and other underground labor cultures.

Francisco Quiñones (2019) recalls his "Berkins-story" as part of a reflection on socially engaged education and its response to the pervasive coupling of sex work and travesti identities. Quiñones weaves together the experience of the Nadia Echazú cooperative, the rise of Berkins as a political icon, and the origin of a travesti-serving, high-school-certificate-granting educational program. Quiñones, who is also a documentarian and filmmaker, highlights the incisive response of the travesti collective when they refuse to be portrayed through the lens of scholarship. At the cooperative, the collective begins manufacturing clothing in 2008, employing at its peak twenty-two trans and travesti members.[48] After Berkins's passing in 2016, they fight against the state's threat to withdraw funding for this venture. In 2021, with the return to office of the Frente para Todos, the cooperative obtains funding to rehab its building in the Avellaneda neighborhood and resumes operations manufacturing COVID kits, including but not limited to face masks.[49]

As Quiñones documents, travestis seek inclusion by redefining their incursion in the counterpublic arena. They call for labor opportunities while showing that having long-term goals for public policies is as important as the number of new jobs that they demand. They approach sex work as a condition rather than a defining trait of who they are. Lacking formal education or vocational training, they sorely urge the state to establish educational programs centered on their community's needs (Martínez and Vidal-Ortiz 2021). For example, they have demanded programs built on the sewing skills of community members and collaborated to found and run a textile co-op. In the last four years, they lobbied federal legislators to co-write and pass a bill securing a travesti work quota at all state agencies across the nation.

The cornerstone of travestis' spatial practice is the double condition of sex work and internal exile. They do business with their sexual resources, and, despite their marginalization as sex workers, they gain critical financial skills. They ultimately steer cash from their clients' pockets to their own. Exile works as both constraint and enablement. The relative penumbra under which they run the solicitation turf keeps them away from gay and lesbian geographies of profit and sanitization: they typically conduct their activities out in the open, on the streets, in locations that are easily accessible to anyone familiar with Los Bosques, whether on foot or by car, and they often find housing in overcrowded, run-down motel rooms when they have just arrived in CABA. They unsettle linkages among decency, residential neighborhoods, and real estate appreciation. Berkins, for instance, voiced discontent with LGBTQ+ rights groups whose advocacy relies on middle-class aspirations. Sex work and spatial marginalization both underscore travestis' skepticism toward the ascendance of worldwide homonormativity and its sanitizing of the public domain.[50]

Argentina extends protections to the LGBTQ+ community under federal law: the same-sex marriage and gender identity bills, and the presidential executive order about the travesti work quota, which passed in 2010, 2012, and 2020, respectively. Despite these protections, travesti reflexivity still decries police harassment and criminalization. Through 2016, criminalization takes place under CABA's city code (art. 81) and, since then, in the form of bribes and other kickbacks that city police members demand.[51] Travestis also denounce myriad mechanisms through which low-level state actors, such as the staff at the city clerk's office, become both participant and adjudicator in matters as complex as gender designation on travestis' personal documentation.

Leticia Sabsay (2011) examines the debates that reshaped the boundaries of public decency in late 1990s Buenos Aires. During what is supposedly an open debate aimed at amending the Code of Urban Public Behavior, the city first decriminalizes and then swiftly recriminalizes sex work. By 2016, the country modifies the federal penal code, which legalizes sex work whenever sex workers carry out this activity within a private setting. This is virtually a state's mandate to avoid illicit associations and human trafficking. Decriminalization at the federal level results in criminalization of the print and web media ads that sex workers employ to promote their services. Criminalization derives from the penal typification of any involvement of third parties in the sex work market, since their incursion corrupts the private context in which solicitation remains legal.

Routine presence of travestis in Palermo's Los Bosques park continues as a symbiotic link between urban development in a cosmopolitan setting and decriminalization of sex work. The issue, though, is that decriminalization takes place without proper or effective regulation. That is, although sex workers become de facto heads in their own small enterprise, dignity and safety in the labor market crudely and unfairly evolve into the worker's burden. Unlike any other enterprise regulated by labor policies, sex work turns into an industry for which the state offers no protections. Decriminalization in this fashion entails the hyperprivatization of sex work. Sabsay's (2011) study argues that travestis, like many of the sex workers whom I interviewed or organized with, find their life stories signified by the divide between public and private. Sabsay claims that scandal, as a discourse figure, proscribes sex work with the purpose of establishing ontologizing mechanisms. Indeed, figures of scandal conflate the visibility of sex work with the presence of travestis in the street. I would like to extend her argument to interpret homonormative projects. Homonormativity foregrounds whitening tolerance for the city's gayscape by mounting a frontier between, on one end, queer and gender subjects who fit decency standards and, on the other, travestis qua travestis rather than as partakers in indecent behavior.

Travesti reflexivity reformulates homonational and transnormative frontiers, showcasing *sideways* journeys whereby indecent and deviant sex workers model collective agency away from usual avenues of consciousness-raising—such as the pathways from factory to union, or from the domestic to the public sphere. In so doing, sex workers expose the twenty-first century's eugenicist regulations over urban space. Not only do travestis fight for their solicitation turf, but they also mobilize against the streets' privatization and sanitization. Berkins, for example, contests the decency threshold expected in public discourse as she prompts unemployed pariahs to take to the streets in coalition with other insurgent city residents. Theirs is a transgression of the public/private fiction, enacting spatial competence against neoliberal, eugenicist, and ornamental integration. As a result of enduring fears of abuse, travestis often go out together, even during daylight hours. Working the street extends into the late hours of the night, with many not retiring until seven or eight in the morning. Maneuvering cross-generational networks while searching for housing, they develop strategies that diverge from an individualizing model. These practices deepen our understanding of travestis' heterogeneous and shifting competence within and outside the ontologizing frontier that Sabsay describes.

An Anti-colonial Standpoint on Gender Formation

In her personal presentation, Berkins performs a "brothel-like" (*prostibular*) stylization of the self (Fernandez 2004). This domain of travesti aesthetic, self-presentation, and well-being manifests material culture at its most intimate scale—corporeality—and it points to the continuity and recalibration of embodied dissidence. Often, cultural, sociological, and anthropological critiques emphasize the precarious conditions in which gender nonconforming individuals access healthcare and other gender-affirming technologies and procedures. They articulate viewpoints that are crucial to advance a public-health approach to the well-being of trans, travesti, and gender nonconforming individuals. For many travestis who engage in sex work, the body is a means of both self-definition and survival. The standards of aesthetic competition in the sex trade—voluminous hips and lips, perky breasts, and delicate waistlines—combine efforts to align self-presentation with the clients' surgical, biochemical, and behavioral demands.

Writing in 2021, Florencia Guimaraes complains about the healthcare system as a hurdle race through interconnected microaggressions, from providers who refuse to acknowledge gender self-definition, which is a constitutional right in Argentina, to the systemic lack of adequate training in transgender healthcare, or from the yearslong waitlist for state-funded gender confirmation surgeries to blatant denial of emergency care for travesti and trans individuals: "Without a doubt, this is one of the most severe experiences of rejection that we suffer, which bears directly on our well-being and integrity and leads many of us to self-medicate or, even, seek body–enhancing procedures in the underground market that, as our history shows, may have painful consequences" (51).

Travesti embodiment retrofits technologies of racial formation in the

Americas. In a country such as Argentina, it builds on the bodily project of racial mixing and the ways that it systemically drafts the nonhuman as a background signpost against the foreground of the genre of the human. Bestialization and hypersexualization of nonwhite bodies is intrinsic, as chapter 2 shall demonstrate, to the alteration of the nuclear family and its rise to the station of biopolitical device. In our discussion of the eugenicist foundation of Argentina, we mentioned that white-centered taxonomies of life and deviation cast the lunfardo world as polluting underground. Not unlike gauchos from the interior arriving in the city at the end of the nineteenth century, travestis from the northwest settle in Palermo's zona roja in the twenty-first century.[52] The Afro, Indigenous, and criollo roots of milongas, bordellos, and cabaret performances reflect back on the travesti aesthetic, fostering an oppositional consciousness critical of bourgeois femininity. Silicone-injected buttocks, padded hips, fishnet stockings, and six-inch stilettos are but a few of the markers fashioning the aesthetic of *traviesa* and *minón*. Both slang words invoke the embodiments that travestis aspire to shape and are pushed to achieve.

The term *minón* in Spanish represents the superlative of the lunfardo word *mina*, which, over a century after its inception, still refers to the ambiguity of femininity among Argentina's low-income and popular sectors. That is, it contests the defining, yet impressible, boundary of whiteness as an undeniable link between husband and wife within the nuclear family. *Tanguería* is the noun that designates the venue where tango performances take place. At the turn of the twentieth century, these venues valued working-class cisgender women who were known as prostitutes, cabaret performers, and entrepreneurs (Pellarolo 2008). Their counterparts, *compadres* and *malevos*, support these women's marginal positions and their undoing of docility. In a world where income doesn't always derive from wages, women who enter the low life secure resources through their talents as waitresses, entertainers, and tricksters.

Sexual autonomy among popular sectors exposes the fragile nature of femininity and masculinity as markers of proper racial standing. Any relative autonomy among lunfardo women slips into tango's lexicon by way of *mina* (literally, precious metal mine), recording the rise of new subjective forms. Sirena Pellarolo collects tango lyrics singing tales of women moving from self-abnegation in peri-urban areas to sexual autonomy in the outskirts of Buenos Aires. To fuel an affair with one of them might have offered compadres an opportunity to strike *gold (minas)*. Legacies of gender and racial encodings continue to shape a brothel-like aesthetic. The very embodied matter of minas transfers through contemporary slang into the neologism *traviesa* (naughty), which artfully stands for travesti subjectivities. This neologism capitalizes on the common sound "trav" shared at the outset of both words, serving as a linguistic bridge that connects and symbolizes these identities.

Sylvain Poosson (2004) tracks the origins of tango and its environment back to the roots of Afro-Argentine culture between the eighteenth and nineteenth centuries. His account speaks to the contradictions of a country whose positivist intelligentsia moves as a pendulum across the ideologies that support and abhor immigration.[53] Blackness and the lifestyle of rural people, plainsmen or gauchos, figure as surrounding for the pendulum's magnetic field. Through a meticulous engagement with literary, epistolary, and musical documents, Poosson finds glaring evidence of Afro-diasporic elements in the dance, rhythm, and beat of tango. Furthermore, he suggests that the word itself, *tango*, derives through a linguistic change from the term "tambor" (drum) and its role in African and Afro-Argentine dance and music (92). Donald Castro (2001) concurs, and in a majestic analysis of narrative sources, he investigates the ruling elites of Buenos Aires and their disdain toward the "lascivious" cultural production of urban Blacks, mainly dance and music. Even in the first three decades of the twentieth century, when dominant Europhilic scripts of the nation considered Blackness all but alive, Castro finds mentions of the act of dancing "a lo negro," which "refers to the sexual focus of the dance where couples dance not *abrazando* [embracing] but *enlazando* [leg hooking]" (87).

In the study of transgender prostitutes that Don Kulick (1998) pursued in Salvador do Bahia, Brazil, the buttocks, or *bunda*, are the major marker of bodily transformation. Kulick is adamant about the salience of "fleshy thighs, expansive hips, and a prominent, teardrop-shaped *bunda*" (1998, 70). These features are, in his anthropological view, landmarks of feminine beauty within Brazilian culture. What is strikingly missing from his ethnographic analysis is a complex engagement with the colonial imaginary that pervades cultures rooted in the Atlantic passage, such as Brazil's (Silva and Ornat 2014; Wekker 2006).[54] In Argentina, this imaginary is today's currency for mainstream culture. The leading newspaper nationwide, *Clarín*, gave free range to this colonial legacy with Caloi's (2012) comic vignette *Clemente*. Its main character represents the patriarchal voice of whitening criollo sarcasm in the face of a changing global city.[55]

Clemente safeguards middle-class femininity, which entails gendering Argentine bodily projects as humanlike, by transferring his infatuation into a perverse cross-racial fantasy. La Mulatona is Clemente's soft-porn playmate for over four decades. As her name suggests, Mulatona has

Afro-Argentine roots. Her name comes from the superlative of *mulata*, or hybrid offspring resulting from the crossing of white Europeans and enslaved African people. However, we must note that Caloi creates the vignette decades before Afro-Argentines, since the early 2000s and through conscious organizing efforts, give way to new waves of visibility for the often-forgotten "racial impurities" of the nation (Ocoró Loango 2015). In addition to being a racial classification, *mulatona* carries much of the pejorative sentiment of racial slurs. Caloi depicts her as a sex object, with exuberant glossy lips, abundant curves, and what looks like kinky hair in an *M* shape. The vignette underscores Clemente's counterpart by visually marking the loose motion of her hips and breasts.

Caricatures such as *Clemente* follow the global proliferation of a damning iconography of Blackness. They exploit the readiness of narrow, superficial, and stereotypical meanings of Blackness as a contradictory doubling of visibility, the too-visible Black figure without depth and its consequent sidelining of Afro-Argentine peoples.[56] Mulatona and travestis share this place of racializing hypersexuality, both too visible and yet purged from having any depth across publics and counterpublics. The semantic field of Blackness and its lust is exemplified with the use of the noun *quilombo*. Borrowed from Portuguese, it originally refers to autonomous communities of fugitives from slavery (Anderson 1996).

The slang term *quilombo* in several Latin American countries currently designates the place where prostitution thrives. Blackening cultural and spatial production is a leading strategy in Latin American states, since it anchors national unity to the myth of racial, white-centered mixing. The festivities for the celebration of 25 de Mayo, which marks the establishment of the first Argentine government in 1810 and the country's independence from Spain, are integral to the school system. Elementary school performances held during *días patrios* (literally, patriotic days) function as laboratory to splice the national subject and its genetic, phenotypical, and cultural pool. At the confines of the nation, as is the case of my native Jujuy, colonial history under educational curricula reproduces deep-seated anxieties about Blackness. Every patriotic school performance I viewed during my childhood includes at least one Black character, often charged with subalternized occupations, such as water porter, kitchen's aide, or street vendor.[57] No matter the phenotype of the student who plays the character, teachers make sure to blacken the student's face with cork black. Indeed, as recently as in 2007, I witnessed this minstrel-like act when I attended my nephew's school celebration for Independence Day.

What cork black does for stage performances, spatial practices do for the lived experience of anti-Black segregation. The neologism "negros villeros" (Black shantytowners) seeks to name the racialization of labor and spatial hierarchies in Argentina. Throughout the twentieth century, and due to capital's biopolitical regime, large swatches of the world's population face not just scarcity but a total despotism of abandonment. Entire pockets of urban poverty are commonplace. They are enmeshed in processes that render the state of exception into rule at the turn of the twenty-first century (Grinberg 2017). In Argentina, impoverished and dispensable sectors of the population make a living through nonformal occupations, such as domestic work, garbage diving, and per-day hand labor. They face a housing crisis, and for this reason they have learned to squat in abandoned places, which they eventually build up. They take residence in these territories, where they often lack electricity, water, sewage lines, and other public works. This is not a process of urban blight, or gradually falling into disrepair. *Villas* are shantytowns whose residents, regardless of phenotype, are often perceived and understood, because of their social position, self-presentation, speech, and taste, as "negros villeros." The iconography of Blackness as lascivious, noisy, and ignorant contributes to this racializing mode of spatial segregation. Blackness and shantytowns amplify the ontology of quilombo, progressively encapsulating travestis into the zone of nonwhiteness.

The ongoing harassment that travestis face at the hands of neighborhood associations such as Defendamos Buenos Aires deploys the semantic of quilombo to ontologize, in Sabsay's (2011) terms, travesti embodiment as intrinsically trash, a toxic pollutant whose organic station resembles sewage debris. No wonder Defendamos Buenos Aires trolls travestis' political arms. They look in horror as fellow city dwellers fall under the spell of Palermo's zona roja. They are horrified by the inexplicable infatuation of honorable family men, or seasoned bachelors, with quilombo and scum. I submit that they fear the outlawed practice of scat, which BDSM communities explain as the sexual arousal and pleasure that participants derive from feces or brown showers. The notorious flow of clients in Palermo's zona roja speaks of travestis as the present-day minón, an almost irresistible bodily project whose fecal allure has no match. Travestis materialize the excremental debris that the city unloads, but for which many a resident lusts. Albeit ontologized as excrement, travestis actualize the anarchic and racialized bodies of yesteryears, the abyss, the gravity-curving black hole, between gender and nongender.

Without reducing travestis' social formation to the perils of minas from the turn of the twentieth century, the affinity between their migration patterns should not go unnoticed. From the interior of Argentina to the margins of Buenos Aires, exile brings about a social metamorphosis for both. If travestis reclaim not only the vernacular—traviesa—but also the racializing embodiment of hypersexuality in Argentina's colonial memory, they do so to the extent that expansive hips and teardrop-shaped buttocks function simultaneously as the materiality of racial otherness and oppositional consciousness. Travestis inhabit scandalous embodiments. Concurrently, as they embrace quilombo modes of being and doing, they criticize the sanctity of criollo, white-centered, human-approaching bodily projects.

Prior to transitioning, Ana Paula lived in Jujuy. We became friends around the year 2000, when she was dating one of my gay (white) friends. Against Argentinean standards that used to mark *him* as "negrito" (blackie), she describes the process of "hacerse [becoming] travesti" by underscoring the imprint of racialization on embodiment: "un negrito como yo, quién me iba a querer?" (a *negrito* like me, who was going to want me?).[58] Her statement pries open the technologies of desire and the ways that they bear on morphing one's bodily presentation at the crossroads of race and coloniality. Above all, her *becoming travesti* acknowledges first the splitting of the psyche at a time when LGBT counterpublics begin to reach their peak and, second, the uneasy position of embodiments who spiral down a cartographic gap. Rejected and unfit for gay sensibilities, Ana Paula inhabits the multiplicity of embodiment at the outskirts of same-sex desire. LGBT counterpublics render her at once too visible and invisible, because she embodies Blackness. She recalls her pretransition past not as a cisgender, or sexed, bodily project. Rather, she understands too well that *negrito* stands far from the human station of masculine or effeminate gay gender. She was unfit for homonational inclusion precisely because she lacked gender. She dwelled in the not quite monstrous, not quite human, but somewhat sacred embodiment that I shall unpack in the following chapter.

Before becoming travesti in her early twenties, racialization made Ana Paula undeserving of homonormative rehabilitation. Coloniality, in its most intimate expression, pushed her to the abyss, beneath the human. The turn toward hypersexualization, which of course relates to underground pollutants, to the fecal allure of travesti embodiments, entails an ontologizing process. Ana Paula partakes in the negotiation of these contradictions, steering her transition toward a brothel-like aesthetic. She fostered a complex, anti-colonial, not always successful standpoint. She learned to claim erotic agency within hypersexualizing racism.

Sideways Relationality

Travestis who become part of sex work networks in CABA occupy embodiment, space, and time in oppositional fashion. They trespass on the blueprint within which the body and its space-time should function. They upturn not only heterocisnormative and patriarchal but also homo- and transnormative extraction. Indeed, they encroach the genre of the human; they trespass on and reconfigure it as obsolete. They clog black holes and sewage pipes by attending to the curvature of the social where neither humans nor animals reside. As explained thus far, travestis germinate their embodiments on the edge of a political, aesthetic, and carnal abyss. From within this abyssal bodily project, they fend off the collusion of heteronationalist publics, homo- and transnormative counterpublics, and white supremacist politics.

I don't deny that travestis petition the state under mechanisms of neoliberal regulation, reaching some level of public and counterpublic legibility. Yet, they extend, expand on, and further offstage reflexivity. A case in point was their successful campaign to pass the 2012 Gender Identity bill.[59] They contributed to writing into law a comprehensive approach to self-identification and autonomous access to LGBTQ+ healthcare. An analysis of the legislature's debate, and their broadcast on national TV, conveys the narrow narrative that the mainstream circulates. They narrate LGBTQ identity as nature's truth. LGBTQ counterpublics, in turn, strategically expand these narratives to encompass nature, choice, and rights. Marlene Wayar instead builds on offstage reflexivity to decry the bill's lacunas concerning trans and travesti identification. The morning following the bill's passage by Congress, Wayar secured space for a provocative headline in Argentina's foremost center-left newspaper, asking point-blank, "Whatever happened to the T?" (Wayar 2012). Her question points to the bill's paradoxical nature, as it simultaneously acknowledges gender self-identification as a human right while denying LGBTQ individuals the opportunity to obtain state-issued ID cards with a gender designation other than male or female.[60] The congressional bill enabled individuals to seek an amendment to sex designation in their birth certificates, removing any medicalization or bureaucratization of this process. While social institutions can no longer deny an individual's gender self-presentation or self-identification, Wayar turns sideways. She refuses to apply for an ID that would coerce the normalization of the *T* into "male" or "female."

As Berkins puts it, transversalidad functions as a method of spatial and temporal production. When travestis take to the street and seek connections with *okupas* (trespassers), street vendors, picketers, and other sex workers, they engage black holes and sewage lines sideways. I link transversalidad to the act of pilgrimaging through and between abyssal possibilities. Akin to the behavior of black holes, travestis assemble fugitive embodiments and dwellings, somewhat there but always already falling out of view. Exclusion engineers the treatment that abyssal subjectivities receive, either as stagnant buildup at the bottom of the nation's species or as toxic waste to be scoured away. Poured over into the void, they traverse the realm of fugitivity, combining at once stasis and regeneration, and twilight and climax.

Henri Lefebvre suggests that we develop spatial practices by navigating "particular locations and spatial sets characteristic of each social formation" (1991, 33). In their practice of transversality, travestis magnify offstage competence in response to spatial sets, such as commodification of Indigeneity, gentrification of gay-friendliness, sanitization of green spaces, and fragmentation of LGBTQ organizing, among many others. These practices underscore that travestis' abyssal competence simultaneously co-implicates and recalibrates one another's embodiment, experience, and space-time. Travestis such as Lohana, Marlene, Florencia, and Ana Paula pass through sewage lines with this sideways competence and, in so doing, puncture their ontological status as debris, toxin, disposable, and trash.

Berkins reflects on self-affirmation with a transversal orientation. As she puts it, she turns sideways to face picketers, street vendors, and human rights activists. Her practices disclose the trouble that neoliberal, Euro-centered spatial sets have with nonconforming flesh. She summons other marginalized subjects to acknowledge an intimate proximity felt, if only momentarily, at the brink of the abyss. Instead of addressing the mainstream to mediate meaning among minorities, Berkins underscores the salience of seeing, feeling, and embodying *travesti* in and through histories of resistance. Such insurgent memory arises from human rights and class struggles ("I stand by...with the human rights flag"). She performs transversalidad by inspiring those walking side by side with her ("I put it out for discussion, for contestation") to affirm affective, social, cultural, and organic interdependence. Ultimately, as the next chapter shall tease out, transversalidad entails sideways competence and maneuvering within, against, and beyond a colonial/modern heterosexualist gender system. That is, it asserts sideways selves in their decolonial disfigurations and reconfigurations of flesh.

More will be said about abyssal and sideways selves and their decolonizing bodily projects later, but for now let us turn to Ana Paula and her lucid anti-colonial standpoint. Her remarks about the emotional damage that racism performs ("a *negrito* like me, who was going to want me?") echo our previous characterization of sideways selves as both twilight and climax. She sees herself caught between the place of gayness, in which Blackness and Brownness render embodiments unfit for homonational inclusion, and the site of travesti fecal allure, whereby racialization endows them with hypersexualization. Ana Paula falls sideways under the black holes' gravitational curve and, from within this state of stagnation, she bears skins that shall house painful yet sustaining possibilities.

Sideways relationality makes connections among travestis redefining space and time. Over a century ago, racialized lunfardos encoded flesh at the nation's outskirts. Today, travestis tap into this void's esoteric archive. Walking the streets, participating in the sex trade, residing in tight-knit close quarters, they all invoke marginal subjectivities that eugenics politics scours away through Buenos Aires's gut. Sideways selves pollute mainstream and counterpublics, and yet, they also transition from the reality of pollutant debris into the enigmatic, dissident, decolonizing abyss. They create unprecedented ground for resistant, oppositional, and abyssal practices, including but not limited to streetwalking, cruising, squatting, and trespassing. Travesti transversality interweaves doing, pausing, reflexivity, subterfuge, masking, transitioning, organizing, and other operations that infuse embodiments with esoteric potential. From within this abyssal void, from within its perplexing sociality, arise sideways relations and selves and their decolonizing bodily projects. At the crossroads of twilight and climax lies an outside to the normalization of queer, feminist, and trans motivation and theorizing.

Teoría Travesti Latinoamericana and Jotería Studies

Travestis' transversal reflexivity pays much-needed attention to the embodied technologies of reconfiguration, denormalization, and decolonization. In *Travesti: Una teoría lo suficientemente buena*, Marlene Wayar crafts an ingenious theory of power from the standpoint of travesti experiences across Latin America (2018b). Two major nodes in the web of her theorizing are *nostredad* (roughly glossed as "*us*ness" or "*we*ness") and *transitud* (transness). Nostredad refers to the disperse *we* that sex work elicits as a learning and pedagogical experience. Nostredad presents an outward-looking orientation that both places travesti at an abyss—where other epistemic, bodily, and political projects simmer—and centers travesti embodiments, experiences, and knowledges. The spatial connections and borders where Wayar and I encounter each other speak to the far-reaching endings of nostredad.

Wayar is the founder of Futuro Transgenérico, a cultural and political organization at the forefront of travesti and trans struggles in Latin America and Argentina. I first meet Wayar in 2002 at a preparatory meeting for that year's CABA Pride Parade. However, we begin to work more closely sixteen years later. Since then, we have cofacilitated workshops, seminars, and performances; presented together at academic panels; and cotaught graduate seminars. At the Latin American Studies Association, I served as cochair of the Sexualities and LGBT track for the 2018–2019 term. During our tenure as cochairs, Dr. Suyapa Portillo Villeda and I proposed and organized "América Transgénerx / América Transgender," the first-ever roundtable in the association's history to be led in its entirety by Latin American and Latinx trans* activists.[61] Our intention was to reverse the usual extraction of resources, from south to north, that academic institutions follow. Back in 2017, Dr. Portillo Villeda had tried unsuccessfully to gather support from the Sexualities track to center trans politics at the annual meeting. Putting the roundtable together, coordinating schedules, facilitating supporting documentation for visa purposes, and seeing through each visa process was at times challenging and exhausting. Wayar and I began to weave transnational collaborations and conversations through this process.

In 2021, I joined the collective Futuro Transgenérico on a hemispheric project of trans/travesti oral histories. Designed by Wayar, the project brings together eight activists from the Spanish-speaking Latinx and Latin American worlds, for example, Bamby Salcedo (TransLatin@ Coalition, Los Angeles), Cecilia Gentili (Trans Equity Consulting, Miami), and Jennicet Gutiérrez (Familia:TQLM, Los Angeles and Tucson).[62] With the joint support of the Palais de Glace, an art space and museum under the umbrella of Argentina's Ministry of Culture, and the Latin American Graduate School of Social Sciences, the oral history project seeks to collect transnational and context-specific evidence about the structural conditions in which trans and travesti individuals face precarity and debility.[63]

Sex work and streetwalking live at the heart of Latin American travesti theorizing, a domain of practice, experience, and knowledge where decolonizing bonds germinate. Wayar conveys that a *prostibular* (brothel-like) self lies at the center of nostredad. Among the lessons that fellow trave-stis learn through the practice of streetwalking, Wayar highlights their adeptness in responding to abuse and harassment. What might not come as a complete surprise is that the art of sex work, conducted openly by travestis, demands more than just a physical gesture or posture indicating availability. It also involves the deliberate interruption of the performance of availability. In Wayar's words, this practice entails, for travestis, an acceptance of the roles they must play within the solicitation arena: creat-ing their own place while also sustaining the client's. What Wayar glosses as the sex worker's "web" implicates a much wider, more dispersed, dis-continuous, and yet enduring sociality.

Through streetwalking, travestis bring into being the dwellings where, I suggest, black holes foster decolonizing bodily projects. For example, Hotel Gondolín is one such assemblage of life-sustaining projects. In the 1990s, Gondolín was a family-owned hotel near the zona roja in CABA's Villa Crespo neighborhood. Travestis arriving in a big and expensive city often lacked the credit or references to access housing. In this context, they paid top dollar to sublet Gondolín's overcrowded rooms. At the height of the 2000 economic crisis, the hotel owners let the building lan-guish in disrepair. Travestis swiftly organized themselves to take it over in 2001. Today, it functions as a cooperative association. Architect Facundo Revuelta (2022) describes it as a "home [. . .], community, a shelter, [and] an emblematic space of self-sufficiency and travesti-trans pride."

Black holes become sites where travestis assemble novel ways of responding to dispossession. Wayar's theorizing links sex work to what I describe as black holes: abyssal subjectivities that encourage and summon nostredad. Latin American travesti theorizing steers nostredad toward its most outward-looking orientation, placing abyssal subjectivities at the crossroads of various decolonial projects. In fact, nostredad reconnects myriad scales of spatial, temporal, emotional, embodied, political, and spiritual arenas. Consider the social physics of nostredad at the round-table "América Transgénerx / América Transgender." Our main intention was to shift from theorizing *about* to theorizing *with* kinspeople. Our coming together relied on an unusual way of assembling dispersed yet deeply resonating voices, experiences, practices, and hopes. Sideways selves gained an operative meaning, I believe, within this constellation that we call nostredad. It became important for us to call upon our abyssal subjectivities across transhemispheric webs of care, mutual recognition, and political determination.

"América Transgénerx / América Transgender" sought to nourish these webs through a three-pronged aim: making collective sense of structural barriers faced by trans and travesti populations across the Américas, exchanging lessons that our collectivities had learned by strategizing against specific manifestations of the politics of death, and countering the disciplinary neglect to which travesti and trans theorizing is subjected within LASA and other academic organizations. The roundtable featured activists, intellectuals, and artists: Jennicet Gutiérrez, a transgender Latina organizer from Jalisco, México, who at the time resided in Los Angeles, California, and who works with Familia: Trans Queer Liberation Movement; Indyra Mendoza Aguilar, the coordinator of Cattrachas, which works as a feminist-led observatory of gender violence, and a network focusing on research and communication to advance LGBTTI rights in Honduras; Pilar Salazar Argueta, a Guatemalan journalist, community radio host, and activist; Nahil Zerón, a historian and feminist trans man who works at Cattrachas analyzing the sociohistorical context of LGBTTI struggles in Honduras; and Susy Shock and Marlene Wayar, whom I have already introduced as activists, performers, and authors. Portillo Villeda and I were the roundtable's conveners but also participated in it. Video journalist Pilar Cabrera documented both the prep and the roundtable.[64]

We knew of each other, but only Portillo Villeda and Mendoza had sustained an ongoing collaboration, for several years. In preparation for this roundtable, we had to learn each other's idiolects and forge a shared language emphasizing our differences. We set up our bunker in one of the hotel rooms. First, we discussed the sources that we each used to describe the situation of the trans and travesti population in the various territories that we hail from—Jalisco, Los Angeles, Buenos Aires, Guatemala City, Jujuy and Syracuse, and Tegucigalpa. Second, we meticulously examined the possibility of going beyond the typical roundtable format. We chose to choreograph an artivist intervention, mixing *copla* singing, prayer, minilectures, dialogues, and dance.[65] Finally, we established that the politics of life and death would be the main theme, as it is the most pressing for travesti, trans, and jotería populations across the Latinx and Latin Americas.[66] The term *Américas*, in plural and with an accent on the *é*, acquired an even more sideways tone through this energizing yet at times tense collaboration.

In a kindred spirit of nostredad, we committed our energies to discussing coloniality and its underwriting of the untimely demise and horrific murder of two fellow trans individuals, Roxsana Hernández and Vicky Hernandez (unrelated to each other). We saw their expendability as a direct result of fascism, border militarization, and dictatorial masculinism. Roxsana was an asylum seeker from Honduras who lacked citizenship and arrived at Tijuana's San Ysidro Port of Entry (SYPOE) during the second week of May 2018. Tragically, she died while in the custody of US Immigration and Customs Enforcement (ICE) by the twenty-fifth of that month. Having traversed three international borders, she entered the US immigration system and was transferred through three different facilities across three states before ultimately arriving at the Cibola County Correctional Center in New Mexico (Gutiérrez and Portillo 2018, 393). Cibola is notorious for its "icebox cages," commonly referred to as "hieleras" by the Spanish-speaking immigrant community.

Vicky, another transgender woman, was assassinated by Honduras's state forces on the eve of June 28, 2009. The date is consequential, since it marks the constitutional crisis that illegally ousts democratically elected President Manuel Zelaya. On behalf of Vicky's three surviving family members, Cattrachas pursued a legal case against the Honduran state for over a decade. By the time we met in Boston, the Inter-American Court of Human Rights had determined that they were going to hear the case. By June 2021, the Court issued its ruling, which became the first-ever decision on transfemicide reached by an international human rights tribunal.

LASA's roundtable was a unique opportunity to make a nostredad statement, and we did not take it lightly. As documented by several activists and scholar-activists, it is crucial to trace the compound structures shaping the perils of Roxsana and many other Central American and Latin American trans and nonbinary immigrant persons.[67] Marlene, for instance, asked that we reflect on the condition of exile that trans, travesti, and gender nonconforming individuals typically share across primary social institutions, such as family, school, and healthcare. Childhood becomes a socially constructed site of pervasive exclusion for gender nonconforming bodies. Families quickly shun anyone who shows early signs of deviation from the rules that tie biology to gender expression. The Argentinean writer Juan Solá illustrates this visceral rejection of *children who never were* in the marvelous novel *La Chaco* (2016). Ximena, the main character, flees her native town in the interior of the country, Resistencia, to live as a travesti sex worker in Buenos Aires. Displacement has a central place within narratives of trans exile. Ximena's childhood is no exception. Subjected to harassment from her bullying classmates, she feels disoriented upon hearing her teacher's admonishment, "Don't you ever fight the girls" (2016, 3). However, Ximena comes to the disheartening realization that the teacher doesn't count *her* among the girls with whom boys should not fight.

At Boston, Marlene reminds us that many young girls are also travestis. "Our fathers and mothers, they send us into absolute exile, into *la nada* (the nothing)" (personal communication, 2019). Notice that in its original Spanish, *la nada* shares a semiotic field with the terms *void* and *abyss*. While the rest of society is talking about migrating in search of a better life, "we say that we are migrating away from the heterosexual and catholic family" (personal communication, 2019). Pilar Salazar Argueta also makes us aware of the overarching influence of religious fundamentalism on the myriad strategies of death haunting travesti/trans existence across the Americas. She examines an extermination machine that arose in Guatemala's early 1980s. She links this machine to Catholic and evangelical groups. Fundamentalist religious groups rallied behind Bill 5272 to deny children access to integral sexual education.[68] According to Salazar Argueta, these strategies extend the genocidal thirst that Spaniards brought with them some five hundred years ago.

As much as Latin American travesti theory centers streetwalking as a response to dispossession, so are other ways of knowing, doing, and politicizing. As such, they give rise to nonconforming bodily projects. If streetwalking points to abyssal and sideways selves, so do other ways of politicizing flesh against colonial legacies across the Américas. Nostredad in Boston moves outwards for its reliance on and implication in decolonizing genealogies of embodiments. Jennicet, Suyapa, and I live and make community in the United States as well as within the webs of kinship that link our histories to Central and South America. Moreover, the perils of both Roxsana Hernández and Vicky Hernandez make visible the continent's power lines, which build on coloniality's geography of death both south *and* north of the Rio Grande. Nostredad among sideways selves charts cross-hemispheric resonances with decolonizing genealogies of jotería studies. It is at this juncture, I submit, where an *é* of and from the Américas lives.

Referenced as a political project, a collective movement, and even a site of personal and collective identification, jotería studies offers rigorous inquiries and methodologies about nonconforming desire, eroticism, and love. Jotería methods undertake an oppositional stance that examines and challenges white-centered projects of normative gender, class, ability, land, aesthetics, and nation. Emerging from feminist, trans, queer, and Chican@-Xicanx-Mestiza-Latinx activism and academics (Revilla and Santillana 2014), these methods seek to correct persistent forms of violence that bind *familia*, community, and nation within Xicanx and Latinx cultures (Galarte 2021). Originally centered on reclaiming the word *joto* from its queerphobic use among speakers of Mexican Spanish, jotería relates to the collective project of affirming nonnormative histories and knowledges embedded in Mexican American, Xicanx, Latinx, and Afro-Latinx communities.

We previously analyzed cartographic gaps, black holes, sewage pipes, and their logics of invisibility. We also recognized these geometries for their connections to women of color and queer of color critiques. The coalitional project of third-world feminism resonates with jotería studies and its ongoing labor to situate individuals face-to-face, allowing them to confront in and through each other's flesh the peculiar estrangements that capitalism exacts. Jotería makes tangible the need for another, the hard-fought companionship that community often denies to its children under the name of the heterocisnormative, whiteness-centered familia.

Chicana feminist intellectuals urge familia to listen to its jotería. In her 1981 essay "La Güera," intellectual and artist Cherríe Moraga recommends starting with the flesh, inviting familia to engage in a thorough exploration of the ways that oppressions take residency in our minds, hearts, and skins; how they create isolation instead of radicalization; and how they may lead us to betrayal by ranking each other's structural subordination (Moraga and Anzaldúa [1981] 2022, 27). The method, or mode, of linking, connecting dissent to multiple systems of power, what theorist and practitioner of differential consciousness Chela Sandoval (2002, 2018) calls *methodologies of emancipation*, invokes a sense of *we*ness. Jotería studies enacts and models this project of *we*ness at the turn of the twenty-first century.

Michael Hames-García expands on the "face-to-faceness" of ways of making sense of jotería flesh (2014, 137). In their insightful introduction to the journal *Aztlán*'s dossier "Jotería Studies," Hames-García invokes the generational wisdom and shift that inspire jotería roots. They refer to "multigendered queer Chican@s and Latin@s [who are] trained and nurtured by women of color feminisms and feminists [. . .] [and who] fought and loved in coalition, inclusion, and multiplicity" (138). As if they were speaking to Moraga face-to-face, Hames-García references the ways that oppressions operate in their shaping of "either 'us' as male-identified queer Chicanos or 'us' as multigendered queer Chican@s" (138). *Us* or *us*ness, in the style of nostredad, implicates the margins or intersections from within which jotería recognizes and acts upon the possibility of an oppositional togetherness. Jotería, in its yearning to affirm multiplicity, challenges Latinx and Xicanx familias to dispute fragmentation and homogenization of nations, languages, sexualities, and genders.

Meeting face-to-face at NACCS (National Association of Chicana and Chicano Studies), MLA (Modern Language Association), ASA (American Studies Association), and LASA (Latin American Studies Association), but most important, "on the margins of Chicana and Latina feminist spaces" (Hames-García 2014, 138), jotería calls upon a tentative yet enduring sense of selfhood. The *we*ness that first occupies jotería's psychic space for Hames-García resonates with Moraga's words, "the 'ism' that's sitting on top of our heads" (Moraga and Anzaldúa [1981] 2022, 29), the experience of outsiderness ranging from feeling dismissed to blatant exclusion. *We*ness comes to existence as "identifiable but not yet fully formed" (Hames-García 138). Jotería consciousness rejects insulation into the comforting experience of shared oppression. In this sensibility lies jotería's commitment to defying fragmentation of selves, as either more or less authentic, or ranking the selves' oppressions. Hames-García understands that the salient labor of jotería occurs face-to-face, centering multiple voices, examining affect as sites of reliable knowledge, and stretching kinship constellations. By practicing this radical politics of flesh, jotería carries togetherness away from homogeneous identities, or from the Eurocentered encasing of jotería into its putative Mexican-Chicano Spanish equivalent.[69] Indeed, jotería steers the politics of flesh toward nondominant differences (Lorde 1984).

Through my own engagement with jotería spaces, specifically the Association for Jotería Arts, Activism, and Scholarship (AJAAS) since 2011, I feel called to participate in the collective redefinition and recalibration of a sense of Latinidad that fosters both (1) critical listening dispositions about differences within and across Afro-Latinx, Latinx, Xicanx, and Latin American and Central American subjectivities and (2) ways of making sense of differences premised on plurality and partiality, in the borderlands (Calvo-Quirós 2014) and against fragmentation (Alvarez 2014). At AJAAS, and other jotería spaces, I am becoming fluent in oral histories, personal testimonies, and other technologies of healing and loving. While I remain implicated by anti-Black and anti-Indigenous racisms, I seek to link my diasporic sense of Latinx Brownness to a decolonial jotería consciousness and praxis. I understand this praxis to thrive in anti-capitalist eroticism, fostering intimate ways of restoring justice to nondominant differences. As if from within the void of black holes, I embrace jotería for its enriching of sideways selves and for its potential to cross-pollinate abyssal subjectivities face-to-face and across the hemisphere.

The border theorist Gloria Anzaldúa speaks of jotería within an imperfect yet astonishing project for mestiza selves. Pejoratively glossed as "mixed-race," *mestizo* refers to contentious transactions. It harks back to whitening anxieties and miscegenation panics. For Anzaldúa, instead, mestizas move away from hardening the politics of blood quantum and land theft, or the erasure or extermination of vibrant Indigenous and Native communities.[70] Jotería also activates mestizaje as we dwell on the thin edge of barbwire where borderlines bleed. Nostredad entails the combination, even fusion, of jotería, mestiza, abyssal, and travesti subjectivities. It is a way of engaging altered states of being, knowing, and living. *Nepantla*, Anzaldúa calls this altered state, after the very Nahua cosmologies of Abya Yala's beating heart.

It is in jotería and travesti spaces where nostredad grows and sheds skins, where we become critical listeners, co-interlocutors, and siblings across solidarity struggles. Skins incubate a "queer materialist perspective" (Revilla and Santillana 2014), switching to felt awareness of what it means to be hurt and immobilized, knowing too well that you could not possibly stand by as oppressions push jotería into exile. Coalition-building, they call it. Not the abstract or mantra-like term uttered ad infinitum as a symbol of "woke" feminism. I mean the lived and expansive repository of technologies of the flesh, the disintegration and reconstitution of who we may become to each other, what we may learn about our differences, and how we may contribute to each other's well-being.

My sister identifies as cisgender, but I am not sure whether I am allowed to say that she has chosen to make kinship as more than or less than heterosexual. That is a telling that belongs to her. The sister I grew up with is direct, outspoken, determined. By fifteen, she is selling cosmetics off a catalogue. I come to her when I want something that my dad doesn't want to pay for. She is aware that working-class teens work. But barely anyone in her classroom does. Me? I live in the world where I go to my dad, aunt, or sister to get what I want. She is six years older than me. Mom passed. My sister looks after me. Me? I take for granted that someone is looking after me. Flash forward to her senior year of high school. It is time to decide whether my father will support her moving out of town to attend college. She is not afraid of getting a job, but for an eighteen-year-old, moving to a large city for college means so much more than books and meals. It is her independence, autonomy, even perhaps her departure, leaving us behind, that my father fears most. In the thorough ordering of gender for the working class in Argentina's periphery, my father envisions marriage for my sister, but not before helping her get through teaching certification at a local school. Closer to home, she would participate in sustaining our family's life. That is, helping with managing my teens, which I am sure dad never enjoyed. My sister doesn't see herself going through teaching certification. She leaves home overnight, not a word to my dad. She never goes back.

Today, I live in central New York, have a job at a private research university, and have access to healthcare, credit, and disposable income. Dad had some aspirations for me. However, not even in his wildest dreams could he have imagined what a college education has afforded me. Not even the myth of meritocracy could have done that kind of number on him. Today, my sister lives in the third largest city in Argentina, owns a convenience store, does not have access to private healthcare or credit. She works between sixteen and eighteen hours a day. She spends all those hours standing on her two feet behind the store's counter. She doesn't make enough to afford an attendant. She did not marry. Nor did she attend college. These are the realities that racializing patriarchies produce across the globe, with their variegated differences. I live today as what many may perceive as a trans woman, but I most definitely grew up with cisgender and ethnic privilege at home and across social institutions.[71]

Siblinghood by Way of *Nostredad*

I have offered a slice of the histories underlying siblinghood for my sister and I. My intention is to tease out life situations, such as siblinghood, where we typically learn to understand intersubjectivity through its many textures. I revisit the relation with my sister to illustrate curvatures of the social as they refract on our meeting each other anew, face-to-face, through a tender and dispersed *we.* I don't seek to center siblinghood in theorizing nostredad, but rather, with a healthy skepticism toward the hardening of blood quantum, I encounter our relation through nostredad and jotería's denormalizing lens.

I have thus far examined the pedagogies, the ways of being, doing, and knowing, *we*ness and jotería. I posit that they enact an ontological turn, a rigorous attention to the materiality of margins, intersections, borders, and, we should add, streetwalkers, dwellers of black holes, and shitholes. I encounter a broad understanding of siblinghood in these pedagogies of crossing, as an almost otherworldly activity, a ritualized act that demands the liminal and altered disposition of many a sideways self, such as *jotas/os*, *jotx*, travestis, and mestizas. In her dazzling ode to eros ideologies, Laura Elisa Pérez speaks of this liminal state as an act of reconstitution of selfhood, or reintegration of mind, body, and spirit, for, she explains, "we have a natural need to love, to unfold, to become, to be tended, to be supported, parenting or gardening ourselves into greater and deepening integrity, self-realization, wholeness" (2019, 6–7). Indeed, we seek to become generous and artful gardeners with deep integrity, affirming self-realization through the act of supporting, as siblings sometimes grow to do, each other's well-being.

Allow me to recall Marlene Wayar's insights regarding travestis, who, despite a world filled with brutal hostility toward their existence, learn to acknowledge the role they play in supporting others, including their clients, all the while forging their own paths. What Wayar (2018b) glosses as the "web of one's own" implicates a sociality of nostredad, *we*ness, black holes, and shitholes—a sociality, however discontinuous, that endures, summoning thereby kin people, those of us that Pérez names as gardeners, those of us who encounter each other face-to-face, jotería-style. The sense of "nature" that Pérez has in mind when she invokes a "natural need to love" doesn't raise universalizing claims to goodness and wholeness as traits of the human. Rather, to paraphrase Chela Sandoval's use (2002), it works as a homeopathic antidote for the dehumanizing disintegration of mind, body, and spirit. That sense of "nature" points to altered, hallucinating ways of knowing and being that I shall later engage in my discussion of decolonizing *remedios* (remedies).[72]

I rehearse a nostredad and jotería engagement with the dispersed sociality through which my sister and I access an unprecedented depth of awareness. I reject subjecting *we*ness to colonial legacies and their shaping of the nuclear family. I recognize in Pérez's gesture toward the "natural need to love" an appeal to an otherwise geometry of healing and caring. What jotería and travesti social formations provide is a novel project of nonconforming embodiments, self-realization, and collective care. We breed embodiments that slip into skins housing more than an individual self. I attend to this creative act as I do the garden that grows right outside the window of the hilltop residence where I live in central New York.

The house where I live sits on unceded Haudenosaunee lands. The tulips inching out of the front yard's soil early in the spring came with the house. The availability of tulips in the Americas has a short history dating back to the nineteenth century. The garden requires hours of maintenance and extra nourishment. Syracuse's industries and residents have over time damaged any semblance of environmental balance. Those extra nutrients come from a gardening store. I sometimes put gloves and a hat on, and I spend hours weeding the garden. Some other times, I put a call out for a gardener to service the yard. You may also find me spraying a vinegar concoction to ethically invite wild upshots of green to die out. To an extent, the garden and I mediate a mode of production that the notion of racializing capitalism helps define. Garden, land, tulip bulb, water, nutrient, and gardening time are commodities that I get by participating in this mode of production. Without settlers, no tulips, but most important, no property for me to own or lease. Without settlers, no capitalism, but most important, no labor for me to sell or buy. Yet, I cannot deny that I also attend to the garden as less an agent of capital and more a life-form, a kin member, who seeks to gift the environment and its many inhabitants *just* companionship and stewardship. This is not easy to realize. It requires both determination and imagination. Above all, it asks that I shift my sense of self from that of a settler to that of a nonsettler. That is, I seek to contend with the contradictions—material, cultural, and social— that shape what brings together Haudenosaunee land, the garden, and I-more-than-individual. Restoring justice to this contradictory nostredad is recognizable and y e t not fully f o R m e d.

The natural need to love my sister summons me to rehearse this gesture or intention toward justice. Few ways of knowing and living against injustice are as prolific and inventive as Latin American travesti theorizing and jotería studies. They infuse dissidence into the journeys through which many sideways selves, such as myself, come to meet head-on coloniality's mode of producing sibling flesh. Without a colonial understanding of gender, I am neither a cisgender boy nor a trans woman, neither my sister's brother nor her sister. Without a colonial understanding of gender, I am neither a monster nor disposable, neither my sister's nightmare nor her less-than-human subordinate. Restoring justice to our siblinghood demands that we sustain each other, interactively, maybe intra-actively, as kin people at the very outskirts of coloniality. This is the politics of black holes, sewage lines, and streetwalking. As I shall discuss next, this is a decolonizing politics of sociosomatic matter, an uncharted and sacred bodily project.

CHAPTER 2

The Coloniality of Transgender

The Decolonial Physics of Social Relations

Sideways selves practice habits of flesh that remain hidden from most. As I initiate readers into specific ways of witnessing and critically listening to their habits, I seek to expose the links between official systems of knowledge and colonial legacies. Colonial systems of knowledge often deploy *gender* as a universalizing and supracultural lens for social and heuristic analysis (Lugones 2020).[1] As this chapter will show, sideways selves further feminist deconstruction by decentering the genre of the human within explanations of embodied differences and formations.

As the practice of travesti streetwalking demonstrates, sideways selves deepen the contradictions found in the physics of social relations. They also invite us to reflect on how they bear on our accounts of bodily projects. Debris, trash, void are to be banished from view. Sideways selves leave an impression in the world, but this impression exists between banishment and trace. Habits of the flesh encode the matter of social stasis, rhythm, distance, and proximity into practices, including those that track responses to banishment. One such habit within streetwalking practices is the formation consisting of a row of three in which travestis synchronize their stride by maintaining a two-step distance in front and behind each other. Streetwalking perfects this practice, as without this precise strut calculation, all three could be confused by potential clients' signals. Tricks register within an invisible radius of desire and transaction. Habits stretch out across the social, not without conflict though. Clients in the sex work trade also participate in enhancing or deflating travestis' strutting pace. For any sex work transaction to be successful, streetwalkers will become either background or foreground. Clients are competent in acting out these transactions, usually pursuing travestis as series of bodies. They search for and extract from them sexual release before swiftly moving on.

Sideways selves combine the paradox of absence and trace, pushed out and yet pressing back. Reduced to thing, behaving as not-thing. Brought to the foreground, then banished from view. From within these contradictions arise nonconforming habits of flesh. They compel us to address the significance of embodiment and its mattering. Conventional explanations used by feminism to interpret embodiments consistently revolve around the dichotomy of culture versus nature. What the embodiments of sideways selves make patently clear is that the divide between culture and nature, subjectivity and reality, no longer carries the same weight as it once did. I submit that new materialisms and, more importantly, performative, agentic, thing-centered materialisms reframe the ways in which feminist inquiries address the social production of embodiments, including dominant and resistant productions. Sideways selves enact materialisms that challenge feminist attachments to anti-realist accounts of power and agency. Furthermore, Latin American travesti/trans theorizing and jotería studies allow us to reframe agentic and performative materialism. They help us question the fraught relations that feminist new materialisms maintain with anti-colonial and decolonial feminisms.

From the standpoint of interdisciplinary philosophical reflection, sideways selves have critical potential. They instruct us on the alternative reality of embodiment and nonconformity. It might feel counterintuitive to talk about alternatives to the dominant order in terms of the *reality* of embodiments, since these terms create healthy skepticism about metaphysics. In feminist circles, metaphysics has enjoyed a bad rap.[2] Feminists are troubled by the metaphysical belief that there exists a world of objects independent of our experience and knowledge. Feminism dislikes an inquiry whose claim to certainty rests on the idea that the natural world has an order outside the realm of social construction and, therefore, independent of oppression and ideology. More recently, however, materialist feminisms reframe this debate by displacing the contradiction between an unadulterated biomaterial world and a thoroughly social domain. They emphasize nonconforming insistences of other-than-human life-forms, among them, what we refer to as nonhuman animals. This shift in focus from human to nonhuman life-forms reveals that life, and its thoroughly material reality, generates potentially more biophilic ends than has been generally imagined (Mortimer-Sandilands and Erickson 2008; Alaimo and Hekman 2008). The accounts of embodiment that I shall outline share this turn toward realism.

Feminist social constructivism benefits from the rich complexity of thing-centered or nonhuman-animal-centered materialism, specifically because embodied differences emerge through social formation, including the formation of the human against the background of matter that is reduced to nonhuman condition. The debate continues over whether the new materialisms of things and nonhuman animal forms genuinely address racialization and its shaping of the nonhuman.[3] We must contend, however, with dispossession, with, for example, having to work a job on the brink of death. We seek new realist versions of materialism if we are to make sense of streetwalkers, stateless migrants, and the habits of the flesh that they foster with their practices. Because of the condition of dispossession, which reduces embodiment to both animal-like and beneath-animal matter, a realist and materialist approach gains salience at the crossroads of Latin American trans and travesti theorizing and jotería studies. Unlike new materialisms for which race and racialization remain diffused, this new materialism that I pursue offers a more explicit direction into the realities of dispossession, such as the nonhuman as fungible (Snorton 2017), toxic and dead (Chen 2012), or unfit for ideological rehabilitation (Schuller 2018).

This chapter pursues three modes of querying the materiality of nonconforming bodily projects in Abya Yala. First, I decode colonialist systems of knowledge that deploy *gender* and *transgender* as a universalizing and supracultural lens for social and heuristic analysis. Second, situating sideways selves within abyssal geographies, I recognize a standpoint that decenters the project of the human in explanations of transgender bodily formations. Critical to this standpoint are embodied responses to an ongoing project that turns people into subjects for colonial/modern exploitation. In other words, of importance to this decolonizing standpoint is the critique of the ways that transgender, as a bodily project, accrues human susceptibility. These responses concern a dominant orientation among transgender bodies today as they are utilized between bodies vested with human-impressible gendering force and those stuck in evolutionary *ungendering* time. I call this sociosomatic entanglement the *coloniality of transgender*. Third, by engaging an agential realist approach, the coloniality of transgender framework adumbrates the possibilities that lie beyond *trans* and with *trans of color*. These possibilities politicize the domain of impressible nonhuman flesh. Through an examination of these possibilities, the resonance between agential realism and Indigenous, Native, and Afro-diasporic lifeways gains prominence. Finally, I turn to the configuration of sacred bodily projects, such as Cuareca and

Kuna life-forms, as they allow us to refocus on sideways selves and their recalibration of ancestral habits of the flesh.

Realism, Embodiment, and Ontological Pluralism

For quite some time, feminist philosophers were puzzled by what looked like an intractable tension between gender as sexed subjectivities that become varied and multiple, and sex as an ineradicable rift between male and female (Alcoff 2005; Grosz 1994). The idea that biology determines the absolute binary between cisgender man and woman, combined with the idea that bodily differences proliferate without a predetermined end, supposedly explained major contemporary accounts of the reality of embodiment. The former accommodates a tradition that is known in Western philosophy as the metaphysics of substance, that is, the idea that the world consists of entities defined by essential characteristics and that they unequivocally exclude any ambiguity between one thing and another. According to the essentialist view, biology marks bodies as either male or female. The latter accommodates a tradition that, by contrast, is known as the metaphysics of events, that is, the notion that the world consists of processes whose dynamics create constant change and, hence, support a world of ambiguity and fluidity.

On one end of these two views, essentialism considers that gender underlies long-standing ideologies about the hierarchical order of differences between cisgender men and women. Sexist and patriarchal hegemonies rest on constructing biology-based differences as clear-cut and absolute. Subsequently, they justify a culture that subordinates anything that falls beneath the male or masculine station. Conversely, a process-centered view of gender underpins anti-sexist and antipatriarchal counterhegemonies that support the notion of performance-based differences. As performative, they unfold in shifting and ambiguous fashion and, consequently, have the potential of affirming a culture of insubordination against male/female hierarchies.

Feminist scholarship and political work contend with the complexities of sexed and gendered embodiments. Yet, they often operate under the belief that reality is one, and its interpretation multiple. In fact, biology-based, culture-based, and performativity-based approaches may align with the gravitational force of this monism. Not only essentialist but also social constructionist and performative accounts of sex and gender may recapitulate claims against ontological pluralism (Lugones 2003c; Sealey

2020; DiPietro, McWeeny, and Roshanravan 2019; Hoagland 2004; Taylor 2022; Dembroff 2018). As this section shall demonstrate, I embrace ontological pluralism, since it is true to the experience of social groups who lack autonomy in the colonial/modern ordering of the world. I feel deflated when some feminist theorists demand that nonconforming embodiments materialize deconstructive viewpoints about sex and gender. My realism tells me that resistance ongoingly repurposes the many modes with which it meets domination and oppression. In fact, minoritized individuals and collectives engage with essentialist and constructivist views according to context or at once within the same context. Moreover, what is typically understood as a context may prove insufficient for capturing complexities that arise from the contradictions of *oppressing⇔being oppressed⇔resisting*.[4] Thus, subjectivities who lack autonomy in the neocolonial order of the world do not become empowered just because some contexts create legal, institutional, or market conditions that favor self-realization as deconstructive expression of free will. Social backing of resistant intentions for minoritized selves may stem from marginal, oppositional, and alternative realities regardless of whether the self finds themself within a context overriding dominant or nondominant arrangements.

Sideways selves and their bodily projects exist beneath the domain of both the human and nonhuman animal. They decouple gender and sex from what Jamaican philosopher Sylvia Wynter calls the genre of the human, or Man (2003, 269–272). According to Katherine McKittrick (2015), this genre is "tied to epistemological histories that presently [. . .] [naturalize] Western bourgeois tenets" (10). In that sense, "the human is therefore wrought with physiological and narrative matters that systemically excise the world's most marginalized" (10). Far from submitting to a purely subjectivist account of decolonizing resistance or agency, sideways selves point to contexts, situations, practices, and histories wherein flesh, in its most concrete mattering, originates from disfigurations or modified versions of the genre of the human. To put it in Alexander Weheliye's terms, the disfigurations that sideways selves realize make us aware of "the atrocity of flesh as a pivotal arena" (2014, 2). That is, within this arena, embodied projects craft new and capacious sociosomatic and sociogenic (dis)(recon)figurations.

I seek to retain a realist emphasis in the metaphysics of sex and gender that I review next. I converse with Sally Haslanger's model mainly because of its commitment to a critical version of realism (2000, 2012). I also aim to challenge some of her metaphysical commitments, as they often lead feminist practitioners to align with the less inclusive aspects of her proposal. I put aside the ascriptivist and conferralist approaches to gender metaphysics of the last decade, which offer bold accounts of gender as a social unifying role or as an individual and communal social property, respectively (Witt 2011; Ásta 2018). Both provide novel ways of thinking about social kinds. My interest, however, doesn't lie with revisiting whether sex and gender are social kinds, or what kind of social kinds they are.[5] Instead, I proceed with an account that, stemming from Black feminist studies, women of color feminism, and their praxes, supports decolonial and pluralist objectivism.

Haslanger's feminist metaphysics speaks to the materialist turn that sees in everything that lives the outward-looking orientation of relations and their connections to a changing whole. The material world, according to this view, is enmeshed in social formation, as much as social construction is interwoven in the biophysical realm. No longer is the supremacy of perception or the mind taken for granted. Her proposal condemns post-structuralist accounts of sex and gender for their underlying theory of reference. She challenges post-structuralist ideas that link the very act of naming what lies beyond discourse with understanding it. That is, Haslanger's realism questions the belief that discourse always already prefigures and, thus, constitutes an extradiscursive realm. By supporting the belief that the world includes some pregiven objects, critiques such as Haslanger's lead feminist philosophy to metaphysical inquiries about the nature of sexed bodies (see also Alcoff 2005; Grosz 2011; Wittig 1992).

Concerning sexed distinctions, Haslanger refers to nature as an infrastructure that, regardless of the sociopolitical regime, neatly determines in a causally significant manner an effective way of relating to the bodies we are given. Clearly, her metaphysics combines a version of essentialism, that there is a something that makes something the thing it is, with a version of constructivism, that there are schemas with which we make sense of things, such as bodies, according to political and social contexts. An objective type or infrastructure, which stands independent of human perception, prompts grouping of things. Grouping functions by convention, of course, but also, Haslanger argues, by the mere ontology of the world, by properties that are structurally more relevant to what the world is. These properties "play a fundamental role in determining what the world (as a whole) looks like and how it evolves," regardless of what conventions we hold about it (2000, 123). Instead of relying on the putative force of nature to dictate what bodies can be or do, her metaphysics seeks to identify bodily properties that are ontologically fundamental and that they relate to bodily distinctions in a nontrivial and causally meaningful way.

Haslanger's model makes room for a contextual account of objective types, as she claims that "one's gender may not be entirely stable, and that other systems of oppression may disrupt gender in particular contexts: a woman may not always function socially as a woman; a man may not always function socially as a man" (2012, 234). At least in certain contexts, she argues, an objective type compels the stabilization of the sex and gender system and allows a woman thereby to socially function as woman. A person is observed or imagined, she says, within a context that stabilizes gender, whenever a person is said to have "the bodily features presumed to be evidence of a female's biological role in reproduction" (235). The capacity for pregnancy and, as such, the chromosomal distinction between female and male is the objective type that Haslanger offers.[6] Primarily, she refers to "endosex," or sex characteristics that physically match what is expected for female or male bodies.[7] In her own words, the subordinate positions that women occupy as a group are "marked and justified by reference to (female) sex" (2012, 230).

In the most politically salient read of Haslanger's metaphysics, strands of the feminist movement find responses to their concerns about the flattening of sexual distinction, and its epistemic and ontological valence. For example, Monique Wittig's works, embraced in the 1970s by radical lesbian feminists, examine both the state of being born a woman and the process of becoming one. Wittig describes a phallocentric economy that consigns femininity to the anomalous mark of nature, a "physical defect" of sorts (Heisler Weiser 2021, 230–258). She makes evident that "female," or "woman," follows the political ideology, the "straight mind," that renders the negative inscription of the body (that which is not male) into a natural kind (Wittig 1992, 27–28). While at times Haslanger's proposal approximates Wittig's, the former reserves references to sex, such as chromosomal distinctions, to an objective, experience-independent reality. In other words, Haslanger contributes to the normative sociosomatic looping between XX-bodies and cisgender women.[8]

Contextual and social constructivist aspects of Haslanger's account correspond to the process of stabilization. By this process, she means normative assignation. Because of the type of realism that she espouses, I am inclined to think that normativity doesn't translate into heteronormativity, homonormativity, or transnormativity. Instead, I understand that she refers to two interconnected processes of normativity. First, the most realist normativity, which entails the ascription of a certain unity to a set of features. Let's say that we are not compelled by the reality of our bodies to ascribe a core place to kidneys in the unity that we call sex-gender. We are likely to be compelled by the reality of our bodies to ascribe a core place to ovaries in the unity that we call sex-gender. We could refer to this process in Haslanger's model as first-order ascription.[9] Second, the way in which ascription operates makes room for contexts in which ovaries cohere with the unity that we call sex-gender. Yet, it also makes room for contexts in which they do not cohere with such a unity.[10] This normative coherence is what we could call second-order ascription.

In her later work, María Lugones claims that coloniality entails reconceiving sex as nonambiguous and dimorphic (2020, 25–47). White and Euro-American colonizers established a hegemonic order within which gender functions as a bodily trait of humans. As such, it stands opposite other bodily projects that colonization subjugated. She highlights that coloniality shapes the link between first-order and second-order ascriptions. I understand Haslanger's model to function within the bounds of coloniality's reconceiving of sex-gender as dimorphic.[11]

The unity of "gender," or "woman," involves two modes of attribution. Firstly, it entails features that compel us to ascribe them a core role with regard to that unity. Secondly, it encompasses contexts in which these features, those that elicit the presumption of evidence of female sex, may or may not cohere according to first-order ascription. Lugones claims that coloniality reserves the role of reproduction of the species for Euro-American women, while colonized "women" become various versions of not-women and, thus, automata or reproducers of unwaged labor force (2007, 203). I am not sure whether, in Haslanger's argument, contexts and systems of oppression are interchangeable. I assume that they are not. However, it seems that systems of oppression do create various contexts, such as those that Lugones describes within coloniality.

In the United States, a dominant patriarchal order marginalizes and discriminates against women across various contexts, including contexts in which the sex and gender system tracks incompatible features (for instance, endosex, secondary sex characteristics, self-identification, legal designation, and societal perception). Out of the interplay of systems and contexts, restricting and enabling arrangements codetermine realities, including incompatible realities. That is, contexts bear on the mattering, the sociosomatic entangling, that gender and sex designate. I must note that contradictions may arise among second-order ascriptions, from one context to another. Stabilization performs a socio-ontological looping between contradictions. Their tenor may bring into question first-order ascription. Let me provide an example regarding sexual and reproductive rights across two contexts.

In context A, the state of Texas's Senate Bill 8 prohibits access to abortion procedures as soon as a heartbeat can be detected in the fetus.[12] Within context A, *abortion* refers to procedures that bodies perceived to have certain features—sexual resources capable of attaining pregnancy—may access as long as available technology does not detect a beating heart other than the pregnant person's. According to S.B. 8, pregnancy is a "human female reproductive condition" with the following features: it begins with fertilization, it is carried out by a "woman," and it must be calculated from "the first day of the woman's last menstrual period" (2). Basically, by the time the pregnant person becomes aware of the interruption of the menstrual cycle, which amounts to a potential pregnancy, there is no time to seek an abortion procedure. Notice that the bill refers indistinctly to "human female" and "woman." It should also be noted that, at least as an implied reality, S.B. 8 remains silent about pregnancies carried to term by bodies other than women's or by technologies replacing the gestational sac.[13]

Within context B, New York State's Reproductive Health Act permits access to abortion care for any person aged eighteen or older prior to week twenty-four of pregnancy.[14] After week twenty-four, the Reproductive Health Act names the fetus's viability, as well as the gestating person's health and life risks, as factors to be considered, by care providers and the gestating person, to reach a decision about abortion. Within context B, *abortion* refers to procedures that bodies perceived to have certain features—sexual resources capable of attaining pregnancy—may access at age eighteen and for twenty-four weeks, if the gestating person arrives at such a decision autonomously.

Discrepancies between context A and context B are compatible with the system of oppression that we call patriarchy, or, more specifically, heterocisnormative patriarchy. These discrepancies between contexts also point to something being amiss in Haslanger's objectivism. I am thinking about first-order ascription in her proposal. Within context A, the bodily features that matter as core for first-order ascription—the unit that may seek abortion procedures—remit to the presence of certain reproductive resources but also to the undifferentiation between technology and nature and between gestating person and fetus. While anti-rights language in S.B. 8 is effectively an assault on cisgender women's reproductive autonomy, the ban clearly targets more than just "human females'" or "women's" bodies. Ironically, this is the unintended sex and gender inclusivity of the state's abortion law. It also targets trans, gender nonconforming, and nonbinary-gender bodies if they were to seek abortion procedures.

Within S.B. 8, the context targets both cis and noncis bodies. It doesn't differentiate between technology that provides ultrasound detection of a heartbeat versus technology that provides chromosomal designation of a gestating person, or between nature as encoded by chromosomal information versus as the capacity of a gestating person to house a second heartbeat. It does not follow that S.B. 8 targets only "female" bodies, since the context, according to glaring evidence, implicates the use of technology, medical criteria that read technology as nature's truth, and both legislative and medical practice that regards physiological differentiation as matters of the state's prerogative and not of personal autonomy.

Undifferentiation between technology and nature within S.B. 8 may lead us to infer that certain intersex individuals count as gestating persons.[15] Available genetic technology tells us that some intersex people can potentially get pregnant. Thus, if the bill doesn't differentiate between technology and nature's truth when it comes to the fetus's heartbeat, it follows that it must agree with the genetic truth when it comes to intersex bodies' capacity for pregnancy.[16] As it concerns gestating person and fetus, it's the presence of the fetus's heartbeat that defines the existence of a gestating person in the letter of the bill. It doesn't matter what the exact chromosomal difference of the pregnant carrier is; what matters is whether that body could grow and house a second heartbeat within it. Thus, the bill includes intersex bodies among those that could potentially carry a second heartbeat within them.[17] S.B. 8 advocates would be hard-pressed to explain why intersex individuals pose an exemption to the bill, unless they sought to clarify the social role that technology plays in the demarcation of pregnancy as a condition that pertains only to a "woman [who] is carrying the developing human offspring" (2). Moreover, due to its archaic understanding of gender, S.B. 8 conflates intersex, nonbinary, and even trans bodies into the legal and medical category "woman."

In conclusion, context A consists of medicolegal enablements and constraints, as well as heterocissexist oppression, that seek yet fail to stabilize first-order ascription. Our analysis reveals that reconceiving sex—only females possess the objective infrastructure to get pregnant—is always already materially transformed by second-order ascription: only women menstruate, house a second heartbeat within them, and are responsible for carrying to term a developing human offspring. Second-order ascription bears on the stabilizing looping, to the extent that a realist feminist metaphysics reveals the sociosomatic entangling at work under sex and gender distinctions. If, according to Haslanger, a woman is a person said to have, within a stabilizing context, "the bodily features presumed to be evidence of a female's biological role in reproduction," S.B. 8 shows that bodily features that provide evidence of such a role in reproduction undergo a thoroughly social, yet not merely social, constitution process. Bodily features are much more socially produced than originally imagined by Haslanger's metaphysics.[18] S.B. 8 helps shape an entangling of technology, chromosomal information, reproductive tissue behavior, expert knowledge, legal definition, and decision-making as they codetermine bodily features.

My contention about Haslanger's objectivism is twofold. A discrepancy between contexts A and B tells us something about first-order and second-order ascriptions and the ways that second-order ascription, fully contextual for Haslanger, bears on first-order ascription, thoroughly ontological in her proposal. Attending to the significance of language use for metaphysics, and following second-order ascription, I don't deny the importance of exposing the myriad ways in which anti-rights state laws target cisgender women and, specifically, pregnant cisgender women. I seek, however, to underscore that second-order ascription—the fact that we typically read abortion-restricting laws as concerned mainly with (cisgender) women—may narrow the terms in which metaphysics makes sense of first-order ascription. This complicated looping between first-order and second-order ascriptions allows us to state that embodiments may in fact present and be perceived as, or be legislated into or out of, playing the female role in biological reproduction. As a sociosomatic entanglement, this role provides evidence of the thoroughly, yet not only, social mattering of gendered and sexed distinctions. By now, it should be clear that I seek a realist materialism that is less hung up on sorting what infrastructure is truly causally significant in the demarcation of sex-gender and more engaged with the ways that sociosomatic entangling bears on what makes certain infrastructures, and what disqualifies others, from being causally significant.

I mentioned that my contention about Haslanger's objectivism is twofold. The second contention that I have in mind is the discrepancy between contexts A and B. This discrepancy tells us something about the explanatory accuracy of the notion of "system of oppression." If systems of oppression operate as thoroughly social yet matter-altering relations, it follows that our account of them should give uptake to sociosomatic complexity. If we understood systems of power as assemblages, or as intermeshing, interlocking, fusing, compounding, codetermining, entangling entanglements, as implicating both discursive and extradiscursive domains, contending with variability, indeterminacy, and position-relative agencies both biophilic and not, the metaphysical valence of systems of oppression would greatly vary. It would allow us to comprehend the mutual implication of an adulterated biomaterial world and an impure biosocial domain. Thus, the discrepancies between Texas and New York with respect to abortion law would lead us to navigate the ongoing loop between first-order and second-order ascriptions and, simultaneously, to hold on to the conflicting, multiple mattering of sociosomatics.

I have thus far shown that social kinds, such as gender, codetermine nature and culture in much murkier ways than Haslanger's objectivism has it.[19] Heterosexuality and cissexism have the sociosomatic force to situate and locate subjectivity and its embodied particularity. This force is such that those presenting as gender nonconforming may be denied emergency care, and their gender *dissonance* in such life-or-death situations can't be evinced from the (a)typical embodiments that racialization codetermines (Snorton and Haritaworn 2023). More than the interweaving of nature and culture, nonconforming bodily projects call our attention to sociosomatic expression. By sociosomatic, I mean the irreducible entangling of biomateriality as social, and sociality as biomaterial. Specifically, I turn to transdisciplinary reflections from within habits of the flesh on the brink of dispossession, to make sense of sociosomatic entanglements. Shifting this analysis to the human/nonhuman divide, of undergoing reduction as the defining of one's innermost fiber, I understand that the sociosomatic captures a realist and materialist ecology of *always already biophilic⇔always already sociogenic* entangling.

I would like to remain mindful of Donna Haraway's ethical turn in her study of situated knowledges (1988). Feminist epistemology is multifarious, interpretive, and shifting. It commits feminist practitioners to "becoming answerable for what we learn how to see" (583). Therefore, I seek a form of realism through which I continue to answer, and remain answerable, for the realities that multiply marginalized communities learn to see. For the decolonial praxis I enact, what matters is to show that coloniality/modernity reconceives sex as dimorphic, which anchors nonhumans to sexed nature, and produces gender as a modality of human impressibility. As we shall later see, deciphering sociosomatic entanglements among sideways selves casts new light on decolonizing modes of impressibility, of living and doing on the brink of the abyss.

Snuff, Desire, and Sociosomatic Entanglements

Travesti and jotería communities face the disfigurations of the human genre in contemporary times. Alongside diasporic and transient embodiments, they carry the carnal contradictions of coloniality. They also situate the debate about bodily nonconformity away from gender and the widespread belief that it makes legible anti-colonial disfigurations of the flesh. I offer *snuff* as a window into these disfigurations. Snuff works as a scopic regime for which travestis as well as migrant selves disembody life.[20] Snuff as a sociohistorical gaze entails the redistribution of distance and proximity, symmetry and asymmetry, between a background form that retreats from view and, concomitantly, a foreground that enables the background to disappear. In the sex work trade circuit or in the militarized US-Mexico border, as we shall see, snuff provides analytics that reveal the coupling of death and desire. It sheds light over the sociogenic and biophilic production of dying life, of the emergence of streetwalkers and migrants as cursed with extinction. Against the logic of snuff, travesti and jotería migrants present, most of the time, sideways through their bodily work of dissent and survival.

Travesti activist and intellectual Marlene Wayar (2018b) employs a materialist approach as she makes sense of the tie between social abandonment and sex work. She refers to the "performativity" of the body as everyday habits that travestis acquire through sex work. In her view, the body is an energetic center of material possibilities. Travesti embodiments assemble energies in an oblique fashion, altering the sanctity of residential neighborhoods and enabling a meeting ground for clients and sex workers. Wayar reminds us that the context of sex work begins with the bare nakedness of the body before the eyes of clients (2018b). In this solicitation turf, clients acquire a clinical gaze. Through dense engagement with travestis' bodily habits, I understand that the clients' gaze combines the distance of observation—the type of seeing that French philosopher Michel Foucault (2002) characterized as devoid of attachment to an unknown reality—with the closeness of sexual transactions. The customer-cum-clinician plays out his fantasies while guiding the scene with zealous precision.

Working the corners, according to Wayar, is like a primer course on the underbelly of a political arena (2018b, 120). The choreography of street solicitation prepares travesti sex workers for the grammar of tense, sudden, and fleeting exchanges. Almost in the same vein as the Situationists, the French revolutionaries who sought to intervene against alienation in everyday life, Wayar conceives of the choreography of solicitation as a set of operations.[21] They "consist of turning the raw into art, in a steady yet unthreatening fashion" (2018, 120). The solicitation choreography combines an expenditure of creativity—humor, laughter, parody—with the chilled groove of someone anticipating the end of their shift. The fear of death and assault hangs in the background like it does in those fictional and documentary genres that make of snuff the ultimate and most extreme iteration of art horror.

According to Neil Jackson, snuff "combines explicit images of mutilation and defilement with hardcore sex" (2016, 4). Johnson and Schaefer describe it as a movie genre that depicts murder, dismemberment, or suicide, through visual strategies that seek to please viewers (1993, 40). The 1970s saw an infiltration of this aesthetic in popular culture, creating conditions for a renewed fascination with conventions that hybridize both realist horror and pornography. In 2022, the Argentine journalist Ariel Pukacz published his first novel, under the title *Snuff*. His lead character, a cinema professor, reclaims the reception of the genre in Argentina by recruiting visual arts students to participate in the production of a documentary. The plot builds on the fact that Roberta Findlay filmed *The Slaughter*, an exploitation film classic, in Argentina in the year 1971. Bought by another director, the film later received a second release in 1976 under the title *Snuff*.

Wayar points to the horror that hides behind this strand of pornographic imagination, that dangerous excitement of a snuff viewer who gets one step closer to the violence of the sex work context. Travestis infuse humor into the serious affair of negotiating sexual transactions, she states, as if the smarts of sex workers drove them to contend with their own vulnerability through wit. She lends an ironic tone to this reflection, enhancing the vantage point of underemployed gender nonconforming sex workers. She anticipates the explosion of masculinism as a matrix of sexual control, one that moves from purchasing sexual access to claiming ownership of the choreography of intercourse, to scripting the juxtaposition of skin and organ. I read Wayar as decoding the entanglement of bare nakedness and social gaze. She predicts, with ironic horror, the promise that snuff carries out. It hints at the looming climax that lies with the annihilation of the pleasure's source. Indeed, it is in retreating from the asymmetrical symmetries of the solicitation turf that the snuff viewer consumes another.[22]

An environment shaped by solicitation readily allows for hybridizing realist horror through numerous subgenres. Equally unsurprising is the replication of this trend on social media platforms, where it manifests in the portrayal of the most disquieting political events of our times. Both the uproar surrounding and fascination with the Pueblo Sin Fronteras caravan of 2018 is a case in point. The Center for Immigration Studies published Kausha Luna's coverage of the caravan, which was posted online on March 30, 2018. While I do not offer a thick ethnography of social media responses to this coverage, a random selection of Facebook comments provides a sampling of a visual rhetoric verging on realist horror. Facebook is, after all, a global giant that at once replicates and shapes, through algorithms, its users' stylistic preferences and topical choices.

Several of the comments refer to the caravan in warfare lingo. They see the caravan as a planned attack taking place on the border, or the "Achilles' heel" of the United States (David W, June 2018). Michael A states, "this is an invasion force, treat them like one" (June 2019). Not unlike the military that develops alternative deception operations to buffer or protect its main offensive, these Facebook users toggle with different scenarios. For each, they orchestrate the most lethal assaults on asylum seekers, whose humanity they deny with labels such as "filthy scum, dirty, foul mouthed brats" (Tibi H, June 2018), "asymmetrical [attackers]" (David W, June 2018), "illegals" (Mickey C, June 2018; Janice J, June 2018), and "hoards [sic]" (Michael P, June 2018). Their craving for bloodshed extends beyond mere expediency or matter-of-factness. Instead, it is a deep yearning for a prey whose suffering fulfills a voracious appetite for a spectacle. This spectacle blurs the boundaries between debility and the verge of death.

Also in 2018, trans activist Jennicet Gutiérrez and historian Suyapa Portillo coauthor a report for NACLA (North American Congress on Latin America) in which they bring attention to the plight of transgender Latinx migrants. They focus on the untimely death of Roxsana Hernandez, a Honduran and stateless asylum seeker who arrived at Tijuana's San Ysidro Port of Entry (SYPOE) the second week of May. By the twenty-fifth of the same month, she had died while in ICE's custody. She had made her way through three international borders and, upon entry into the litmus space that is the custodial branch of the United States immigration system, she was transferred through three facilities, located in three different states, before landing in Cibola County Correctional Center in New Mexico (Gutiérrez and Portillo 2018, 393). Run by Core-Civic, one of the country's largest investors in the prison industrial complex, Cibola is infamous for its icebox cages, known as "hieleras" by the Spanish-speaking immigrant population.

It is crucial to trace the compound structures that shape the perils of Roxsana and many other Central American and Latin American trans immigrants. Several activists and scholar-activists, such as Isa Noyola of Familia: Trans Queer Liberation Movement (TQLM) and de la Garza (2019), have documented this issue. While in custody, Roxsana continuously requests access to life-sustaining prescription medication, a consultation with a physician, and minimal palliative care to treat a worrying bout of diarrhea, vomiting, chills, and coughing. A posthumous official report states that Roxsana was hospitalized with pneumonia and dehydration. Upon her death, both ICE and the Honduran authorities disclose her HIV-positive status as the cause for her sudden demise. There is no way of knowing when Roxsana learns of her status. HIV-related complications such as Pneumocystis pneumonia do not typically develop unless the immune system has dramatically weakened.

Honduras faces notable gaps in HIV-related care, and as of 2022, the status of CONASIDA, the national program for HIV/AIDS in the country, remains uncertain.[23] In the absence of official reports, international humanitarian organizations frequently step in as unofficial data collectors. They tell us that approximately 40 percent of Honduran people living with HIV may not know their status. Antiretroviral medication, as well as viral load testing, are available in the country's capital (Retes 2020). A person like Roxsana, living in San Pedro Sula, would have had to endure a round-trip bus journey lasting approximately eight hours to access adequate monitoring and treatment. If she had earned the average monthly income, which equates to US$188, Roxsana would have had to allocate a third of her earnings to cover the cost of the trip. She made a living by cooking tortillas and beans and selling them out of the one-bedroom apartment that she shared with her three sisters (Gutiérrez and Portillo 2018).

In her compelling study of the borders of AIDS, Karma Chávez describes what she calls the alienizing logic of the United States (2021). This logic builds on narrowing membership and belonging within American national identity by displacing the source of disease, infection, or, more generally, social chaos onto the presence of immigrants in both imagined and material border territories. Chávez shows that trans communities, among gay and other queer ones, serve as scapegoats of American exceptionalism through "detention and deportation, incarceration and institutionalization, and estrangement and isolation from communities" (11).

The hashtags #JusticiaparaRoxsana and #JusticeforRoxsana, together with demonstrations across major US cities, brought attention to the aftermath of Roxsana's passing. Her death was long and painful, and her battle to hang on to life protracted. Uncanny as it may sound, the last snapshots that we can recover of her already short life come from witness statements, an autopsy, and accounts from relatives and activists who worked, despite the USA and Honduran bureaucracy, to return Roxsana's body to her family. At times, the neglect to which Roxsana was subjected eerily resembles the odious visuals that circulate on Facebook about the fate of immigrants and refugees. It is no mere coincidence that she perished gasping for air, the lungs rotting her insides. Furthermore, according to accounts from fellow detainees at Cibola, this processing facility subjects them to inhumane treatment. Dominique Mosbergen's report for *HuffPost* in 2018 indicates that efforts to probe into Roxsana's death, conducted by her family and the Transgender Law Center, led to a private autopsy. The forensic pathologist found obvious signs of abuse on her body, citing hemorrhages in the wrists, allegedly inflicted by handcuffs, and protracted suffering before finally being admitted to a hospital. The autopsy report also includes references to signs of "blows and/or kicks and possible strikes with a blunt object."

Vitriol and hateful social commentary circulate on Facebook and may go unnoticed for many. Hybridizing realist horror, of which snuff is but one iteration, feeds the growing insensitivity toward the suffering of another. Imperial, neocolonial, and racist or nativist discourse constructs this another as both infrahuman and infra-animal. Being a person who cohabitates with a Boston terrier by the name of Inti, I am no stranger to receiving targeted ads that appeal to my animal-loving profile. There is no doubt that these ads confer, upon nonhuman animals, the type of dignity that immigration and customs agencies routinely deny to refugees and asylum seekers. Sexual assault and coercion are among transphobic expressions that weigh heavily on transgender people who choose migration. However, they remain vulnerable to this violence while they wait for their asylum cases to be adjudicated.

According to the United States Department of Justice, transgender adult inmates housed in federal prisons and local jails reported experiencing sexual victimization between 2007 and 2012. Startlingly, at federal facilities, 24 percent of incarcerated individuals reported victimization by another inmate, while around 17 percent reported such incidents involving staff members. In 2014, ICE detained Monserrath López, a twenty-three-year-old transgender woman from Honduras, for approximately six months. Human Rights Watch documented her testimony, in which she disclosed that after reporting a sexual assault by a male detainee to facility staff, she was threatened with solitary confinement.

Until 2016, the federal system sorted most transgender detainees into facilities according to gender designation received at birth. In more recent years, California's Santa Ana facility has become the regular housing unit for most trans women detainees at any given time. Those who end up in facilities with cisgender men often receive offers for transfer to other locations where insufficient medical care and harsher mistreatment run rampant. One such case captured national attention in March of 2020 when the Associated Press reported on the dire situation of Alejandra Alor Reyes. She was physically harassed and sexually abused multiple times over a nine-month period while a detainee at an Arizona immigration facility for cisgender men.

Necropolitics is a concept that explicates the centrality of death within institutions that shape the political order of human life, such as borders, prisons, war conflicts, and policing activities (Mbembe 2019, 6). Most important, as Haritaworn, Kuntsman, and Posocco argue (2014), an anti-colonial queer lens invites us to recognize "the unremarkable, the ordinary and the mundane" (2014, 2) as sites of particular importance in the reconstitution of life, its viability and dispensability. By incorporating snuff as analytics of travesti/trans, jotería, and queer Latinx migrants, specifically for what it reveals about the conditions through which they engage the sociogenesis of embodiments, I suggest that the mundane and ordinary become crucial—much more so as it concerns the link between the pleasure of certain people and its ties to the demise of others while they carry on with an ordinary life. Displacement and migration become ordinary for gender nonconforming individuals. While the liberal democratic order sanctions pockets of abandonment and precarity as cursory and not exceptional, it is mundane sensibilities that transform bystanders into snuff consumers, or hate-based Facebook posters into hate-crime instigators. Indeed, we are implicated by the sociosomatics of queer necropolitics, of the centrality of death, dispossession, and dispensability in the social production of nonconforming bodily projects. For the hate-based Facebook posters, it is not remarkable that another immigrant goes missing or dies in ICE's custody. They show that nativist desire implicates the sociogenic production of dispensable bodies.

The reality of destitution, the disappearing of gender nonconforming streetwalkers and migrants such as Roxsana Hernández and Vicky Hernandez, speaks to the atrocities of flesh as a pivotal materialist arena. Attending to these atrocities, we arrive at the examination of nonhuman and nonanimal flesh. Shifting our attention to this atrocious materiality, we may contend with understandings of life that run the gamut of the failure of ethics, from the mere lack of hospitality that a military border perpetuates to the hostile withdrawal of care that nativist bashers glorify.

Temporalities coexist and superimpose upon one another in the environment of streetwalking, from the Afro-diasporic dance moves that come alive in the *lunfardo* world of tango to the communal attachments, perhaps Indigenous-based attachments, upon which travestis devise collectivist housing and employment strategies. The disintegration of this communal seed is one with the rise of racializing, ableist, heterosexualist, and heteropaternalist capitalism. Its necropolitical force relies on long-standing, deep-seated habituations of flesh. As shown by the central gaze of the snuff genre, the annihilation of another requires first the coproduction of the conditions of destitution and consumption. As Wayar (2018a) warns us with ironic wit, the coloniality of streetwalking exacts the acceptance, from travestis, of the bodily and psychic role that they play in sustaining the client's place while creating their own. What Wayar describes as the web of one's own reveals and implicates its sociality, which, though dispersed and discontinuous, remains enduring. Her reflection speaks to the impressible nature of embodiments.

In a powerful treatise on the nineteenth century's sentimentalism in the United States, Kyla Schuller (2018) examines the tropes of sentimentality across Lamarckian evolutionary discourse and its afterlife in contemporary movements and epistemological frameworks. Sentimentalism was deployed, Schuller argues, to intervene in the capacities of the civilized body. Sentimentalism cultivates the body's responses to the sensorial world according to emotional reflection rather than instinctive, primitive, undeveloped, animal-like reflex. Colonial taxonomies of evolution recruit emotions as pivotal sociosomatic entanglements. They guide the sociomaterial production of conforming, whiteness-centered embodiments. At once, they outline an ableist boundary, dispensing with those bodies whose impressible nature responds poorly to civilizing adaptation.

While Schuller focuses on the United States, Nancy Stepan (1991, 64–65) provides evidence of a robust link between eugenicist taxonomies and neo-Lamarckian heredity theories in Latin America. This is why I turn to Schuller's notion of relative "impressibility" (2018, 12) to theorize sociosomatics in this chapter. After all, both travesti and jotería bodily projects have emerged partially in response to colonial and eugenicist taxonomies across the hemisphere. Referring to the "energetic accumulation of sensory impressions" (3), *impressibility* captures the degree of sociosomatic responsiveness of a living body. An ableist framework arises through the disciplining of sensorial susceptibility. Technologies of life and death differentiate between bodies vested with the ability to accrue human impressibility and those deemed stuck in evolutionary nonhuman time. Later, I will expand on this ableist framework, which I link to notions of sanity and derangement in the eighteenth-century work of German philosopher Immanuel Kant.

Thus far, I hope to have shown that essentialist, constructivist, and performative accounts of embodied differences service various projects that align with but also challenge systems of oppression. Resistance to systems of oppression may even recruit the energetic accumulation and expenditure of those who often occupy dominant and privileged positions. The very materiality of sideways selves becomes the site of resistance against, in opposition to, and beyond the paradox of absence and trace, of being reduced to thing and behaving as not-thing. Latin American travesti/trans theorizing and jotería studies steer the analysis of nonconforming habits of flesh toward atrocious ways of knowing and being in the world. From within this standpoint, they outline alternatives to white-stream feminist, queer, and trans thinking and their ways of addressing the reality of gender embodiments. No longer do claims about plasticity, fixedness, or even vitality return to feminist theorizing and praxis an indisputable description of the subversion of rationalist, extractivist, and oppressive realities. Since I recognize a radically different, subaltern, decolonizing cluster of ways of knowing and being among nonconforming bodily projects, I seek to expand on their materialism. Most important, I turn to Indigenous and Native lifeways, as they underwrite materialisms within everyday experiences and activities among travestis/trans and jotería exiles and migrants.

I feel adamant about the violence that underpins Eurocentered frameworks since they are likely to translate sideways selves into the supraordinary categories of "transgender epistemology" and "activism." I am appalled as I observe how white-stream, feminist, and queer politics inadvertently contribute to the necropolitical challenges faced by travestis and trans exiles and jotería migrants. The legacy of colonialism establishes metaphysical assumptions that conflate transgender with sideways, abyssal projects of bodily nonconformity. As various strands of decolonial thinking demonstrate (Roen 2006; Harding 2019), metaphysical assumptions lead us at once to place and exclude certain elements within that weblike network where social and biomaterial structures produce bodily nonconformity. In a response perhaps compatible with Sylvia Wynter's framework, I would like to interrupt the Eurocentered trend within white-stream feminist, queer, and trans studies, by which they assume that *trans* revalorizes bodily nonconformity across geopolitical, temporal, and spatial realities. Wynter warned us against the enticements of human-centered revalorization (2006). From within a radical social context of decolonial thought, I honor what feminist science scholar Sandra Harding calls the ontological turn. Harding defines this turn as the insistence on the social fact that "different cultures live in different realities, and thus purely epistemic solutions to cross-cultural communication remain colonial" (2019, 61).[24] White-stream feminist, queer, and trans studies miss the point when they pursue *understanding* travesti/trans and jotería bodily projects. These studies' Eurocentrism disregards a political and ontological opacity that emerges from complex and multiple realities.

I am inclined to think that various claims about ontological differences between cultures and realities may unwillingly endorse both political relativism and homogeneous versions of cultural differences. The bodily projects of sideways selves demand that we avoid immobilizing viewpoints about incommensurable differences. Similarly, if sideways selves are said to mobilize resistant positions, we should tread lightly to avoid overgeneralizing accounts of both dominant and nondominant dynamics. For these reasons, I insist on the significance of biophilic and sociosomatic configurations.

Examining the encodings of matter, at once sociosomatic and biophilic, may allow us to arrive at a framework that alters our core beliefs about reality. Thus, instead of claiming that sideways selves foreground novel versions of posthumanist materialism, a materialism that doesn't have gender at its heart, I ask that we pay attention to sideways selves as they move us to reassess what the project of the human portends for our beliefs about the world. We need not be understood. If they were ethical co-inspirators, as they often claim to be, white-stream feminist, queer, and trans scholars would ask instead how our bodily projects alter their beliefs about reality.

Next, I query the framework of agential realism for its capacious explanations about the nature of reality. I would be staunchly misrepresenting quantum physics for the sake of my argument about colonialism and gender if I assumed a misleading transliteration of life sciences and social phenomena. I suggest, instead, that we look at agential realism for what it reveals about enigmatic and sometimes otherworldly forces of nature. At a later juncture, I shall invite us to consider whether the bodily projects of sideways selves, specifically those underwritten by Afro-diasporic, Indigenous, and Native knowledges, indicate that we owe nature, and its magnificent, complex, sociosomatic, nonconforming poiesis, the respect that contemporary societies pay to quantum physics.

Decolonizing Agential Realism

In *Meeting the Universe Halfway*, Karen Barad (2007) theorizes the paradigmatic shift that quantum physics performs across epistemological, ontological, and ethical inquiries. Quantum physics is a field of study that evolved over the last century greatly assisted by technological developments. At a basic level, quantum physics makes predictions about how matter works at the microphysical scale, which places such predictions at odds with how things seem to work at the scale of the cosmos or the world around us. If Newtonian physics once made us think of space and time as absolute, and of ourselves as mere observers of invariable laws, the theory of relativity and quantum mechanics provide new languages to make sense of variability, indeterminacy, and position-relative measurements. It matters to Barad to explicate the role that the putative knower plays in enacting or codetermining the phenomena that knowing enterprises are supposed to describe. She contends that scientific and technological practices behave as enactments that can no longer be severed from the reality that we seek to decipher.

Phenomena, at least at the quantum scale, comprise entangled agencies. This new language rejects the core principles of atomism. The Newtonian paradigm finds comfort in the notion of "interaction," which entails the metaphysics of individualism or of discrete objects with inherent characteristics. Single particles effect their own influence upon others. That is, they interact with each other. Barad introduces the notions of ontological entanglement and agential realism to make profound points about the relative import of interaction for our cursory understanding of the world's nature.

Barad truly shifts the paradigm through which we make sense of our being enmeshed in everything that the world is. They rely on two of quantum physics' theoretical contributions as they reshape the inside/outside divide that allows human-centered physics to cohere. It is worth noticing that shifting from atomism—for which atoms are the fundamental indivisible component of the universe—to quantum physics bears on other ways of knowing reality, such as metaphysical inquiries and Native and Indigenous philosophies. Barad's starting point states that there is no pregiven material world but rather specific material configurations. By configuration, quantum physics signals the conjoining dynamic of microparticle, observation, and measurement. When an experiment calls for the observation of how two particles behave, the phenomenon is not reduced to the particles and their separate reactions toward each other. Rather, it involves an entire configuration shaped by the particles' system and the measuring apparatus.

What is usually glossed as the correlation of properties (e.g., temperature, mass, speed) between two separately determined systems can only function as a measurement, in principle, from within an atomist account of the world. The understanding of experimental measurement involves obtaining information about a particle to a desired accuracy, but this accuracy shows great range of variance at the scale of microparticles. Through the study of this variance, quantum mechanics reveals that the technologies of observation are as significant as the objects under observation. They constitute physical reality as entangled components, agential components, of phenomena (Barad 2007, 309). Through this ontological revelation, quantum physics delivers us from a universe of predetermined and separate entities. The notion of ontological entanglement speaks to the in-the-making quality of these microphysical systems. Furthermore, it also reconceives a world of interactive systems through an ontology of "intra-action" (139–140) or "general relation of reciprocal indeterminacy" (403). No particle is fully active, or agentic, but for its being implicated by agencies or intra-actions of (1) other particles in the making, (2) apparatus of observation, and (3) the cutting that performs the slit of space-time where cause and effect emerge.

Two major implications that we must draw from Barad's philosophical contribution are (1) posthumanist critiques of a metaphysics of substance and (2) an agential realism that reframes the relation between epistemology and ontology. Their performative framework challenges the presupposition that agency lies only with humans or with the side of subjectivity vis-à-vis objects and things. Conversely, it also contests the idea that technologies that mediate between the domains of things and people demand representational understandings of reality. So, if there were any reservations as to why the interdisciplinary humanities benefit from engaging agential realism, it should be evident by now that it critically redefines subjectivism and representational accounts of reality. Indeed, it advances posthumanist debates in several directions.

Barad works across science studies and the humanities, with an agential realist approach. Neither the objects of science studies nor of the humanities are predetermined, an agential realist perspective holds (Garratt 2017, 163). Rather, they are ontologically implicated by each other's agencies, which are ongoing, open-ended, and in a reciprocal intra-action. One may be inclined to argue that, unlike the experiments of quantum mechanics, critical theoretical inquiries have human practices as their central focus and that despite the leveling of the realm of things and people across object-oriented ontologies, it is human beings who get to make choices about knowledge and about how we get to know ourselves and things. Barad, however, asks that we pause for a second and learn from behavior that, without having humans at its center, manifests different degrees of agency. This behavior defamiliarizes the typical boundaries that neutral, human-driven, observation establishes. For the quantum performative framework, observation and the macroscopic technologies that magnify it enact knowing practices, which, in their intra-acting, constitute the measuring agencies (effects) and the measured object (an emerging rather than a stable cause) of quantum phenomena (Barad 2007, 27).

Performative materialism emerges from various theoretical endeavors. As a groundbreaking engagement with posthumanist views across the life sciences, it undergoes thorough translation in its motion upwards from the realm of quantum particles to the molecular scale where life assembles reproductive resources, genetic material, enzymes, organs, neurons, and many other basic units that generate the matter of embodiment. Note that my earlier example about abortion laws captures some of this motion upwards. So does Schuller's proposal about *impressibility* (2018), Snorton's transubstantiation (2017), or the one that I put forth as *bodily responsiveness*. To the end of unpacking this assemblage of intra-acting biophilic and sociosomatic agencies, I find useful two interdisciplinary models: *enactive cognition* and *molecular biology*. Together, they help us recognize manifold entanglements among what lies within the body and without. These models offer materialist, thing-oriented ontologies. Ultimately, they arrive at enactments of embodiment that Indigenous, Native, and at times non-Western cosmologies have engaged all along: agency does not reside in the seat of human motivations and intentions.

Peter Garratt (2017) situates the philosophical contributions of biologists Humberto Maturana and Francisco Varela (1980) within theories of distributed cognition. They challenge "the standard boundaries of cognition" by examining concepts like "brainhood," which reveals how "thinking" disrupts the inside/outside split while assembling interconnected objects, including the mind, that function as both a localized unit and a broader enactive whole.[25] Maturana and Varela introduce "structural coupling" to explain how living organisms world themselves through autopoiesis and self-organization. This concept describes self-creation modalities where the environment and organism coproduce each other. Communication, in this context, happens at the site of material co-constitution rather than between separate entities. Like agential realism, Maturana and Varela explore the molecular scale of life generation and its implications for our engagement with knowledge and reality.[26]

The second model arises from biology's renewed focus on uncertainty and indeterminacy within living cells. The connection between molecules and genetics is not new: biophysicists and biochemists showed interest as early as the mid-1920s, when genetics was still marginal. The potential of quantum physics in this area, however, remained largely unexplored. It took microbiology nearly fifty years to overcome the postwar legacies of antisemitism and eugenics that hampered its progress. Nevertheless, during this time, proponents of a quantum-responsive biological domain began to appear. In the 1940s, Nobel laureate Erwin Schrödinger suggested that genetic information might contain a molecular code that requires quantum theory to maintain the fidelity of inheritance (McFadden and Al-Khalili 2018, 8). Over the following decades, organicism in biology and quantum physics demonstrated that traditional chemistry alone couldn't fully explain vital phenomena without recognizing a hidden principle of uncertainty. By the late twentieth century, scientists were gathering evidence of quantum dynamics in biological processes (2018, 10).

In 2019, Catherine Offord, writing for *The Scientist*, reported previously undocumented behavior in photosynthetic bacteria tied to subatomic-level dynamics resembling particle entanglement. This puzzling subatomic behavior has historically raised doubts about its relevance to living systems, due to the extreme conditions required for quantum experiments. However, recent discoveries (Thyrhaug et al., 2018) highlight how enzymes and photosynthesis leverage quantum advantages. Additionally, Deboleena Roy's argument (2018) underscores the importance of considering the effects and revelations stemming from scientists' interactions, breakthroughs, and failures in the context of subatomic particle research (76). It is not coincidental that there is growing interest in that motion upwards from the realm of quantum particles to the biological scale, where life assembles, I insist, sociosomatic resources.

Agential realism offers a much-improved remedy to the subjectivism/objectivism conundrum within interdisciplinary humanities. The impressible, responsive body, which I proposed as faithful analytics of sideways selves, accommodates a materialism of entangled agencies. It refutes not only the language of atomism but also the subjectivist pretense of liberal and full self-realization. Verging on the language of sacred wisdom that Native and Indigenous lifeways use to recognize natural forces, the agential realism paradigm highlights our being enmeshed in everything the world is.

Extrapolation from microparticles to social practices is not a leap that I recommend. I would like, however, to remind us of Evelynn Hammonds, who turns to astrophysics as she elucidates complexity, uncertainty, variability, and hidden forces across systems of power. Her argument reveals that hidden forces, whose gravitational pull the Newtonian paradigm cannot possibly detect, leave their imprint on the behavior of space bodies.

I appreciate Hammonds's gesture, since it underscores not only materialism in feminist theory and praxis but also that this strand of materialism allows for feminist research to align with ontological notions of multiple and coexisting realities. In line with Sandra Harding's (2019) assertion about an ontological turn, the physics of black holes indicates that competing realities intra-actively coproduce and codetermine Black queer women's sexualities. Their realities at the very least shuttle from being hypervisible—black + female + queer within the additive logic of white-stream queer studies—to (in)visible: the politics of dissemblance, among others. An astrophysicist paradigm, a white-stream queer paradigm, and an anti-colonial feminist paradigm codetermine the slits of space-time through which we come to make sense of Black women's queer sexualities. In sum, agential realism furnishes new practices for social analysis whenever we begin by acknowledging, as Native and Indigenous thinking does, that bodily responsiveness ensues from coexisting realities. These realities assemble, and are at once assembled by, intra-acting sociosomatic agencies. They codetermine each other at their various scales, however hidden they may remain to our current epistemic and observational practices.

Travesti/trans exiles and jotería migrants reside at this site of ontological variance, in relational reciprocity with theoreticopractical paradigms such as those articulated by the categories "black holes," "shitholes," and "sideways selves." Migrants' and exiles' lives occupy relative positions in their reciprocal entangling with these paradigms. This is perhaps why, as we previously discussed, debris and excrement equally implicate void, nothing, dispensability, but also toxin, pollutant, allure. The realities of transitioning embodiments implicate molecular and hormonal modification as well as the coupling of such a modification as sociosomatic entanglements. If sideways selves are to teach us something about what makes feminist lives more vibrant, they will teach us about theoreticopractical modalities of reciprocal regeneration, coupling, and recoupling. Most important, they will make tangible that material co-constitution incubates the mysteries of autonomy and conjoining agencies: that is, enigmatic and contingent habits of the flesh.

The Coloniality of Transgender

Decolonial feminism posits that *gender* operates as a metaphysical, ontological imposition over Abya Yala, which the conquest launches and Eurocentrism consolidates. The framework advanced by María Lugones (2007) shows that Eurocentrism and racial classification shape all conflicts about the generation of life. Coloniality and its codetermining of the human through the nuclear family center heterosexual and cisgender bodies in the reproduction of white supremacy. Reconceived sexed distinctions differentiate those who reproduce white supremacist and bourgeois values from "inferior others" who occupy the "primitive" condition of enslavement, servitude, and bestiality.[27] Coloniality places the latter beyond gender and, therefore, in close metaphysical proximity to transgender. Due to this proximity, transgender bodily projects *could* materialize a body politics external to coloniality and, hence, give rise to nonconforming bodily projects in opposition to and beyond heterosexualism.

In line with the materialist framework described thus far, I understand embodiment as a sociosomatic production in its most contradictory, realist sense, neither fully a commodity nor completely a creative work. Crucial to this social production is what I call *bodily responsiveness*, or the capacity of flesh to assemble sociosomatic matter. Flesh behaves as an agential configuration, at once codetermining and codetermined. As decolonial hope, *transgender* could manifest nonconforming bodily projects with respect to colonial gender. Because I too am hopeful about the project of trans embodiments, I pursue a collective intuition felt among trans of color populations. This intuition tells us that *trans of color*, as a bodily project and as an identity, feels like an oxymoron. With this, I mean that negatively racialized populations rarely find ourselves at ease within trans identification, embodiment, and activism. Notice that in CABA's vice zone, *travesti* and not *trans* arises as both a bodily and identity project. Without subsuming *trans* under the designation *jotería*, Latinx communities may use the latter term as a collective reference to their queer, nonbinary, and trans members.

I present the notion of the *coloniality of transgender* to explain the lack of ease with which travestis and jotería inhabit the sociosomatic space of trans of color. As previously mentioned, global patterns of racialization cast off the nonhuman because it remains stuck in time, unable to accrue any evolutionary boost because deranged and perverse. If trans is a bodily project, and if the project of the human currently offers trans rehabilitation into sanity and ability standards, accruing evolutionary time and leaving perversion behind opens routes into biopolitical ease. Travestis and jotería, as well as queer and trans Latinx migrants, are denied this route.

Broadly speaking, what María Lugones calls the heterosexualist colonial/modern gender system is a Eurocentered and bestializing pattern of global power that shapes all conflicts about the generation of life. Coloniality, and its representation, arrangement, production, and disciplining of the human, takes place through the nuclear family. Sanctioned as the site for the entangling of intimacy, food, care, and property, the nuclear family centers heterosexualist and cisgender bodies in the reproduction of white supremacy. Lugones understands that the nuclear family orders the generation of life on both ends of the human/nonhuman divide. She calls these ends the light and dark sides. I am reluctant to read Lugones's use of *dark* and *light* within the colorist taxonomy of racism. I don't understand light to stand for white nor dark for black (or nonwhite, for that matter). Rather, she seems to argue, alongside Evelynn Hammonds, that we need to focus on the correlation, or codetermining, of visibility and obscurity. What remains hidden, as in the astrophysics of black holes, constitutes not so much *what* we perceive but the *modality* in which we come to make sense of what we perceive.

In the "dark side" of the colonial/modern gender system, I understand that flesh, already agential, entangling, and discontinuous, cogenerates the nonhuman according to the politics of impressibility. While disfigurations of the human purge, they bring into being an inferior, in-the-making embodiment of nonMen and nonWomen. Denial of wages and personhood offers evidence of the systematic, structural, fundamental logic of the human/nonhuman dichotomy. This logic codetermines sexed animalized bodies, who, disappearing into the background, stand in opposition to Men and Women. The dark side's entangling agencies often proffer the background against which the bodily project of Gender becomes evident. In the light side of the colonial/modern gender system, the human enshrines, makes visible, educates, brings to the foreground Husband and Wife and their sensible responsiveness to the ruling white supremacist economy. Notice that I add to Lugones's framework here by thinking of both sides as codetermining, agential, variable, heterogeneous, and, most important, as sociosomatic webs with a clustering category, or set of key knots, at each of their centers.

I examine the myriad ways through which the human/nonhuman emerges as an impressible response, an entangling where genderless embodiments both appear and fade away. It is by contending with these bodily agencies and material conditions that we may interpret sideways selves and their potential to foster anti-capitalist, nonmonogamous, neurodivergent, and anti-racist relations. Theorizing nonconforming embodiments within the "dark side," I witness and learn from the materialism of impressible flesh. Making sense of flesh beyond gender and nongender, I seek to magnify an intuition that Lugones explains as follows: "Women racialized as inferior were turned from animals into various modified versions of 'women' as it fit the processes of global, Eurocentered capitalism" (183). By following my intuition as a Latinx trans person, I dwell precisely on and in the assembling of *disfiguring* flesh. I focus on the ways in which trans points to both disfigurations of the genre of the human and modified versions of Gender. In that sense, trans of color embodiments both fit and escape the processes of global, Eurocentered capitalism.

My contribution relates to the onto-epistemology that Lugones suggests. To this end, I introduce a three-pronged model to explicate coloniality and flesh entanglements. When I use the term Gender in my model, I refer to entanglements that ongoingly rehabilitate bodily projects to serve the white supremacist purpose of the nuclear family. As it concerns negatively racialized bodies, such as Afro-Latinx and Latinx embodiments, Gender leaves us at a crossroads. We are pushed to desire and invest ourselves in the business of Gender. Lowercase and italicized, *genders* stands for the safe and yet confusing habituation of racialized flesh as individualizing and assimilating. The whitening nuclear family entices Afro-Latinx and Latinx bodily projects into *genders*, and, at the same time, it removes us from the Gender domain. As we are enticed into and yet removed from Gender, we engage with more than one bodily project. While *genders* captures individualization and assimilation, (between quotation marks) "genders" stands, instead, for sociosomatic entanglements through which we participate in the coproduction of neither human nor animal embodiments, both close to and yet outside the nuclear family, and both within and yet beneath animal embodiments. Hierarchies simmer within the "dark side," with various modified versions of *genders* circulating and spreading among heterogeneous bodily projects, including those where "genders" prevail at the very outskirts of the nonhuman station.

Under the hegemony of the Westernizing Man>Woman divide,

transgender emerges as a bodily project whose provenance aligns with the reality of beyond-Gender. Since trans populates the outskirts of the light side, it harbors the possibility of giving rise to embodiments that betray coloniality. However, because trans harbors this decolonial hope, I would like to make visible the category's coloniality and, thus, recognize the extent to which trans bodies fit the processes of global, Eurocentered, capitalism. As part of what I call the coloniality of transgender, I seek to emphasize the global and Eurocentered patterning of bodily projects as it recruits *transgender* through an impressible, white supremacist education. Not surprisingly, this pattern brings transgender to bear on the colonial/modern gender system, potentially utilizing it as a buffer that prevents the danger of *underdeveloped monstrosity* and time-stuck *idleness* from taking root in the sensorial responsiveness of Gender and *genders*.

My argument about the coloniality of transgender moves in the following manner. Bodily responsiveness functions as the capacity of embodiment to ongoingly assemble its sociosomatic matter. (Capitalized) Gender regulates impressibility. For a modernizing project of sanity, which I shall link to the rise of a Kantian notion of reason, whiteness entails carnal habits that cast off the dangers of disabled and ambiguous, not-quite-human *genders*. It allows for modified versions of *genders* to receive an education in human impressibility at the expense of, or with the purpose of expunging, polluting debris, or, in other words, the abyssal bodily projects of "genders." It is my contention that transgender bodily projects sit ambiguously between disability, a lack of sanity, and the self-realization of *genders*. As a site of self-realization, of human-impressible education, transgender hides the coloniality of gender. As a site of disability, transgender hides the racialization of bodily impressibility, because, as we shall see, state-sanctioned policies seek to rehabilitate trans bodies to fit *genders* differences. Between self-realization and rehabilitation, transgender further obscures an ungendering of the many bodily projects that coloniality renders dispensable.[28] Conjoined by coloniality, sideways selves such as travestis/trans and jotería reside as exiles within but also at the outskirts of the zone of nonbeing. From within this site, sideways selves enact "genders" who dislodge the centrality of the human/nonhuman divide.

In his noted treatise on the racial history of trans identity, Snorton demonstrates that gender differentiation operates as a capacity or modality of cultural and political maneuvering (2017, 56). Theft of both land and body, he argues, lies at the center of the colonial, transatlantic enterprise. This process—grammar, framing—rearranges reality to the point of severing body and desire (Spillers 1987, 67). For this magnificent gene-alogy of Black transfeminist studies, the body inextricably relates to tem-poral and spatial rearrangements brought about by colonialism. In fact, Snorton follows Hortense Spillers in her examination of the organic ori-gin of the body under captivity. By way of colonial violence, the body transmogrifies, becomes constituted by and in, materializes through and for transatlantic exchange. Often standing for each other under colonial rule, race and gender cease to index specificity. They mutate and pass themselves off for the other, since the colonial order ongoingly amends, modulates, denies, and revises forms of not-being.

Akin to Lugones's claim that women racialized as inferior were turned into various modified versions of "women," Snorton's interpretation of fungibility speaks to the interchangeable revisions to the body as "they passed in and out of carceral states" (64). Moreover, both Spillers and Snorton point to ontological rearrangement not merely as the oblitera-tion of "liberated subject-positions" but also as the modulation of flesh in its wounding of personhood. Flesh, always already agentic, responds to and participates in transubstantiation. It registers the wounding of per-sonhood and its transformation into the body "in its material and abstract phase" (Spillers 1987, 66). A fugitive orientation, or an escape into vari-ous modified versions of "women," as Lugones put it, registers the socio-somatic entanglements that sideways selves sometimes illustrate amid dispossession and dispensability.

In my argument, these many modified and amendable versions of "gen-ders" entail the examination of sociosomatic entanglements among san-ity, disability, and transgender self-realization. As amendable, "genders" fade into view against the background of white supremacist histories. (Capitalized) Gender habituates impressible flesh to the nuclear family. The binary Husband and Wife functions as a sanity-defining entangle-ment. It differentiates hierarchies of life relationally. That is, the more the binary habituates the body to human-accruing transactions, the deeper the rift with the nonhuman and yet more intimate their codependency. The more enticing the habits of white-centered sanity become, the stron-ger they resonate with nonhuman, animal, and less-than-animal flesh. Enticements into *genders* unfold through this disciplining of impress-ibility. As contingent configuration of Gender, transgender habituates the body to seek self-realization through ability-securing individualiza-tion, accrual of *human* features, and extraction of species differentiation. That transgender self-realization implicates the rise of the middle-class, ableist, white-supremacist, two-sex body model is a consequence of the coloniality of transgender, of the captivity of racialized and gendered bodies.[29]

As I weave my argument about Abya Yala's bodily projects, I shall examine (1) posthumanist feminist approaches and their use of *transgender* as a distortion of nonconforming carnal configurations; (2) the ways that a Kantian project of ableist bodily formation bears on humanizing transgender plights against racial, gender, and disability discrimination; and (3) the traces of Indigenous materialism on a sacred praxis of flesh habituation whose expression contests the coloniality of *transgender*.

The Posthuman Turn and the Distortion of Abya Yala's Nonhuman Configurations

We can trace foundational categories of sex, gender, and sexuality back to the eighteenth and nineteenth centuries (Laqueur 1992; Wiesner-Hanks 2012). In the West, *transgender* and *transsexual* rise to the station of an individual body only in the second half of the twentieth century (Stryker 2008, 18–19, 123–124). In its dominant configuration, *transgender* presents a main biological basis (Banner 2010, 845), seeks to arrive at the trans-man or trans-woman binary (Irni 2016, 522–523), and asserts the supremacy of cissexist masculine values (Serano 2007, 15). Far from altering this paradigm, the transgender body is either cornered as a gender altogether different—a third gender—or made to reinforce the binary.

Dominant sociosomatic configurations make self-realization increasingly more viable for trans individuals, while they allow cisgender subjects to experience trans phenomena as if they were foreign to them. Trans happens to others and not to all of us. White-stream trans and feminist studies contend with these contradictions, emphasizing the proliferation and variation of bodily projects that I am calling *genders*. For example, Stryker, Currah, and Moore describe genders as "potentially porous and permeable spatial territories (arguabl[y] numbering more than two), each capable of supporting rich and rapidly proliferating ecologies of embodied difference" (2008, 12). They reject the idea that *genders* are containers of *a single kind of thing*. They posit that trans embodiments are neither deviations nor accidents that merely qualify *man* or *woman*. While these approaches call our attention to a materialism of impressibility, they also show that impressible variation remains compatible with neoliberal biohacking.[30]

Transfeminist critiques challenge the traditional paths that trans embodiments follow to express personal and collective dissent against biopolitical regimes. For example, they claim to dislodge a eugenicist and racist engineering of gender from the metaphysics of substance through performative and posthumanist accounts of *genders* (Butler 1993; Barad 2007; Hayward 2008; Kelly, Boye, and Rice 2021). They make us aware that the white supremacist legacy of race as a physiological signifier also provides the backing for gender essentialism and its hierarchies.[31] This anti-colonial stance, however, often collapses into the next stage of post-humanist trans thinking. I am referring to animal studies and the breadth of lessons about sociosomatic configurations from which trans studies draw (Hayward and Weinstein 2015). One case in point is the variation of reproductive capacities among nonhuman animal life-forms, and their fascinating challenge to cisgender bias across life sciences.[32]

Trans thinking of this kind supports the enterprise of provincializing the human, showing that its materiality is one among many other entangling entanglements.[33] In their relinking of social constructivism and concrete embodied practices, deconstructive approaches in trans thinking advance new materialisms and reveal proliferating ecologies of bodily impressibility. They dislocate a humanist project of neoliberal patterns of omnipotent self-fashioning.[34] They examine the key agency of matter across nature/culture and human/nonhuman interfaces (Braidotti 2002, 2013; Haraway 2008; Mortimer-Sandilands and Erickson 2010; Grosz 2011). The human no longer remains at the center of their understandings of *gender*'s biomateriality. However, this posthumanist turn may not always revise its Westernizing attachments. For example, notions such as *vitality* have great currency in feminist animal studies (Schueller 2005),[35] or in political theory about animal rights (Agamben 1998), or in explanations that flatten the role that racialization plays in the historical split between human (*bio*) and nonhuman life (*zoe*) (Braidotti 2006, 2013, 2020). These warnings should caution against such attachments if the deconstruction of hierarchies between animals and nonanimals was to pave the way for a posthumanism that challenges the cross-cultural relevance of gender and transgender (Gramling and Dutta 2016; DiPietro 2016b). Howard Chiang rightly argues that provincialization of the human does not necessarily result in engaging embodied practices other than those favored by Euro-American theories (2012). To avoid colluding with colonialist legacies, deconstructive approaches may need a post-posthumanist turn.[36]

With the introduction of questions about the flesh of nonbeing, a novel model for decolonizing transgender embodiments arises. It shifts our attention to hierarchies of vitality and away from Eurocentric, however posthuman, debates on bodily proliferation. By hierarchies of vitality, I understand asymmetrical habits of flesh, incursions in and out of black holes and abyssal geographies. Nonhuman and racialized encodings of flesh give uptake to minoritized "genders." While "genders" express opposition to the vitality that the human genre promises, *genders* avail themselves of the revalorization that a protracted access to the nuclear family affords them. The Jamaican philosopher Sylvia Wynter warns against the revalorization of nonhuman flesh within the "present sociogenic code or genre of being human" (2006, 116). She examines the emotional order of truth, an elementary biocentric regime, that conflates any counterhegemonic valorization of subjectivity with the organic and individual experience of being human (114).

Hortense Spillers (1987), C. Riley Snorton (2017), Zenzele Isoke (2018), and Gladys Tzul Tzul (2018) also propose that feminist and denormalizing struggles consider a (post)posthuman history of flesh. Through this attempt at historicizing human, nonhuman, posthuman, and (post)posthuman habits of flesh, the coloniality of a transgender framework invokes an otherworldly materialism and body politics. Coloniality extracts matter from captive and indentured flesh, and, through this very extraction, the "unbearable wrongness of being" (Wynter 2006) retroactively alters the genome, organic origin, and enigmatic nature of peoplehood. Sideways selves—travesti/trans exiles and jotería migrants—remember ways of knowing and arranging the real. In so doing, they foster a body politics, an impressionable responsiveness, that underwrites contemporary nonconforming bodily projects.

Consider one primordial scene of Abya Yala's colonial history. When Vasco Núñez de Balboa arrives in the Cuareca region of the isthmus of present-day Panamá in 1513, his envoy discovers that forty Cuareca Natives are "stained by the foulest vice" (*nefanda infecta venere*) (Martyr [1511] 1912, 285).[37] According to Spanish chroniclers Fernández de Oviedo y Valdés (1535) and López de Gómara (1552), this referred to the Cuareca practice of *sodomy*. The Spaniards instill Catholic dogma into heuristic operations that conflate contagion (*nefanda infecta venere*) with the lasting effects of carnal practices (i.e., anal sex defining the entire character of a person) (Valdés 1959; López 1943). Records note that the Cuareca forty flaunt their vice without shame (Horswell 2005, 71–72). To set an example, Núñez de Balboa orders all forty to be torn to pieces by mastiff dogs (Martyr [1511] 1912, 285). In the 1590s, the German-Belgian artist Theodor de Bry documents this debauchery in one of his engravings, chronicling the launch of an unprecedented regime of viability. The violent, genocidal attack on the Cuareca forty modifies conceptual and perceptual logics concerning anal practices.[38] It sets in motion an entangling of bodily responsiveness that from then on carries the imprint of voracious mastiff dogs. This colonizing regime of impressibility renders the Cuareca forty the linchpin between pre-Columbian and colonial anal sex.

At the time of the reduction of the Cuareca peoples to an infrahuman condition, bodily projects adopt new habits of impressibility. The violent canine attack becomes intertwined with an intimate act between individuals, disrupting the previously upheld degrees of asymmetrical reciprocity within Cuareca relationships, which had centrally featured anal intimacy up until that point. This sudden overturn of anal communing feeds molecular intensity to colonial perversion.[39] Anality,[40] which at one time fostered communal responsiveness, turns into an act of destitution that, simultaneously, produces Indian flesh. It shifts the Cuareca site of communal anal praxis to that of dogs' prey at the bottom of the species pyramid.

Deborah Miranda (2010) examines the existence and extermination of *joya* members among California Natives at the time of the expansion of the missionary project. Spaniards violently give the linguistic designation *joya* to members of Native communities, mostly Chumash, who did not fit the presupposed Man/Woman binary. The newcomers view joyas as carriers of dangerous behavior capable of undermining hierarchies imported from the Old World. Not unlike Núñez de Balboa's company, when Spanish soldiers arrive in the coastal region of California, they associate the Chumash population's acceptance of same-sex relations with sinful acts.[41] The egalitarian structures existing within this community, which the Spaniards will taint with accusations of sodomitical transgressions, pose a challenge to the colonial regulation of bodily impressibility. That the Chumash and other California Natives integrate various anatomies into labor specialization provokes great uproar. As Miranda states, the shock makes "mission priests [...demand] that *joyas* spend all their time in 'masculine' company" (265). Thusly, Gender cordons off Native and Indigenous bodily projects from ever approaching, accumulating, or storing Spanish or even mixed-race impressibility. Above all, it prevents labor specialization from continuing unless the Chumash came to see Spaniards as Gendered.

Miranda's research suggests that the destitution of joya peoples materializes an unprecedented assault on Indigenous views. It uproots the spiritual and political roles that joya embodiments held precontact (256).[42] Miranda's findings concern an ontology of embodiment that resonates with non-Western metaphysics. It points to worldly and nonworldly cohabitation, a discursive and practical framework in which reality takes shape. The joyas, and also perhaps the Cuareca forty, stood in relation of proximity to the divine, because, for Amerindian philosophies, the cosmos and its forces unfold as modes of being across worlds. Cuareca peoples commit their embodiments as an interweaving of everything there is. Kindred to agential realism, Native and Indigenous lifeways recognize that selfhood, being, and embodiment are enmeshed in everything these worlds are and do. No absolute, atomlike distinction exists within this enmeshment. Thus, there could not have been heterosexual or cisgender bodies in Chumash lands. Anality was neither a psychological nor a theological conduit for "primitive perversity."

When coloniality rearranges species differentiation between mastiff dogs and the Cuareca forty, it also shatters Native and Indigenous practices. It halts the generation of embodiments as the cosmic entangling of politics and spirituality. Impressibility enacts the *how* of embodiments, their verb rather than noun, and their mode of regeneration rather than transformation. Eurocentered deconstruction of the two-sex body model pays the most attention to individuals who challenge the normative positions of receptivity/rejection and submission/domination. Conversely, the decolonizing approach builds on ancestral ways of cultivating impressibility, thereby recalibrating in habits of the flesh reciprocal, yet asymmetrical, ties among everything that exists.

If, within the two-sex body model, *transgender* applies propelling force to bodily orientations, then it is not far-fetched to think of impressibility as having a central role in contesting the typical reality of the subject. I suggest that sideways selves maintain a codetermining and ancestral relation with the zone of nonbeing of the Cuareca forty and joyas. Sideways selves fail to accrue human-impressible variations, both those that fit the nuclear family, such as Husband and Wife, and those like *transgender* that, while less central for the light side, remain attached to the genre of the human. As we shall see next, carnal habits among nonhuman embodiments unveil the links between Gender, the ascent of the man of reason, and the bodily project of sanity and ability within colonial/modernity.

Kantian Sanity, gender's Rehabilitation Technologies

Transgender plays a role in the process of naming cognitive and physical deficiency. It functions as a node in the periphery of the Gender web within the light side of the colonial/modern system. From the periphery, the confusing reality of trans embodiments comes into focus. While peripheral and sometimes monstrous within the light side, *transgender* remains attached to the project of the human. The problem before us is rather simple. At a time of the transgender tipping point, the United States of America has established disability policies concerning the potential rehabilitation of transgender individuals. Rehabilitation continues the project of revising, amending, mutating, and reconstituting sexed and gender differences and distinctions. In so doing, transgender bodily projects recapitulate the sociosomatic teachings that the settler-colonial state pursues, by supporting and promoting ableist, modified versions of *genders*.

Since I inhabit a transing embodiment, I am implicated by disability. The Gender Expression Non-Discrimination Act (GENDA) of 2019 extends protections against disability discrimination for people who live with "gender dysphoria" in New York State, where I reside. I also present as a person who is racialized through migrations, having moved from peri-urban environments to Latin American and Latinx urban centers, from third-world to first-world economies, and from affluent Latin American metropoles to postindustrial cities in the northern, English-dominated hemisphere. Feeling inadequate within the human or transgender domains results not from my gender dysphoria but from racializing legacies.[43] Impressibility unfolds as a resource for both punishment and protection. My Brownness and accent: the symptoms of incompetence. My gender dysphoria: an index of split humanity. My sense of living with a disability combines the fixity of race and the iterability of gender. The more I become transgender, the more positively I respond to the modern assemblage. Yet, my disabled status keeps me from the zone of full humanity. The more that my embodiment is defined by race, the less human-impressible I become. As a trans person of color, my trans status propels my embodiment to the domain of disability protection—human, but not quite. My racial identity, contradictorily, leaves me always already lagging behind animals, unable to accrue any species gains from evolutionary time. Thus, it is not surprising that identifying as a trans person of color feels like claiming residency in an oxymoron. As it happened to the Cuareca forty, I remain placed beneath animals, or, as Mel Chen reminds us, "the class [of creatures] against which the (often rational) human with inviolate and full subjectivity is defined" (2012, 95).

At the end of the eighteenth century, Immanuel Kant argues that reason safeguards free will by instituting the limits of being, its sanity and insanity (2006). He warns against any voluntary "attempt to observe one-self by physical means, in a condition approaching *derangement*" (114; emphasis mine). In Kant's view, reason anchors sanity to an individual's "faculty" to resist and fend off external impressions and influences.[44] Anyone giving in to external forces will be cursed with the fate of objects and animals, for they lack the faculties necessary to discern what, if anything, to retain or accumulate from outside, infrahuman encroachment.

Critical disability studies challenge this Kantian hierarchy. Eunjung Kim suggests that ableist regulations shape the subject's boundaries in accordance with cognitive and physical deficiency (2015). Kim develops the notion of "curative violence" to account for a historical, social, cultural, and technological process through which cure becomes at once "remedy and poison" (2017, 14). In her analysis of cultural practices and institutions in South Korea, Kim observes uncanny concerns about the health of the body social. She examines political claims among, specifically, disabled Korean women and their struggles to access lives free of violence, including curative violence. Modernization of an ethno-nation-state, argues Kim, implicates the biomedical and medicolegal power to "physically transform a disabled individual" (4) and recover the citizen subject for the *normal* evolution of polities.[45] To cure, as Kim writes, may result in destroying the person whose well-being is at stake (14).

Kim's work demonstrates that *cure* often functions under the guise of modernizing, ethno-centered devices and that the state employs curative violence to "properly govern the body and its social relations" (3). We shall see that coloniality recruits twenty-first-century legislation to "cure" trans individuals. Indeed, remedy and poison are simultaneously employed to govern ethnic, racial, and national capabilities, thereby extracting citizenship out of the stagnant divide between humans and nonhumans.

Kant's appeal to reason works as prophylaxis against an individual's weakening ability to govern the body. Modernity in Kant's thought ties the project of *the human* with *his* ability to domesticate impressibility. Hence, the anxiety about derangement. Ethnocentric and racist links to state power find conduits, in Kant's proposal, to impress bodily responses by which flesh becomes at once an individual and a national subject. Cultural studies on global masculinities—from the sixteenth century's *ego conqueror* to marital and restrained manliness under Manifest Destiny—provide ableist and white supremacist portraits of the impressible nature of Kantian Humanity, Masculinity, and Femininity. As illustrated by Spillers and Snorton, the modern individual emerges as the sociosomatic by-product of theft as well as the amending of being, which I call *genders*, through captivity, chattel, and other carceral conditions.

The Westernizing two-sex body model objectifies what remains outside the realm of typical humans, which entails apt responsiveness to race, gender, class, and ability. Objectification entails typification of life, its deadening through rationalization, including at times medical regimentation. Legally and socially speaking, *transgender* registers as other than Gender and, through transgression of traditional metaphysical categories, as *handicapped*. In the West, the monster figure also functions as gatekeeper of the Kantian subject's racializing sanity. Noël Carroll understands the monster figure as "a composite that unites attributes held to be categorically distinct and/or at odds with the cultural scheme of things in unambiguously one, spatio-temporally discrete entity" (quoted in D. Smith 2016, 432). In my view, the monster figure manifests mutations and revisions to the reality of sexed and gendered differences and distinctions. It performs the fusion between neither *masculine* nor *feminine* and transgender.[46] A trans-monstrous formation gives rise to the medically and legally transgender disabled body, a peripheral knot in the web of abled-bodied citizenship. Trans-monstrosity disallows the differentiation of a *genders* territory from its opposite, thereby foreshadowing anxiety for modern subjects who fear their own impressible, not-so-cisgender not-so-racially-legible bodies.[47] As I suggest below, however, transgender approximates the human-impressible station of Kantian sanity via the coherence, perhaps the curative violence, to put it in Kim's terms, of disability status.

In few places is that stubborn comparison between disability and whiteness as distinctive as in the US military's contrasting handling of racial desegregation and the lift of the transgender ban. The government concedes that civil rights hang in the integration of historically marginalized populations, non-White people, and nonheterosexual and noncisgender peoples. Since the late 1970s, the movements for racial and gender equality make it hard even for the Armed Forces to dismiss the "implicit link between military service, citizenship, and an entitlement to society's benefits" (White 2012, 202). A 2016 report by RAND (Schaefer et al.), a nonprofit consulting on political decision-making, examines the integration of women and other excluded minority groups in the forces. Glossing over the 2013 lift of the Combat Exclusion Policy, the report claims that acceptance of non-White people, women, and gay and lesbian populations increased once the access barriers were removed.[48] As evidence, RAND states that "there were no issues with physical strength of African

Americans or the intellectual capacity of women," nor were the concerns about either capacity—physical or intellectual—applicable to "openly gay or lesbian personnel" (Schaefer et al., 39). This statement implies that in cases where race is the determining factor for the exclusion of the African American population, physical strength is not the primary concern. At the same time, in cases where intellectual capacity is not the issue when gender determines the exclusion of cis women, physical capacity is the primary concern.

The blatant misstep of the report reminds us of the categorial invisibility theorized by proponents of intersectional thinking. The report conspicuously implicates that there are no African American cisgender women whose exclusion is simultaneously determined by both race and gender. Or, by inference, that there are no AfroLatinx or Latinx transgender women or transgender men, whose exclusion is determined by both race and gender. Consistently, the misstep follows the path that scientific racism and sexual pathology have opened through their accounts of race and gender. Inclusion of these underrepresented groups, according to the report, would in fact respond to the stereotypes that construct women as fragile, *lesser human* specimens, and African Americans as feeble-minded, *other than human* specimens.

Drawing on the analytics of black holes, we now discern that the legal redress that the Armed Forces means to provide depends on the splitting between the impressible responsiveness of human life (*bio*) and nonhuman life (*zoe*). Whereas *bio* potentially responds with gender-accruing impressibility, *zoe* instead remains stagnant or irresponsive. As much as black holes banish woman of color or queer of color populations from liberal rehabilitation, trans of color populations remain suspended, as it were, fading in and out of view or, in other terms, constantly being revised, regimented, typified, to become dispensable for redress. We are cognitively and physically deficient, neither fully *gendered* nor sane. As shown below, at least the United States and some countries in Latin America are attending the transgender tipping point, which entails a time when *trans* comes into view for redress. However, medicolegal apparatuses seek to address *either* cognitive *or* physical deficiency, but not both at once. They open a path for redress if they find responsive aptitude, either cognitively or physically, but not simultaneously. If black holes spell out ontological impossibility, which is the zone of nonbeing, then *trans of color* remains beyond the reach of redress. We exist at the nonvisible crossroads of cognitive and physical irresponsiveness.

The military's efforts to undo the harms of racist and sexist exclusion allow us to examine the often overlooked coupling of scientific racism and sexual pathologies. Particularly, because this coupling underlies the ban against transgender individuals seeking to serve openly in the armed forces. Heterogeneous parties rally behind the struggles to lift the ban. The LGBTQ movement's goal to eradicate discrimination in healthcare, education, and sports for transgender people often lends strength to lifting the transgender ban in the military. To many, though, it feels counterintuitive that transgender civil rights provide implicit endorsement of the state's violence against alleged enemies. Look no further than to the border patrol, and you will find trans servicepeople enforcing immigration law. They are, in fact, targeting "undocumented noncitizens," among whom many, like Roxsana Hernández, present as trans or as noncis.

Strategies to increase racial and gender inclusion show that transgender status sits ambiguously between the military's encodings of race and gender as sources of intellectual and physical deficiency. The Kantian socio-ontology of insanity and deficient citizenship constructs transgender status as a monstrous formation. Transgender status entails mental and physical health conditions that act as barriers to standard activity. The Medical Evaluation Board and Physical Evaluation Board assess whether personnel with a physical ailment, such as that resulting from gender confirmation surgeries, or a mental health diagnosis, such as gender dysphoria, will remain fit to serve (Department of Defense 1996). Under the military's mission to secure operational readiness, the criteria for allowing transgender personnel to serve openly requires assessment of both physical and intellectual fitness before and after an individual acquires the target gender (Schaefer et al. 2015). Despite the incendiary rhetoric at the start of Trump's second presidency, this analysis remains relevant.

The two-sex body model endures as legal regulation of impressibility. Allowing transgender status within the armed forces sanctions this binary model as an ableist finish line. This trait figures prominently in the transnational comparison that RAND carries out. The report finds that first-world nations allowing transgender people to serve openly seek to provide for their "stability" in the target gender "without significant symptoms or impairment" (40). Transgender individuals receive accommodations as a direct result of the state's investment in cleansing the monstrous out of the trans body—that is, regulating impressibility and deriding its possibilities. The military accommodates temporary deferrals if transgender individuals acquire the coherence of an incommensurable target gender (either man or woman). The legal treatment that *trans* receives carries its embodiment from the zone of monstrosity to the zone of *genders*, amending its existence through whitening and, ultimately, making it legible through appropriate responses to intellectual and physical deficiencies.

Eventually, legal redress confronts trans status with the regulation of *bio* and *zoe*. Whenever *zoe*, which is nonsalvageable and nongenderable, stains bodily responsiveness, trans remains species-stagnant. Thus, the oxymoronic responsiveness of *trans of color*. Human impressibility in Kant's rationale for sanity aligns with those anxieties that *zoe* triggers; for, if Europe was to arrogate itself sovereign self-definition as *bio*, it had to project deficient responsiveness onto the body of the colonized. Kant's purpose, not unlike that of California's missionaries or the Spanish colonial envoys, was to rehabilitate the material and subjective weaknesses of the body into the human or near-human station.

The possibility of fleeing derangement offers trans-monstrosity an out, away from pathologizing conditions.[49] It also appeals to the redress that *genders* promise. The standard accommodations extended to individuals who claim transgender status reduce the responsiveness of transitioning bodies to human self-definition.[50] The closer to human-impressibility trans individuals get, the less *thing* they become. The more skilled they become with the sensibilities of Husband>Wife, the further from the reach of "genders," of sideways selves, they get. Indeed, trans embodiments have a white supremacist history. As black holes do, the bodily project of *transgender* under coloniality hides sociosomatic arrangements that fall beneath the human station. Whereas trans-monstrosity stands for *bio*'s disabled and freakish responsiveness, joyas and the Cuareca forty, and perhaps travestis and jotería, negotiate impressibility from within *zoe*'s stagnant state of disrepair.

Sideways selves may share habits of flesh with ambiguous nonhuman animals or even life-forms beneath animal flesh.[51] Indeed, coloniality produces differing hierarchies of *zoe*, curvatures and fleeting lines through which flesh fades in and out of trans-monstrosity and infra-animal habits. An enigmatic force resides with these hierarchies. What if we quit mistaking the West's "deficient" and not-quite-human trans monsters for all nonconforming, transing embodiments? What if we ceased to conflate transgender bodies, which the military targets for rehabilitation, with those nonconforming embodiments that the Cuareca forty and joyas continue to retroactively underwrite?

Much of white-stream feminist and transfeminist scholarship and political practice equates trans-monstrosity with the zone of nonbeing, nonhuman animal, and infra-animal flesh (Banner 2010, 864; Gannon 2011, 24; Smithers 2014, 641–642).[52] Their slippage is not what I would describe as a case of molar covering up, of transgender subjectivity being imposed upon precolonial or non-Western nonconforming embodiments (for example, *hijra*, *waria*, *nádhleehi*).[53] This kind of slippage is a matter of nominalism at best and Eurocentrism at worst. Rather, I am raising an ontological claim linked to bodily impressibility.

Within the white supremacist order that ongoingly rearranges life, embodiments become legible as sane, heterosexist, cisnormative, aptly responsive to hierarchical, either/or habits of individualizing flesh.[54] Not-quite-humans retain legibility as split beings whose partial humanity renders them *genderable*. At the black holes, they may come into view as *genderable*. They come in and out of *genders* through openings, asymmetries, distances, proximities that monstrosity enables.[55] This is the case for transgender individuals serving openly in the US military. Reminding ourselves of Wynter's account of sociogenesis, we can now acknowledge that coloniality produces the Cuareca forty or joyas as lacking this *nature* for rehabilitation. They may share a kindred condition with today's trans people of color and, as we shall see next, with travesti and jotería communities.

The coloniality of a transgender framework brings to the fore the body politics that the white supremacist nuclear family suppresses. Body politics stands in sharp tension to the politics of individualization that religious and philosophical regimes sanction within colonial modernity. Madina Tlostanova and Walter Mignolo refer to these regimes as "theo- and ego-politics of knowing" (2006, 213). Akin to Spillers's notes on the tortures inflicted upon flesh, I understand body politics as portals into the modulations of sociosomatic entangling and their rearranging of experience, knowing, and being. Such modulations point to *ungendering* in a retroactive fashion, harking back to socialities wherein Gender was absent. In what follows, I examine intertwined slices of this repository of *ungendering*.

Abya Yala: Anality / Communal Impressible⇔Voracious Hunger / Dekunafication

Travesti and jotería communities carry the mark of abomination. We perceive perverse embodiments as tied to our communal resistant existence.[56] Our *abominable perversion* supposedly relates to various impressible agilities. They bring into being asymmetries among habits of flesh. Examining these asymmetries, we begin to differentiate trans-monstrous susceptibility from Abya Yala's body politics.

Consider the proximity between dogs and Indigenous inhabitants of Abya Yala prior to and after the colonial encounter. Pre-Hispanic records show that canines were widely present in everyday life. Maya K'iche' and Nahua Mesoamerican cultures recognize the ritual and symbolic functions assigned to dogs. Activist and intellectuals, such as Gladys Tzul Tzul (2018) and Aura Cumes (2012), offer advice about intercultural philosophies. I interpret their advice on interculturality as follows. In grasping the meaning of the link between persons and dogs within the context of colonial encounters, we must veer away from imposing modern metaphysical notions of *individual* and *nonhuman animal* over Indigenous person and dog, respectively.

Words designating dogs abound in the Nahuatl language—*xoloitzcuintli* and *chichi*—and the Mayan-language: *pek'* and *tzul* (Yucatec), *tzi* (K'iche' and Pokonchi), and *tchii* (Ixil) (de la Garza 1997). While not identical across pre-Columbian cultures, there are at least three prevailing religious characteristics for dogs: their ceremonial role as substitutes for the person's body;[57] their presence as calendar signs, especially *nine dogs*, which indicates transfiguration of one life-form into another;[58] and their link to anything malformed or misshapen.[59] Undoubtedly, dogs play unique roles across the borderlands, where life spins multiple transitions.

Before the conquest, Nahua and Mayan cultures reach the Western end of present-day Panamá. The topography of the region facilitates exchange between Mesoamerican communities and the area closest to Cuareca lands (Popolo 2017). While many may find shared traits between Indigenous cosmologies, it is up to these communities to determine what carries over into intercultural translations, much more so because cross-cultural liaisons often pose the threat of ethnographic appropriation (Bruchac 2018, 176–190) and the dismissal of Indigenous and Native sovereignty. They attest to the very violence of conquest. For those of us who come from mixed-race backgrounds, the decolonial endeavor of sovereign translations entails the provincialization of our own praxis and the interculturalization of all geopolitical dialogues (Arvin, Tuck, and Morrill 2013; Walsh 2022). This sense of interculturality is not foreign to my own upbringing.

Despite benefiting from racial privilege in Argentina's northwest, starting at age nine, I lived in the same house as L. Patagua, a Casabindo-descendant "woman" who chose my father as her life partner until his passing.[60] Within the intimacy of home, I was torn by the mixed feelings I harbored about my stepmom. Technologies of *genders* made me feel confused. My family's middle-class aspirations taught me welcoming responsiveness toward white-centered ways of speaking, motioning, dressing, cooking, arranging space, and laboring. For instance, I vividly remember my disappointment when I first visited my stepmom's place. She was still in the dating stage of her relationship with my dad. Her kitchen's cabinets had no covers. There were two rows of almost bare shelves. A plastic container of salt lived there as if a tenant on a moving day: all gone but the tenant. The spatial distribution of L.'s kitchen told me something about her being; the lesson was painfully piercing to me. L. was no mom. Indeed, L. lacked the accoutrements, or the responsiveness, of white-centered femininity among the aspiring working-class in northwestern Argentina.

First, I was confused about L.'s racial ambiguity. If she were to become my stepmom, how could she, how could I, care for each other? Second, I was frightened due to my own racial ambiguity. If I were to become L.'s step*son*, how could I explain to my neighbors, friends, classmates, and acquaintances that I intimately cared for her? A decolonial endeavor lies at this rupturing juncture, the simultaneity of debasing ontologies and intimate ties. Provincializing one's center of subjectivity is an ongoing, inter-, intra-active process of translation, of learning to wear someone else's skin without claiming sameness of experience, without arrogating someone else's skin as one's own. Intercultural translations may equally entail an inscrutable abyss where someone else resides. Indeed, they demand a quota of sobering acceptance toward sometimes intractable opacity that another claims, retains, and cultivates.

I turn to intercultural and ancestral social practices among Indigenous and Native peoples of Abya Yala. I am reminded of the delicate but often cruel attachments that undergird my subjectivity, at once migrant, Brown, settler. I keep these attachments within the terrain where intercultural translations take place, where "terror and loathing of difference [. . .] lives," where "the deep place of knowledge" (Lorde 1984, 113) both hides and waits. Disciplinary ways of making sense of social histories, cultural practices, and systems of knowledge typically run afoul of the realm of intercultural translations. Disciplinary undertakings rely on a Eurocentered scaffolding, the subject/object split, and the myth of cross-cultural equivalences.[61] When I approach social, bodily, and cultural practices that I have not witnessed myself, I draw on third-party accounts, secondary sources, and, most important, firsthand narrations, through which all evidence is cast under a refracting light.

As it relates to Indigenous cosmologies in the Darién Isthmus region, where the attack on the Cuareca forty took place, we find fragmented traces among third-party accounts and secondary sources. Kuna ways of living and understanding provide fertile ground to examine cosmological overlaps.[62] Due to Indigenous migrations in the seventeenth and eighteenth centuries, Emberá, Wounaan, and Kuna cosmological systems coexist in the former Cuareca region. Nowadays, Kuna territory spans from the San Blas archipelago on the Atlantic shore to the Darién Forest. Kuna culture gives cosmological significance to shape-shifting from one life-form to another.

Kuna do not follow the Western divide between human and nonhuman, which is central for the colonial order of things; rather, they point to gradations of vitality across Kuna and non-Kuna life-forms. An agential realism of entangling entanglements resonates with this Indigenous system of knowledge.[63] Within it, asymmetries and indeterminacies manifest mysteries of the regeneration of life. Moreover, as indicated to Carlo Severi (1987, 74) by Paolino, one of the community's chiefs in the mid-1980s, Kuna and other Mesoamerican peoples acknowledge dogs' roles in supporting bodily transitions, such as burial rites. "The skull of a dog" is placed by the brazier that Kuna communities attend to while they burn an adult corpse prior to burial (74). The brazier signals the passage into death. Energy from the dog's skull keeps threatening animals away during this metamorphosis.

Spanish envoys turned dogs into torturing, snuff-enacting weapons. Indigenous cosmologies, by contrast, associate dogs with everyday tasks and ceremonies, in which they facilitate the passage between life's end and dawn. That is, dogs intercede in the impressible indeterminacy of bodily matter. Emberá and Wounaan cultures also uphold cosmologies in which everything in the universe, tangible and not, is interrelated (Velásquez Runk 2009). Afterlife mutations begin with the corpse-burning ritual. After burial, dogs chaperone their Kuna kin throughout otherworldly designs. Impressibility entangles environment and embodiment across worldly and otherworldly asymmetries among Kuna embodiments. Kuna peoples use the word *kurkin* when they speak of the amniotic sac, but also of vital intelligence or intangible spiritual force (Fortis 2010, 484). Kurkin grows the fetus through birth, guiding the transitioning of matter from non-Kuna life to Kuna personhood.[64] For their roles in everyday ceremonies and burial ceremonies, dogs are clearly attuned to kurkin designs and the spinning of bodily skills. Transitioning is key, since it gives expression to perennial faculties of entanglement for non-Kuna-animal and

Kuna-animal life-forms.[65] Kurkin fosters maturing differentiations, which in turn teach newborns how to embrace and be embraced by spiritual lifeways (Fortis 2010, 490).

The Spaniards' voracious hunger for infectious flesh prompts an assault on the Cuareca forty. De Bry's engraving, which we have previously analyzed, constitutes a primordial scene of snuff. Conquest dissolves habitual patterns of flesh that once nourished companionship and affirmed balance among various asymmetrical configurations, including Cuareca-Kuna and dogs.[66] The dusk of pre-Columbian anal praxis slides into the netherworld right at the onset of unfavorable events. Anal impressibility becomes a mark of destitution, launching cascading effects of dekunafication.[67] Building on Sylvia Wynter's sociogenic argument, I submit that geopolitical tension lies between dehumanization and dekunafication, since Kuna peoples were never counted as humans. By contrast, and through Spaniards' intrusion, dogs become more skilled in snuff technologies that conquest sets forth. Dogs begin to partake in the very human erotics of conquest and its mundane sensibilities. Canines slowly retreat from the realm of reciprocal yet asymmetrical entangling that they used to share with the Cuareca forty. Kuna peoples literally bumped into a massacre, where the sacred nature of their bodily transitions got shattered, where more-human-canines mauled Indigenous peoples' faculties for regeneration.

Given the evidence thus far provided, I would like to reconsider the rhetoric of the tipping point regarding trans phenomena today. At the height of visibility for trans experience and politics, I would like us to consider whether contemporary trans bodies are becoming more human-impressible and less monstrous, and whether, through this process, they also retreat, as mastiff dogs once did, from the realm of bodily sibling-hood that they share with an oxymoronic station such as trans of color.

Naguala, **Sacred Shape-Shifting**

Abya Yala, the deep Indigenous, Latinx, and Afro-Latinx Americas, fore-grounds sacred and otherworldly materialism. Communal, balance-affirming impressibility among dogs and Cuareca peoples points to tangible and intangible configurations that transmogrify into one another. Perhaps it is the late artist, writer, spiritual activist, and intellectual Gloria Anzaldúa who pointedly captures nuances in the material configuration between mundane and spirit worlds. Through a sustained engagement with the practice and study of *nagualismo* (Anzaldúa 2002, 549; Keating 2009, 229), Anzaldúa furthers our understanding of unearthly realities and how they bear on posthuman, decolonial, and (post)posthuman materialism. Her spiritual search traces the knowledge that comes to be embodied in the praxis of healers and shamans who shift shapes by adopting nonhuman animal forms (DiPietro 2020).[68] Anzaldúa incites dis-ease with secular accounts of gender nonconforming formations. Therefore, we can relate her praxis of nagualismo to critiques of white-stream posthumanism.

Nagualismo is a Nahuatl-derived term. Linked to "shape-shifting" subjects, it refers to Anzaldúa's own pedagogy in the search of "an embodied yet expansive consciousness with the capacity for 'hyperempathetic perception'" (Zaytoun 2016, 395). The path of *conocimiento*, Anzaldúa explains, seeks to synch psychic, physical, emotional, and spiritual agencies of subjectivity across an in-between bridge that we may call, for lack of a more vibrant image, self and other. In Anzaldua's thinking, *naguala* outlines a process of self-awareness and consciousness. It underscores subjectivity's engaged presence in the actions of everyday life, or the configurations of inner and outer aspects of the self. What distinguishes her account of naguala is that subjectivity doesn't reside in the individual's consciousness—one's own dreams, intuitions, ideas, and emotions—but resides in the entangling of shapes, forms, and energies whose cores are more codetermined than not. Reminiscent of Maturana and Varela's notion of structural coupling, naguala unfolds precisely through this conjoining of environment and selfhood.

I turn to nagualismo because it resonates with posthumanist materialism and offers a strong critique of the Kantian rationale for sanity, extending Anzaldúa's teachings to the study of Abya Yala's body politics. Naguala offers three significant insights, I believe, about nonconforming bodily projects such as sideways selves: (1) Xicanx, Afro-Latinx, and Latinx narratives draw on agential realism whose origins they trace back to sacred knowledges of Abya Yala (see also Barad 2014, 172); (2) feminist and queer knowledge emerging from the everyday life of Afro-Latinx and Latinx communities influences our account of nonconforming bodily projects without becoming wed to the Euroamerican category *transgender*; and (3) a decolonial shift occurred in the ways of knowing and politicizing embodiments. These three insights combined respond to affinities between submerged Indigenous lifeways and contemporary sideways selves.

In her 1987 study of Indigenous Mesoamerican psychology, Anzaldúa (1999) examines five centuries of wounds bleeding across the Mexico-US border, where she was born. Torn from several directions, she sees herself as one of the *atravesados*, border-dwellers who practice an extraordinary faculty that she calls *la conciencia de la mestiza*, or mestiza consciousness. Anzaldúa's account of mestizaje rejects the Indigenous mold that the settler imagination determines. She does not consent to the Indigenous lineage of Xicanas going extinct, as white supremacist and sometimes Native American exigencies dictate.[69] "New mestizas" see beneath the surface of amnesia, because they dwell in a twilight region of psychological unrest, never quite at home on either side of the tangible and intangible borders that define our times.

Think of travesti streetwalkers as Anzaldúa's atravesados. Typically purged from the sanctioned space of childhood and home, they foster an enigmatic faculty to find company at the crossroads of exile and migration. Anzaldúa refers to the site of minimal existence, the fragile grounding of atravesados, as a thin edge of barbwire. Streetwalkers respond to their precarious situation by occupying the sex-work strip with their synched strides. Sideways selves perform *transversalidad* and, by so doing, they come to impress embodiments with affective, social, cultural, and organic interdependence. They bring into being a collectivist responsiveness that they now call *travesti*, a praxis of offstage stasis and mobility. They are atravesados, neither humans, nor animals, nor monsters, but an enigmatic force of nature, a sacred *nostredad* or *weness*.[70] As such, they fade into view on the cusp between *genders* and "genders." Somewhere in-between the political and theoretical space over posthumanism and decoloniality, sideways selves commit to bodily portals into the less- and more-than-human, less- and more-than-animal. In sum, they contest and respond to that sociosomatic entangling that I call dekunafication. Atravesados, *traviesas*, *travas*, travestis, and jotería emerge from an otherworldly materialism, inspiring and pressing upon, and at once being inspired and pressed upon by, the bodily portals of the Cuareca forty and joyas.

Mexican Indigenous spirituality imbues atravesados' everyday faculties based on acts of shamanic transition across material domains. First, Anzaldúa activates nagualismo with her own writing, since it transforms both narrators and readers (1999, 89). In that sense, naguala behaves as glyph or graph, an imaging of sacred force spinning its mysteries. She then reflects on the historical continuity of Mesoamerican shamans who hold the power to morph into animals. She even dives into her own relation to serpents and their mythical force within Nahua cosmology. Nagualismo underwrites myriad grammars of modulating impressibility among everything there is. Under this light, De Bry's engraving serves as an illustration of a landmark entanglement of transculturation. It is a snapshot of trans-mogrification, of dogs into animals and Cuareca into less-than-animal flesh. For a subalternized sociality such as the Cuareca's, the Spaniards' assault perniciously invades the domain of impressibility but also the faculty shamans held to revise, amend, and mutate matter. While conquest renders bodies into things as a mode of captivity, Cuareca realities instead encourage the transubstantiation of worldly and otherworldly existents.

Anzaldúa returns to discussing shape-shifting in the foreword that she wrote for the *Cassell's Encyclopedia of Queer Myth, Symbol, and Spirit* (Conner, Sparks, and Sparks 1997). She defines spiritual mestizaje as "a spirituality that nurtures the ability to wear someone else's skin" (Keating 2009, 230; Delgadillo 2011, 98). This ability refers to the recurring trait of bodily and sensual participation in the world, what Native philosophers call the key strategy of science and knowing (Cajete 2000, 26). Anzaldúa's naguala figures in the sociosomatic arrangement of the world through recurring patterns or habits of flesh, by wearing someone else's skin and, concomitantly, aiding another in wearing one's own. Shape-shifting may account for the modes of being and doing that sideways selves foster, since they enact an agential and ecological materialism wherein conjoined, reciprocal mutability becomes paramount.

Naguala praxis summons soul work across species—Kuna, dogs, Cuareca, and shamans—even before the colonial introduction of "species" as a racializing category of developmental stagnation. Through pedagogies of crossing, to paraphrase M. Jacqui Alexander (2005b), sideways selves learn nagualismo style by wearing someone else's skin. The crux of mattering otherworldly possibilities lies with stepping into nonhuman, animal, less-than-animal skins, enacting and reactivating communal asymmetries such as those that dogs and Cuareca kin might have once embraced. Cuareca's impressible responsiveness participates in code-termining dogs' habits of flesh as much as dogs transmogrify into and through Kuna life-forms. There is no romancing the burial of mummi-fied dogs as artifacts that accompanied Kuna peoples after death. However, and despite the sometimes deeply contradictory asymmetries among everything there is, we may find alternatives to the theo- and ego-politics of knowing by turning, naguala style, to inter-skin and intra-skin mattering. Indeed, naguala functions as an intra- and interactive disposition of subjectivity, a transmogrifying economy of ungendering flesh.

By engaging Olmec and Toltec ways of inhabiting the world, Anzaldúa expands on the kinetics of consciousness and the *nagualizing* of embodiments. Her rendering of conocimiento outlines an Indigenous-centered method that synchs spirit, flesh, and consciousness (Anzaldúa and Keating 2002, 540–578; Pitts 2016, 357–359; Zaytoun 2015, 70). The liminal infrastructure of naguala conocimiento shares features with Kuna ceremonies. It attests to germinating impressions among Kuna, dogs, and otherworldly and posthumous matter. The multiple realities affirmed by spiritual mestizaje frames Anzaldúa's wisdom as follows: "*Simultáneamente me miraba la cara desde distintos ángulos. Y mi cara, como la realidad, tenía un caracter multíplice*" (Simultaneously I saw my face from different angles. And my face, like reality, had a multiplicitous countenance) (1999, 66; italics in the original; my translation). Anzaldúa denormalizes the sense of sight when she adds quotes in the statement, "I 'see' my face" (66), as if she were providing evidence of otherworldly sensations, glyphs, graphs, inside her skull. Unlike white-stream queer and feminist readings, pluralism, multiplicity, or nonconformity for Anzaldúa does not lie with the capability of all and any flesh to subvert normative boundaries. When facing the ancestral obsidian in which Anzaldúa looks at her countenance, not multiplied as reflection but multiple as many pluralities, she affirms and at once recalibrates Nahua and Mexica ways of being, knowing, and doing. Temporal cycles warp in the borderlands, she suggests, because past and present produce more than the dialectics of thesis and antithesis or the contradiction latent in interacting.[71]

Naguala's shape-shifting foregrounds a version of pluralist materialism more capacious than those in which singular units are said to have many facets: "Gloria, the everyday face; Prieta and Prietita, my childhood faces; Gaudi, the face my mother and sister and brothers know. And there in the black, obsidian mirror of the Nahuas is yet another face, a stranger's face" (1999, 66).[72] Confronting an obsidian self-reflection becomes simultaneity of oppositions, emphasizing asymmetry, mobility, and latency. Akin to Indigenous shamanic mattering, Anzaldúa's stranger's face summons the faculty of impressing and being pressed upon, spinning intra- and inter-skins among infrahuman and other (in)animate forms.

If sideways selves taught us lessons about the deeply ancestral modes of pluralist and agential materialism, they would behave as twenty-first-century shamans and nagualas of nonconforming bodily projects. Through their lessons, we come to witness the ways that Gender and *genders* fade out of view through decolonizing body politics. The inversion of oppositions between Gloria and her many faces disarticulates any longing for an immanent principle of life's singularity (one) moving toward plurality (many). This modality of shape-shifting is incongruent with the modernist, white supremacist, ableist, two-sex body model. Foregrounding incommensurable body parts, such a model might at best arrive at its deconstruction by moving toward many *genders*. La naguala, as do sideways selves, instead inhabits communal asymmetries such as trans of color and jotería, from within the twilight terrain of plural agencies and configurations, ongoingly in-the-making, indeterminate, and yet specified. They regenerate, rearrange, and revise "genders" as portals into what the colonial/modern gender system cannot fully discard. This enfleshment of communality points not shared humanity but to the specificities of beneath-animal dispossession.

This chapter queried colonial systems of knowledge that deploy *gender* and *transgender* as a universalizing and supracultural lens for social and heuristic analysis. By exposing the collusion of coloniality's systemic oppression and various accounts of gender differences (essentialism, constructivism, and performativity), we faced the need to retrace, gather, and cultivate a realist approach, the sociosomatic looping, for making sense of *transgender* in a decolonial fashion and from within oppositional and post-oppositional formations. Sideways selves contribute standpoints that decenter the project of the human in transfeminist explanations of embodied differences. Critical to this standpoint is what I call the *coloniality of transgender*. This standpoint shows the conjoining of the genre of the human and the configurations of Gender and *genders*. It also enriches our understanding of the colonial/modern gender system by weaving together Latin American travesti/trans theorizing, jotería studies, and agential realism. With an agential realist approach, the coloniality of transgender framework adumbrates the contradictions and possibilities that lie with *trans of color* as a way of living in and politicizing domains of embodied impressibility.

Among impressible possibilities, this chapter offered a novel way of theorizing nonconforming bodily projects by juxtaposing the entangling entanglements among trans and human, nonhuman, and monster configurations and agencies. An ancestral yet vibrant repository resides in the bodily responsiveness of colonial, postcolonial, and contemporary ungendering formations. Through the examination of such a repository, the resonance between agential realism and Indigenous and Native lifeways becomes salient. Finally, the configuration of sacred bodily projects, such as Cuareca and Kuna life-forms, leaves traces in various habits of the flesh. Naguala subjectivities, among them Cuareca and joyas, provide knowledge, experience, and practice where ancestral traces intensify their decolonial potential. Knowledge, experience, and practices mobilized by ancestral, yet vibrant habits of flesh disqualify subjects from rehabilitation. Akin to contemporary disability justice activists, many of us defy a regime that sanctions and demands normalcy and a lack of singularity. We are not looking for a cure or to be cured; we foster awareness of painful injuries and the discomfort of embodying *genders* and "genders." In other words, we exist within and beyond the twilight mutations of *husbands* and *wives*. We are inclined to adopt and adapt to the conditions of degraded, stagnant, unripe flesh. This awareness, however, speaks to the potential of incubating a radical stance toward the genre of the human. Sideways selves arise from within (post)posthuman histories of travesti/trans and jotería exiles and migrants, stemming from their disabling survivance. They respond with impressive skills as they enact the *crip* capacities of flesh. Sideways selves tap into long-standing repositories that reinterpret and recalibrate the state of disqualification and stagnation. Like the struggles of disability activists, sideways selves and their bodily projects reclaim an imposed "crippled" nature—not quite human, not quite monstrous, not even animal, but somewhat sacred.

CHAPTER 3

Stressing Verbs, De-stressing Nouns

Unlistening to Gender

In the Quechua spoken in Perú, *rikuni* conveys the action of seeing for the first-person singular. *I see*. Third-person objects emerge from the context of a situation, meaning that there is no way of establishing whom we are seeing unless we track pragmatics elements of the speech situation. But the issue seems larger than Quechua's purported lack of object pronouns (such as *myself, you, her, him, you, them*). Unlike what occurs in most Indo-European languages, Quechua manifests a relational, codetermined and codetermining, materiality of selfhood. A language such as Spanish, with a history of subjecting expressions to colonial grammar, is ill-equipped to accommodate Abya Yala's speech. Indigenous expressivity relies, as we shall see next, on entangling verbs that point to circumstances and open-ended configurations. Rikuni, in the style of Indigenous expressivity, tends to specify relations through an ongoing engagement with circumstance and variation.

This chapter listens to the expressivity of sideways selves as they de-stress colonial/modern grammar. Specifically, they de-stress nouns, toponyms, and gender markers. Sideways selves disbelieve the notion that trans, queer, or travesti speakers offer the proper object of gender nonconformity and its expressions. To begin this defamiliarizing route, we follow the expression *chachawarmi* across the jarring echo chamber of Gender, *genders*, and "genders." Typically glossed as "gender complementarity between husband and wife," *chachawarmi* is an Aymara term that at once accommodates and resists heterosexualist ideologies. I submit that it conjoins muffled articulations of "genders" with the nonhuman and its many versions.

By way of this cacophonous entangling, I shall recognize decolonizing habits of speech. They sound nonconforming realities where Indigenous and mixed-race "genders" reside. Linked to ceremonies and rituals, memories of chachawarmi inhabit the space-time through which I learned to make sense of self and community. While many of the speakers from Argentina's northwest share bilingual contexts, such as Aymara-Spanish, Quechua-Spanish, and Guaraní-Spanish, a great majority retains and re-creates stronger competence in other sociocultural languages. Specifically, I am focusing on Andean Catholicism and Andean Spanish among these languages. I posit that both serve as oppositional and post-oppositional languages.

Part of Andean Catholicism, Carnaval is an annual ancestral festivity about the resolution of material and social conflicts. Within its religious context, I turn to traces of decolonizing languages and sounds. Traces of what I glossed as rikuni above persist among speakers of Andean Spanish and their referencing of Carnaval's ritual philosophy. They allow me to join the weaving of an extended web that includes Andean villages in the high-altitude plateau, Jujuy's capital city, and San Pedro, my hometown in the greener area valleys. These traces incite critical listening skills, since neither cognition nor perception alone could apprehend decolonial styles of expression.

Chachawarmi

Aymara-speaking peoples of Bolivia live within what they call the "chachawarmi" opposition, which is a duality of generative and symmetrical forces (Harris 1978; Silverblatt 1983; Lugones 2010; Rivera Cusicanqui 2004; Platt 1980). More than forty years of scholarship examines an Andean gender system where this pairing is central (Arnold 1988; Bouysse-Cassagne 1978; Cereceda 1986; Duviols 1979; Silverblatt 1987). Chachawarmi drives germinating powers among everything there is. It allows for growth and resolution of conflict and imbalance. This principle of dual opposition appears in much of the oral tradition recounting the origin stories of Native Andean peoples but also in the archeology of spatial, ecological, and zonal complementarity (Arguedas and de Ávila 1966; Duviols 1979; Lane 2009; Saintenoy 2013; Schaedel 1988; Stanish 1989). Among Quechua-speaking peoples of Ecuador and Peru, it is the pair *qariwarmi* that encompasses this cosmological principle.

A note on decolonization is critical whenever mixed-race people, such as my case, undertake the study of chachawarmi. Gender complementarity works both rhetorically and practically in at least two simultaneous fronts and not necessarily without contradictions. On one end, complementarity stands for balance between different *gender* poles, chiefly (cis) men and (cis) women. On the other end, complementarity seems to justify exclusive areas of sociocultural competence defining of the roles of (cis) men and (cis) women. That it points only to cisgender bodies may result from the imposition of colonial metaphysics.[1] Most important, different collectives, groups, and institutions employ the notion of complementarity with disjunctive aims.

Anders Burman identifies one major distinction between chachawarmi as sociocultural ideal and as political practice (2011, 74). Those of us committed to decolonizing projects closely examine the rift between both. Activists and community members in the Andean region often justify gender inequality under the guise of the chachawarmi ideal (Paredes and Guzmán 2014, 91). This is likely a consequence of intersecting processes of epistemic colonization and indigenization. Aymara feminist intellectual and activist Julieta Paredes illustrates this contradiction. She describes the paradox of colonial gender among Aymara state officials in Bolivia under the hegemony of MAS (Movimiento al Socialismo).[2] She notes that participants in Indigenous-centered projects of state decolonization embrace institutional transformation, which involves dismantling Eurocentered foundations of public authority. However, as a decolonial feminist who has herself worked in a leadership government position, she insists on the need to depatriarchalize intersubjective, interpersonal, and institutional domains of life. She is rightfully concerned with the risk of obscuring complex power systems that hide behind the cultural ideal of chachawarmi and, thus, leave the political and material marginalization of Aymara women intact (Paredes and Guzmán 2014, 91).

Cultural supporters of chachawarmi enthusiastically pursue decolonization but mistake depatriarchalization as foreign to an Andean way of life. That is, they cast gender equality as culturally foreign. Political supporters of chachawarmi consider, instead, that patriarchal power must have been colonially imposed or, at the very least, enhanced. They claim that colonialism and its legacy corrupt pre-Hispanic ideals and practices of complementarity and equality. This entanglement of cultural and political aspects of chachawarmi divides supporters along the lines of denial and atavism. The former group imagines contemporary patriarchal regulations to rule outside Andean life, while the latter affirms that complementarity remains undisturbed by contemporary social hierarchies.

I begin with chachawarmi because I would like to pursue an agential-materialist approach to embodiment. Chachawarmi functions both as a cultural ideal and a political practice, but it lives simultaneously in embodied ways of being that are far from static or passive. They emerge from concrete histories and thus may point to patterns of conflicts dating back centuries, even from before the arrival of the Spaniards to Abya Yala. To the representational and political analysis of chachawarmi, I add the rich historical record of its material embodiment. Exploitative and extractivist, the Man>Woman divide colonizes impressibility by establishing variations of *genders*.[3] They reduce negatively racialized *nonbeings* into commodities and unwaged labor force. Against this thorough habituation of the body, chachawarmi arises with its ambiguous contradictions as a representational, political, and material site of negotiation. Dual complementarity populates everyday life's ceremonies. It reveals imperfect approximations to ancestral memories that remain much more dispersed across ethnic, class, and social lines than originally thought.

In the Argentinean northwest where I grew up, several cultural artifacts, practices, and events express long-standing memories of dual complementarity among mixed-race Jujeñxs. The Carnaval season marks an ecstatic, almost explosive, collective commitment to the rehearsal of ancestral ways of being and knowing, among them, phenomenological, representational, and political aspects of dual complementarity. Urban dwellers and residents of peri-urban and rural areas in this state flock to the Humahuaca Gorge for a ten-day celebration of Carnaval. Over the dried heat of February, the locals, many of them speakers of Aymara, Quechua, and Andean Spanish, lead dance rituals, cooking parties, and musical gatherings.

Carnaval festivities are not exclusive to the arid region of the Bolivian-Argentinean plateau. In the greener lands of the subtropical valleys, also known as the Yungas, the Carnavales of San Pedro de Jujuy attract a large following, even from distant states. In the higher lands of Tilcara, however, a handful of families maintain a system of cargos and promises that they consider intrinsic to Carnaval. Through this system, they pass on, from one generation to the next, Amerindian knowledges about these rituals within the region's agricultural and spiritual calendars. Complementarity underwrites this system as an array of activities to help ring in the Carnaval season and foster its blossoming.

In the course of exploring Carnaval as an Amerindian and mixed-race landmark of dual complementarity, I will be defining Andean Catholicism and examining its relation to decolonization as a political practice. I explain Andean Catholicism as a praxis of decolonization of subalternized knowledges that is constitutive of what I call sideways selves. Walter Mignolo's understanding of border thinking speaks to specific epistemologies of decolonization (2012).[4] In this account of border thinking, I connect Andean Catholicism to struggles about knowledge and politics that recalibrate complementary opposition in everyday life. The nexus between border thinking and dual complementarity acts as a tool for deciphering and revealing truths. Politically, this insight challenges both the Western-driven impoverishment of reality and the purist demands—sometimes Indigenous but often centered on whiteness—about what is considered genuinely Native.

Andean Catholicism reframes germination between Native, Indigenous, and mixed-race ways of knowing and being. Germination at the crossroads of racializing projects plays a central role in Carnaval festivities. Germination emerges as a manifestation of opposing dualities, traversing scales of existence, from personal memory to communal ceremony and from embodied knowledge to spiritual dexterity. Indeed, germination and its numinous, otherworldly contours provide ancestral, anti-capitalist, and even de-Westernizing technologies for subject formation.

Carnaval mediates ancient but politicized knowledge about germination. It works through the differentiation of bodily appearance and dexterity, through attire and choreography. It contends with the colonizing matrix of *genders* and its apportioning of distance and proximity among styles of being. As important as Carnaval in contending with the coloniality of gender is the linguistic variation Andean Spanish. Speakers of Andean Spanish gravitate toward a verb-centered reality, one in which germination enacts an ongoing present tense. A phenomenon known as *lo aspectual*, or *loísmo*, inscribes everyday utterances within a project of carnal germination. Loísmo, I shall argue, deflates the noun-based metaphysics of Gender and its hold over *genders*. Andean and other Indigenous forms of Catholicism, as well as Andean and Mesoamerican Spanish, converge in the politicization of everyday bodily projects. They record carnal and linguistic expressions whose economy and grammar lean on verbs, situations, and circumstances. Both Andean Catholicism and Andean Spanish will assist in expanding the scope of sideways selves as analytics of decoloniality.

Andean Catholicism and Border Thinking

It would not be possible for me to talk about Carnaval and Andean Catholicism without acknowledging the prevalence of folktales and mythmaking in my own upbringing. Ubiquity of local myths in everyday practice is widespread across much of the Bolivian-Argentinean plateau (Smietniansky 2013; Bossi 1998). Orality gives meaning to religious and economic memory. Rehearsal of oral traditions through storytelling and *copla*-singing remains at the heart of Carnaval and other religious ceremonies throughout the year.[5] My family's participation in the world of orality shapes our class and racial formation. Occidentalist views on the so-called primitive mind of Amerindians doesn't hold as much truth-value for Argentineans with my family's background as it does for fully assimilated populations.

I occupy changing locations across the field of social formation in Jujuy. I am the first to graduate college within my extended family. Both my father and mother received a high school diploma. My father managed to later complete his education through a trade training program offered by the Fábrica Militar de Aviones (Military Aircraft Manufacturing). Despite their families speaking languages other than Spanish, my parents' generation recognized the significance placed on monolingualism by the nation-state. It is a core foundation of the whitening of the country's middle class. On my father's paternal side, they speak Calabrian Messinese, a dialect from southern Italy. His mother spoke Habla Rural Chilena (rural Chilean speech) (Cid Uribe and Céspedes 2008). On my mother's paternal and maternal sides, they spoke Levantine Arabic. This language ran mostly through ethnic networks, and my mother was a monolingual speaker of Spanish by the time I was born.

It was a regular occurrence for my family to visit *curanderas* (healers), while my paternal grandmother maintained a large supply of home remedies. My parents appreciated several of the qualities of popular medicine. Most importantly, the shared peasant values within both my parents' families influenced us to perceive our interactions with curanderas as an extension of mutualism. In other words, it reinforced the sense of community, where individuals were taught that their place in the world revolves around caring for one another. We also learned to reject the often-obscure style of communication that doctors employ, whenever we had to see them. Indeed, tending to our health taught us the foundations of Andean Catholicism.

On the occasion of a frightening mishap when I was crossing the street at age six, I ended up fainting. A pickup truck that turned a corner at high speed touched my left knee as the driver slammed down on the brakes. It didn't run me over, but the world came to a screeching halt in a millisecond. Given Argentina's open and freely accessible socialized healthcare system, one might assume that my parents would have rushed me to the nearest emergency room. However, they didn't perceive my fainting episode as a symptom of a physical ailment like a bone fracture or concussion. Instead, they took me to a local elder, who maneuvered metal bells over my chest as she cast fright out of my spirit.

My family garners working-class, subaltern, and peasant life experiences, albeit syncretic and fragmented. Links between spirituality, well-being, and Indigenous knowledge figure prominently in our mixed-race lives. From the viewpoint of spirituality and aesthetic, Laura Elisa Pérez explores syncretism as a site of renewal and various forms of agency. Her approach rejects the colonial ideology that reduces Indigenous, Native, and African cultures to "vestiges of the precolonial [that] survive as largely incoherent fragments within the engulfing colonial culture" (2007, 95). Pérez revisits the notion of syncretism in the theory and practice of Native American and African diasporic religious cores. These religious cores illustrate a de-Westernizing consciousness that lives in the material realm of political agency. Practitioners in Pérez's account of syncretism screen dominant theologies of past and present, adopting a critical stance through which they assess whether adaptation, disguise, rejection, absorption, or recreation lend historically marginalized communities a far-reaching set of spiritual technologies (2007, 94–95).

Andean Catholicism presents a deeply syncretic nature. It outlines the intersection between competing cosmological principles and differing strategies of territorial exploitation and cultural domination. By "Andean Catholicism," I refer to subaltern practices that respond to and engage with the twinned dynamics of territorial expansion and transculturation. Between the fourteenth and sixteenth centuries, both the ruling Inka elite from Cuzco and invading Spaniards advanced over what is today the northwest of Argentina. They targeted sites with strategic economic value for mining and agricultural trade. Inkas moved into this region approximately 150 years prior to the arrival of the Spaniards. They brought with them a theological system based on the cult of the Sun and its ever-present manifestation in everything related to nourishment and survival. Omaguaca and Tilcara peoples of this region were receptive to this cosmological and territorial upheaval, since their own worldviews gravitate around sacred forces of nature. They also share a view of reality that privileges relations and their ongoing change, rather than fixed and stable kinds (Lussagnet 1948, 554).[6] They do not fear a slip or shift but, rather, welcome its seismic waves. This feature, which consists of embracing change as a cyclical opportunity to achieve a higher balance, proved fatal to the autonomy of Indigenous peoples.

Spaniards' invasions establish an iconography of conquest. Conspicuously, the Catholic imagery sanctions the corruption of the sacred constellations of land and deity, which served until then as the guide for Indigenous peoples' life paths. *Wak'a* is a Quechua term that encapsulates this sacred entanglement and which, through the crucible of conquest, comes to point to the material existence of various degrees of the divine, including a shrine, a deity, or an event (Kusch 2010, 53). Andean dwellers facing conquest place Christian images next to their guacas, which are sacred objects, deities, or worship sites. Despite being forced to show respect for Christian imagery, Andean dwellers employ several strategies to dechristianize this religious pantheon. Among these strategies, the superimposition of wak'as and Catholic saints had perhaps the unexpected effect of multiplying Amerindian religiosity.

Andean Catholicism became an intricate system of thinking and doing. Following Walter Mignolo, I understand that these systems push Indigenous and mixed-race peoples to craft and enact "border thinking" (2012). Contemporary Christian imageries follow an Andean style in this area. Border thinking eats at the absolute knowledge that Western theology propagates through settlement and conquest. In a way, border thinking reshuffles clashing spiritual lineages and performances. It brackets, as it were, the truth that catechism seeks to render universal, an omniscient surveyor that keeps count of an individual's sinful acts, an essential rift between divine and human natures, and retreat of communal ceremonies. In countless rituals, still taking place in the Humahuaca Gorge nowadays, Andean dwellers witness a mysterious unfolding world, the entirety of the modern and colonial history of this region being constantly refashioned (Angelo 2014, 281). They come to acknowledge that everyday rituals perform political struggles and that, upon these conflicts, an intangible world reveals its teachings.

As Mignolo argues (2012, 12), the keystone of Christianity within modernity/coloniality is to remove salvation from the realm of practical and personal experience. Christendom disallows the reception of supranatural revelation that even today cements Amerindian ways of knowing. By contrast, for Omaguaca and Tilcara peoples, germinating opposition between worldly and otherworldly domains manifests in everyday entangling of objects, events, and shrines. Today, mixed-race Jujeñxs and Kolla communities map this crucial germinating relation with the performance of rituals. What I gloss as Andean Catholicism, thus, is not an abstract account of the hybridization of Indigenous or Amerindian cosmology. It doesn't refer to an underlying psychological structure as the paradigm of structuralist anthropology has it. It invokes instead the performative in its most relational and entangling potential. In the style of border thinking, Andean Catholicism punctures space-time, activating liminal enactments of subjectivities in transition. Transculturation takes place through this performative entangling, one that doesn't privilege humans but rather takes stock of myriad forms of activity across carnal, physical, and spiritual embodiments.

In my view, an agential materialist approach, which we have previously described, supports systematic and rigorous study of enigmatic forces that cross, assemble, conjoin worldly and otherworldly domains. In so doing, this approach takes border thinking to the realm of body politics, of sociosomatic practices—such as singing, dancing, cooking, and speaking, among others. This is of paramount significance, because the linguistic utterance of chachawarmi is not widely recognized among mixed-race speakers across the Latin and Latinx Americas. It continues to live, however, in and through embodiments and their impressible and habitual memories. As partakers in this bodily repertoire, mixed-race communities may help us decode ways of being and knowing that recalibrate our competence to remember otherwise.

While my family did not possess substantial wealth in terms of financial or entrepreneurial exigencies, we were never deprived of the resources that enriched our well-being. My grandmother was not only an apocryphal source behind an unwritten book of recipes for home remedies but also an officiant of healing rituals. Together, they instilled in me a sense of humbling ingenuity. My grandmother was far from helpless when faced with unfamiliar symptoms or manifestations of ailments. She ceremoniously applied a principle of analogy to recommend a sensible treatment. If a new symptom bore resemblance to an ailment she had encountered before, she would proceed with a tried-and-true remedy. For instance, when her grandchildren came home with a skin rash, she would soothe it with iced lavender tea. When bug bites led to allergic reactions, she applied her trusted home remedy for skin inflammation. This inherited subaltern knowledge underwrites lessons with which I learned of the supranatural, entangling, and codetermining link between environment and embodiment. While I wouldn't encounter the concept of dual complementarity until later in life, my grandmother made me an engaged witness and co-inspirator of the principles of growth and the latent healing potential it harbored. She was instructing me on the carnal aspects of border thinking, the fleshy dexterity that allows subjectivities to veer sideways and away from the Eurocentered matrix of knowledge and physiology.

Sylvia Marcos studies this principle of dual complementarity in Meso-america, and its secret revelations about the nature of everything that exists. She examines analogy as one of the features of healing practices, which I also learned from my grandmother. Marcos's approach owes much to the labor of the curanderas, *graniceras*, shamans, and midwives of Morelos state in Mexico. Doña María is one of the healers with whom Marcos worked. From her, she learned of the curative practices that eggs facilitate. This practice draws several analogies that rely on hidden connections that the healer must decipher to provide both diagnosis and treatment. Once cracked, the egg's behavior manifests the relation between disease and the body in which it takes root. At the same time, the egg white and yolk show the link between the body and its environment (2006, 5). Like Doña María, my grandmother had enormous trust in nature's diagnostic properties and an analogy principle. Her treatment for seborrheic dermatitis is one case in point. This ailment runs in my family. It generates an annoying scaly netting that sits on the outer layer of the scalp. It can also be found in skin regions with higher sebum secretion. My grandmother suffered from this skin condition. So did my dad and I. She swore by the properties of lemons to maintain dry flakes under control. Her teachings slowly developed in me, as they had in my father years prior, a great respect for hidden connections of nature. She wasn't wrong about lemons. A 2015 study highlighted the role of citric acid as a natural pH adjuster, particularly in the context of the shampoo industry, where pH balancers play a vital role in preserving scalp health (D'Souza and Rathi 2015). Her approach was not unfounded. She practiced a healing process that sees in the person who seeks healing advice, the outward-looking, weblike relation through which the body social manifests distress or well-being.[7]

Germination, Reciprocity, and Indigenous Sovereignty

The conceptualization of an Andean and, sometimes, peasant Catholicism authorized my grandmother to acknowledge interdependence through various ecologies. This is not an unknown feature of vernacular or radical theological and spiritual praxis. Nature's magnificent talents cast their spell on generations of mixed-race and peasant peoples. Our relation to Western rationality remains one of skepticism and disenchantment. Not far from where I grew up, an elder cisgender woman in the village of La Banda del Durazno, Salustiana Párraga Arraya, recounts her childhood experience with Catholic priests to Asunción Ontiveros Yulquila (Onti-veros 2003, 76). She remembers an incident in the 1950s. It taught her lessons that she doesn't want to forget. This incident underscores the sig-nificance of the Andean *cargo* system, which is a set of communal activi-ties heading into the preparation of offerings to local, often syncretic, deities.

She recalls the admonishing reproach that the Catholic priest levied against Kolla parishioners. Her extended family, like most others in La Banda, shared in the communal duty (cargo) of providing offerings (*ofren-das*) to Pachamama and gifts (*cuartos*) to San Juan.[8] The priest expects observance of the catechism. He insists on casting Salustiana's network of material and cultural reciprocity, which underwrites ceremonial offerings, as a waste of time and energy. He likens them to idolatry according to the rationale that catechism instills in the ruling class of mestizos through-out Abya Yala. Extirpation of idolatry was an inquisitorial mandate from the onset of colonization and, by the late 1500s, evangelical reduction in the New World swept the spiritual ground upon which Indigenous peo-ples found their meaning (Fuerst 2018). Salustiana abhors that the priest's admonishment perpetuates the coloniality of Catholicism. His preaching targets what he cannot understand, while simultaneously casting Salustia-na's bodily expenditure as sinful, primitive, and nonhuman.

Taking on communal responsibilities operates within an economy that integrates multiple ecologies and affirms reciprocity and comple-mentarity.[9] Communal responsibilities implicate bodily and energetic expenditure, which remits to complex, inclusive, and all-encompassing germination. Whereas the priest reads an idling nature that makes Indig-enous practices deviate from proper forms of worship, the Kolla com-munity of La Banda enacts a more humbling, less predatory incantation. Worship is measured through the longevity of the numinous, other-worldly interconnection among all aspects of what there is. Rodolfo Kusch offers insightful approximations to the notion of the numinous within an Andean world. An Argentinean philosopher and anthropologist, Kusch lived in proximity to Aymara and Quechua communities. He links the numinous to the knowledge of revelation that, within this region, Indigenous peoples find in the signs of the divine (2010). These signs are not expressions that stand for, but rather point beyond to a reality that, unstable and changing, the community needs to summon through ritual. Salustiana's practice of border thinking underscores that reciprocity con-tributes to this ritual aspect of knowing. Reciprocity doesn't configure a transactional system but instead points to an underlying cosmological arrangement, an entanglement that codetermines worldly and non-worldly affairs.

The priest didn't understand that germination is an anchor for Andean Catholicism, that it far exceeds the biology of reproduction, and that it works as a signifier of abundance due to its numinous nature. Germination, such as the sprouting of a new crop of baby potatoes, points to an otherworldly contouring, an invisible yet tangible energy whose manifestation secures the continuity of Andean lives (Kusch 2010). Mysterious and divine, this contour frames the way that Andean dwellers make sense of seeds' germination. For my grandmother, a mysterious alchemy in healing frames lavender flowers. For Salustiana, the ritual offerings to Pachamama, feeding her flowers, grains, coca, and tobacco leaves, seek to name, in the dexterities of soul and body, an economy of energies with unknown name and unmeasurable value. The priest blatantly ignores the mundane manifestation of vital ties to which Andean dwellers tend. He lives at the crossroads of multiple and conflicting terrains but fails to engage border thinking and its potential to bend subjectivity sideways.

I have turned to Andean Catholicism and the embodied ways in which it underwrites healing practices among mixed-race, criollo, and Indigenous populations in the Bolivian-Argentinean plateau. As an embodied political practice, healing expands and augments border thinking, endorsing epistemological and material struggles that recalibrate complementary opposition in everyday life. Within a Eurocentered context of hostility toward Andean Catholicism, dual complementarity presses upon mixed-race and Amerindian subjectivities. It operates underground as a technology of consciousness, guiding an interpretive nexus between earthly and nonearthly affairs. We see this technology at play in Salustiana's defiance of the admonishing priest and my family's questioning disposition toward allopathic medicine. Andean Catholicism activates an ongoing political opposition to Westernizing structures, to an awful process of impoverishing working-class Amerindians and mixed-race peoples. It is not surprising that *germination* emerges prominently as tangible manifestation of this political stance. As I explain below, the salience of germination within Andean Catholicism allows me to identify an insurgent and de-Westernizing claim about territorial and bodily sovereignty.

Threads of inquiry that I have woven thus far make evident the following methodological note. Chapter 2 pursues the idea that bodily impressibility is disciplined by the coloniality of transgender and that, within this pattern, the nuclear family regulates conflicts over the control of resources associated with the regeneration of life. Notice that

Andean Catholicism enables Salustiana Párraga Arraya and other members in her community to relate with each other through an economy of sociosomatic germination. Unlike the nuclear family, which reduces life generation to reproduction between *genders*, practitioners of Andean Catholicism steer worldly conflicts around germination—such as scarcity, drought, climate change, infertility—toward an otherworldly domain of faith in one's web of co-responsible neighbors, associates, and acquaintances, both human and not. Indeed, they do not eliminate but certainly decenter Gender and *genders* from the core of life's web. Theirs are bodily projects of anti-capitalist and, thusly, decolonizing nonconformity.

In Salustiana Párraga Arraya's web of reciprocity, intra-ethnic and interethnic arrangements require that Andean dwellers accommodate the needs of soul and body by committing themselves to material expenditure. Through this act of *gastando* (spending), she rekindles and modulates vertical and horizontal forms of spatial, temporal, and labor integration and complementarity. Far from a transactional and extractivist capitalist paradigm, *gastar* integrates ecologies of sacred communality, an entanglement of active objects, worldly dwellers, and thing shrines.[10] Salustiana retroactively shuts down the priest, since she grounds her enactment of Andean Catholicism in a sovereign claim. In her view, it should not matter to priests how parishioners spend their resources. "After all, it is us who spend, not him," she states (Ontiveros 2003, 81).

On the Edge of *genders'* Intersectionality

Salustiana Párraga Arraya directs her sovereignty claim toward members of her own community. She speaks of the systemic violence to which many women in La Banda have been subjected. In the Andean Spanish that is typical among this region's speakers, she conveys how Indigenous, Kolla women feel as they face structural violence.[11] Her memory reaches all the way back to the 1940s when she recalls that

> todas las mujeres se hacían pegar mucho con los maridos. Decían, que lo que dice el marido tenía que hacer la mujer. Por algo se casa… decían. Tenía que servir al marido en la mesa…todo como si fuera un doctor. El varón no hacía nada. Trabajaban[,] s[í], pero [é]l no lavaba su ropa, no cocinaba, no planchaba, nada nada nada…Todo hacía la mujer. Una no hac[í]a las cosas de la casa, él ahí nomás nos daba una cagada y listo. (Ontiveros 2003, 82)

(women got themselves many beatings at the hands of their husbands. Whatever husbands dictate, the woman must do, they used to say. There is a reason for them getting married, they said. She had to service the husband at the table…as if he was a doctor. The male didn't do anything. They did work, but he didn't do laundry, or any cooking, ironing, nothing, nothing, nothing…Women did everything. If she didn't take care of the house chores, he gave us a beating right there and then.)

Her statement indicates that violence operates through institutional, psychological, and interpersonal scales. The coloniality of violence harms the potential of Andean Catholicism and its fostering of interpersonal and interspecies germination. What Salustiana seems to interpret as interpersonal ("whatever husbands dictate, the woman must do") she nonetheless links to long-standing social and material hierarchies such as the divide between productive and reproductive labor ("They did work, but he didn't do laundry, or any cooking, ironing"). She illustrates hierarchies between Indigenous men and women—"genders"—by commenting on the social valuation that whiteness projects onto medicine as a liberal profession. Almost with a hint of irony, Salustiana mentions the state of confusion that racializing patriarchy has cast upon Andean "husbands." Kolla themselves and excluded from the racializing and gendering project of the Argentine nation, "husbands" expect to be treated as "doctors" and, thusly, receive from their "wives" an ongoing transfer of material and emotional resources.

On the surface, Salustiana seems to gloss a mainstream feminist critique, which unveils an unequal distribution of responsibilities within the household. I would like, however, to suggest an alternative reading. Her Indigenous intersectional thinking asserts that both Kolla *men* and *women* go missing in the map of anti-sexist interpretations of the household.[12] She challenges the structure of expectations to which racialized *men* have no access ("she had to service the husband . . . as if he was a doctor"). She half-jokingly names the insidious workings of *genders* shaping Kolla men's consciousness. She clearly denounces *genders* as the site of indoctrination of Kolla subjectivities into split beings: nonhuman as Kolla, yet genderable through sexist privilege. As I further explain below, she also employs linguistic resources to which Andean Spanish imprints a deeper decolonial logic.

Joking ironically about the oversized expectations of their "husbands,"

Salustiana's comment renders visible a geometry of power relations. Within it, Indigeneity refracts the reading of gender, sending it outwards and close to the boundary where *men* or *women* can no longer apply.[13] Her intersectional comment shifts gender epistemology, centering the oftentimes unintelligible location of Kolla subjectivities and embodiments. No resources are meant to transfer from the waged or unwaged labor of criollo *husbands* and *wives* into the Kolla domain. Extraction works the other way around. Objectification operates through patterns of subordination whereby Kolla subjectivities lose autonomy and sovereignty. They become bound to the prosperity of the nuclear family.

Unlike the process of dispossession that colonialism brought about, Kolla communities rely on germinating attachments to land and nonearthly beings for their sustainability. Returning to the black holes' lens, *refraction* seems to be the key for making sense of Indigenous forms of sustainable reciprocity. Refraction illuminates the ways that *gender* curves the gravitational pull of subjectification, from a project that services the nuclear family to another that foregrounds "genders." Black holes simultaneously unveil the enduring impact of the Husband>Wife dynamic over Kolla and mixed-race communities, as well as the decentering of gender in these communities' material relations to land, collectivism, and otherworldly events.

Salustiana's border thinking centers Kolla reality and maps a refractive reading of embodiments and genders. Her speech treats as interchangeable the markers for gender and number when she is talking about marriage and the social hierarchies that it implicates for Kolla "women" and "men," respectively. Unless speakers constantly keep abreast of the speech situation, Salustiana's use of *gender* pronouns and nouns is fairly ambiguous. From singular to plural, Salustiana underscores more than grammatical confusion. She switches between epistemological and ontological horizons, from one where an individual is the agent to another where reliance on social bonds takes over. Consider the following two examples that we borrow from the same extract that we previously discussed. She indistinctly straddles singular and plural markers for the nouns *male* and *husband* as well as *woman* and *wife*. In the first example, she states that "the male [sing. masc.] didn't do anything. They [pl. masc.] did work, but he [sing. masc.] didn't do laundry, or any cooking." In the second example, she asserts that "women [pl. fem.] did everything. If she [sing. fem.] didn't take care of the house chores, he [sing. masc.] gave us [pl. fem.] a beating." Her speech use contends with an Indigenous worldview for which boundaries that negotiate personal and communal attachments lie beyond Western notions of private property, individuality as engine of moral action, and *gender inequality*.[14] Salustiana's expressivity rejects the need for severing self and community. If one person seems to be driving the action in her statement, it carries a greater web of connections. *Women* in plural provides that backing for what *she* does. Moreover, when it comes to gender markers, ambiguity becomes even stronger. Consider this ambiguity in the following two syntagms:

> Women got themselves many beatings at the hands of their husbands.
> Whatever the husbands dictate, the woman must do, they used to say.

In the first phrase, it's unquestionable that the noun *women* (plural, feminine) serves as the subject of the action. In the second phrase, the tacit subject allowed by the Spanish language compels speakers to seek out an antecedent to anchor the gender of the elided subject of the action. That is, the conjugation *decían* (they said) points to either *ellos* (masc. pl.) or *ellas* (fem. pl.) as paradigmatic substitution.[15] Most would agree with the coordinates that pragmatics outlines. Since the plural feminine (*todas las mujeres*) carries out the action in the previous syntagm, we should probably assign the same gender (*ellas*) to the tacit subject of the conjugation "decían." Pragmatically speaking, ruling Spanish grammar sends speakers looking for Gender (*ellas* or *ellos*). Salustiana's subaltern and disorienting register sends some speakers looking for *genders* instead.

In her speech, Salustiana introduces an even more complex formulation of the subject in the adjacent third syntagm. The original Spanish phrase, "Por algo se casa, decían" (There is a reason for them getting married, they said), poses a challenge when one is replacing the tacit subject with the feminine pronoun *ellas* (they) due to the conjugation of *decían* (said), which makes the substitution less straightforward. Notice that the syntagm contains another unit of meaning that troubles gender expectations. The verb *to get married* works as reflexive in Spanish (*se casa*).[16] For the third-person singular, Spanish grammar allows for two gendered pronouns, *he* or *she*. The conjunction of the reflexive form *se casa* and the tacit subject averts the definition of the gender of the person who is getting married. Who is marrying whom, and who said or used to say what about whom? This is the murkier formulation that Salustiana offers.

In my English transliteration of the original Spanish (*There is a reason for them getting married, they said*), I chose to work with the gender-neutral pronoun *they*. Within this formulation, speakers may consider the *genders* binary for both, people with reasons to get married and people who used to make such statement. Strict and purist language ideologies pertaining to Spanish leave speakers uncertain due to the absence of a definitive paradigmatic association between subject and reflexive verb (*se casa*, in this context). We remain uncertain regarding the *gender* of the person or people who had reasons to get married. As Salustiana recalls the words of others, concurrently shifting the subject of the action and, as previously discussed, frequently toggling between different number markers, we can only recognize her inclination to deflate gender nouns and object pronouns. How is this de-stressing effect in Andean Spanish related to germination, Andean Catholicism, and the decolonization of Gender and *genders*?

If Gender, as I argue, accrues universality as an ableist projection onto how we configure our bodies, it follows that Gender casts off colonized and negatively racialized peoples for their *disabilities*. That is, as nonhuman, they respond *poorly* to the cognitive demands of imperial languages, their metaphors, and their conduits. They fail to learn how to properly express human/nonhuman hierarchies. Indeed, they misunderstand the Spanish language in its attempt to solidify *husband* and *wife* (or *marido* and *mujer*) as authoritative descriptions of dual complementarity or chachawarmi. From a sociolinguistic prism, Salustiana flips gender and number upside down, making them reversible. What strikes most as incompetence allows Salustiana to veer away from social and species hierarchies that establish and magnify Eurocentered Gender and *genders* ideologies.

The next example, concerning heteropatriarchal violence, provides further evidence of border thinking in Salustiana's speech. Andean Catholicism indicates that germination holds a central position in Quechua and Aymara philosophies. Salustiana seamlessly weaves this philosophical tenet into her arsenal of remedies for addressing both interpersonal and physical manifestations of structural violence. Far from romanticizing germination as an ancestral remnant, Salustiana exposes the underside of interpersonal violence. She suggests that the subject of harm does not lie with an individual but with a communal aspect of the self, one which has turned damaging and unfavorable. It leads me to think that remedial action against gender-based violence is better served by (1) unpacking the systemic hostility among Gender, *genders*, and "genders," and (2) decentering Husband>Wife and *husbands>wives* within the subjectification of Andean communities. Below is her statement,

> Women got themselves many beatings at the hands of their husbands.
> (Todas las mujeres se hacían pegar mucho con los maridos.)

In this utterance, Salustiana follows the standard Spanish grammar, differentiating between "women" and "husbands." However, the typical agency of transitive verbs in Spanish, such as "to beat" (*pegar*), demands an indirect object upon which the agent exerts the action (A beats B [*A le pega a B*]). Apparently, Salustiana mitigates the nature of the transitive verb by placing "women," who are in fact the recipients of the beatings, as initiators of the activity that results in the beating. This formulation, I am sure, must sound as startling evidence of victim blaming and self-delusion to white-stream feminism.[17] For now, and only temporarily, let's acknowledge that Salustiana's point may demand a decolonizing way of listening to her and yet unlistening to *genders*. Her point requires a contextualization of local conditions for liberatory action, practice, and agency, within contradictions and heterogeneities that intersectional and transnational approaches both capture and miss. In missing the underside of Salustiana's contradictory words, white-stream feminism may intensify the hold that Gender has over the circulation of feminist theory and practice. Intersectional and transnational approaches in turn may equally distort those words by failing to deflate *genders* and its heuristic force as an anti-colonial feminist device.

It is evident that the complaint of Salustiana against the priest resonates with the point that I am raising about white-stream feminist views of domestic violence. In Salustiana's spiritual practices, the priest sees confirmation that she and her Indigenous contemporaries are undifferentiated members of a (Kolla) social group that remains stuck in evolutionary time. Thusly, they don't quite gain or accumulate proper responsiveness as assimilating *husbands>wives*. White-stream feminism sees, in her account of domestic violence, confirmation of Salustiana's membership in a differentiated social group (females) of an (Indigenous) collective that remains stuck in patriarchal time. Colonial temporalities collide. Catholicism and white-stream feminism contribute to this interlocking maze.

Salustiana's sense of selfhood bends with its decolonial orientation. It doesn't seek to restore Indigeneity into appropriate impressible patterns of assimilation and humanization. It meets unfavorable conditions by embracing Andean Catholicism's web of sacred germination. Her linguistic response foregrounds asymmetries among community members, including *husbands* and *wives*. This emphasis on ecologies of reciprocal agencies allows her to conceptualize a web of sacred germination as they meet the unfavorable conditions of Gender and *genders*. Shortly, we shall return to further engage Salustiana's linguistic resources against this puzzling legacy.

Pujllay, in Search of the Devil

My grandmother's repository of healing practices and home remedies stands in sharp contrast to modernization. It disavows the Argentinean middle class's preferences for a purportedly scientific and neutral view of healthcare and anatomy. Her praxis, rural and mixed-race, resonates with Salustiana's communal understanding of Andean and Mesoamerican Catholicism. Peasant worldviews reject a common infatuation with Westernizing rationality among resenting middle classes. The Church and its monocultural, colonizing mission feeds this resentment. It is one with the culture of ignorance fostered by the nation-state and its white supremacist structure.

In this context of resentment, Carnaval season creates conditions for the release of an underground knowledge. Carnaval calls forth the *pujllay*. Devil-like, pujllay fosters a fugitive subjectivity who escapes annual captivity with the goal of showing off its trickster, playful, and jocose talents. During the two February weekends when Jujuy celebrates Carnaval, a procession of cars packs Route 9, transforming what is typically a ninety-minute trip into a three-hour ritual. Route 9 connects the city of San Salvador with the town of Tilcara, the primary hub for Carnaval festivities. This congested traffic illustrates the steady pace of thousands who flee the city.

Urbanites flee to the quebrada in an emotional turn toward the city's complementary opposite, the gravitational pole where geographies of white nationalism and Amerindian "barbarianism" collide. Poles in this rending are entrenched in the cartography *for* difference, for the ethnic Other and sexual Other. From within border thinking, fleeing the city refashions modern and colonial histories, ritualizing multiple political conflicts and bodily possibilities. To spend one's life in the city locates epistemological, political, and cultural conflicts for urban dwellers. It also creates conditions for the germination of its complementary opposite. This shift toward germination takes the form of an intersubjective disposition. It lives in the healing practices of my grandmother, the communal responsibilities of Salustiana's family, and the urban flight during Carnaval season. In these practices lives a numinous aspect that presses subjectivity into border thinking. The unknowable and the uncertain reside there, not as a universal plight for humans to find salvation but as a double critique of Western Catholicism and rationality as well as Amerindian rigidities.

As the saying goes, "El diablo nos llama"—the devil is calling us to partake in an unearthly ritual where he will be set free. At this ritual, the devil escapes into our world, lurking and indulging in acts of mockery. He festers with vices and, for Carnaval participants, models a way of embodying the intangible needs of an otherworldly domain. Release precedes restoration. Disorder conjures a new balance. Opposition demands complementarity. Dancing, cooking, singing, and eating are events that consume the harvest of annual cycles of balance and abundance. They usher the world into productive, germinating asymmetries. They anticipate carnal needs of an intangible world. Not unlike those of Salustiana or my grandmother in Argentina's northwest, or Doña María in Morelos, Mexico, ceremonies decipher natural forces, with all their contradiction, disorientation, and uncertainty. Contemporary recalibration of chachawarmi as embodied memory lives in the most dispersed sociality through which "genders" politicize the traces of anti-capitalistic, germination-seeking, and reciprocity-affirming economies. Under tectonic layers of coloniality simmer the transitional fossils of wandering evil. The provocations of its shadowy imprint seek to remind the disempowered and historically minoritized—especially Indigenous, Afro-diasporic, mixed-race, peasant, and working-class sideways selves—that earthly life owes its blossoming to otherworldly affairs. Carnaval heightens this otherworldly aspect of germination, which in turn pushes up from below against Andean Catholicism. Sideways selfhood arises as a post-oppositional response, a *nostre-dad* formation that pairs with and at once deviates from chachawarmi.

Individuals of mixed-race heritage who present as white actively participate in ceremonial practices within the city, preparing themselves for the upcoming weekends when they will travel to Tilcara and partake in the pujllay release celebration. Flocking to Tilcara mediates an opposition between urban and rural poles. It offers an ideation upon which to project the outside of entrepreneurial, individualistic, and city-dwelling subjectivities. Simultaneously, it challenges the ideation of Amerindian cosmological principles as abstract or undisputed over centuries of colonial imposition. Carnaval enables these subjectivities to sift through latent desires, veering sideways in-between modernist and atavistic attachments. "Le ha saltado el indio" (the Indian within has awakened) is a popular and pejorative saying that serves as an admonishment. It reminds many of the fact that obtaining whiteness or Western status doesn't always occur for mixed-race people, that being from Jujuy carries the curse of proximity and closeness to stagnant Indigeneity.

Populist state policies also participate in staging Indigenous identity for show and consumption. This reduction led the missions of many a priest. Among countless of her ancestors, Salustiana harbors contempt toward this official version of Catholicism. For the priest and his Occidentalism, she resides at an exiled continent where species do not evolve. He perceives her actions as acts of either mere obedience or disobedience. Many who internalize the cartography *for* difference, including sometimes Indigenous and, much more often, mixed-race peoples, would likely consider Salustiana a faithful enactor of ancestral dual complementarity. In that sense, proponents of what Anders Burman (2011) calls cultural, but not political, support for chachawarmi follow some version of atavism. Melting-pot politics colludes with atavist rigidities. They promote a public representation of Indigenous culture as glorified fossil of nativist tradition (Tucker 2011, 407; Rivera Cusicanqui 2013; Vargas and Aruquipa Pérez 2013). From within sideways selves' twilight, a parenthesis about truth and knowledge, Salustiana and my grandmother enact political responses to their exiles. They exist in neither a human nor an Indian continent. They carry Tilcara with them through dexterities of flesh and soul.

Soltáme, Carnaval (Let Go of Me, Carnaval)

As a child during Carnaval season, I would wear masks. Masquerading meant putting on costumes centered around masks. My parents took us shopping for Carnaval supplies, including confetti and snow spray, at a school supplies store. Inspired by popular animated cartoons, we often used spray-painted paper or fabric to accessorize our costumes. These costumes were reserved for evening parades, where troupes and floats marched through downtown while attendees played with snow spray, paint, and talcum powder. Steamy summer afternoons furnished the stage for water-balloon battles.

San Pedro de Jujuy is an intermountain subtropical valley in a region known as *ramal*. The town combines features of Carnaval celebrations from both highlands and lowlands. Themes traditionally associated with Qapaj Raymi (Harvest Festival), such as maize roots and sunflower stems, belong to high-altitude festivities (Podjajcer and Mennelli 2009, 77; Ontiveros 2003, 165). Meanwhile, *comparsas*, or troupes, in the lowlands choose themes that represent the warm temperatures of the green Yungas. In the Guaraní language spoken by Indigenous communities in this region, *arete guazu* refers to Carnaval season. These communities carve masks out of the wood from the silk floss tree (Ceiba speciosa). Masks serve as an interface between this world and the netherworld. An elder musician known as the *arete iya* plays a significant role in the Guaraní culture and offers their *oka* (patio) to host the welcome ceremony for Carnaval (MEDN 2016, 21).

Major cities in the *ramal jujeño* hold their Corso at the end of February. Neighborhood associations, social clubs, and Indigenous collectives walk the parades with their own floats and troupes. Locals refer to parades as Carnavales Nocturnos (or Evening Carnavals). It helps them differentiate between a mestizo style of partaking in festivals with spectators and an Indigenous style of more intimate gatherings centered on family and ethnic ties. As shown next, Carnaval festivities foreground the process of materialization of mestizo, mixed-race culture and its proximity to Kolla, Quechua, and Guaraní cosmologies.

Gabriela Karasik (2000) carries out ethnographic research on *las diabladas* (devil's troupes) in border towns across the Argentinean-Bolivian plateau. According to Karasik, materialization refers to Indigenous communities adopting and employing a novel mode of relationship with their own cultural domains. This mode of materialization consists of "curating, recovering, and exhibiting" culture for the role it plays before an imagined national audience (2000, 161). Segments of the criollo population also partake in these performative acts since national modernization demands an interactive field of ongoing circulation and ratification. An increasing context of social unrest, which skyrocketed in the aftermath of neoliberal state planning in the 1990s, fuels the dynamics of ethnicization.[18] It refashions various labor and social conflicts, including job precarity, greater immigration control, and the internationalization of basic consumption. Carnaval sets up the stage upon which these disputes take place. Harvest and renewal season presents the most concrete materiality for intercultural quarrels.

Despite growing up in San Pedro, I never heard words such as *arete guazu* in connection to Carnaval in my childhood. The greater ethnicization of Carnaval occurred after the 1990s. However, for families such as mine, the project of modernization entails at least two simultaneous processes: (1) avoiding the position of racial Others and (2) holding on to an exoticizing proximity to the nation's racial Others. Local media begin to popularize Quechua terms such as *Qapaj Raymi* and *Inti Raymi* by the first years of the millennium. This is consistent with the process of materialization that Karasik documents.

Prior to the 1990s, my family enhanced our ambiguous racialization. Many of our everyday practices decentered the mestizo belief system of Catholic praxis and supposed racial neutrality. For example, I learned the staple dance formations from each region, lowlands' *pim-pim* and highlands' *carnavalito*. Originating in vernacular religious beliefs, the devil's face was as popular as comics and cartoons among children's masks. Families like mine had two roads to choose from, either remaining spectators before these quarrels over intercultural materialization or participating as curators, consumers, or allies of Indigenous cultures.

After my mother's passing, which occurred in 1984's summer, my father drives us for about ninety minutes each way to consult with an Indigenous healer and fire whisperer. We arrive carrying groceries. They live deep in *el monte* in a humble dwelling. Three cramped rooms are arranged in a crescent shape, all opening onto a shared patio. She talks to me about the importance of making plain signs for my mother's spirit. She says that these signs help with grief and mourning and with learning how to find clarity in our minds and hearts. Her teachings appeal to the habits of the psyche and body, to the dexterity of the soul in coping with pain and loss. She spoke of the transmutation of ill feelings by securing the favors of elements. Unlike the lessons about austerity and guilt that I received in catechism school, she talked of communion between trees, skies, rivers, clouds, and us, humble co-participants in this ecology.

There is little doubt that appropriation and distortion undermine the symbiotic link between mixed-race and Indigenous Andean cultures. Appropriation is like the flip side of a process of cultural resilience and survivance. Indeed, my family fosters cultural and material habits that the nation cast as marginal to Western ways. These habits also usher my transition into the devil's mood and its religious context. Yet, within these syncretic practices lie the dangers of appropriation and absorption, of cannibalizing the demands of a spiritual world we can neither afford to give up nor fully embrace. It is no wonder that I chose a popular saying as the heading for this section. *Soltáme, Carnaval* (let go of me, Carnaval) manifests an enticing proximity between an Indigenous pujllay and his repenting defectors. Mixed-race selfhood seeks redemption, a return to lifeways despised by coloniality. The ironic challenge faced by seasonal pujllay visitors is that no route could lead back to lost origins.

During February siestas, trucks with massive speakers blast invitations to the grand opening of Carnaval at the town's largest club. These announcements employ words that Andean Catholicism has used for centuries to disguise pre-Hispanic beliefs and practices. Welcoming Carnaval requires the collective unearthing (*desentierro*) of its devilish spirit. An unearthing performs the transition from a favorable time without conflict to the unbridled battle of cosmic forces. Ritual dances such as *la diablada* (devil's polka) rehearse struggles among all that lives, but most important, among forces that manifest material abundance and scarcity in the Andean context (mining, drought, trade, harvest, and crops). Diabladas reenact the central Carnaval struggle between devils and angels, culminating in the devils' surrender to the Virgin of Socavón.[19]

At my father's factory workplace, many guys crack jokes about Carnaval season. They fantasize out loud, often verging on explicit sexual tones. Banter displays competing memories of flirtatious and sexual behavior. Since innuendo assumes the world to be cisgender and heterosexual, this kind of banter gives marriage special treatment. Its foundation of oppressive regulations makes it an easy target of many who are only Catholic in name and not at all in practice or belief. What matters to the factory workers is to relish the return of a season of tolerance toward casual sex. Banter, however, casts light over the underside of marriage in a region where Andean Catholicism thrives. That is, it makes explicit the double standard of whitening criollo values. For factory workers, including my father, marriage-market behavior across racial groups defines and restricts desirability for masculinity and femininity.[20] As discussed in chapter 1, assimilation is key in gendering the working class. Behavior that accommodates expectations about earning power, labor fitness, and romantic commitment differentiates cisgender men from cisgender women across racial differences. The higher the earning power and labor fitness, the more desirable the romantic commitment of cisgender men becomes. Racialization of labor and educational opportunities in Latin America translates social mobility into a whitening mechanism (de la Cadena 2000). Though not all my dad's coworkers were considered white criollo or mixed-race, the influence of gender-related expectations for assimilation is evident in the tone and content of marriage banter. Therefore, banter pits romantic commitment against sexual satisfaction, acknowledging the influence of a whitening dynamic and the enticing relief that Carnaval offers.

Elena Humana reflects on marriage and her outsider position with respect to this institution. Critiquing the nuclear family's hypocritical morality, she occupies an oppositional stance that heightens her position as an Indigenous, Kolla woman. She stands against the backdrop of national modernity. By the year 2000, when Asunción Yulquila Ontiveros records Elena's life story, she has sung coplas along with Del 1800 Band and her friend Salustiana Párraga Arraya for over forty-five years. She states, "I get drunk, sing, dance, I do it all, I am not lying around on the floor though. People respect me" (Ontiveros 2003, 120). Her standing in the community disputes the *genders* criteria that dominate the marriage market of the criollo population.[21] In La Banda El Durazno, Elena's sense of self deepens with communal attachments that highlight her savvy as a stellar co-creator of Andean material culture. Her community doesn't get confused by the contractual promise of modernity, for which individuals transact their freedom both into and out of marriage. In her analysis of a wedding in the Ecuadorian Andes, Sarah Radcliffe also articulates a viewpoint similar in fashion to Elena's. She argues that the rural Indigenous wedding ritual reaffirms not just familial but also federal and more-than-human attachments among earth- and otherworldly beings (2019, 133).

In Elena's decolonial imaginary, ornamental inclusion of Carnaval stands in sharp contrast to the sovereign claims that she channels: she gets drunk, sings coplas, and dances Andean polkas. Great dissonance exists between the banter among my dad's coworkers and Elena's incisive humor. Her remarks about the communal role of copla singers point to decolonizing aspects of Andean selves, also at play during Carnaval season. She sees herself as enhancing physical and spiritual dexterities inside a de-Westernizing reality. Carnaval appeals to mixed-race peoples precisely because it magnifies decolonizing aspects of selfhood.

I am keenly aware that the logic of domination in Argentina's map *for* difference sways criollo practices toward distortion, appropriation, and amnesia. The risks demand reflexivity from within this sociality of criollo, mixed-race, and Indigenous attachments. Carnaval creates differing conditions for the materialization of Andean Catholicism. Subaltern and decolonial perspectives, such as those of Elena, Salustiana, or my grandmother, both broaden and narrow the intimate bonds between mixed-race and Indigenous realms. In contrast, the banter at the factory reflects varying degrees of cultural agency. Unlike Elena and Salustiana, my dad's coworkers seldom align their banter with a more oppositional stance. Rather, they respond to what they perceive as a tantalizing feature of Andean Catholicism, a temporary upturn of racial and gender codes regarding sexual propriety and appetite.

A pervasive criollo expectation is for Carnaval to fade away or go under for twelve months. Banter and sexual innuendo activate the desiring plexus of my dad's coworkers in their steering of criollo subjectivities toward the dangerous and yet forgiving Carnaval season. In this reorientation of desires, the devil grins from the other side of the ultimate frontier. He may not let anyone return to the straight time of the nation's *genders*. Banter could occupy an oppositional space in which factory coworkers confronted their complicity with masculinism. It would reveal compounding harms among masculinity, racial privilege, and capitalist exploitation. Thus, pleading *soltáme, Carnaval* (Carnaval, let go of me) makes perfect sense. Servicing patriarchy not only activates the individualizing habits of whitening masculinity, but also disintegrates more communal and dispersed ties to sacred germination, to an otherwise relation between desires and embodiments.

Elena Humana does not sanitize the legacy of racializing patriarchy. She acknowledges the duplicity of bodily responsiveness. She understands too well that sexual innuendo combines the process of whitening ancestral carnal practices while *gendering* flirtation. Drawing on alternative body politics, Elena may inhabit drinking, singing, and dancing as practices of erotic embrace, participating in the mutual exploration of *servinakuy, vida-michiy,* or *amicharse*.[22] In that manner, Elena confronts the duplicity of sexual innuendo that, through the filter of whitening culture, reads these practices as signposts of an approaching and explosive sexual release. Instead, she comes through onto the other side, honing her skills in drinking, singing, and dancing, as these habits garner respect.

Unlikely Pairings: *genders* Lying between Indigeneity and My Family

Cisgender women from the generation of my mother, Yamile, and my aunt, Haydée, did not show much interest in Carnaval season. They had an even more distant relation to the somatic and spiritual dexterity that Elena Humana and Salustiana Párraga Arraya foreground. While major sociocultural differences endowed both Yamile and Haydée with racial privilege, their alignment with prescriptive, human-impressible femininity was not straightforward. Social pressure about looks for cisgender women in Argentina illuminates the contours of gendered femininities. They underscore that racialization, and its twinned bodily stereotypes, creates distinctions among middle-, upper-, and working-class strata as well as among poor, immigrant, and national segments of the population (Sutton 2010; Miranda 2020).

I was born during the last dictatorship in the country (1976–1983), and the disciplinary power of the military Junta shaped embodiment and appearance for years to come. This normative pattern follows a white European ideal. It pushes women to retreat into the home and adopt proper feminine looks, which emphasize docility and submissiveness (Sutton 2010, 67). It also rewards wearing makeup, dresses, and skirts in opposition to the subversive look of jeans and slacks.

My late mother, Yamile, wore comfortable and loose clothing, which helped with the chores that consumed her days. My sister, Cristian, says that our mom "dressed as a homemaker from that time (1970–1980)" (personal communication 2016) and that she devoted most of her day to tending to our needs. An accomplished cook, she also excelled at cleaning, washing, ironing, sewing, embroidering, baking, school tutoring, and gardening. Through it all, she executed a balanced budget, overseeing the monthly envelope that my dad received at work. She was up by seven in the morning even though my sister and I went to school in the afternoon shift. She never made it to bed before any of us.

My sister finds it relatively easier to view Yamile as an embodiment of Argentinean familial culture. In contrast, I recall that our mother paid less attention to her physical appearance compared to many of my classmates' mothers. While she would wear nicer clothing for school recitals, she rarely followed makeup or hairstyling routines. Neither my sister nor I conform to the white European ideal embraced by mainstream Argentine culture. Instead, we both inherit our Lebanese ancestry from our mother's side, and we are acutely aware of how our features, including our noses, eye shapes, and under-eye skin tones, present obstacles to racial assimilation.[23] To an extent, our mother showed indifference toward those racial standards of beauty. I must add that she spoke the variation of Argentinean Spanish associated with the country's central region. This linguistic competence, coupled with the education that she received at a Catholic institute, conveys prestige before the working-class, poor, and mixed-race population of Jujuy. Yet, when compared to my aunt's aesthetic, Yamile's feels relatively at ease switching between contexts that encode her embodiment as middle-class, to others where she embodied more fully her minoritized class and racial status.

My mother shopped at the local produce market, carrying heavy bags from one stand to the next. She also customized and embroidered aprons to sell among acquaintances. She undertook many other labor-intensive endeavors. My aunt, Haydée, by contrast, observes the boundary between appropriate and deviant femininity to a tee. While she ran her own clothing store for many years, which entails tracking inventory, traveling to larger cities to restock inventory, and managing customers' expectations, she felt obligated to display racial and class markers of authentic femininity. Unlike my mom, Haydée has an Italian maiden name and a Spanish-sounding married last name. This fact alone makes me think that she should have felt less anxious about fitting feminine stereotypes. However, sharing the same upbringing as my dad's, she too comes from humble beginnings and did not receive any formal education past elementary school. Their immigrant parents completed basic schooling, learning to write and read. My aunt would face a much higher risk were she not to observe proper scripts of femininity. Wearing makeup, coloring and styling her hair to the beat of fashion magazines, and staying on top of cosmetic and beauty standards amounted to more than expectations of her chosen industry. They furnished a social shield against the gaze of a milieu to which she only timidly belonged.

A sticky situation arises when we examine socially and personally empowering Indigenous worldviews. Defined as the Other of Eurocentric cultures (Taussig 2010; Pérez 2007; Ahenahkew 2016), Salustiana Párraga Arraya and Elena Humana bring into view the agency that both Yamile and Haydée accumulate. Focusing on my mom and aunt, in itself a way of othering Salustiana and Elena, allows me to assess responsiveness to proper and deviant *genders*. A refractive effect occurs when the beam of our social reading deviates from the domain of cisgender femininity toward its always already "primitive" other. I am aware that I may wind up underscoring this otherness, which would align my feminist approach to primitivist views. I attempt to tread lightly as I highlight the agency of mixed-race cisgender women like my mother and aunt. A Westernizing feminist reading affords Yamile and Haydée an agentic assessment of contexts, normative and alternative scripts. This reading works off the theoretical and methodological reduction of Indigenous *women* to stationary social positions or identities. Haydée and Yamile appear as Salustiana and Elena are banished from view into the black holes of disability. The latter two, however, instruct us with a phenomenal feminist lesson. They refuse to become fodder or sociological lip service. Elena makes it abundantly clear when she introduces her own intersectional geometry into an account of drinking, singing, and dancing.

Salustiana and Elena wear clothing that belongs to a different sociocultural register. They cut, sew, and weave their own garments, all the while attending to other value-producing activities in their social units, such as herding sheep, growing potatoes and fruit trees, and preparing the fermented beverage *chicha*. They also spin wool and dye fabrics with which they manufacture what they wear. The design of their clothing highlights neither the bodily standards sanctioned by white European ideals nor the proper looks of docile and domestic femininity. Their attire remains outside the light side of cisgender femininity.

Cree scholar Cash Ahenakew discusses "the practical difficulties that arise in the enactment of an egalitarian simultaneity of incommensurable worldviews in a historical context of severely uneven grounds of negotiation between Indigenous and non-Indigenous peoples" (2016, 328). Wary of these difficulties, I explore the geopolitical rift between Kolla *women*'s concerns about embodiments and those of my mom and aunt. Salustiana takes offense at an insensitive priest who doesn't appreciate the generative connection between spending in ritual worship and the cosmos's germinating powers. She highlights more than the tense coexistence of incommensurable worldviews; her epistemology embodies a paradigm of multirelationality, revealing an ecological correlation among everything that exists. This ecology includes hostile worldviews, such as the priest's. For Salustiana, spending entails bodily expenditure and energetic reciprocity, without which her dexterity lacks community and belonging. She engages the priest's admonishment within a framework of energetic accountability or what Gerald Vizenor (Anishinaabe) calls *survivance*. The latter works as an affirmative disposition among Native and Indigenous peoples that rejects the settler imaginary of tragic victimry (2009, 84). Salustiana's insights prompt me to reconsider my own understanding of my mom's and aunt's bodily practices in relation to Salustiana's and Elena's, aiming to restore justice to how non-Indigenous peoples relate to Indigenous models of accountability.

In my childhood, I used to believe that Carnaval was a festival where kids played a central role, had the most fun, and received the most attention. My parents were not familiar with the ceremonial calendar of the central Andes' cosmologies. However, when our childhood neighbors hosted a daylong barbecue during the second weekend of Carnaval, I gained insight into how mixed-race individuals approach Indigenous ceremonies. Approximately twenty adults, along with their children, spent hours enjoying alcoholic beverages, dancing to pim-pim and Cumbia music, eating, reenacting singing performances, and playing tag with body paint. They playfully protested by blowing colorful whistles when tagged. Their dance formations reflected gendered pairings, and the performances playfully reenacted mischievous belligerence and flirtatious interaction common among Carnaval participants.

While both my parents and our neighbors were mixed-race, often we were counted as white in the local racial structure. The grandfathers of the neighbors' kids worked in the liberal professions, the one as a doctor and the other as a school principal. Their standing more emphatically backed an allegiance to whiteness. Holding prominent roles in a rather small town, they were imbued by Jujuy's hybrid realities. An ornamental and folkloric tinge laced their cheerful and playful recreation of an Andean bodily aesthetic. I found a startling memento from one of these white-centered recreations among old photographs of me as toddler.

The photos likely date from around 1981–1982 when my dad took us on a work trip to Salta. At a small amusement park, we snapped a picture of me next to a fountain, with a children's Carnaval troupe in the background. The troupe's theme was the 1970s American show *Roots*, aired for Spanish-speaking audiences in 1979. These kids, likely part of a neighborhood float, wore shackles, torn shirts, and blackface makeup. The disruption of cultural norms, a feature in Andean cosmology often seen in mixed-race interactions during Carnaval, can sometimes lead to racist disorienting exchanges, even when attempting to align with the struggles of marginalized racial groups, inadvertently resembling minstrelsy.

When I turned nine years old, my aunt moved from San Pedro to the state's capital city, San Salvador de Jujuy. I visited my aunt and cousins every summer and on winter breaks. There, I became aware of the multigenerational nature of Carnaval's complex networks. Going to the convenience store between 2:00 and 4:00 p.m. on any weekday during this season felt like being thrown into water warfare. Being out in the street makes anyone the target in a water balloon practice of sorts. Balloons fly from several stories high in the direction of people's traffic down in the street and, while very few reach the intended target, when they do, they are awfully painful. Saturdays and Sundays get even worse. No matter age or class status, walking solo or in groups means that you are game. Any troupe targets you. No one claims to be out of Carnaval's reach. Often traveling on the back of pickup trucks, troupes jump passersby, snow-spraying them, covering them with body paint, or hosing them down with water buckets or a flurry of water balloons. This spasmodic quarrel crosses social boundaries.

Jujuy's residents form Carnaval troupes through existing social networks, often based on school districts and neighborhoods, which extend beyond their socioeconomic backgrounds. Carnaval temporarily reshapes Jujuy's societal asymmetries, valuing families with deep roots in the region, regardless of their economic status. Their symbolic capital lies

with their knowledge about the spirit of Carnaval. Competence in Carnaval traditions leads to invitations and strong connections, often resulting in the establishment of a kinship system known as "padrinazgo" or
"madrinazgo," where close friends become godparents to each other's
children. This system opens access to networks of affluence through
work-related recommendations or business leads.

Contemporary sociocultural conflicts play out through Carnaval's seasonal ritual in the Argentinean-Bolivian plateau. In that sense, Carnaval
is an encompassing phenomenon, a carnal economy that enhances border
thinking, fosters sideways selfhood, and redefines the relation of ancestral, Indigenous praxis to contemporary political and cultural conflicts. As
a site of redefinition, Carnaval offers technologies of adaptation, creation,
and alteration. It relocates nationalist bodily projects to struggles over
cultural, environmental, and economic resources, encoding the opposition between racializing capitalism and its outside, individualism and
the commons, and colonizing religion and Andean Catholicism. Sideways relationality comes into being through these technologies. From
the situation of border thinking, sideways selves employ and recognize
new geometries of subject formation. They pivot away from the thumb
of Gender and *genders*. Mixed-race families see themselves through
the prism of Carnaval and reassess their standing at the confines of the
nation-state. Sovereign Indigenous practices such as those that Carnaval magnifies reaffirm the subaltern politics of life, of "genders," against
supremacist histories of land theft, cultural dispossession, and religious
reduction.

Capitalism, individualism, and Catholicism coexist under a global patterning of all available bodily projects.[24] Yet, within and across this patterning stand embodiments and the fullness of their impressible stasis.
Interfering with each other's productive outpouring, they germinate.
Salustiana's and Elena's bodies are the first thrown into the productive
space of my mother, Yamile, and aunt, Haydée. Anxieties about racialized
and working-class labor, such as my mother's entrepreneurial approach to
homemaking, or my aunt's zealous performance of middle-class femininity, point to the contrast that Salustiana and Elena embody. Simultaneously, accruing the appearance of authenticity of whitened subjectivities
leaves my mother and aunt exposed for their attachment to precarious
yet sanctioned places. They occupy their place within the cartography *for*
difference, for *differences of the same*.

Marginal in this geography, Salustiana and Elena, or even my grandmother, sit flat under layers of Darwinian, Lamarckian, eugenicist, and

human-impressible sediments. Arrested in their development, however, Salustiana and Elena incubate dormant flesh. Denied, they never quite find a footing at the *genders* station. Andean Catholicism, border thinking, and Andean Spanish underwrite Salustiana's and Elena's embodiments, troubling the ossification of pre-Columbian styles of being. In the relationality that recreates an Andean commons against and beyond the cartography of the sexual and racial Others, and against and beyond the exigencies of ethnicization, Salustiana and Elena sprout away "genders." Enfolded in linguistic resistance, as we shall see next, they navigate the puzzling legacy of the coloniality of gender. As we examined in Salustiana's use of Andean Spanish and her approach to heteropatriarchal violence, engaging language from within the site of border thinking is a way of rendering sense-making sideways.

The Colonization of Indigenous Expressivity

The linguistic variation Andean Spanish results from the ongoing contact between Spanish and two Amerindian languages, Quechua and Aymara. Currently, large populations who live in the Andean region, and who are either in a bilingual or monolingual Spanish situation, use Andean Spanish. Speakers of Andean Spanish cover a large area, from Cuzco in Peru to Santiago del Estero in Argentina, respectively the core and the southern outskirts of the former Inka kingdom. Roughly, they are found in the Andean highlands, but recent migratory patterns disseminate this variation across mountains and coasts.

As discussed in a prior section, Andean Spanish addresses and calls upon border thinking and its technologies for the emergence and redefinition of sideways selves. Traces of border thinking in actual speech can be found in not only grammar but also, and more significantly, pragmatics and sociolinguistics. If we limit border thinking to linguistic changes in words or syntax, we perpetuate the colonial linguistic ideology. Coloniality, a power pattern influencing Andean Spanish speakers, shapes contemporary communication dynamics. Gabriela Veronelli highlights that the colonized, initially transformed into a brutish labor force during the conquest, undergo desubjectification concerning language and expression. Integral to this process is the loss of an authorized tongue. Veronelli also understands that delegitimization occurred through the rise of grammar as "an instrument to teach a language" (2015, 114). In conjunction with the fifteenth century's rise of Spanish grammar, Amerindian peoples become "primitive" in the sense that they lack the minimal amount of cognitive expression in their utterances.

Coloniality's speech situation undermines the range of expression of Amerindian languages. Spanish missionaries set fire to Toltec *amoxtli* (typically glossed as "books") and Andean *quipu* (textiles or knotted cords). But in no way were they the first to target Indigenous expressivity. Pre-conquest interethnic conflicts resulted in the destruction of painted codices and knotted strings.[25] Material memory and cognitive expression among Indigenous populations took on another meaning, however, once colonial notions of racial differences were introduced. These notions earned semiotic currency on the far edge of the Ocean Sea as Castilian ships sailed westward. This psychic encounter, between vessel and island, charts a field of unmet expectations. Colonial envoys had to quickly learn a language they primarily viewed as a tool for conquest. This created a perplexing contradiction for Spaniards, who lacked a basic understanding of their surroundings and refused to acknowledge cognitive, epistemic, and expressive repertoires among Taino stewards of Guanahani lands.

Columbus's first voyage crew includes a botanist, a surgeon, and a translator, all serving cognitive needs of conquest. Colonial exploration seeks a direct water route to exceptionally valuable spices in the East Indies. Discourse in the description of flora is crucial. Columbus has a limited understanding of the plants that he finds along the maritime route (Kingsbury 1992). A surgeon in fifteenth-century Spain is far from an expert in medicine, with an apprenticeship-based knowledge regarding noninvasive excision techniques and the use of herbs. Practitioners of medicine, by contrast, obtain university titles and are well versed in classic and Arabian medical writings (Pérez Marín 2020, 32–33). Luis de Torres, acknowledged as *converso* by the historical record, performs as the official translator of the first travel. He has fluency in Hebrew, Arabic, and Portuguese. The utility of his polyglot skills when encountering Native languages like Taino, Igneri, Arawak, Carinaco, or Carib remains uncertain (Gužauskytė 2014, 69).

In letters to the Castilian crown, Columbus laments his linguistic limitations, especially as he prepares for the second voyage. He recognizes that his inability to establish a linguistic bridge could jeopardize conversion, maritime dominance, and wealth extraction. We should consider the botanist, surgeon, and translator among the members of the crew with the greatest symbolic capital. They are nonetheless an exception compared to the bulk of seamen on board. Most late medieval seamen barely have an education in navigational skills. In all, the success of conquest hinges on the need for transparent communication. Regulation of expression becomes a milestone in the path to accumulate accurate knowledge about plants, herbs, and spices; recognize symptoms of illness in the new world; and explain to the Native population colonial asymmetries. In sum, expression bore the burden of justifying the inferior nature of Indians.

Toward the end of the fifteenth century in Europe, a changing environment shapes the pursuit of maritime expeditions. It combines venture capital and enterprising mentality. New opportunities among commercial seamen require expansion, of either the known world or the routes connecting the world. Columbian vessels carry this psychic life into the quest for a mystical place, aiming to reshape the conquerors' identity through a transformative shift in time and space. Some scholars view Columbus's travel writing as an instance of messianic and mystical discourse, while others focus on his meticulous accounts as a geographer or surveyor. In fact, as Margarita Zamora argues (1993), Columbus proceeds less as the fact-checker who gathers proof of the existence of an unknown world and more as an ingenious broker who classifies what already occupies a symbolic place, the Indies, to boost the Old World's identity.

The changing nature of the conquering self bears on Columbus's disdain toward the expressive capacities of the inhabitants of the Indies. Thus, he shapes the pragmatics of colonial communication in deeply othering terms. He seeks the assistance of Indigenous functionaries, but he doesn't have an ear for their expressivity, since, according to his messianic view, they could not have had anything unheard of or unknown to teach him. This colonial enterprise brings about the thorough transformation of the meaning-making situation in which Spaniards and Amerindians meet.

Colonizers quickly establish hierarchies about expressivity that assist Catholic indoctrination. The time of friars and missionaries was not distant, but Columbus wouldn't live long enough to see it with his own eyes. Spaniards come from different stations in life and are far from the discourse of diplomacy. Some share with Columbus the stature that the Castilian monarchy vests upon them. The majority, however, barely knows how to read and write. Upon arrival, they recruit members of the newly dominated communities who had, precontact, key roles in procuring and safekeeping knowledge of history, natural resources, and politics. It is not surprising that the encounter magnifies the mismatch of semiotic competence and impressible responsiveness. On the one side, we have seamen whose sole purpose is to either find new riches or return to Spain alive and in one piece as soon as possible. On the other, we have Indigenous astronomers and spiritual leaders whose initial openness to visitors verges on self-delusion. In the end, Native recruits become cultural and linguistic interfaces of two worlds that were ill-equipped to make sense of each other's purpose.[26]

Toponyms and the Denial of Expressivity

The multilayered reality of expressive domination demands a multipronged approach. Andean Spanish endures today as the living struggle over expressive domination. By the time Hernán Cortés and Francisco Pizarro invade Aztec and Inka territories, respectively, the mechanics of war and settler administration have implemented a colonial pragmatics of communication. For colonizers, marking off new lands and making them intelligible for extraction was crucial.

Gužauskytė states that "toponyms, names of people and deities, and nouns played an essential role in establishing a very basic kind of linguistic communication between the conquistadors and the natives" (2014, 71). Given their predatory representation of space, it makes colonial sense that Spanish explorers turn to toponyms as a linguistic priority. Toponyms seek to erase the reciprocal standing that land holds next to other sacred and yet tangible forces. As Arvin, Tuck, and Morrill argue, settler colonialism entails the twinned dynamic of land theft and forced labor (2013). Denial of Indigenous sovereignty proceeds against conceptualizations of land that are woven into ceremonial and spiritual arrangements about authority, economy, knowledge, and subjectivity (Marker 2004, 106).

Oppositional responses to linguistic domination impede, condemn, criticize, and reorient the colonial assault on sovereignty. This phenomenon is not unique to Andean Spanish. It is also documented in Spanish-Nahuatl and Spanish-Otomí variants (Ibañez Cerda, Corripio, and Mora-Bustos 2017, 131–132). Several phenomena related to contact between cultures endure across centuries, reactivating and recalibrating material, cognitive, and spiritual modes of arranging the real. In Indigenous languages, such as Nahuatl, Aymara, and Quechua, the salience of glyphs, textiles, and knots points to semiotic and representational domains that find their potential in connotative relations. Unlike the sequential ordering of the written word, the visual and oral languages of Mesoamerica and the Andes adopt a multidimensional spatiality, a weblike network of moving and tense possibilities. No single unit encapsulates pure and denotated meaning within this network of relations. Rather than naming with definitive boundaries the objects of the world, these languages point to circumstances that qualify process-realities that are not fully realized. Reality unfolds in all its specificity, context, and circumstance through languages such as Nahuatl or Aymara, which rise to the domain of memory and circulation through visual and oral semiosis. They demand a deeper involvement from speakers and their sensorial plasticity. Colonizers imprint a much more restricting semiosis to their linguistic competence. They rapidly turn to toponyms based on their need to compartmentalize, level, and divide lands.

Meaning without Things, Meaning without *genders*

In his *Nahuatl as Written* (2001), James Lockhart describes the importance of the articulation between language and cognition. He suggests that Nahuatl nouns require quite some help from particles that de-stress action and realization. In other words, Lockhart understands that nouns are more like verbs in Nahuatl and that this is the reason "they have obligatory affixes which proclaim them to be nouns" (2001, 1). Rodolfo Kusch makes a similar observation about Aymara and Quechua, for they "are flexible in turning nouns into verbs and vice versa, and they have an abundance of particles that indicate the idea of realization" (2010, 77). Both Lockhart and Kusch refer more broadly to a conception of the cosmos, but not in the abstract way that Eurocentered rationality frames cause and effect in its pursuit of the control of reality.[27]

Semiosis in Nahuatl, Aymara, and Quechua presents as verb-centered and processual, incomplete, entangling, codetermining, and, therefore, unfolding.[28] These languages purportedly lack objects and, to an extent, cannot define the boundaries of things the way that, for example, toponyms typically do. That nouns are more like verbs speaks to a conception of reality that is about dwelling in all the uncertainty of duration and event. In this instability, energies repose but also lean toward favorable or unfavorable events. They point to what germinates in verbs, in their circumstances and modalities.

Speakers of Andean Spanish continue to activate the processual metaphysics of a world without things, of an abundance of events. This metaphysics repels imperial linguistic features, whose semiotic universe begins and ends with thingified relations. Contact in the legacy of coloniality rehashes contradictory tension between border thinking's linguistic technologies and the rigidities of nouns and toponyms. Andean Spanish registers several phenomena that reactivate one's faith in the unfolding of events, their stasis, repose, and germination. I mean faith in the sense that an Indigenous way of thinking points to the location, or residence, as it were, of the holistic subject, of an entangling of worldly and other-worldly affairs that remains exposed to an overturn. Among these phenomena, I examine the use of clitics, ambiguous particles that are present in some languages, such as Spanish, and that are neither a word nor an affix. For their significant link to verbs and what verbs can do, clitics play an important role in locating the context, and actual possibilities, of an event. Clitics emphasize the duration of events whether they occur in the present or past.[29] Their salience lies with pointing out an action's circumstances, since clitics designate both people and objects connected to the verb. The functions that I am describing fit well into semiotic domains of visuality and orality where the speakers' needs and resources lean heavily on a weblike network of moving and tense possibilities. Clitics are signs that stand for the implementation of the verb, since only contexts, and not denotation, specify it.

Declension describes morphological changes that words adopt according to their syntactic function. Inflections mark cases of the noun, such as dative, accusative, or genitive.[30] Some authors argue that Spanish lacks declension cases, as in Latin. However, Spanish does allow word inflection by adding atonal affixes before or after a morpheme, a feature that functions similarly to cases, for many linguists. For example, Pablo Chaves, another member of the Del 1800 music band in which Salustiana Párraga Arraya plays and sings, uses both cases and clitics in the style of Andean Spanish. Recounting the practice of herding the Andes *suri*, which is an alpaca-like animal within the camelid family, Chaves states, "If the suri's kick hit the leg of a mounted horse, the leg would break" (*Si lo llega [a] agarrar una patada al caballo montado, lo quiebra la pata*). In this utterance, there are two and not just one clitic (Si *lo* llega…*lo* quiebra). Notice that this atonal particle (*lo*) is affixed before the verbs, *llega* and *quiebra*, respectively. A closer transliteration for Chaves's conditional utterance is "if the kick *were* to latch onto or grab the mounted horse, the kick would break the mounted horse's leg."[31] As mentioned earlier, clitics are pronouns that designate both objects and people. Speakers use clitics with frequency, for they make communication more efficient and economical. In this example, the particle *lo* substitutes the mounted horse. As we shall see, Andean Spanish thrives in a peculiar use of the clitic *lo*.

Lo Aspectual

In the more literal translation of Pablo Chaves's utterance, the noun "kick" works as the subject of the action. The kick latches onto or grabs the mounted horse, which is the direct complement or object of the action: "*Si lo llega [a] agarrar*" contains the clitic *lo*. In this first clause, *lo* supposedly replaces the object (mounted horse) that receives the kick's action or force. *Lo* is the standard's pronoun for the direct object, upon which the subject exerts action. The second part of the utterance (*lo quiebra la pata*) also contains the pronoun *lo*, but standard Spanish would consider it to be grammatically incorrect. It is crucial to investigate this error and tease out this use of the clitic *lo*, known as lo aspectual.

Based on number and gender, clitics that replace the direct object are the following: *la* (sing. fem.), *lo* (sing. masc. and neutral), and their plural forms, *las* and *los*. In the syntagm *lo quiebra la pata*, the clitic *lo* refers to the mounted horse but not to the horse's leg (direct object). The question that helps us identify the direct object is "What is broken by the kick?" The horse's leg. By contrast, *lo* in *lo quiebra* refers to the indirect object, which is where or to what the verb's action is performed. The question changes too: "To whom is the kick going?" To the mounted horse. Regardless of gender, the clitics that replace an indirect object are only two, *le* (sing. masc., fem., or neutral) and *les* (plural masc., fem., or neutral). Why, then, is the clitic *le* missing from Chaves's utterance? Because he speaks using Andean Spanish loísmo. The use of *lo* replacing the mounted horse, as in *lo quiebra*, is grammatically incorrect since the clitic for the indirect object should be *le*. The switch from the clitic *le* to *lo* is a widespread feature of Andean Spanish that is known as lo aspectual.

Broadly speaking, grammatical case underscores the function between two elements. Consider the relation between the verb *latch onto* or *grab* and the nominal syntagm *mounted horse*. These are verbs that require a mandatory object (such as eating, because we eat *something*). Nouns, or a nominal syntagm, receive an accusative case from verbs that demand an object. The nominal syntagm *mounted horse* receives an accusative from *latch onto*. Clitics further shrink the distance between verbs and the pronouns that replace direct or indirect objects. One way in which they do so is by coupling the pronoun's sound to the verb's. This is what linguistics defines as an atonal pronoun, or the type of word that composes one single tonal unit with the neighboring verb. Clitics cannot be stressed. Rather they gravitate so close to the verb that a clitic lends prosodic force to the action. Consider how salient this feature may be for speakers of Andean

Spanish, whose affiliation to the world of verbs incubates insurgent and anti-colonial forms of expression.

Within coloniality's tense negotiation over expressivity, Andean Spanish speakers confront the disorienting linguistic ideology of toponyms and nominalization. Rodolfo Kusch (2010) reminds us that verbs incite an Indigenous expression centered on processual reality. He establishes this for the Aymara and Quechua languages; so do James Lockhart (2001) and James Maffie (2014) with respect to Nahuatl. For a contemporary Spanish speaker, whose sense of linguistic competence lies with imperial grammar, clitics convey the universal drive for efficacy and efficiency in human communication. That assemblage that we call *the human* links nominalization, or the thingification of reality through toponyms, to the domain of clear-cut demarcations. For contemporary speakers of Andean Spanish, whose linguistic competence battles against colonial erasure, clitics may efficiently convey contextual expression among everything that exists.[32]

Why do speakers of Andean Spanish rely on *lo*, which typically sounds singular and masculine to the speaker of the privileged Spanish variation? What ways of knowing and living support the use of loísmo, or lo aspectual, to designate the indirect object (*le* or *les*)? What can this persistent use tell us about border-thinking negotiations, about speakers of Andean Spanish as border thinkers? Within a reality that does not subject bodies to nominalization, that refuses to see toponyms in bodily parts, what would it mean for speakers of Andean Spanish to employ a pronoun that relies on a gendered grammar of anatomical boundaries?

Loísmo: De-stressing Nouns, Ungendering Language

I understand loísmo to work along both dominant and resistant worlds of sense. From within the dominant sonic world, this use has three goals: masculinizing the neutral clitic *le*, heightening the universal masculine slant with which Spanish represents reality, and redirecting an action to the discrete timeline of past, present, and future. From within a post-oppositional sonic world, loísmo ungenders the use of clitics, foregrounds the contextual and nonrepresentative reality of Andean Spanish, and expands the present tense of the action in which clitics are involved.

Hailing from Peru herself, Gladys Merma-Molina (2007) has extensively researched lo aspectual in Andean Spanish. Her research traces the incidence of this linguistic feature as far back as the seventeenth century's *Relation of Francisco Tito Yupanqui*. She also identifies three major theses about the origin of lo aspectual: (1) Quechua and its linguistic contact with Spanish, (2) not just the Quechua language but mostly the contact zone, and (3) various causes, including contact between Quechua and Spanish. As Merma-Molina, I too come from a region, Jujuy, with a considerable percentage (approximately 70,000) of bilingual speakers of Spanish and Quechua (Giménez Folqués 2017; INDEC 2012). This number is the equivalent to 10.5 percent of the state's population. The percentage is, of course, higher in Peru, where 19 percent of the country's population speaks Quechua. Some Peruvian districts are 90–95 percent monolingual in this Andean language. Lo aspectual arises from these histories of expression, and, as we show next, it modifies the structure of the actions and, thus, verbs. It remains widely present in speech among not only bilingual speakers but also monolingual Spanish speakers (Merma-Molina, 2007). Andean Spanish not only degenders or neutralizes the gender of indirect objects, but also infuses circumstance to the way language carries out an action through expressivity.

In Pablo Chaves's utterance (*lo quiebra*), the clitic *lo* (masc. and sing.) replaces *le* (neutral and sing.) in reference to the mounted horse, which is the object that receives the suri's kick. Neutralization of gender and number is typical in Andean Spanish (Merma-Molina 2007; Giménez Folqués 2017; de Granda 1993). Often, linguists explicate this phenomenon in terms of the *lack* that they identify in the Quechua language because the object of the third person is always absent. For example, *rikuni*, a way of saying *I see* in Quechua, consists of the morpheme *riku* for the verb *to see* and the affix *ni* that stands for the first-person singular that carries the verb. Yet, there is no morphological designation for the third-person object—known as objective pronoun in English (*him*, *her*, *it*). Because of this absence, contemporary linguists argue that loísmo derives from Quechua's lack of gender and number.

This theory of deficiency brings us back to Veronelli's claims about colonial expression. Contact between grammar-based imperial languages, such as Spanish, and subjugated languages, such as Quechua, demands a decolonial approach to bilingualism. A comparative decolonial analysis contests the language ideology that views Quechua as lacking gender and number because it does not follow the grammar of an imperial language. Moreover, we could also question whether loísmo relates less to what Quechua lacks and more to what it affirms. Spanish grammar as a technology of coloniality prescribes reality, naming people and deities along gender and number lines. In the case of toponyms, gender and number had an essential role to play in settler societies. They established a very basic kind of linguistic communication between conquistadors and Natives' communities.

In Quechua, *rikuni* points to the action of seeing, for the first-person singular only, within contexts that specify whether *I see them*, *I see her*, or *I see him*.[33] Instead of establishing the foundation of communication through the individualizing anchor of *her* or *his*, Quechua relies on transitions that mark or modify verbs while being carried out. Suffixes and transitions of the verbal lexeme designate the objective pronoun. This linguistic form contrasts with Spanish, for which clear-cut demarcation remains central. Andean Spanish, instead, centers location and circumstance. It underscores connectivity. The conceptualization of toponyms in the colonial framework, which tends to demarcate resources for extraction, denies the sacred nature of Andean land. The first-person singular in that colonizing conceptualization does not *see* in the style of rikuni, for rikuni entails, first and foremost, the dispersal of the one who sees in the sacred sociality of earthly and otherworldly beings. Loísmo is far from a deficient mistake or slippage.

In addition to this feature, Quechua speakers simplify the clitic structure when they substitute their mother tongue with Spanish. The substitution consists of using a pronoun that is clearly gendered masculine (*lo*) in Spanish to replace the gender-neutral pronouns for indirect objects (*le*, *les*). Standing within the linguistic ideology of Spanish, loísmo counters the neutralization of gender. That is, for a Spanish speaker who speaks a *prestigious* variation, loísmo may sound like all clitics are masculinized. In fact, it sounds as if Andean Spanish heavily relies on an exceedingly emphatic masculinization of the things in the world. As Germán de Granda explains, however, Spanish remains psychologically removed from the existing object marking system of Quechua speakers (1993, 277). Therefore, we may want to query loísmo from within an Andean system of knowledge, which as previously established closely relates to an agential realist paradigm.

Right next to the verb, *lo* in the case of *lo quiebra* fades into the sonic intelligibility of Spanish as a marker of *gender*, as if the *gender* of the suri whose leg may kick the mounted horse was masculine. When I state that *lo* fades into sonic intelligibility, I mean that it resonates with expected elements of speech under the hegemony of Spanish. In that sense, *lo* refers to either Gender or *genders*. Let's keep in mind that toponyms inform the zero degree of whitening subjectivity. Simultaneously, like black holes, whose presence leaves imprints on more visible, legible stars, *lo* fades into an alternative sonic realm. It pivots the center away from colonial, binary toponyms. It deflates Gender/*genders* and their regulation of expressions regarding bodily responsiveness. Andean Spanish retains aspects of expressivity that affirm the nonhuman, that is, the physical and spiritual dexterity of "genders." It refuses to collapse embodiment into what some linguists call gender case. For this reason, I posit that loísmo points beyond the masculine or feminine encasing of reality.

We distort the expressivity that underlies loísmo whenever we anchor its linguistic force to gender pronouns. In short, the ideology of standard Spanish being dominant, loísmo takes away the gender-marking force of *la* (for the direct object) or the gender-neutral force of *le* or *les* (for the indirect object). However, through the decolonizing shifts that Salustiana Párraga Arraya and Pablo Chaves enact, loísmo infuses speech with an otherwise reality, with the verbalization of life forces that, as we see next, reveal the sacredness of the Andean cosmos.

Spirits Speak in the Present Tense

Clitics' neutralization of the third person consists of formal, semantic, and pragmatic parameters. The first parameter concerns Quechua's "lack" of gender and number, and the fact that it doesn't bear on the speakers' choice of *lo*. The second refers to the resignification of binary oppositions, such as animate and inanimate, through which the clitic *lo* redistributes positivity between, for example, the suri and the mounted horse.[34] The third speaks to the deference or respect that speakers intend to show toward social distance and proximity. This pragmatic component aligns with speakers who need to negotiate the rift between Spanish, which includes morphological changes to mark the tense of the action, and Quechua, where a great number of utterances foreground the present as prevailing tense. In such cases, speakers of Andean Spanish employ *lo* to further emphasize the end of an action, or its latent state. They signal how close or far an action is with respect to the situation's time. This feature is yet again another manifestation of the ways that loísmo redistributes agentic force, since Amerindian realities privilege the contentious tense of the present, its openness and reversibility.

Consider Chaves's second use of the clitic *lo* when he says *lo quiebra la pata*. We previously established that *le* should be the grammatically correct clitic for this utterance (*le quiebra la pata*). Andean Spanish speakers employ *lo* and, thus, bend the tense of the activity that they describe. While *quiebra* corresponds to the present tense of the suri's kick—as it latches onto the mounted horse's leg and, in that process, breaks it—the previous syntagm (*if the suri's kick hit the leg of the mounted horse*) follows a hypothetical or potential tense.

The prevalence of the present tense in Andean Spanish is evident in Chaves's utterance. He uses the present tense to formulate a hypothetical or conditional. In the standard utterance, the verb *quebrar* requires the conditional form *quebraría*. The clitic *lo* in Chaves's utterance conveys the simultaneity of two temporal realities that contradict each other, the hypothetical future and the actual present. For a cosmology in which time entails germination, and for which germination does not entail a clear-cut beginning and end to life, it follows that verbs retain the most contingent or precarious openness. Speakers engage bilingual resources, such as loísmo, as they point to an eventual yet unstable, and uncertain, termination of an action. *Lo* works as if the Andean Spanish speaker was stating the contingent or ongoing present tense of the world and its entangled participants. To the Andean Spanish speaker, *lo* sounds more like "in this way," *así*. Participants in reality become así to the extent that they realize the present tense and its entangling rendering of the right here and right now.

I agree with the idea that Spanish remains psychologically removed from border thinking. I understand that Andean and other Native and Indigenous knowledge systems support decolonial connections among clitics that destress the *genders*-centered reality of Spanish. I hope to have shown that the behavior of clitics, especially within loísmo, can help us visualize the psychology of border thinking and the ways that it assists sideways selves in their navigation across Gender, *genders*, and "genders."

In the world of orality and sounds, tonal stress differentiates between commands and questions. As we previously discussed, clitics function as atonal pronouns that both qualify and follow the verb because of the proximity between them. Andean Spanish speakers employ clitics as they trespass on imperial grammatical rules. Atonal pronouns provide the materiality where Spanish and Andean Spanish meet. At this crossroads, Andean expressivity betrays the clitic *lo*'s formal and semantic parameters. *Lo* latches onto verbs, in the style of Quechua's expressivity, for, as *rikuni* demonstrates, verbs emphasize, through their circumstances and modalities, dispersed subjectivities. Communication becomes much more demanding in this fashion, yet *lo* signals that all potential speakers carry a shared responsibility. If you could halt—bracket, as it were—the grammatical function of the pronoun *lo*, what would you hear? What would you learn from the histories and pragmatics of Andean Spanish?

Dispersed subjectivities recoil in germination, brooding while fading in and away, employing loísmo to specify the link between elusive nouns and ever-present verbs. Indeed, Indigenous expressivity shows that *lo* does not have to align with a noun-centered reality.

We have learned much about decolonial battles over expressions. They remind us of Salustiana Párraga Arraya's damning comments about the Catholic priest. Her demands also work as subterfuge and refusal. She may not contradict him in verbal quarrel, but she turns the realm of communication sideways, bending discourse with an attitudinal shift. Comparable to Salustiana's change of orientation, Andean Spanish speakers pivot the clitic *lo*, not so much because they disappear or alter the clitic's appearance but, rather, because they infuse *lo* with subterfuge, a kind of ruse that makes what sounds familiar, already known, reveal unheard or uncharted tones.

As mentioned earlier, Anders Burman identifies contrasting perspectives on the use of chachawarmi in contemporary Bolivia. Advocates of chachawarmi as a sociocultural ideal perceive it as a model of complementarity that remains unaltered by modernity. *Chachawarmi, chachawarmi, chachawarmi; esposoesposa, esposoesposa, esposoesposa.* Those who push chachawarmi into the political plane pay attention to how it resonates with, but also at times contests, patriarchal and white supremacist hegemonies. Often, chachawarmi points to heterogeneous, overlapping, and tense realities that run very close to coloniality's Man/man and Woman/woman. Many of us dwell in the liminal space of not quite *men* or *women*, not quite "men" or "women." We engage *genders* and their many variations. Verb-centered realities gestate embodiments beyond Gender and *genders*.

Liminal languaging invokes futurity, not necessarily of the posthuman but rather from within nonhuman contingencies. What is now also coexists with the tense of what might have been, what did not conclude. Proximity between clitic and verb defines crucial features of Andean Spanish. I turn to this proximity and wonder whether it has become a form of cognitive and sociocultural dexterity. As mentioned before with respect to Chaves's utterance "lo quiebra," the closeness of the atonal prefix imbues the verb and, recoupled, they enact a new kind of togetherness. It wouldn't be surprising if additivity, as a grammatical principle of Andean cultures, enabled recoupling between clitic and verb. Based on the entangling of loísmo and additivity, I submit that the man/woman divide and chachawarmi remain close to each other. Recoupled in the present, they behave at once as a localized unit and as a vaguer yet enactive whole.

This closeness reminds me of Elena Humana's standpoint about her own bodily practices—such as dancing, getting drunk, and singing. She affirms a communal ontology of the self. She affirms this communal reality of the self against, but also in the proximity of, *genders*. In recognizing and interacting with Elena's dexterity, the community shows her respect. They entangle Andean sociality with deficiency, lack, hypervisibility, or even hypersexuality. An economy of cargos or offerings to San Juan, or the expenditure of Elena as she sings, dances, and gets drunk, continues to activate bodily memories, to recalibrate chachawarmi. As clitics that dwell in verbs' surroundings, chachawarmi remains near a sacred ecology of everything there is. It points beyond the bodily exigences of *men* or *women*.

Gender coexists with but doesn't annihilate chachawarmi and its many versions of sideways selves. This decolonial shift equips the present with Indigenous thinking's refracting lens, which offers a sensorial apparatus attuned to process-based, verb-centered realities.[35] Salustiana, Elena, and mixed-race people such as my grandmother carry out outstanding feminist labor. They present and expand processual accounts of embodiment, of the very matter upon which sacred social relations unfold. The last twenty years have given us major developments in feminist theorizing. Specifically, they help us understand ontologies of things, objects, and life-forms other than human. We are, thus, confronted with the risk of conflating two streams of feminist materialism: white-stream posthumanism and Indigenous, Native, and decolonizing materialism. Andean Spanish and its additive loísmo allow us to revisit this schism. I comment next on this risk by pursuing a set of questions about what has been dubbed performativity theory.

(Post)posthumanism, Decolonizing Feminism without Regrets

Previously, we discussed James Lockhart's (2001) and Rodolfo Kusch's (2010) engagements with Nahuatl and Quechua. They suggest, as Germán de Granda does (1993), that Indigenous realities stress realization and action. That nouns are more like verbs within these realities speaks to an ontology that is about dwelling in all the uncertainty of incomplete material processes. Performative materialism introduces an account of ontology as processual and, specifically concerning gender, as enacted by speech acts through the following discursive and material dynamic: (1) ongoing repetitions that generate the appearance of a surface that matches the inner self, (2) a matrix of power that gives coherence to the link between surface and inner self, and (3) naming operations that ensue from such a matrix. The self does not precede the performative, but rather the performative invokes the self and its varied contingencies into the appearance of being. From de Beauvoir's *The Second Sex* (2011) to Butler's *Gender Trouble* or *Undoing Gender* (1990, 2004) and Halberstam's *Female Masculinity* (2019),[36] white-stream feminist thought foregrounds the productive force of language and the materiality that verbs, especially performative verbs, emphasize and realize.

Feminist philosopher Judith Butler contributes to this genealogy by examining the patterned and performative doing through which gender comes into being. Butler delivers an account of a process that invokes the gendering of the subject in alignment with and against a matrix of compulsive heterosexuality (1990, 25, 112). They focus on "those deemed illegible, unrecognizable, or impossible" (2004, 44), their material and discursive practices, and lived experience. Most significantly, Butler's metaphysics of events questions the preexistence of the subject and, why not, the human (2004, 13). Gender is assigned neither in a past left behind nor in the nowhere of always already. Gender constitutes the "I" through the duration of the present and as a response to the sociality of recognition and illegibility.

I turn to white-stream feminist theorizing to briefly demarcate the resonance between its performative materialism and the one that underwrites Andean and Mesoamerican Spanish.[37] The ontology of a processual and uncertain self lies in both versions of this materialism. Butler's proposal highlights her commitment to the psychology of recognition, the Hegelian underpinning of her philosophical architecture. Subjective dislocation prominently figures in Butler's materialism. Yet, the secular trappings of the notion of the self remain unchallenged. Butler posits that the "I" emerges through the intertwining of self-description and the ongoing saturation of the self by norms. Language presents as the means of articulation and self-disclosure for the "I," a continuous activity whose origin the "I" cannot pinpoint. A gendered "I" doesn't preexist the very languaging through which the "I" becomes intelligible, or through which it contests the appearance of an original "I." Nor does the "I" invoke its matter without assistance from many copies seeking an intelligible social membership.

Andean and Mesoamerican Spanish foreground verb-centered realities. Underwritten as they are by sacred ecologies, they point beyond both the human and the domain of *understanding* the human. The performative in Andean and Mesoamerican Spanish lays claim to an otherworldly sociality. It exceeds the secular dialectics of recognition and illegibility. Sideways selves never quite reside in that borderland of recognition merely between individuals and social norms. Sideways selves don't go around empty, seeking to be recognized and individualized. As Salustiana did with the admonishing priest, sideways selves reject the thingification of personhood. They constantly remind us of the numinous entangling of the right here and right now, of the budding germination that Salustiana and my grandmother foster in the presence of enigmatic forces.

Butler's approach subsumes the reality of oppression to the dialectics of recognition. Primarily, in their view, selves are enthralled with each other's vulnerability and, thusly, learn to keep each other's destruction in check (2004, 149). Placing the "I" among competing understandings of difference, Butler restricts selfhood to the dilemma between identity and emancipation. This approach services rather than rejects the secular cast that lies with recognition, flattening the communal and spiritual materialism that, for example, Salustiana or her Andean Spanish enact. Whether it is due to Butler's reliance on psychoanalysis or vexed relation with white-stream feminism, we cannot know for certain. However, performative materialism furthers secular representations of selfhood. It compels the self, theoretically speaking, to a life overridden by individualized reactions to norms. Ultimately, this account of performativity reaches for the posthuman through an anti-identitarian bent but remains caught by Enlightenment's rationality.[38]

Andean Spanish and Andean Catholicism illustrate futurity beyond Butler's account of a performative "I," beyond the encasing of selfhood into either the phenomenology of becoming—various and competing lived iterations of the human—or the epistemology of difference: various interpretations of the human. Anna Carastathis (2016) and Vivian May (2015) make similar critical claims about intersectionality by arguing that interlocking systems of power and intersubjective agency socially and materially produce complex multiplicity.[39] They refer to multiplicity not merely as a matter of differential understanding. Rather, as it happens within the spirit-centered world of Indigenous germination, the matter of selfhood transmogrifies "at the root of our very Souls" (Alexander 2005b, 308). Futurity in its piercing irony registers the (post)posthuman ecologies of materialism.

Evelynn Hammonds reflects on the interface between political agency and knowledge production (2004). Practitioners of Andean Catholicism and Andean Spanish dwell in this interface. For Hammonds, black (w)holes radiate out the cacophonic sounds of a politics of dissemblance, of making something pass for something else. She is concerned with the ways that the genre of the human bears on collective self-definition. She suggests that Black female sexuality remains in the void of distortion and silence, trapped by both white-stream feminist agency (311) and dissembling forms of Black erotic sociality (306). Similarly, speakers of Andean Spanish who engage loísmo inhabit black holes. They adumbrate polymorphous, conflictive, entangling, codetermining, and asymmetrical responsiveness. Unlike Butler's perspective, the approach of Hammonds to the illegibility of difference doesn't subsume racialization under the performative differentiation of the human. Nor does it support an epistemic corrective as the route to finally recognize the nonhuman *in its current iteration.*

Recognition of the exteriority of the self doesn't disentangle whiteness from the project of performative selfhood. A Hegelian politics of recognition occupies the tender ties through which whiteness seduces desire into a constant comparison between human and nonhuman. Hammonds summons instead a "polymorphous" eroticism of differently located Black "women." She seeks to make us aware that Black "women's" many variations don't derive from the human or the nonhuman but rather derive from a decolonial idiom of other-than-worldly undercommons. Sideways selves who practice Andean Catholicism and who speak Andean Spanish reside in such an undercommons. It is here where we renew our commitment to polymorphous domains of "genders," to a sacred eroticism of flesh.

Rikuni

In Quechua's rikuni, speech conveys the action of seeing for the first-person singular. Third-person objects emerge from the context of the situation, manifesting an intrinsic and yet relational materiality of selfhood. Implicated by rikuni, selves span and lie across degrees of life-forms, from the most concrete germinating aspects of the cosmos, such as a sprouting potato, to a thunderstorm or rain, or to fellow communal dwellers who share weaving responsibilities. Speakers of Andean Spanish engage loísmo not so much because Quechua lacks gender. Instead, Andean Spanish loísmo accommodates (post)posthumanist subterfuge. It occupies more than just the form of language. It trespasses on the domain of expressivity. Sounds such as those that emulate an atonal pronoun come to express an otherworldly, sometimes even sacred, relationality of entangling agencies. They encode the practice of interspecies entangling, unlistening to Gender and *genders* as they appeal to the enigmatic kinship between worldly and nonworldly affairs.

CHAPTER 4

Hallucinating Knowing

In this chapter, we delve into the concept of "hallucinating knowing," a multifaceted cognitive, practical, and spiritual device. Hallucinations, within the realm of narrative and performance, emerge as critical sites of exploration within Afro-Latinx and Latinx feminist theories. Intimately connected to diasporic communities and their collective repositories of knowledge, hallucinating knowing points to ongoing responses within and against an ordinary world ruled by the genre of the human. Consequently, it fosters the development of an extraordinary and more-than-human type of consciousness.[1]

Sideways selves draw on hallucinating knowing as they learn healing practices with which to fence off coexisting realities of *genders* and "genders." Under the current global pattern of coloniality, fascist, racist and xenophobic sentiments leverage Gender and *genders* to exile Afro-Latinx and Latinx subjectivities into cognitive, traumatizing unrest. A twilight sense of displacement is the primary condition of these subjectivities. As such, displacement takes varying forms according to historical contexts and scalar mediations, from the disintegration of Cuarecas' ways of life in the sixteenth century to the illegality of Brown bodies at the turn of the millennium. Since hallucinating knowing evinces bodily, and thus cognitive, responses to displacement, it also instructs us on how to recognize, and perhaps dismantle, mechanisms and theories that naturalize and justify racializing forms of subjugation.

Three thematic threads intersect in this study of hallucinating knowing. First, I turn to anthropological literature about cognitive practices and representations of the mind. I bring this thread into broader conversations about racializing aesthetics, nonconforming embodiments, intercultural translations, and multiple realities. Second, I engage debates about ways of knowing in feminist philosophy. Specifically, I consider competing accounts of multiplicity and its hallucinating existence within Afro-Latinx and Latinx feminist philosophy. Finally, I explore intergenerational liaisons between Latinx performance and the spoken word as they endeavor to heal the pernicious legacy of Gender and *genders*.

For the sake of brevity and to help readers, I will use the acronym ALXFT when I refer to Afro-Latinx, Latinx, and Xicanx feminist theories. Since the acronym covers a large geopolitical and geographical region, I preface any of the interpretations that I provide by stating that there are shared features among strands of ALXFT, which I have practiced and discussed over the years. Shared features extend an invitation to examine critical narratives that, by weaving contexts and characters alongside historical conflicts and feminist, anti-racist, and crip standpoints, offer concrete passageways into ALXFT. Between 2011 and 2014, I joined a network of Afro-Latinx, Latinx, and Xicanx performers, artists, and poets in the San Francisco Bay Area, where I became more intimately aware of ALXFT. Within a project of co-interlocution and autoethnography, I began to reflect on this network's wisdom and make sense of practices and narratives of hallucinating knowing.

Broadly speaking, I submit that multisensory and hallucinatory ways of knowing inform ALXFT and their anti-colonial perceptual repertoire. I seek to show that hallucinating knowing refers to a situational competence by which ALXFT represents bodily responsiveness among, for example, Afro-Latinx, Latinx, and Xicanx characters. With this competence, characters accommodate and, yet, contest the psychic unrest inaugurated by heterosexualist colonial rules. Characters allow us to examine, through the lens of bodily responsiveness, sideways selves and the ways that they deflate *genders* and recreate "genders." These characters' narratives explicate ancestral links between bodily responsiveness and Afro-diasporic and Indigenous thinking—specifically Nahua, Yoruba, and Creole. Altered states of consciousness figure within these systems of knowledge, for they play a salient role across healing and religious practices, such as brujería, curanderismo, and Vodou. Finally, I trace the expansion and recreation of hallucinating knowing within the artwork of Xicana playwright Cherríe Moraga and undocuqueer activist and spoken word performer Yosimar Reyes.

Race and Aesthetic Consciousness

Pilgrims become transient citizens of the world in the 1600s when they mistake Wampanoag territory for empty lands waiting to be ravaged.

The US Immigration and Customs Enforcement (ICE) agency continues this settler-colonialist and predatory project today. Unlike pilgrims, undocumented immigrants in the twenty-first century are cast as illegal and reside thereby at a place of fracture. They feel torn across boundaries of nation, race, class, gender, sexuality, caste, and disability. Within this historical juncture, the shattering of subjectivity underlies the undocumented, migrant, and diasporic condition of Afro-Latinx, Latinx, and Latin American populations. Various archives of feminist, queer, and trans of color praxis foreground feelings and knowledges about negotiating life as trespassers, as not quite fitting into the rule of viability and legality. Trespassing selves carry forward extraordinary consciousness against legacies of destitution and illegality.

When conquistadors arrive in the Cuareca region, they disintegrate pre-Hispanic systems of ecological sustainability. Removing dogs from the domain of asymmetrical reciprocity creates an unprecedented region of species exclusion. In this pivotal moment for the ascent of the genre of the human, ecclesiastic and juridical powers bent on conquest damage the bond between Native and Indigenous peoples and their environments. These powers intervene to maximize colonial resources, secure long-term and forced compliance from Native populations, and redefine the meaning of life. Catholic theologians by the mid-sixteenth century debate whether natural law protects Indians from unjust and unfair assault over their personhood. They produce a mode of rationality that, in pursuit of administrative expediency, makes evident the changing meaning and reality of human nature. At stake is not whether an ecclesiastic worldview assigns a soul to Indians, which would grant them a pathway for salvation, but rather whether the possession of a soul entails a cognitive design, a perceptual apparatus that supports an aesthetic judgment characteristic of the human species.[2]

A crucial point about aesthetic judgment as a way of knowing must be addressed here. It shall serve our goal to expand on the historical connections between diverging ways of making sense of reality, one that is based on the rule of god and the other on the rule of man. Typically glossed as the distinction between theology and secularism, both the notion and practice of knowing can be said to follow natural *divine* law or anthropological *rational* law. According to whether a society follows one or the other, the procedures, materials, and resources that knowing combines vary.

During the long sixteenth century, a pivotal shift in political rationality emerged.[3] This period witnessed the establishment of two juxtaposed viewpoints around the New World. Europe at once embraced both colonialist and democratic perspectives. By contrast, an anti-colonial stance originated in Abya Yala.[4] Spaniards commit to the daily atrocities of conquest, turning an encounter into a battleground (Maldonado-Torres 2008). They became adept at justifying their violent actions under the banner of "just war" doctrines. Pursuing justice through conquest was the cornerstone of the Catholic Church's mission to evangelize Amerindians. The colonizer's arrogance raises significant questions about the relations between self and other. What counts as justice for invading forces translated into injustice, suffering, and harm to those under attack. Central to this debate were the cognitive faculties used by colonizers to assess the nature, standing, and origin of those who were subjected to colonial rule.

In the now infamous debate that Carlos V convenes in 1550, Spanish Dominican friar Bartolomé de Las Casas and theologian Juan Ginés de Sepúlveda present opposite arguments. They battle over the right of the Spanish Crown to conquer Indigenous lands and subjugate their inhabitants to serfdom. Regardless of whether we portray Las Casas as benevolent humanist and Sepúlveda as Machiavellian sympathizer, both their arguments formulate new versions of knowledge and knowing. They draw a relation of correspondence between visual expressions and the world of inwardness or interiority that houses moral agency or choice.

Bartolomé de Las Casas implored colonial representatives to confront their insensitivity toward the relentless atrocities they inflicted upon Indigenous populations. If Spaniards *look like* civilized peoples, why doesn't their behavior express civilized interiority? This was a key question among the many that he asked. In his *Short Account of the Destruction of the Indies* (1552), the friar flips the available definitions of *civilized* and *barbarian* (Las Casas 2004). He demonstrates that Spaniards are the kind of humans who have become *inhuman* due to losing their grip on sentient cognition. They can no longer employ aesthetic judgment in a civilized manner, since they are desensitized to the suffering of Amerindians. For Las Casas, Spanish conquerors behave as barbarians and, thus, remain within a colonialist perspective. It is worth noting that decolonial theologians, such as Santiago Slabodsky (2010), challenge the conflation of barbarism and the dismissal of Europe's internal others. In Slabodsky's analysis of intellectual and religious Jewish histories, he claims that the barbarian was "a fierce and self-actualized creature who challenged Christendom" (153). Sentient knowing and affective capacities take on a geopolitical valence, since Europe's otherness refers to non-Western religious beliefs among Native and Indigenous peoples, Arabs, Jews, and Africans (Slabodsky 2010, 153).

In his study of Las Casas's rhetoric, Diego von Vacano (2012) states that "aesthetic experience, understood here as sensory cognition based on feelings, is thus not merely a capacity to witness something, but to be moved in a way that will connect a person to others' suffering and their condition as human" (419). Spaniards' perceptual apparatus, we may infer, absorbs the material condition of coloniality and habituates their body and psychology to this new condition. They respond with destruction and violence to the nascent divide between human and non-human, or even between nonhumans and infrahumans. Las Casas argues that resignified aesthetic markers, such as size and shape, elicit among Spaniards a sense of superiority. It enables them to ignore pernicious and barbaric consequences as they arise from arrogant and violent acts. By contrast, in his sometimes exaggerated benevolent rhetoric, he portrays Indians as lacking the physical shape that manifests the required strength for conquest.

On one end, Las Casas implies that Spaniards are the kind of humans who have physical and aesthetic markers for sentient knowing, but they have lost restraint. Instead of thinking of restraint as an ethical virtue, Las Casas aligns it with an aesthetic process based on a feeling, for which empathy toward another person's suffering seems to be the right fit. On the other end, Indians are the kind of protohumans who demonstrate empathy, albeit with a few exceptions, but lack physical markers to inflict as much suffering as Spaniards do. Las Casas implies that Indians lack virtue because they don't possess the strength for which restraints would be needed. Lacking force, they need no restraint. Needing no restraints, Indians do not develop virtues.

I am trying to track the rise of a colonial way of knowing that shows the more molecular and intimate ties through which the human and non-human, or the notion of race, comes into being. In chapter 2, I outline the sensibility standards that Kant identifies in the rise of modern subjectivity. I also submit that such standards, three centuries later, help us understand the ascent of *transgender* as an embodiment that aligns with ableist and racial conformity. What chapter 2 describes as bodily responsiveness makes explicit that there is a link between form and interiority. Habits of the flesh stand for the most concrete expression of sensibility. In the debate between Las Casas and Sepúlveda, they both characterize physiological distinctions within sensible habits. Las Casas comes across more as a racialist exploring anthropological differences, much like contemporary ethnographers, rather than an advocate of biologically determined distinctions among social groups. While delving into cultural alterity, Las Casas intervenes in the early stages of discourse that link outward appearance and behavior. Eventually, positivism would infiltrate these elements, harking back to imperial aesthetic values, and rigidify bodily morphologies as markers of natural hierarchies and classes.

I posit that the humanist friar pursues anthropological rationality. He underscores that sentient knowing builds on the contrast between social groups, on differences that carry radical and irreducible alterity. Those who are morally insensitive owing to their "lack of compassion and emotion in the face of cruelties" (von Vacano 2012, 417), Las Casas argues, are anaesthetized (90). For Las Casas, emotion, specifically pain, is essential to the development of moral sentiments among civilized humans. An aesthetic experience such as pain leads to intellectual activity, which in turn may inform moral judgments. Though the theological perspectives of Las Casas and Sepúlveda came before Kant's Enlightenment contributions, intellectual histories don't always follow a linear progression. Interestingly, Kant's views on aesthetic stereotypes and archetypes bear similarities to Las Casas's defense of Indians. However, a significant divergence in their aesthetic theories is Kant's ambiguous position on the inherent classifications of beings, particularly concerning the demarcation between human and nonhuman animals.

As evidence of their relative innocence and civilized propriety, Las Casas cites a delicate, less robust constitution of Natives. What the friar deems a delicate constitution would make Native populations prone to illness and unable to pose physical threats. Las Casas suggests that the interior world of morality relies on the shape or morphology of a person. Indeed, this is the role that aesthetics plays in the crucible of conquest. While, as we see next, Kant also links aesthetic knowing to moral agency, the German philosopher develops a brand of teleological thinking that deflates the more experiential or anthropological components of aesthetic valuation. His theory is supposed to supersede Las Casas's aesthetics. That is, over two hundred years later, Kant's study on appearance ideals sends this debate in a different direction. His direction conveys not just the emergence of racial categorization but its hardening. He saw that race would evolve into a category capable of absorbing discourses based at once on experience and nature.

According to John Hoffman (2016), Kant's thinking about aesthetic ideals manifests contradictory notions about human differences, from endorsing a monogenetic theory—races belong within a single

species—to speaking of racial appearance as sufficient to "denote different kinds of humans" (58). At its core, Kant's aesthetic theory advances
normative claims about the judgment of taste, appearance, and morphology, because he assumes that the general architecture of our cognitive faculties follows a natural and necessary order. He appreciates this
approach, because it allows him to introduce universalizing claims to a
world that, from experience, looks full of heterogeneity. Kant delves
deeper into the teleological significance of aesthetic categories. He further posits that our inherent cognitive processes form the foundation for
determining distinctions between aesthetic species. While Kant acknowledges the spectrum of sensible standards we inhabit, he contends that we
universally discern these standards using the same method: by drawing or
prioritizing an average, often a stereotype, among bodily attributes and
proportions.

When compared to each other, Las Casas's and Kant's approaches
regarding racial differences lead to strikingly diverging conclusions.
However, they both rely on perceptual procedures through which species, or its differing racial kinds, encode aesthetic value. Las Casas sounds
the alarm before his contemporaries, because they are losing their grip
on reliable perceptual procedures. They cannot empathize with members
who closely resemble their own kind. Interestingly though, Las Casas
remains unmoved by the multiplicity of sensorial devices by which Indians examine and learn the mysteries of the world. Kant, instead, explicates
a modernist intuition that would soon become a universal prototype.
Perceptual procedures operate within the necessary telos in which race
defines different species kinds. Las Casas develops a humanist stance that
enshrines similarities among humans at the expense of a deeply sensorial
brand of knowing. This depth reaches beyond compassionate feelings,
which Las Casas valued as intrinsically human and, thusly, essential to
making morally sound aesthetic judgments.

Indigenous and Native systems of knowledge equally evaded Kant and
Las Casas. Kant was blunter in his disavowal and othering of nonteleolog-
ical, nonhuman, and deeply sensorial ways of knowing. Next, I introduce
elements from contemporary anthropological and intercultural studies of
the mind. By looking at the boundary between the human and nonhuman
as well as base and extra-ordinary consciousness, I reframe the account of
aesthetic perception reviewed thus far. Neither an anthropological nor a
teleological justification of aesthetic judgment dispels racializing legacies
about knowing and sensing. Hallucinations, within ALXFT, offer an otherworldly remedy against such legacies.

Colonial Conditions and Extra-ordinary Consciousness

As experiential and phenomenological, perception presents the world to our situated and embodied senses. Typically, sensual stimulus appears external to our perception. We often neglect the fact that our social and interpersonal histories are always already at play in our own perceptual field and situation. Unlike a Kantian approach, today's anthropology and neuroscience tell us that cultures create specific framings of the relation between the mind and its boundaries. Some non-Western cultures emphasize interconnectivity, while Westerners rely on clear-cut distinctions (Luhrman 2011; Barrett 2004).

Sensory overrides induce altered states of consciousness, involving the experience of sensation in the absence of a source to be sensed (Luhrmann 2011, 72; Chiu 1989, 292–293).[5] When your internet connection slows down over video calls, images get pixelated, and voices loop and crack. Sometimes, the connection speeds up, getting the parties caught up. In a synesthetic boost, we perceive internally what is not offered to the senses. Whether we trust them or not, cracks in our consciousness prompt cultural invitations to draw on both previous perceptual lessons and sensual repertoires. Did we hear that, or did we just make it up? Are we hallucinating? The answer lies with history, it seems, much more than with psychobiology alone.

Perceptual learning comprises cultural conditioning that greatly shapes whether we experience hallucinations. To an extent, both Las Casas and Kant can be understood as spokespeople of a milieu in which coloniality shapes perceptual learning. Sensual repertoires relate to the way that we are expected to experience hallucinations and to the role that culture plays in heightening one or more senses over others (MacLean 2001, contra Noll 1983). Apparently, hallucinating consciousness is more widespread than stigmatizing psychology has it. With this, I mean that cultural prompts may shift and alter consciousness much more often than we would like to admit. We don't need recreational or nonrecreational drugs to alter our states of mind.

Habits of the flesh build upon layers of perceptual encoding and decoding. Stuck in evolutionary time, such was the case of *travestis, jotería* migrants, but also Salustiana Párraga Arraya and Elena Humana; sideways selves ongoingly transact with Kantian, sanity-conducing, sensual repertoires. Heterosexualism and the nuclear family mobilize contexts, situations, and other laboratories of human-impressible perception. For example, streetwalkers, jotería migrants, and diasporic border-crossers participate in realities wherein the condition of debris, excrement, and exile entails forms of hallucinatory existence. As racialized exiles and immigrants, sideways selves acquire awareness that grows perplexingly more ambiguous, fractured, and yet, as this chapter shows, necessarily more accurate and reliable. What I am calling *genders* pervades the affective education of sideways selves, and yet, from within this carnal economy, they make a dwelling out of "genders." That is, in disparate and sometimes incongruent ways, they reject the project of human-centered rehabilitation. If we followed Las Casas's and Kant's aesthetic theories, "genders" would likely involve cognitive processes deeming jotería and travestis nonhumans due to a lack of sentient, morally sound judgment.

Colonizers suppress Indigenous practices, among them orality, animist spirituality, pictographic knowledge, and sustainable farming, because they see them as symptoms of degeneration, species stagnation, or lack of humanity. Those living under coloniality experience this extraordinary violence as ordinary (Fanon 2008; Maldonado-Torres 2008; Mbembe 2003; Quijano 1991). Paradoxically, colonial rule also determines what counts as ordinary, and it marks anti-colonial consciousness as nonhuman or evil-like and, in other words, as the very sign of savage nature.[6] Colonial imagination mounts an institutional architecture for the instruction of sanity and perceptual ability. It employs a range of institutionalization techniques, from witch-hunting, inquisitorial processes, and confessional tortures to eugenicist conversion treatments, carceral surveillance, and mental health clinics. This aesthetic allows dominant subjectivities to keep their grip on baseline and ordinary consciousness while it condemns racialized, gendered, and disabled selves to a hallucinating condition.

Material life that was fulfilling for pre-Columbian communities remained in their perceptual field even throughout the process of colonial suppression. For instance, Mexica scribes and painters, who understood continuities between worldly and nonworldly domains, heard, saw, read, and painted stars and divine wisdom (Gruzinski 1992; Dussel 1994; L. Pérez 2007). Talking objects, idols, or effigies are present in the colonial record of Cozumel and Chichén Itzá (Aguilera 2009, 166). Montesinos (1882) and Arnold (2006) explain the process of catechization of Andean textual practices, among them textiles and *kipus* (cord-based annotation). Colonial rule subjected these practices to great scrutiny and developed myriad strategies to remove them from the domain of spirit communication. Moreover, conterminously to this suppression of multisensory meaning-making, both Renaissance and Cartesian perspectivism made of sight the king of an impoverished sensual kingdom (Jay 1988).

As this chapter suggests with respect to practitioners of ALXFT, an ancestral, hallucinogenic, multisensorial domain of expressivity underwrites an ongoing opposition to normalizing habits of the flesh. This opposition, as it interrupts the deployment of the genre of the human, fosters the consciousness and embodiment of "genders." In their responsiveness to the geometry of black holes and sewage lines, sideways selves put in perspective sociosomatic entanglements. Indeed, they illustrate coming in and out of *gender* and ungendering. Under the colonial/modern gender system, sideways selves accumulate, store, dispense, release, and spend carnal impressions. Facing rehabilitation and disposability, sideways selves push the boundaries of sensorial and carnal repertoires.

In the context of colonial history and historiography, Ann Laura Stoler (2001) uses the term "tender ties" to describe the interaction between rule and intimacy. "Dense transfer points" (Foucault 1980, 103) between regimes of imperial truth and microsites of intimate governance partially convey what I have in mind when I think of sideways selves and their bodily responsiveness. In addition to this Foucauldian lens on self-governance, in the sense of the care of the self, I point to post-oppositional responsiveness, since it frames habits of the flesh that draw on discontinuous, yet ancestral, perception, consciousness, and cognition. As we have discussed in the previous chapter, an agential realist framework shares features with Indigenous and Afro-diasporic systems of knowledge and their sacred realities of inter- and intra-activity, of entanglements and configurations between worldly and otherworldly domains. If Bartolomé de Las Casas had not been bent on rescuing humanism from its unintended cruelties and perversions, he might have found Indians to be enactors of a different kind of revolution. He might have also confronted the narrow account of anthropological differences that he held. Instead of claiming that Indians could receive proper civilizing education, he might have reflected on the violence with which ecclesiasts and settlers swiftly demonized Natives' ancestral repositories of more-than-human perception. Pressed against this violent uprooting, practitioners of Afro-diasporic and Indigenous systems of knowledge fought to pursue hallucinating knowing. Indeed, they trespassed on the puzzling terrain of aesthetic derangement.

Deranged *Loquerías*

In "El Desorden," Laura Elisa Pérez fosters a perceptual disposition that hangs unhinged from a secularizing normative order (1999). Instead of avoiding what's deemed pathological by the condition of coloniality, she delves into ALXFT's disorderly ways of knowing. She examines noninstitutional spiritualities in Chicana artists' literary, visual, and performance arts from the 1960s onward. She demonstrates that their artmaking reappropriates emblematic religious images from the Mexican American community. Pérez contends that Chicana artists access altered consciousness by disrupting the heterosexist, male-centered, and monotheist legacy of colonialism, nationalism, and Manifest Destiny. They not only reject colonial imposition but also create multiple oppositions to its rule. They embrace what is extraordinary, such as nonconforming eroticism; what is nonsensical, such as virgin warriors; or also what is aesthetically dubious, such as what they call *domesticana rasquache*.[7] Reoccupying Aztlán, they respond to cultural invitations and hallucinate.[8] Becoming hallucinating subjects, they develop technologies of knowing, not despite anxiety, fear, and confusion but rather because of them. Apparently, they thrive in *el desorden*, or what Kantian rationality deems cognitive impairment. I shall extend Pérez's argument to examine bodily responsiveness among sideways selves who thrive in derangement.

Anti-colonial feminist genealogies recognize ALXFT's emphasis on cognitive plasticity. They recognize that colonial plasticity works as a method to assess, work on, and transform an imposed condition of insanity. Mapping feminist methodologies of emancipation in the twentieth century, Chela Sandoval (2000) indicates that Fredric Jameson's manifesto against postmodernity fails to tell the truth of lesbians of color. She shows that in the 1960s and 1970s, lesbians of color activate a "differential consciousness" kindred but also homeopathically resistant to dominant modes of postmodern circulation. Gloria Anzaldúa summons this rebellious disposition with the term *loquería*, or "the crazies," also locating this psychological labor among lesbians of color who "choose" the path of queerness (1999, 41).

Anzaldúa's theory of *conocimiento* offers a path of spiritual liminality (Delgadillo 2011), inspiring (r)evolutionary selves who learn to wear someone else's skin. She refers to heightened awareness of interconnectivity with the practice of wearing someone else's skin. She has in mind ecologies of interconnectedness among everything there is. Sandoval explains that globalizing capitalism builds circuitries of extraction and compliance, which themselves operate as interconnecting webs. By "differential," Sandoval refers to oppositional combinations that shift interconnectedness toward emancipatory relations and subjectivities. Anzaldúa includes *atravesados* among selves that learn to wear somebody else's skin. I submit that hallucinogenic competence prompts memories, gestures, insinuations, insights, and other cognitive acts with which atravesados learn to wear another's skin. This practice of knowing, learning, and deciphering is intrinsic to the positionality of "the perverse, [. . .] and those who cross over [. . .] the confines of the normal" (Anzaldúa 1999, 25). Wearing another's skin challenges boundaries between subject and environment, but it does so by shifting interconnectivity, as Sandoval suggests, from an equalizing to a differential mode.

Navigating out-of-bound, disorienting realities is a constant within ALXFT. *Borderlands / La Frontera* equates leaping into the dark to the clash of cultures that "makes us *crazy* constantly" (Anzaldúa 1999, 80–81; emphasis is mine). María Lugones reflects on women of color in the United States who dwell in ontological confusion. They inhabit a state that feels like "schizophrenia" and, thus, acquire epistemic flexibility as both outsiders and travelers across multiple worlds (2003b, 86; Ortega 2001, 2016). In several of Cherríe Moraga's plays, the theme of insanity figures in the daily struggles that Xicanas wage to reconcile a colonial past with ancestral decolonizing memories. Ana-Maurine Lara (2006), Josefina Baez (2012, 2017), and Rita Indiana (2019) offer Afro-Dominican narratives of diaspora and displacement, centering characters and their life stories as they negotiate archives of ritual possession, multilingual disorientation, and time-traveling.

Kantian anxiety delineates prevailing subjectivities. Under the pretext of heteropatriarchal and ableist dominance, colonialism's legacy compels marginalized Afro-Latinx and Latinx communities to navigate the risk of what Kant termed "artificial insanity" (1964, 17).[9] This process develops cognitive mechanisms to both accommodate and challenge the state of derangement. ALXFT counter this anxiety with an affirmative turn toward multisensorial responsiveness, an enigmatic and deeper understanding of cognition, and a more communal feeling of trust over the shared experience of derangement. From within the social physics of absence and trace, practitioners of hallucinatory knowing face the threat of sensual atrophy. They adapt to this condition by embodying epistemic duplicity, inhabiting deranged loquerías as both true to experience and confusing and (un)reliable.

Cognitive duplicity permeates hallucinating knowing among practitioners of ALXFT. It stands at the crossroads of psychic bewilderment, between excitement and torture. Earlier I discussed an instance of cognitive duplicity when I glossed my friend Ana Paula's decision about transitioning. She doubles sensorial responsiveness. Coloniality disallows, expunges, disintegrates Ana Paula's erotic and bodily range. Desirability, itself a sensorial response, absorbs colorism and racism. They torture Ana Paula pretransition. A white supremacist education of desire recruits affluence, job security, and neoliberal consumption to repurpose narratives of national and global belonging across Argentina's gay and lesbian communities. Homo- and transnormativity marginalizes Ana Paula's transitioning, leaving her literally hanging between racial stagnation and gender assimilation. In response to these colonial legacies, Ana Paula finds ways of trusting this bewildering erotic of colorism and racism. She learns to step into an embodiment that at once affirms and abhors travesti skins.

Similarly, Gloria Anzaldúa reminds us that body/mind dualism, and the fear of our own bodies, operates as an injunction against Indigenous, Afro-Indigenous, and mestiza populations and their perceptual capabilities (1999, 59).[10] Ana Paula's self-perception as racialized shares with atravesados an abyssal condition. Across generations and hemispheric distinctions, they have acquired sensorial memories. Moreover, they continually recalibrate and fine-tune their sensory responsiveness, persistently diverting the conventions of the genre and *genders* of the human. Hallucinating knowing encodes differential and post-oppositional responsiveness, pointing to "otherworldly events [and] [. . .] those fleeting images of the soul's presence and of the spirit's presence" (58). I shall now turn to narratives emerging under the sign of ALXFT, and their extraordinary and otherworldly register of "genders" consciousness.

Hallucinating "genders"

I would like to pay attention to migrant desires in Cherríe Moraga's theatre plays. At the same time, I would like to make theoretical room attending to the rift between desires and bodily responses. Often, Gender and *genders* chart desires in distorting ways, appointing the genre of the human before any index of bodily responsiveness. In Moraga's plays, I aim to explore how they articulate Xicana, jotería, and "genders" in terms of subjectivity and embodiment. Her plays reveal, I suggest, links among multisensory consciousness, hallucinating knowing, and "genders" sociality.

From the essay "A Long Line of Vendidas" (1983) to her last play, "The Mathematics of Love" (2015), Moraga envisions sexual dissidence through the deconstruction of the La Malinxe myth. Concerning

Malintzin Tenepal's history, this myth accounts for her primordial role in mothering a new mestiza/o race after having had carnal relations with conquistador Hernán Cortés (Pérez 1999, 102). Both as bilingual translator and mistress, Malinxe presents a bodily project whose sociality lies across excision, denial, death, and desire. As Indian, her bodily responsiveness fades out, goes extinct, disappears into the depth of the black hole (Alarcón 1989; Rueda Esquibel 2003). Yet, she attains futurity as the mother of a new mestizo race, the Chicana/o race of the twentieth and twenty-first centuries. Heterosexualism encodes the naturalization of complicity between invading conquerors, whose racial classifications will rule for centuries to come, and mestizo *men*, whose racial subordination secures the internalization of the human/nonhuman divide. Racialization and *gendering* implicate each other, fused in the production of modified versions of non*women*.[11]

Malinche's myth persists today in the sanitization that *genders* entails, through self-abnegation, purity of mind and body, and sorrowful penitence (Lozano-Díaz 2021, 210).[12] She becomes Guadalupe, the Virgin Mother, as part of a lasting process of colonial imposition. The dark Indian "woman" is the object of colonial desire, but her flesh is betrayed by both colonizers and offspring.[13] Her embodiment is produced through a sixteenth-century surrogacy system. A settler project that seeks to extinguish Indian kin and ancestry surrogates her womb. The child must forget Malinche and, thus, be raised and fostered by another economy of flesh, of gendered kin.[14] It is within this colonizing dynamic that Malinche emerges as "lesbian" (as in "genders") in Moraga's plays. I submit that she stands for a traitor whose original sin works through the atrocities of the genres of the human, whose mouth and lips bespeak a new language of disfigurations.

The Hungry Woman is one of Moraga's plays. It was published in 1995. Its plot and characters draw on existing mythologies: Malinche, Coatlicue, Medea, and La Llorona. Coatlicue is an Aztec goddess, predating the arrival of Spaniards. Medea is the central figure in Euripides's ancient tragedy. La Llorona is a Mexican folktale about a weeping woman. Yarbro-Bejarano examines *The Hungry Woman* and contends that it deconstructs the Chicana lesbian body. By reclaiming Malinxe, she argues, Moraga doesn't seek to heal, repair, or make lesbian existence whole (2001, 5). Rather, by "recognizing how it has been appropriated" and by having it hinge on its various parts—*labios* (lips), hands, face, legs, eyes, and so on—Moraga represents Xicanas' nonconforming bodies in their contingent reconstruction or "potential fatal perils" (5).

Yarbro-Bejarano's close reading shows how *genders* obscure noncon-forming bodily responsiveness. The language of *gendering* makes non-conforming embodiments banish into the abyss of the colonial/modern gender system. In what Yarbro-Bejarano calls deconstruction of the Chi-cana lesbian body, I recognize Moraga hinting at a deeper incoherence. That is, she confronts an oxymoronic condition defining the existence of Xicana lesbians.[15] In my view, an oxymoron stands for synchronicity between absence and trace. It is not surprising, then, that Moraga popu-lates her plays with dystopic, sometimes otherworldly, and yet intimately real "genders" characters. They embody contradictions that at once con-form to colonizing patriarchy and are cast as unimaginable and perverse agents of desire (Brady 2002; Moraga 2011).

Not unlike hallucinating subjects who mistrust their own senses, the leading characters in Moraga's plays painstakingly excavate self-delusion. Medea breaks away from male-centered Chicano history because it con-flates postapocalyptic Aztlán with heterosexist kinship. In a near future where today's ethnic minorities in the United States split from white "Amerika" (Gringolandia) (Moraga [1995] 2001, 1), they each claim their own, separate territories. Medea, who is a midwife, and her lover, Luna, live as exiles in what remains of Phoenix. As lovers, they raise Medea's son, Chac-Mool. Medea's mother, the *curandera* (healer) Mama Sal, also assists with caring for the boy.

Set on a consciousness continuum including a facility described both as "insane asylum" (98) and "psychiatric hospital" (8), *The Hungry Woman* recasts a primordial scene where a male offspring, Chac-Mool, abandons his mother, Medea. Leaving Phoenix is not afforded to anyone, but given the chance, Chac-Mool decides to rejoin his father, Jasón, in Aztlán. In Chicano consciousness, Aztlán is a territory upon which political expres-sion asserts sovereignty claims. Phoenix instead functions as a dumping site where outcasts and queers reside, where pollution and endemic pov-erty make its population feel lousy all the time.

We previously examined restricting spatial configurations among minoritized populations in Argentina. Colonial legacies configure differ-ences as spaces of *different sameness*. In *The Hungry Woman*'s geography, racial Others have secured a land for what they imagine and construct as their own different sameness. They have also thrown out their jotería (19). In the first act, Mama Sal has a conversation with Savannah, who is Luna's girlfriend in the present. This is the present in which Medea, after an unnameable occurrence, has been committed to a mental health facility. Mama Sal tells Savannah that others may call this dumpster of a space "Phoenix." By others, she means those who maintain male-centered rule, the genre of the human, as intrinsic to the definition of sovereign land for Chicanidad. In muffled thinking, she invites audiences to meditate on the way that exile bears on excluded selves and their search of uncharted spaces of communal support. I associate this subjectivity, as Mama Sal does, with liminal, sideways perception. Mama Sal puts it best when she conveys that Phoenix's dwellers call this locale "Tamoanchan," after the Nahuatl word for "we seek our home" (19). The act of seeking for a dwelling responds to the ways that dispossession reifies the link between self, land, and community.

Because of their abject relationship, Medea and Luna got to live their love only in Phoenix. Given Mama Sal's statement, it would be more accurate if we said that Medea and Luna learned to attend to their love by *seeking home*. Given that jotería lacks a place within Aztlán, they "became peregrinos como nomads" (19). Expulsion of jotería is compounded with another form of internal exile that relocates Xicanas from the political to the domestic sphere. Inherent in this displacement are the habits of perception through which *genders* enactments shave off unwanted pollutants. Savannah recalls this violent patriarchal ideology, which subjects *Chicana women* to putting down their "guns" and picking up their "babies" (18). This mandate ties *genders* to Gender and pulls *genders* away from jotería.

Tamoanchan resonates with current dwellers of Phoenix through cacophony. Phoenix is literally a deposit of excrement, making its residents feel lousy. Senses get at once tired and overblown. Perception becomes restricting, fragmenting, and splinters what feels like multiplicity. Multisensory perceiving operates between languishing receptors and compensating pathways. Mama Sal's insights reveal that embodiments who thrive in multiplicity exist neither in Aztlán nor Phoenix but rather in a rupture state. Tamoanchan reminds us of travesti and jotería, their twilight adaptability and search of nostredad.

It must be noted that geographies of base and ordinary consciousness have shrunk in the play's Amerika. Derangement habituates Medea and Luna to an altered sense of memory—so much so that Luna, at the onset of the play, reminisces over *the loving years* that she once shared with Medea. In the meantime, Medea asks a nurse about a woman she can't really remember. She doesn't, because derangement pushes perception to the point of amnesia. Derangement integrates, as a matter of survival, jotería's fading out. Luna embodies jotería possibilities, but their sustainability is wrought with anxiety and fright. The nurse reminds Medea that Luna is that girlfriend who visits and brings her flowers, the one who wears "the man's suit jacket" (4). In reference to Luna's ostensible butch style, the nurse readjusts perception in a haptic-like manner. She assists the audience by anchoring bodily markers, such as *girlfriend* or *man*, with the texture and feel of a suit jacket or flowers, to the coloniality of gender. The nurse punctuates the dialogue as she instructs a disoriented Medea to trust what lies behind the velvety skin of petals: "She's the face behind the flowers. You can't miss her" (4).

Decolonizing devices arise in the shape of hallucinations. Fleeing subjects hallucinate as they seek to make up what fear of derangement pushes them to miss, such as what the nurse indicates lies right there behind the flowers. Hallucinations operate as portals into enhanced stages of brooding and gestation. Subjectivities in flight make their dwellings in regions of historical and cultural disarray, where the line between voluntary and involuntary states of derangement blurs. In such conditions, they adapt by learning to wear each other's skins, by becoming nostredad.

The Nahua expression *in Xochitl in cuicatl* points to a poetic way of knowing, linking ritual chanting with the intergenerational transfer of truth and wisdom (Carrasco 2011, 98; Damrosch 1991). Originally associated with "xochitl" or the glyph for flowers in ancient Nahuatl, this way of knowing pairs the sensorial experience of delicate fragrance and beauty with the central role that chanting—*cuicatl*—has within this oral culture (Leander 1991, 3–6). For some scholars of the colonial encounter, *flor y canto* entailed a specialized profession akin to contemporary philosophers', which the Toltec tradition identified as the *tlamatinime* (sage). By contrast, other theorists, such as Laura Elisa Pérez, consider that philosophy was not reserved to those who received formal education in the pursuit of an abstract form of knowledge. Rather, as a scholar of visual arts, she contends that "pre-Columbian Mesoamerican notions of art and art making [are] represented in [. . .] the Mexica figures of [both] the tlacuilo (glyph-maker) and the tlamatini (sage, decoder of the glyphs)" (2007, 22).

Pérez's approach casts new light on the hallucinating exchange between nurse and mental health patient, between medical knowledge and unreliable loquerías. Moreover, she develops the notion of "spirit tongues" to reveal the connection between knowing and form, which, akin to "flower and song," contemporary Chicana artists embody (22). They foster a sensibility, or personal stance, tapping into the dual nature of reality as both worldly, mundane, and otherworldly. In what follows next, we further examine the linking of knowing and form in the philosophical reflections that Moraga's plays ignite.

Against the Hardening of Blood Quantum

In her analysis of another Moraga play, "Heroes and Saints" (1996), Mary Pat Brady pays attention to the thematic thread of agribusiness, environmental contamination, and chronic health conditions within communities of color (2002). The play centers on Cerezita, whose body reveals the disabling effects of pesticides among farm-working families of McLaughlin, California. Brady makes explicit the correlation between space and sociality in her account of Moraga's treatment of land and racialized embodiment. Much like the situation in Phoenix, where border towns and maquiladoras are tainted by toxic elements, in "Heroes and Saints," pesticides play a role in altering farmers' DNA. In fact, they take residence in the very bodily vehicle of capital's pursuit. Racialization rationalizes the extraction of underpaid labor at the same time that it facilitates capital's access to ghettoized pools of carnal resources. Moraga, Brady argues, seeks to resacralize land, and most important, its relation to embodiment as an energetic expenditure. Moraga finds radical creativity in bodily responsiveness. Resacralizing land draws upon hallucinations wherein mothers, co-parents, lovers, children, and grandparents breathe new life into kinship. Medea's act of ultimate betrayal, filicide, surges against and beyond patriarchal claims to space and place (Brady 2002, 167). Indeed, Phoenix's inhabitants occupy, if only temporarily, the geography of fugitive desires and exiled bodies. Their sideways selfhood seeks an uncharted *we*ness, or *nostredad*, a jotería sociality of kinship rendered anew.[16]

Brady also notes that Moraga delivers an anti-aesthetic methodology. Anti-aesthetics works as a maneuver or antidote against representational approaches. She argues that anti-aesthetics highlights suffering and horror to expose realities unleashed by colonial violence. Instead of claiming authenticity, or essentialist accounts of land and people, Brady finds that Moraga undertakes a rigorous and realist exploration of "how the production of the social entails the production of the spatial in a processual relationship" (2002, 167). As farmworkers revolt against agribusiness in *Heroes and Saints*, Moraga underscores that the process of birthing the next generation has already been brought to a halt. The play invokes memory, and the contradictions of social history, by hanging a child figure from a cross. Cancer-stricken or toxin-ridden bodies, especially infants', provide irrefutable evidence of coloniality's twinned objectification of peoples and land.

Sandra Soto presents a thought-provoking analysis of Moraga's racial theories, which appears to diverge from the central aspects of Brady's interpretation of Moraga's rhetorical maneuvers.[17] In *Reading Chican@ as Queer* (2010), Soto explains Moraga's ambivalence toward her mixed-race heritage. She sees Moraga pursuing a double narrative of outsiderness and homecoming (2010, 20) and "an unusual objectification of race" (27). In Soto's perspective, the crux of the matter lies in the intersection of Moraga's perception of race as a commodity, something that can be acquired, owed, conferred, or withheld, and the prevailing societal architecture of juridical power.[18] Soto's materialism makes room for a critique of racial ambivalence, which the critic finds in Moraga's style of showcasing that Chicana identity is at once slippery and attainable. Brady instead emphasizes the production of space as social, which provides an alternative analytic of power. I join Brady in positing that, by attending to the spatiality of pesticides and poisonous maquiladoras, Moraga queries racialization and its shaping of bodily responsiveness and altered perception. The flapping image of the child hanging from the cross summons the pollution that incubates imminent demise. Race is, indeed, a rarefied object, a social one. It is ubiquitous and acquires chameleonic features. Moraga, however, seems to journey through its rarefying process, including the ways that her agency both fails to match all the pathos of race and, consequently, yearns to become its embodiment.

Soto's criticism of Moraga's body of work concerns racial essentialism (29). Building hierarchies of authenticity is much more manageable, Soto states, when race is understood as essence. Brady instead points to the fact that Moraga undertakes the theorizing of relationality. As Mama Sal, who sees "tamoanchan" as a spatial response to colonial legacies, I see Moraga loosening up the strictures of racial identity, which doesn't preclude its examination.[19] McLaughlin in *Heroes and Saints*, as well as Phoenix in *The Hungry Woman*, illustrate space in its stretching out. Social production entangles grape growers and *maquila* workers, grapes and electronics, and the next generation that is not meant to be—as either effigies or subjects of filicide. This processual relationality implicates all of us, including myself as I type these lines and you as you read them. It is not far-fetched to think that maquiladora workers assemble the microchips at the heart of either this laptop or the digital press. Indeed, we become coproducers of death and unviability through intertwined scales of racializing capitalism.

Moraga's narrative incites an altered state of consciousness among us as we each come to grapple with the twilight sense of belonging in and disidentifying with capital's politics of death. The hardening of Brownness, which Soto sees in Moraga's failed effort at self-racialization, unfolds as one among several other slices of lived experience and geographical displacement. You and I may not claim residency in either McLaughin or Phoenix, at least not in the way in which racialization implicates farm-workers and maquila workers. But we are summoned, physically and sym-bolically, to occupy positions of consent, contradiction, and opposition within the spatiality of racializing capitalism and its energizing of patri-archy and environmental devastation. Self-racialization, in the sense that Medea gives to her positioning as Indian mother, reveals the rarefying of race that Soto warns us against. Moraga's overture doesn't fully partake in this process. An anti-aesthetics of Brownness puts distance between self-racializing subjects and patterns of colonial violence with which they must contend. Moraga chooses to make tangible what, to some, may appear as grotesque or "failed efforts" at authenticity.

The Hungry Woman troubles modernist and arrowlike timelines. It shuttles across temporal portals, including ancient Aztec deities and other mythical figures, such as Coatlicue, Coyolxauhqui, and Huitzilopochtli. A Yaqui Indigenous bloodline runs through Medea's family (Moraga [1995] 2001, 85), countering the notion that a Chicano/a future or pres-ent requires the extinction of Native realities and cultures. A chorus of four women warriors, known as Cihuatateo, performs Aztec rituals.[20] Chac-Mool finds himself torn between allegiance to his paternal lineage as he faces the decision of relocating to Chicano Aztlán with his father or remaining in Phoenix with Medea and Luna. Heterosexualism rules land-ownership in the *father*land, a mandate that reinforces strict bloodline adherence while dismantling nonconjugal kinship arrangements. Bear in mind that Medea, almost shrieking in despair, will later throw a jab at Chac-Mool by yelling, "I'm the Indian, not him [Jasón]!" (85).

Chac-Mool earns his mother's disapproval because he is learning the sensibilities of *gendering*. He is ready to both abandon Medea into exile and reclaim his rights to land. Jasón will instruct his son on the erotics of heterosexualist bloodlines. Because Medea lives in an altered state triggered by pollution and lousiness, she sees Chac-Mool as her claim to sovereignty. Her claim doesn't issue from any greediness over land but from concern over the future of kinship. Medea grows impatient, since she can't model for Chac-Mool how to rise with and from atrocities of flesh. She tries and yet fails to provide an effective alternative to the hard-ening of blood quantum that ethnic nationalism entails (Arvin, Tuck, and Morrill 2013; Lawrence 2003).[21]

At what is probably the height of the dramatic tension in the play, we encounter Mama Sal foretelling imminent death for the next generation.

She talks to Chac-Mool, who has just arrived after a short visit with his father. She tells him how she would like to be cremated and have her ashes spread in the not-so-distant Aztlán. She smokes a pipe while allowing Chac-Mool the space to tell her whether he will stay or go back to Aztlán for good. The next dialogue finds Mama Sal and Medea. Without truly putting it into words, their dialogue infers that Medea has made up her mind and plans to poison Chac-Mool. *Heroes and Saints* also examines poisoning as a colonial imposition that alters Indigenous being at its core. In the case of California's agribusiness, brimming with chemical toxicity, capital poisons and modifies the very genetic makeup where life initiates. Both plays compel us to contemplate the complex relationships that mixed-race minorities maintain with their Native and Indigenous heritage, both historically and in contemporary times. In one instance, Mama Sal's handling of Medea's unspoken revelation employs theatrical hallucination to draw an audience into its grasp. Similarly, Cerezita's ailing health in *Heroes and Saints* serves as another poignant tool of twilight engagement. Indeed, ALXFT render hallucinations into a competence for crip survival and reaffirmation.

While Phoenix holds Aztlán accountable for erasing its jotería, the concept of hallucinating knowing extends this critique to minoritized but heterosexist subjectivities in a broader sense, implicating them for aligning with the reinforcement of blood quantum, reliance on base consciousness as a measure of communal membership, and conflation of cognitive ableism and sovereignty claims. Halluci*nation* unfolds as a device of duplicitous effects. On one end, Chicano subjectivity hallucinates a geography of spiritual, cognitive, and political autonomy. On the other, within this hallucinating geography, the Chicano nation entails the erasure of "Medea/Malinche" and her autonomy. Through this device, the nation comes to be produced, socially and materially, by the tense relationality of contradictions between *gendering* and ungendering. Ordinary consciousness is a stage of awareness inducing a son's proper return to his fatherland. Derangement entails approaching the very hallucinations through which jotería sheds *genders*. Kinship becomes an invitation to hallucinate nostredad.

"genders" and the Betrayal of Racism

It should be clear by now that "genders" signal multiple realities within Aztlán. These conflicting realities contend with the disparagement of female powers among ancient Aztecs, but also the retelling of Mexica and Xicanx histories. Emma Pérez calls this kind of disparagement an "all-encompassing patriarchal 'order of things' " (1999, 122). Chac-Mool's failure to reject the males-first mandate speaks of the heterosexist ordeals, past and present, that prompt Xicanas to hallucinate queer, perhaps even ungendering, bodily projects in Aztlán. Despite feeling tormented, Medea poisons her own son to prevent ethnonationalist patriarchal rule from exhausting his existence. Perhaps, through this betrayal of motherly duty and love, Medea places the Chicana lesbian body between quotation marks, within that tender yet confusing state of "genders."

I consider Medea's despair as a bodily response, simultaneously experiential and epistemic. It synchs hallucinating knowing to the perceptual reality of "genders." Consider the scene where Chac-Mool informs Medea of his reasons for moving back with Jasón. In Phoenix, he feels identity-less, lamenting, "There's nobody to be." Medea reminds him of *jotos*, a support system of adoptive *tíos* (uncles) to whom she introduced him. This system redefines relationships beyond heterosexual bloodlines. However, Chac-Mool remains adamant that this is not his point. His struggle in Phoenix doesn't concern a lack of community but rather the absence of a "father" or a "country." He implies that he understands Medea's plight, since he states that he "can't help that they took away Aztlán from" her. His treading in and out of lucidity is unnerving. He doesn't want to leave Medea, he claims. Yet, he can't figure out how to exist across the multiple realities that sustain Phoenix's inhabitants.

He can't appreciate what he leaves behind. He absolves himself by rhetorically asking, "But what did I do?" This hesitation embodies the ignorance María Lugones terms indifference, which men of color manifest, she argues, toward violence facing women of color (2007). Medea's desperation intensifies during her final moments with Chac-Mool. A bodily response among "genders" may lie precisely with the state of unrest that Medea derives from multiple realities. Responsiveness configures flesh as a competence to see ourselves wearing someone else's skin(s), sometimes lovingly, sometimes in frustration. This act of both sacrifice and defiance throws Medea into a heightened state at the mental hospital.

If you [Chac-Mool] live, then why am I here? I've committed no crime. If you live, why then am I strapped into the bed at night? [. . .] Why are there locks and I haven't the key? Why? (Moraga [1995] 2001, 98)

This monologue enacts several of the features of hallucinations within ALXFT. For Medea, the betrayal by her own offspring represents an unbearable reality, one with which she couldn't continue living. Repeated experiences of abandonment, exile, and dispossession only magnify the traumatic disintegration of her identity as the *dark* Indian mother. Medea's decision posits that the true crime within the Xicanx community is the complicity of the nation's values with heterosexuality and colonial rule, with *genders*. Caressing, understanding stares, muffled hurt feelings, swallowed tears, compassionate dispositions toward a son who has not yet quite grown up, they all may coexist in Medea's responsiveness as dutiful mother. Through this responsiveness, which orients desire and conviviality away from heterosexualism, Medea remains outside *genders*. Thus, she lives in exile. At once, Medea lives in Phoenix and participates in the atrocities of "genders" as a surrogate for Aztlán's bloodline. Her path toward filicide disavows the sensorial repertoires that weaken hallucinating knowing. She approaches the abyss of heterosexualism, of the tender ties through which the human gets lodged into the incomplete geography of Aztlán. She transitions, spinning a new skin out of the interstitial space in-between *genders* and "genders."

Narratives of Mexica origins also remind us of a new dialectics regarding societal foundations. For instance, Gloria Anzaldúa argues that militarization among Aztecs brought about the first intensification of patriarchal rule and the disparagement of feminine roles.[22] Under the watch of her own mother, Huitzilopochtli mutilated his sister Coyolxauhqui (Anzaldúa 1999). Governing Xicanx relations between and among *women*, Huitzilopochtli persists as a background shadow. Chac-Mool may play a similar role in Moraga's Medea. This kinship economy makes *men* get loved, fed, cared for, and heard first.[23] Therefore, between Aztlán and Phoenix, characters in *The Hungry Woman* dwell in and out of *genders* and "genders." Kindred to the dynamic between absence and trace, hallucinating dispositions arise with the wounding of social erotics. The gravitational pull of *gender* speaks from the past, but in a ventriloquist fashion. Huitzilopotchli and Coyolxauhqui, the coloniality of gender framework suggests, do not belong in the sociogenesis of the human, or nuclear, family. Moraga, however, employs the conflict between brother and sister to query painful attachments. She sees this trauma represented by the relation between land and bloodline and its shaping of Chicano *familias*.[24]

Within the material world of bodily responsiveness, what does siblinghood entail between Huitzilopochtli and Coyolxauhqui? Does it perpetuate a kinship system that relies on the sensible education of *husbands* and *wives?* It does not. Ventriloquist voices enable Moraga to displace the critique of the relation between Medea and Chac-Mool onto a broader commentary on gender, lesbian desire, and the politics of death. What remains unsaid, banished from view, is the redeeming potential that "queer" kinship, neither human nor nonhuman, could foster. If only Chac-Mool unlearned *gendered* responsiveness by practicing a novel bodily economy. Perhaps Moraga entrusts tíos with providing a new model of subjectivity for Chac-Mool, because jotería experiences kinship, out of sheer necessity, as a political project against the hardening of blood quantum. If Chac-Mool had learned jotería ways, they would have assisted him in adumbrating sideways selves out of "genders."

Malinxe-Medea occupies a dilemmatic position as racial traitor—if she conforms, she is sold; if she speaks, she sells out. Her position links two temporospatial domains where cultural invitations and injunctions to hallucinate arise for Xicanas. Medea doesn't have the keys to unlock the coloniality-of-gender cage. Refusing identification with conforming and ordinary consciousness is not a matter of choice. Rather, it is a product of colonial differences. Living in opposition to coloniality is like dwelling in an altered state of consciousness. Selves in relation weave decolonial ethics as they untangle kinship from settler morality. Indeed, hallucinating knowing asks that we learn to wear somebody else's skin, that we at once dwell in and wear conflicting skins. If only Medea and Chac-Mool could reestablish between them the social erotics of a differential mode of perception. If they could only detach from the beguiling binds of familial love. In this liminal space, intensified by hallucinations, both humans and nonhumans grapple to reimagine an otherwise genesis of love. Through these hallucinations, they forge new gestures, intensities, and attitudes, allowing mother and son, as well as the distinctions between Indian and mixed-race identities, to reconnect. They evoke a sacred economy of flesh.

Hallucinations in Moraga's play grow unworn skins for selves such as Medea and Chac-Mool, selves who meet each other anew at the abyss of the nonhuman. They may stare into the Aztec obsidian as if looking into black holes, facing each other through the erotic of alluring excrement and debris. In fact, Medea has had the taste of that secret—excrement—between her lips. She has loved Luna. Trash, pollutant, toxic, excrement; Phoenix lives and loves there. If only Chac-Mool could learn the habits of the flesh between Medea and Luna; if only Medea and Chac-Mool could spin an otherwise habit of the flesh, one that incites an ungendering erotic of love.

Curanderas, Brujas, and "Horses" Activate a Feminist Third Eye

Practitioners of loquería draw attention to (extra)ordinary conscious-ness among Afro-Latinx, Latinx, and Xicanx histories. Non-Western cosmological principles—Afro-diasporic, Nahua, Taino, Yaqui, Maya K'iche'—underwrite the perceptual field of hallucinating subjects (Anz-aldúa 1999; Castillo [1993] 2005; Moraga [1995] 2001; A.-M. Lara 2006; Pérez 2007; Humphrey 2019). Malinxes, curanderas, *tlacuilo* and tlam-atinime artists, midwives, *brujas*, "horses," and *hounsis* employ ancestral multisensory repertoires.[25] These repertoires contribute to feminist spiritual praxis by (1) challenging Eurocentered ethnographic accounts of shamanistic perception, (2) foregrounding shamanic "flight" and its enhancement of cross-modal perception, and (3) fostering bruja, curand-era, and *horse* positionalities.

Colonial chronicles and contemporary sources convey that Indigenous and mestiza women typically occupy the role of healers.[26] Practitioners of same-sex eroticism also have ritual and healing roles in pre-Columbian and colonial records (Horswell 2005; Sigal 2003). Medicinal practices imbued in ancestral Indigenous knowledge emerge from ecologies of inter- and intra-connectivity among all that lives (Jones et al. 2001). Ethnicity and racialization are both entrenched in the resilience of Afro-Latinx, Latinx, and Xicanx healing practices against the "frightening of spirit from one's body-mind" (Pérez 2007, 27; see also Marcos 2006, 2; Gonzales 2012, 159–162). Gloria Anzaldúa considers *nepantleras* media-tors who "facilitate passages between worlds" (2009, 248). Moraga, Ana Castillo, and even Anzaldúa have been likened to curanderas who "pull out the subversive "forgotten" memories of another worldview, the sup-pressed countervalues of women and Native peoples" (G. Pérez 2002, 59). The recurrence of spiritual praxis within ALXFT speaks to the affinity between curanderismo-brujería-Vodoun and hallucinating knowing.

Curanderismo shares both shamanistic and healing dimensions (Mor-row 1997, 68; Noll 1983, 444). Practitioners of ALXFT devise feminist remedies to survive colonial legacies and attend a holistic well-being of selfhood (Hartley 2010, 54). Patrisia Gonzales is a community health promoter-researcher who holds empirical knowledge about healing from the vantage point of belonging to Native and Indigenous commu-nities (Kickapoo, Comanche, and Macehual). Countering ethnographic accounts, she doesn't differentiate between shamans and elders, since such description downplays the feminist healing praxis of everyday curanderas and elders (2012, 12 and 217). I bring together shamans, curanderas, and healers, because I recognize that the performative aspect of their practices is linked to the negotiation of the pendular worldly and otherworldly continuum. As selves traverse this continuum, they transmogrify one material state into another. This negotiation also suggests that, within these highly syncretic contexts, practitioners reach altered states. They take on the responsibility of establishing and expanding a sensorial repertoire. In this manner, they perform healing ceremonies, tending to mind, body, and soul. These healing dimensions of altered states open portals into an embodied experience of spirit and sacred communication.

Practitioners of Afro-diasporic religiosity emphasize the importance of flesh, embodiment, and their connections across time and space. They refer to the everyday as sacred, since divination, magic rituals, and healing inform processes where the "transmission and articulation of sociocultural, aesthetic and religious values [. . .] [take] place not just through discourse but mainly from *one body to another*" (Romberg 2012, 211). In the practice of Dominican Vodoun, which we shall touch upon shortly, possession refers to the process by which a person's body serves as channel or mortal vessel for one of the *loa*, or divine or spirit manifestations.[27] Mounting is an act through which a loa inhabits the body of a priest or priestess. As performative, mounting exploits in the present time the liminal terrain between mundane and sacred worlds. By liminal, in this context, I mean the proximity that ceremonies intensify between the most mundane, such as the abundance of food, dance, and singing, and the needs of deities, such as thirst, hunger, or lust.

Curanderas, brujas, and horses resort to visionary states. They employ them as perceptual conduits for their communication with an otherworldly elsewhere (Marcos 2006). Indeed, impressible responsiveness is a technology of spirit-knowing within ALXFT. Rhythmic repetitions, burning copal resin, praying, among other practices, extend sensual invitations into a flight where ritual specialists perform as messengers or horses, and attendants as witnesses (Gonzales 2012; Marcos 2006; Lara 2005). During travel, curanderas and brujas translate visions into treatments, smells into remedies, sounds into colors, and words into touch. In the register of sensual cross-referencing, flying becomes visual, auricular, tactile, olfactory, and even orgasmic. Curanderas and brujas associate shamanic flight with translation of sensual modalities (MacLean 2001). Within Vodou traditions, it is the horse that is metaphorically "ridden" by the loa. Through a deep, sensual connection, the loa manifests, imparting teachings. The attendants are primary witnesses to this ceremonial possession, as the horse frequently has no recollection of the trance-induced experience.

In *The Hungry Woman*, the Cihuatateo chorus punctuates birthing of new beings. The chorus delivers rhythmic chants, leading characters and audience into a heightened state of consciousness. Sounds usher in uncharted selves. They activate transient, shamanic subjectivities. They announce healing techniques against racializing heterosexualism. When Luna visits Medea in the psychiatric ward, they acknowledge that they share dreams, each entering a common erotic encounter materialized through the explosion of a *maguey* (sentry plant) within a vagina (Moraga [1995] 2001, 94). From this twilight domain, they retrieve teachings about eroticism among lesbians of color. Carnal intimacy opens the door for a pedagogy of shamanistic healing when Medea adds, "Is that how I died, Luna? Giving birth to myself?"

Moraga's play leads into more than a decolonial stance. Giving birth to self consists of shedding gendered skins, harking back to stagnant and atrocious flesh. To abolish mother/son demands a (post)posthumanist turn. According to Las Casas, Indians die because Spaniards cannot see themselves in the suffering of Abya Yala. For Kant, alterity must be, out of necessity, subjected to a normative aesthetic process. He seeks similarity not among kinds but among the cognitive procedures of each subject. Giving birth to herself, Medea shows, reaches into (post)posthumanist sociogenic labor. It is about working with and on the organic origins of selfhood. That is, on an enigmatic nature of peoplehood vis-à-vis an ableist valorization of the human. Shamanistic from birth, (post)posthuman subjectivities generate a sacred right-here-and-right-now.

Ana-Maurine Lara's *Erzulie's Skirt* (2006) evokes an Afro-diasporic goddess to narrate the perils of the novel's main protagonists, Miriam and Micaela. Erzulie represents contradictions within Vodou's pantheon, since this goddess weaves together virginity and lust. The novel begins with Erzulie's voice and the omnipresence of water, upon which she travels to liaise with different domains. It is from within the reality of the sea, transparent and fluid yet mysterious and threatening, that Erzulie lends her voice to Miriam's and Micaela's stories. Of Haitian descent, Miriam is the daughter of sugarcane fields laborers. She grows up on a plantation near the country's border. When she gets pregnant, she runs off to the city. There, she will eventually meet Micaela. Born in San Cristóbal, Micaela grows up as part of the working class, learning how to care for her brothers and family. She has almost no access to formal education. In an absurd accident that conveys the fragility of life among the underclass in the Dominican Republic, Micaela's baby brother drowns while in her care. Due to this unfavorable occurrence, her mother casts her out.

Miriam and Micaela meet under the harshest of circumstances. Both reside outside the rural settings where they grew up. They have faced the brunt of coloniality by the time they meet. They barely make a living in the city. Miriam has a son after a failed relationship. She has seen the bloodiest face of anti-Black, anti-Haitian racism in the island. Micaela is full of hopes, and once she strikes a friendship with Miriam, a lifelong companionship unfolds. Eventually, they will settle in a small community back in the countryside, where they open a small market, or *colmado*. In Lara's narrative, Miriam performs as Changó's horse.

A passage about possession is of particular interest, as it concerns multisensory awareness and the role it plays within ALXFT. The evening begins with dancing and rum. When Changó descends upon Micaela, the crowd gathers around her. They light up a cigar for her, and she blows up smoke as she approaches a fire. Miriam calls for Changó to come around. They dance, first forcefully, and then with great excitement. Possession enables Miriam and Micaela to dance together, in front of the crowd, inhabiting an altered state of intense lust. The coloniality of gender reads Changó as male, descending on Micaela. Lara registers this transmogrification by switching Micaela's gender pronouns to Changó's. The ride confronts a sacred reality beyond *genders*, with those intimate attachments that "genders" avail to an Afro-diasporic underclass.

In his analysis of a formative moment between Miriam as a young girl and her mother, Chavel, Carlos Decena focuses on female socialization as part of the ongoing cycle of birthing, becoming, and dying (2016, 186–187). For Decena, it is hair braiding, rinsing and combing hair, and oiling scalp that ignite the transmission and articulation of a way of loving and knowing hair. In the Afro-diasporic vein of ritualized pragmatics, the racialized female subject receives the social body's numinous qualities, Black womanhood, from one body to another. Decena also explains that the narrator speaks from within the metaphor of a cave, playing on the image of Blackness that points to what is already Black, the emergence of Miriam as a Black girl whose "formed head (after combing) crowns a member of a community" (187).

I read the acts of possession, hair braiding, and maguey explosion as routes that usher characters into multisensory awareness, carnal entanglements, and shamanistic states. ALXFT offer sensual dispositions that veer away from the colonizing suppression of other senses (Lloyd 1984; Jay 1988) and from "visuocentrism" (O'Callaghan 2008).[28] Indeed, perceptual plasticity is greatly a matter of resistant histories.[29] Human animals have the capacity, on average, to both hallucinate and experience cross-modal perception. Neuropsychology shows that our perception cannot excise one sensual modality from another (O'Callaghan 2008, 328; Arabzadeh et al. 2008).[30] However, Western cultures deflate our disposition to make references, or transition references, across senses. I would like to submit that inhabiting multiple realities where "genders" lie, working within and on the genre of the human, incites those transitional references. Growing "gendered" skins earns subjectivity a competence to navigate codetermining, often contradictory, realities. Assimilation into *genders* deflates such a transitional competence. As Medea does with the Cihuatateo women, who connect drumming with the scents and visuals of birthing, or Micaela's Changó, who connects loas and their sensual and morphing needs, hallucinating knowing encourages perceptual plasticity and responsiveness.

Socially legitimized in subaltern records of the colonial encounter, a sensual archive fights for its endurance. It resists ongoing domestication of perceptual plasticity and impressible responsiveness. Image-makers, image-readers, painters or scribes, and weavers shared the responsibility of recording and circulating authorized, otherworldly knowledge (Gruzinski 1995; Mignolo 1995; Pérez 2007). Within Xicanx feminisms, this specific "queer mixture" between tangible and intangible realms points to glyphs' spiritual and social function in Mexica tradition (Moraga 2011, 4).

Glyphs often represent prophetic visions that Chicana artists interpret using their "mystical third eye" (Pérez 2007, 34). Modern ethnographies corroborate the prophetic and hallucinating roles of these glyphs. One vivid example can be seen in the art of Huichol people, an Indigenous community from northwest Mexico. Their vibrant yarn paintings and intricate beadwork (MacLean 2001, 2012) serve as mediums for these visionary reflections. For Huichol shamans, radiant colors in their art are more than mere decoration; they embody a divine language that transcends conventional symbolism. As one shaman expressed, interpretation of these colors shifts based on how "the gods speak to [them] through colors" (MacLean 2012, 167). When artists, curanderas, and shamans employ a third eye, they engage colors as both word and song (MacLean 2001, 309), as entangling configurations of spirit-knowing that transmogrifies into formal perceptual qualities.

Concocting Hallucinations

To an extent, Kant's rationalist account of bodily responsiveness curtails alternative uses of the flesh, such as those present in ritual performances. "Genders," I argue, more emphatically gather oppositional and post-oppositional habits of flesh. Selves who relate through "genders" often transfer these habits from one body to another. They contribute to a collective experience of derangement against which Kant warned us. An enigmatic mystery lies with "genders," for they summon solidarity among selves who are learning to wear another's skins. This mysterious experience of selves in relation gains hallucinatory insights from "gendered" subjectivities.

Moraga's last play, "The Mathematics of Love" (2015), serves as a powerful testament to collective witnessing. It holds the promise of mending bonds across generations of Xicana, Mexican, and Nahua women.[31] By exploring themes of time travel and Alzheimer's disease, the play delves into what Kant describes as the complexities of (in)voluntary derangement. Viewing insanity as a profound breakdown of human essence, the play captures the trepidation that Xicanas, armed with their feminist third eye, might feel in the face of spiritual connections. They come to inhabit flesh as selves who intimately relate to each other. Not just through interconnections but also, as agential realism suggests, intraconnections.

The Biltmore Hotel gathers the story's three geographies: present-day multicultural Los Angeles, the nightlife of big-band casinos in 1930s Tijuana, and an eighteenth-century New Spain outpost. The four main characters in this cross-generational dynamic are Peaches, daughter, Malinxe, and Nana. Peaches lives with Alzheimer's. Her daughter mysteriously goes only by "daughter." Malinxe apparently was Peaches's daughter in the past. Nana plays two roles, an eighteenth-century enslaved person and a hotel worker in the present. According to historical accounts, it was her own mother who gave Malinxe away to Cortés. Breathtaking for its shamanic juxtaposition, the play blends bickering and betrayal between mothers and daughters with their ongoing search for reciprocal love. Malinxe shows up as a dystopian, fashion-forward, divaesque traveler who is selfishly absorbed in online dating. Pretending to be checked out, she knows why a treacherous reputation precedes her. Claiming self-determination may grow into deranged, hallucinating love between Xicana mothers and daughters. There lies the otherworldly origin of peopled opposition against heterosexualism.[32]

Alzheimer's is not the only condition prompting contradictory time-lines in the play. Akin to those found in shamanic flight, conflicting timelines manifest an opportunity to heal intergenerational trauma. In her dual role as hotel worker and eighteenth-century enslaved person, Nana illustrates curanderas' working-class sensibilities, setting the stage for revelations that will come along with "sweat and purification" (Moraga 2015). We also learn of Malinxe punishing one of her servants with a thorny plant, and of this excruciating pain opening portals into hallucinations. Malinxe's cruel attitude toward her servant illustrates distance and asymmetry among modified versions of *women* and "women." Heterosexualism thrives in this hierarchical ordering among negatively racialized and formerly colonized subjectivities.[33] Psychic unrest seeps into the body social in the form of hostility. It undermines communication and cross-identification among modified versions of the nonhuman.

Peaches's daughter, who has been mourning the passing of her lesbian lover, crosses into the hallucinogenic decentering of Xicano male subjectivity. Her family impatiently waits for God, "the" son, to begin the celebration of the fiftieth wedding anniversary of Peaches and her husband. Daughter, however, keeps her cool. She has long figured out her brother's charade. God is not about to make an appearance, nor has he done so for their family in quite some time. In fact, his absence has been prolonged. I believe that the play links God, the son, to Cortés, whose arrival the Nahua mistook as godlike. "The Mathematics" employs this trope to challenge vexing histories of paternalistic violence. Within Xicanx families, the characters' emotions reveal that masculinism becomes an essential channel for hardening blood quantum. The play allows Daughter, Malinxe, and Peaches to rehearse collective, hallucinating, and third-eye memories. They steer hallucinogenic concoctions against a colonial hardening of *genders*.[34]

I presented a rather brief account of the relationships among these characters. While brief, the dynamics among Peaches, Malinxe, Nana, and Daughter foreground insights about the coloniality of gender. Their accounts clearly understand coloniality as a condition, a cultural invitation but also an injunction, that casts suspicion upon cognitive and affective capabilities. Under this condition, these characters concoct more-than-human and shamanic hallucinations. They intensify hostility among modified versions of *women* and "women," prompting psychic unrest to open portals into learning how to cross-identify and transition by wearing each other's skins.

"But Baby You Are Not Deserted"

Yosimar Reyes is an acclaimed poet that tours the country, blasting wisdom about immigration, race, and sexuality.[35] We met at the 2011 gathering of the Association for Jotería Arts, Activism, and Scholarship that took place at the University of California, Berkeley.[36] Previously eligible for the Deferred Action for Childhood Arrivals (DACA) program, his work authorization remains precarious. He was the cofounder of La Maricolectiva, a performance group of queer undocumented poets. Self-defining as a Brown boy "from the hood," he grew up in a vibrant hip-hop Black culture (personal communication 2012).[37] It matters to him that his words travel "in a way that is accessible; so, that any other little Yosimar could pick it up" (personal communication 2012). In 2022, he premiered his one-man show, *Prieto*, at the Brava Theater in San Francisco. He was named Santa Clara County Poet Laureate in 2024.

While I frame Reyes as a contemporary contributor to ALXFT, this section covers only a handful of possible connections between Reyes's milieu and these theories.[38] Focusing on Reyes's video performance of his poem "TRE (My Revolutionary)," I analyze its main theme of nonnormative Brown love and its decolonizing and hallucinating ritual.[39] I point out hallucinating affinities between his homoerotic, ritualistic performance of "My Revolutionary" and the tradition of brujería and curanderismo within ALXFT: (1) extraordinary, loquería consciousness; (2) hallucinating knowing; and (3) multisensory cross-referencing as decolonial remedio, or remedy.

Set on the Caltrain commute, the performance of "My Revolutionary" cunningly connects contrasting geographies of conformity and destitution. Among them, we recognize Silicon Valley, San Francisco, East San José, and the East Bay. The performance begins with Reyes standing up, delivering a spoken word poem to commuters. He speaks to the camera but also to passengers on BART (Bay Area Rapid Transit). The ride illustrates the circulation of Reyes's spoken word performance, captured in video to honor Tre, his mentor and spiritual guide.

Research on shamanic prayer and incantation highlights the creation of a sacred environment imbued with rhythmic repetitions and poetic methods (Gill 1981). In *The Hungry Woman*, the Cihuatateo chorus explores an evolving dynamic of love between and among Xicanx mothers, daughters, and sons. In Reyes's tribute to Tre, spoken word transforms the Caltrain commute into a ceremonial space for "genders" incantations. This train journey encapsulates both trace and absence for selves that fade in and out of "genders." Reyes skillfully engages commuters as active witnesses, immersing them in his distinctive style of prayer and chant, calling our attention toward nonconforming Brownness. In this context, his spoken word creates a jarring yet deep resonance amid the bustling noise of Caltrain.

Public transit, like Caltrain, exposes intricate flows of capital and the societal implications of transportation systems. Human geographers refer to this phenomenon as "revanchism," or an intensification wherein conservative stakeholders prevent public transport from becoming an inclusive social good. The term *revenge*, synonym of *revanch*, in this context pertains to the upper echelons of society reclaiming transit systems from perceived disruptions, such as "unruly lower-class riders and antagonistic unionized bus drivers" (Henderson 2013, 160–161).

The Caltrain route, originating in the south bay near San José, eventually connects with the Bay Area Rapid Transit (BART) system. These transit systems date back to the 1960s. Following their growth is like tracking evolving urban dynamics between suburbs and metropolises. As Joseph Rodriguez elaborates (1999, 215–216), BART supporters in its early days championed individualism and regional mobility. Their vision prioritized mobility and consumption freedoms for suburban dwellers, often at the expense of established, ethnically diverse urban communities. These localities, rooted in self-reliance, grappled with the challenges of modern urban planning that prioritized hyperflexible capitalist extraction over community stability.

Reyes's spoken word spreads a sonic trace along Caltrain-BART routes. His poetry aspires to link ethnic minorities across the bay. To occupy the sonic trace, Reyes invokes an emotional and affective labor that heterosexualism, and the genre of the human, expels from *The Hungry Woman*'s Aztlán. He proclaims, "For men like you I would ride a million BARTs, get lost in Oakland, and find your house beneath the brightest star." In the vein of brujas who fly on brooms, or of curanderas' flights discussed earlier, Reyes takes on BART to subvert its meaning.[40] BART and Caltrain provide capital with the daily commutes of thousands of Latinx undocumented immigrants. Contrastingly, Reyes's spoken word delivers an atypical anti-capitalist expenditure. He renders commuters' ride into a loving tribute to queer of color mentorship.

Imposed *illegality* of Brownness activates the surface association between manual labor and its apparently never-ending supply. Not unlike Salustiana Parraga from Northwestern Argentina, Reyes launches a sovereign stanza about his expenditures over Caltrain and BART commutes. Mary Pat Brady (2022) provides incisive commentary on the scales of captivity that contemporary racial capital outlines. She explains that capital redeploys military and economic power as it regulates life, its rhythm and decay. Due to his undocumented status, Reyes was, at the time of this performance, captive of this national territory. California, originally Native land, is now governed by a capitalist ethos that links Manifest Destiny to today's pervasive climate of deportability. As Reyes journeys on BART, searching for Tre's house beneath the stars, he disrupts—with his resonating defiance—the cadence that capitalism affords undocumented Brownness.

Reyes's opening verse serves as a cautionary note against the racialization of landscapes whose tangible nature "numbs the senses [and] cages the spirit." It excavates emotions associated with (extra)ordinary consciousness, specially for those facing the colonial aftermath and its linking of various scales of degendering. He values the teachings that Tre offers about the effects of the city's buildings on Brown bodies. Reyes takes a fierce phenomenological stance to underscore that Tre's free spirit resembles the "winds that we feel sitting on top of the world," or "the tobacco you offered me to blow blessings." Rather than likening Tre's "freedom" to the sensual capacities of all minoritized bodies, "My Revolutionary" digs deeper into anti-colonial resilience. It expands an ongoing tradition of Xicanx healing and curandera arts. The line "You come from the desert but baby you are not deserted" contests the colonizing relation between capitalism and perceptual destitution. With Tre being originally from Ajó, Arizona, the poem links the trail of many undocumented immigrants, who often perish crossing the Sonora Desert, to the danger of becoming "deserted." Reyes cunningly likens the violent enforcement of national borders to the process of personal destitution. In turn, he suggests that destitution entails the domestication of one's senses. For Reyes, as for ALXFT, horrifying geographies seek to erase multisensory responsiveness.

Reyes perceives his mentor, Tre, not just as an instructor but as a healer onstage. Tre embodies the essence of a curandero, revering the profound sanctity of body and voice. He once imparted to Reyes that body and voice are not mere tools but the only true possessions we hold in this world. With these tools, we honor the spirits of "los antepasados [ancestors]." In *The Hungry Woman*, Medea gives birth to herself by affirming an ancestral legacy of sensual cross-referencing. Reyes's poem honoring Tre equally cultivates the powers of bridging realities and temporal lines.

It's conceivable that the Cuareca forty stand alongside Tre as ancestors, as sideways selves. They partake in a social formation where the disfiguration of the human gets worked on and reworked.

Sensual responsiveness is injured by *gendering* and its shaping of atrocious flesh. Within an ethnic community of place, such as Aztlán, *gendering* imbues flesh with human aspirations while simultaneously entrapping it. Running away from Aztlán begets illegality. Without an ethnic nation, such as on the Caltrain, *gendering* paves the way for the exploitation of "illegal" labor. Reyes's singing materializes sacredness in the tangible form that healers give to remedies. Singing, as typically remedies do, tethers an elsewhere of consciousness to the emotional and bodily needs of those, such as the Cuareca forty or the characters in Moraga's plays, who grapple with the constraints of illegality. Singings enchant consciousness into the plurality of worlds, within and beyond "genders." They provide a balm against the relentless scars of illegality.

"To get into the mood of the emotion," Reyes crafts worlds where undocumented immigrants find sites of nonconforming identification (personal communication 2012). In one of his performance's segments, Reyes assumes the positions that most commuters adopt. He illustrates the seriality of the Brown body as stowaway who, passing as another passenger, sits opposite to or with his back to other riders. The performance, however, reveals that "singing," as he puts it, makes tangible the more-than-human force of incantation, of invoking spirit "till this system crumbles, till this border breaks, till the earth shakes." Reyes's poem embraces sacred ("sagradas") words that, he claims, arrive "del más allá" (from elsewhere).

Spoken word poetry harmonizes with the decolonial traditions of oral literature, drawing on key aesthetic elements, such as complementarity, repetition, opposition, duality, and powerful closing lines. These elements mirror the rhythm and cadence intrinsic to the spoken voice, especially in ritualistic environments. Similarly, as negative space in artwork, spoken word crafts singing as the vibrant contour of riders whose existence Caltrain is supposed to exhaust.

Researching *kåntan chamorrita*, a call-and-response, communal oral poetry of Guaham (Guam), Santos Perez describes spoken word as a genre that often takes place at a poetry slam, which is an "interactive event that showcases poetry and its crucial component, performance" (2021, 140). Poetry slams organized by Youth Speaks, a nongovernmental organization that fosters poetry literacy in the Bay Area, gave Reyes the first platform to experiment with his talents. He deepened his competence with code-switching, a northern California Spanglish meshed with hip-hop vernacular. Mostly Berkeley and San Francisco youth dominated the slams of the mid-2000s, and Reyes felt that they had "a language that was so much more developed than where [he was] from."

Spoken word works as a marginal vantage point, enabling poets such as Reyes to usher audiences into performative rites. Kindred to hallucinations, rituals are rich in sounds and other sensual stimuli. They prompt sense-making into an opportunity to test the pervasive boundary between sanity and derangement. Like the Alzheimer's that haunts Peaches, Reyes's multilingual, richly sensual ceremonies strip their partakers of their normative, monolingual, and monocultural status. Hallucinating knowing offers a decolonial and homeopathic remedio to this atrocious condition of illegality and involuntary derangement.

Sideways Selves Who Hallucinate

Perceptual resilience is part of the healing traditions that this chapter documents. Curanderas and brujas archive ancestral knowledge in their own flesh, transitioning one set of sensual clues into another. They also outline new interpretive keys concerning *gendering*, ungendering, and nonconforming flesh. Reyes's ode to Tre troubles typical accounts of homoerotic sensuality. Attraction and desire bind Reyes and his mentor. Yet they germinate within their identification as two-spirit beings.

In Native American and Mesoamerican cosmologies, "two-spirited people are sexually mixed beings who enjoy a living relation with their Indigenous ways and spirituality" (Estrada 2003, 12). Curanderismo as the work of spirit healers, of specialists of the heart, remains the cornerstone of Tre and Reyes's two-spirit relation. The most carnal expression of their erotic and spiritual embrace unfolds with the stanza "You got me and together we are 4 spirits like the 4 directions." Impressible, codetermining entanglements among two-spirited people, among spirits becoming larger and multiplying into four, actualize more than homoerotic mentorship. In fact, they puncture LGBTQ ideals that rely on settler bodily technologies, such as opposite or same-sex desire. Four spirits challenge the notion that personhood anchors its existence to the Western binaries of surface and interiority, of a dichotomous sex-gender system that projects onto the body's surface an appearance of Man>Woman. The carnal sensuality at stake is not that of a whole that seeks another. Rather, atrocious flesh generates patterns of sociability or ways of ungendering love among sacred, multiplicity-affirming embodiments.

Might we call Medea, Peaches, Micaela, Miriam, and Tre kindred spirits? Might we consider Reyes's hallucinating rite a feature of broader epistemic and ontological histories? Do they foster ALXFT, as sideways selves do over decades, if not centuries? Further research may provide more insight into these resilient responses to colonial injunctions. For sideways selves, coloniality entails the experience of being perceived as insane, behaving that way—most of the time, intentionally—and employing this competence to connect with other practitioners of loquería. As shown in this chapter, contributors to ALXFT face one another at the edge of an (extra)ordinary condition. They heal *el susto* by doing intergenerational work, making of Afro-Latinx, Latinx, and Xicanx nonconforming bodily projects a new alien race that doesn't have *genders* at its center.

Against a Kantian legacy linking ordinary consciousness to reliable knowledge, ALXFT generate hallucinating and richly sensual repertoires. Their practitioners employ tongue, skin, ears, eyes, nose, and "the mystical third eye" to decipher, carnally and spiritually, what they need to carry out healing rites.[41] In the flight of altered consciousness, they gain new visions, totally unique, not quite nameable, half-seen, half-heard, half-tasted, and half-felt, a way of sensing that is as much compelling as it is frightening. Afro-Latinx, Latinx, and Xicanx curanderxs and horses stand against the horror of sensual destitution, of the suppression of Indigenous, Native, and Afro-diasporic perceptual repertoires. Under the sign of illegality, from within the geometry of black holes, they present contemporary generations such as Reyes's with our more-than-human, ungendering potential.

CHAPTER 5

Jotería Poetics

Diasporic Selves

The praxis of poet Maya Chinchilla inspires spirit work. Her poetics responds to and honors the domain where the more-than-human resides. Within this domain, she foregrounds natural and spiritual entanglements and their underwriting of artmaking. Chinchilla's poetics style finds its grammar in the binding of life to both nature and politics. In this fashion, it reveals its significance for Afro-Latinx and Latinx thought, practice, and aesthetics.

We previously examined the ways that genocidal, militarized, and snuff-driven violence shapes precarious conditions for Afro-Latinx and Latinx *jotería*. In fact, jotería migrants in the diaspora must battle against myriad forms of displacement, including being pushed over, onto the other side of life, onto an arena where politics renders disempowerment natural. In Chinchilla's poetic exploration, jotería delves into the complexities of life, capturing its intricate entanglements. This chapter will show that her poetics offers a sensorial medium that allows us to discern the decolonizing meeting between precarious life and systemic violence. She dubs this sensorium "jotería." She illustrates with this medium an upsurge of creativity, an actionable poiesis by which jotería communities pursue life against centuries of material, ideological, and political struggles.

Gender nonconforming projects arise in response to dispossession. Often, they put forth visions about life-forms, living things, live things, afterlives, and beyond. Visions that point against and beyond dispossession recreate the very origins of viability, both organic and not, at once natural and otherworldly. Jotería foregrounds modes of being and knowing against the odds of dispossession. They entail intentional engagement with life and its various meanings and expressions. As I engage in a dialogue with Chinchilla's poetic practice, I discern unique approaches, or "maneras," as she refers to them, through which she invokes jotería consciousness. Specifically, I pay attention to the more-than-human function that life plays in jotería's enduring pursuits of liberatory futures. These pursuits, I shall argue, find expression in the soundscape of diasporic and migrant messengers whose poetics Chinchilla honors.

Maya Chinchilla is a poet, activist, teacher, videographer, and documentarian. Based out of Oakland, in the San Francisco Bay Area, she is part of a network of queer, trans, and disabled Latinx and BIPOC performers and activists. Her multimedia approach spans various ways of knowing, living, and politicizing nonconforming embodiments. In that sense, her sensibilities share cognitive and sensorial connections with those ancestral hallucinatory ways that Afro-Latinx, Latinx, and Xicanx feminist theories cultivate.

Jotería poetics invokes dissonance within diasporic Caribbean, Central American, and Latinx communities. It carries traces of the more-than-human across the border between *this* and *other* life-forms. This poetics furnishes unprecedented insights into the materiality of sideways embodiments. As Chinchilla grapples with revolutionary legacies across the Américas and, more pointedly, her family's ancestral Guatemala, jotería becomes company and comrade of her spellbinding stream of heartfelt meditations on social transformation. As dissonant, her poetics reaches beyond not only Euro-American orthodoxies about the meaning and scope of revolution but also limiting visions of third-world insurgency. Pushing contradictions between revolutionary subjectivities and embodiments, Chinchilla delivers critical understandings of carnal responsiveness.

As M. Jacqui Alexander explains in a chapter titled "Making the Invisible Tangible" (2005a), feminist revolutions demand that we learn the work through which sacredness embodies solidarity. Chinchilla with her revolutionary poetics manifests more-than-human capabilities of the self. She invites us, as Alexander does, to re-member the self in transformation. Neither habitually individuated nor unwittingly secularized (Alexander 2005b, 298), the self of jotería revolution journeys through sacred resonances and incantations. This journey requires jotería selves to reassess contemporary accounts of Central America as the cradle of sociopolitical and geophysical havoc, experiment with new languages about diasporic sound and dissonance, and center life with its wide-ranging entanglements within intergenerational pedagogies.

To the end of traveling this journey, I lay out three interrelated conversations. First, I consider Chinchilla's search for diasporic ways of enacting the plurality of Central America in language and, particularly, in the language of social transformation, revolutionary discourse, and migration. I listen critically to her poetics while witnessing its record of dissonance, both linguistic and sonic, through practices such as *voseo*. This practice consists of a set of pronominal and verb forms for the second-person singular among some, but not all, Latin and Central American speakers. Chinchilla's unique appropriation of voseo illustrates visceral and sonic ways by which migrating embodiments press upon each other. Diaspora and its nonnormative sensibilities, we shall see, restore and recreate sonic responsiveness. Second, the chapter follows Chinchilla's *messenger maneras*, a decolonizing method of revolutionary solidarities across the diaspora at the turn of the twenty-first century. Diaspora is a phenomenon that intertwines origin and dispersion as well as center and margin. It provides meaning to "the restoration of a collective sense of identity and historical agency" (Barkan and Shelton 1998) by mediating the dynamics of displacement and belonging. Messenger maneras draw upon long-standing repositories of liberation and intergenerational pedagogies to reflect on and enact revolutionary solidarities across Central American and jotería communities. Third, I engage (in)organic entanglements between nonhuman and human configurations and the ways they bear on Chinchilla's diasporic rendering of Central American identities, territories, and struggles. In her rendering of hyphenation lies an anti-colonial, jotería-inspired stance. It invites readers and co-listeners to reassess the matter, organic and not, that vibrates at the center of the Américas.

Of importance to these conversations is the method of jotería, an embodied consciousness discerning motions and mutations in coloniality's legacy. This method injects dissonance, off-the-record and off-the-center insights, into uncharted engagements with Central American identity in the diaspora. It interweaves grammars of political life, such as revolution and insurgency, together with inorganic grammars of vitality, such as volcanoes' activity and seismic friction.

Colonial depictions of Central America as a hub of chaotic and savage forces are coupled with the diminishing of Guatemala's historical spiritual authority as the center of the ancient Maya civilization. These portrayals narrate the formation and marginalization of Central American identities. Settler logics also contribute to the perception of this region as seismic and earth-shattering. Jotería poetics seeks to reframe these primitivist views, which for centuries have encased Central America in tropes of wilderness, voracious jungles, and revolting earthquakes. By joining jotería poetics, I follow Chinchilla's longing for a more-than-human togetherness. Hers is a longing not just for a widening of contemporary boundaries between notions of the human and nonhuman. Rather, I seek to show the poetic ways by which she reshuffles human and nonhuman boundaries. Ultimately, she disrupts the paradoxical account of Latinx, Caribbean, and Central American diasporas as either primitive-yet-salvageable or stagnant-and-irredeemable. In fact, this reshuffling shall reveal that jotería poetics as embodied consciousness magnifies sideways selves and their hemispheric teachings about diaspora, solidarity, and intergenerational revolution.

Arrebato Earthquake

Maya Chinchilla hails from California. Though raised in the Los Angeles area, she has lived on the San Francisco Bay for over twenty years. Founder of *La Revista* at the University of California, Santa Cruz, and cofounder of the theater and poetry performance troupe Las Manas, her written work has graced multiple publications, including *Las Girlfriends*, *Mujeres de Maiz*, and *Sinister Wisdom*. An accomplished and award-winning filmmaker, she is the director of *Made in Brazil: Dreams at Work*, *The Last Word*, and *Solidarity Baby*, the latter with the support of the San Francisco Film Arts STAND Award and Queer Women of Color Media Arts Project (QWOCMAP). Her vast portfolio lies at the intersection of politics, media, and art, and it underscores the emergence of ecologies of solidarity across boundaries of race, class, nationality, gender, sexuality, and disability. Specifically, Chinchilla examines the flows of migration and the global/local dynamics that shape this phenomenon and its impact on subjective and collective sensibilities and memories.

Many events led to the emergence of Decolonize Oakland in the fall of 2011. I'd also like to think that they prepared the ground where I met Chinchilla and other members of a long-standing network of queer, nonbinary, and trans Latinx and Afro-Latinx performers in the Bay. Decolonize Oakland came to light with a twofold purpose: (1) expressing dissatisfaction with the lack of focus on racial justice within the Occupy Wall Street movement and (2) narrating that the discontent of the 99 percent had to contend with the links between American exceptionalism and settler, imperial, and neocolonial modes of domination and exploitation.[1] Artists such as Melanie Cervantes and Jesús Barraza of the Oakland-based collective Dignidad Rebelde created posters affirming

Indigenous sovereignty in October of 2011. They call Occupy to task by signaling, through their art, an ancestral Ohlone presence in today's Oakland city limits (Talcott and Collins 2012). Almost in unison, the QPOC and POC caucus of Occupy developed a multimedia sphere of discourse. They denounced that occupying was not "enuf" to fuse anti-capitalist and anti-colonial struggles.[2] In the aftermath of the bank bailout of 2008, it quickly became evident that there are unequal tiers among the 99 percent and that Occupy's model of organizing, without a clear leadership, tends to replicate rather than do away with those hierarchies.

At the time, I was living in Oakland's Pill Hill, a section near Lake Merritt where several medical practices and hospitals, not so amicably I must note, share real estate with Afghani-run businesses, recently gentrified housing units, and the adjacent Koreatown. Within fifteen blocks or two BART stations, Occupy Oakland sets up an encampment by October of 2011 on the grounds of the Frank H. Owaga Plaza.[3] Occupy Oakland issued a call for a general strike, scheduled for Wednesday, November 2. I learned of this strike through a post on social media, when one of my Facebook friends shared Dignidad Rebelde's bilingual poster titled *A Descolonizar Oakland: Huelga / Decolonize Oakland: General Strike.* Having recently moved to the East Bay, I was still figuring out the queer of color and nonbinary scene. I had made acquaintances with a few activists when the Association for Jotería Arts, Activism, and Scholarship (AJAAS) met at the Cal campus the weekend of October 14–15, 2011. It was these many intersecting nodes, across small-scale sites of collective fashioning and oppositional collaboration, that allowed me to access a growing feed of social justice events, clips, news, and posts.

I joined hundreds on that Wednesday as we marched toward the Oakland Port around 4:00 p.m. I saw small and midsize clusters of folks who had clearly coordinated their banners, chants, and outfits. I gravitated around LGBTQ+ contingents. I located a makeshift installation of a grave site, whose headstone read "RIP Victims of Monsanto Corporation." I lingered there. I stared in delight at the Day of the Dead knickknacks that one of the troupes had carefully arranged on the floor surrounding the makeshift grave site. From this viewpoint, banners unfurled before me, seamlessly weaving together elements of artistry, design, visual tradition, and powerful slogans. They encapsulated the spirit of the marching crowds. One of the posters connected global and local struggles, such as the Arab Spring's uprising of 2010 with the "American Autumn." Another, hanging on the top of a tent, linked economic disparity with the need to decolonize food justice efforts.

I had heard of Chinchilla's poetry performances, but I had not had the opportunity of hanging out with her. Angela Davis, the fierce feminist philosopher and former member of the Black Panther Party, was speaking to the crowds. Chinchilla and I realized that we were standing close to each other. She was wearing a black tee with the legend "Homie for Justice" printed across her chest. I recognized her from the AJAAS event hosted at Cal, and I timidly nodded. She gingerly leaned on the woman standing to her left, who was wearing her hair parted into a pair of braids. I took the cue as signaling that they were making room for me. An affective constellation sustains this and many other gestures that I recognize as jotería erotics, a political recalibration of nonnormative identities. While Chinchilla's nod felt deeply personal to me, it also speaks to wider grammars of rebellion among converging generations of Latinx and Afro-Latinx activists. Not unlike that gesture, her poetics brims with wisdom on and about the meaning of learning solidarity as a principled politics for life.

Chinchilla opens *The Cha Cha Files: A Chapina Poética* (2014) with an insightful and powerful testament to the force of cross-generational pedagogies. Under the title "Solidarity Baby," the opening of the collection documents the convergence of various rebellious communities and the affects that they instill in Chinchilla's art. At the same time, it documents broader transpositions, particularly the transfer of affectivity from former revolutionary collectivities to contemporary youth of color who share with Chinchilla the experience of being first-generation Guatemalan American and diasporic. At first glance, the concept of solidarity draws attention to notions of empathy as a universal appeal to or plea for recognition. Chinchilla, however, makes available a more layered genealogy of solidarity, which begins with precarious and yet resilient identities, and it arrives, as this chapter shows, at humbling accounts of human/nonhuman cooperation. She doesn't exploit the urgency that social justice activists assign to present-day conflicts and demands. Rather, she introduces audiences and readers to solidarity as an erotic power with long-standing social and spiritual roots.

Chinchilla learned solidarity from an "extended family of activists" (2014, 4), who taught her how to "[take] on telling the truth" (3). She witnessed the Central American Underground Railroad passing through her parents' living room (3). Among memories of her *mami*'s and *papi*'s first lessons in solidarity, she listened to Maya women's testimonies and debates over US-backed dictatorships throughout the southern cone. These, among others, are the transpositions that Chinchilla performs as an invitation into an erotic of solidarity.

An architecture of transpositions and migrations may already be present in Chinchilla's chosen title for *The Cha Cha Files*. It combines *cha cha* and *Chapina*, likely with the intention of highlighting their quintessential functions of intercultural transitioning. Cha cha consists of a dance genre with a highly contested history of migration and multipronged provenance, while *Chapina* signals Guatemalan identity and its unsettled composite of Mayan, K'iche', Spanish, and Afro-Caribbean roots.[4] Together, cha cha and Chapina preamble repertoires of material transpositions, among them those that Chinchilla revisits in her journey from her parents' generation to her own, from one mode of oppositional consciousness to another, and from a limiting to a more decolonially expansive account of solidarity.

In her piercing declaration about the uses of the erotics, Audre Lorde locates the demands of coalition-building among women of color in that "deep place of knowledge" where "terror and loathing of any difference [. . .] lives" (1984, 113). A praxical concern among feminists who theorize coalition is the subtle ways in which structures of oppression shape political orientations between women of color and white women but also among women of color (Johnson Reagon 1983; Sandoval 2002; Lugones and Spelman 2018; Martin and Mohanty 1986). The transformative power of Lorde's erotics partly stems from exploring how marginalization leads to our ignorance about the harms we may cause within our own communities. While Lorde's statements apply directly to concrete mechanisms of distortion and erasure among white women and women of color, they also concern contemporary demands in coalition-building among nondominant differences.

Lorde's erotic praxis couples the crucial act of self-reflection with another fundamental act of empathic understanding. Yet, we should not confuse empathy with tolerance, or with the act of arrogant appropriation of societal margins and their resistant repositories. Women of color thinking is an epistemic and political movement emerging from a shared commitment to support coalition-building among nondominant differences.[5] Erotics as a social means of coalition incites affinities inside difference, as Chela Sandoval (2002) suggests. It summons perhaps the loosest sense of *we* that flesh affords to our perilous moves against dehumanization. Third-world women and women of color feminists in the latter quarter of the twentieth century understood and practiced coalition-building as a reorientation of the flesh and its erotics, embodying posthumanist versions of kinship, togetherness, and community. In Lorde's exploration of these iterations, she encourages us to contemplate a "new spelling" of subjectivity (1982). From my perspective, she engages with feminist coalition-building as a means to redefine the concept of "women" and its erotics, against yet away from the impact of colonial legacies.

In line with our previous discussion of the genre of the human, I understand that Lorde's call for the erotic arises precisely from the experience of moral and political disintegration. Her version of coalitional materialism builds upon connections, usually hidden, among beings thoroughly reduced to disfigurations of the human. To love each other through these connections entails an expansion of selfhood, a redoing of dehumanizing insularity. I believe that this is the call to which jotería responds. Chinchilla's rendering of solidarity entails, as we shall see, the art of translation. It focuses on one's experience with disintegration and its deciphering into languages, images, emotions, and feelings that communicate the potential for cross-pollination. Translation shapes co-interlocution and recognition of mutual implication among constellations of human disfiguration. As Lorde announced forty years ago, loving is a political glyph that tells the truth about the role we each play in our contemporaries' struggles.

Chinchilla's art underscores that solidarity doesn't begin with good intentions or the benevolent act of lending a hand to one another. Rather, it stems from a thorough examination of each other's experiences with disfigurations and the ways that we are implicated by them. In that fashion, she observes that her parents' living room and dining room hosted various survivors of neocolonial counterrevolutionary regimes in Central America and, specifically, Guatemala. She was a witness to their resilient mobilization of rebel sentiments in the face of both despair and opposition. Through these and other acts of faithful witnessing, she helps us understand how to acquire skills for sharing testimony as a co-performative practice. In her poetics, witnessing testimonies becomes a way of inciting solidarity babies into birthing.

Chinchilla's sense of solidarity begins with the humbling gesture of questioning the magnitude of her own disposition. In light of the militant fervor that Chinchilla finds among her parents' comrades, she doubts herself and asks, "What have I ever done for revolution, honey?" (2014, 4). Initially, she perceives the prospects of revolution in the twenty-first century as fragile when juxtaposed with the "militant explosions" characteristic of her parents' generation (4). This expression is among the keywords signaling the reappropriation of the geopolitical and geophysical identities of Central America. Considering that supranational agencies, media, and first-world governments sensationalize gang activity in Central America, and that sensationalizing tropes include *chaos* and *sudden violence*, it is worth exploring Chinchilla's appropriation of the semiotics of earthquakes and *arrebatos*. In this appropriation, I recognize the recalibration of geopolitical positions as a source of dissent and protest.

Her poetics is deeply aware that geopolitics demands innovative "secret plans" (2014, 5) to campaign against its ever-changing mode of domination and extraction. She describes subversion in opposition to Cold War regimes. During this period, leftist movements often saw liberation as an urgent cause, with activists rallying behind slogans like *revolution now or never*. Despite grappling with self-doubt, Chinchilla takes on Lorde's erotics pedagogy. She delves into the deeper place of knowledge where differences between generations spark flames of accountability and hope (Garcia Rojas 2017). Here, tectonic shifts resonate in the insurgent spirits of multigenerational fronts.

From "under literature tables" or on her "father's lap" (2014, 4), Chinchilla listened to the complexities of radical meaning-making and learned, over the years, how to decipher inflections in tonal, emotional, and cultural differences. Her "mami" interpreting the testimonies of Maya women, who spoke the Spanish language of their former conquerors, gave Chinchilla a firsthand experience of the elusive fiction of full transparency (4). Witnessing the K'iche' Maya–accented Spanish of Rigoberta Menchú, she learned of Guatemalan guerrilla fighters, mostly Indigenous *women* and *men*, who hoped to end the winding maze of colonial, modern, and neocolonial violence.[6] Through these acts of critical listening, Chinchilla encounters an "extended family of activists" who leaves skin-deep literacies in her sense of solidarity. She carries the imprints of carnal, testimonial literacies into her coupling of self-reflection and empathic understanding. She sometimes gets paralyzed by the fear of not living up to the revolutionary expectations of her activist and intellectual family. Teasing out the differences between her parents' generation and her own, specifically in relation to the meaning and scope of revolution, enables her to finesse the type of relational affectivity that Lorde recommended over forty years ago (1984).

While Chinchilla acknowledges fear as part of her journey through an uncertain terrain of cross-generational visions of revolution, another emotional dimension emerges from the transition between generations. As Lorde puts it, "sharing deeply any pursuit with another person" (1984, 56) becomes an erotic galvanizer. Chinchilla's poetics is informed precisely by a deeply shared pursuit against injustice among members of her parents' generation. She was raised as a "rebellious daughter" (2014, 4). Having observed satisfaction and camaraderie within her extended family, she expands traditional concepts of poetry to encompass revolutionary spirits inherent in cultural and aesthetic endeavors. Memories of clandestine and booming debates introduced Chinchilla to an erotics of underground translation. She developed communication techniques that encode and encrypt earthquake-like and often sudden dissident acts (Muñoz 1999). Her use of *voseo*, for example, opens a diasporic domain of sonic dissidence, which we engage next.

Voseo's Reverberations, Inciting Sonic Rebellion

Finding inspiration in Central American poetry, such as Guatemala's Otto René Castillo and Cuba's Pablo Milanés, Chinchilla performs an erotic turn in her theorizing of revolutionary praxis.[7] If the praxis of revolution belongs with the in-betweenness of social dissidence, between one another as Lorde suggests, Chinchilla doesn't forgo the possibility of building on the accomplishments of her parents' generation. Yet, she finds that it is equally important "to stay away from letting them impose their guru" on present revolutions (5). She delivers a sonic rendering of this intergenerational collaboration through a singular use of the linguistic pronominal address *voseo* in Spanish.

A line in the poem "Solidarity Baby" encapsulate insecurities and anxieties that contemporary activists grapple with as they compare past revolutionary struggles and leadership with more fluid and fragmented modes of dissent characteristic of the post–Cold War era. The line, "*Si el poeta sos vos que tengo yo que hablarte?*" [If you are the poet, what about do I have to talk to you?], has unique provenance among Latin America's new song movement and its themes of anti-imperialism and social justice.[8] Chinchilla quotes the song that Pablo Milanés pens under the title "Si el poeta eres tú" and whose lyrics pay homage to Che Guevara, who was a renowned Latin American revolutionary hero at the onset of the Cold War period. In turn, Milanés borrows inspiration from Miguel Barnet's famous ode to Guevara ("Che," 1967), which depicts the combatant as a fierce guerrilla genius and visionary. Milanés echoes Barnet while Chinchilla, spanning generations, echoes both of their voices.

The poem's reclaiming of sounding words channels subaltern subterfuge. It seeks to destabilize the politics of citation between both poems and their memorializing of Guevara. More prominently, Chinchilla infuses Guatemalan Spanish into Milanés's words by utilizing the regional linguistic form of *voseo* to address the second-person singular.[9] Unlike *tuteo*, which relies on the familiar pronoun *tú* for the second-person sin-gular, *voseo* employs the pronoun *vos*. The latter, though less widespread, has a regional penchant associated with Argentina, Uruguay, Paraguay, some regions of Colombia and Chile, and, of great importance in Chin-chilla's case, parts of Central America like Guatemala. Voseo also shapes the alignment of pronominal and verb forms. It's worth noticing that *tuteo* is the form of address employed nearly exclusively in Guatemala's largest neighbor, Mexico.[10]

Within speech acts, interlocutors may opt for voseo based on power relations, such as gender, class, race, ability, and sexuality (Tricola 2011). In Guatemalan Spanish, speakers frequently transition from *tuteo* to *voseo* when conversing with peers they have a close social relationship with, marked by trust and familiarity (34). This switching dynamic creates a sonic context in which trust between speakers signifies a mutual recogni-tion of authority, not in a hierarchical sense but as a reciprocal bond.

Linguists who study Guatemalan dynamics of voseo query the con-ditions under which it originates. They are interested in explaining the widespread use of voseo in a country where approximately 50 percent of the population is monolingual in the Mayan language. They suggest that the Mayan language K'iche' also offers formal and informal manners of address for the second-person singular. They highlight the possibil-ity of continuity over the interphase between Guatemalan Spanish and its historical proximity to the most common Native language in the area (Pinkerton 1986). Notice that, at this intercultural linguistic crossing, shifting between *voseo* and *tuteo* may respond to sociolinguistic elements such as those that we previously surveyed regarding Andean Spanish speakers. With their practice of loísmo, speakers of Andean Spanish make Spanish-sounding words carry the sensibility of an Indigenous language that does not have noun-like particles at its center. Among Central Amer-ican speakers who were unlikely to engage voseo in the localities where they grew up, scholarship shows that they opt for this manner of address when they change towns or, particularly, if they migrate to the United States and reside in a state or city with strong Latinx presence (Sorenson 2010).

Voseo offers an affective gesture that moves in diasporic fashion for Central Americans. This gesture brings diasporic sonic embodiments into being. That is, although there may be minor differences in the way Central American speakers construct and phrase voseo, it nevertheless generates a new geopolitical landscape of sound for Guatemalan speakers. Once outside their native country, Guatemalans in the diaspora turn to voseo as a site of recombination of familiar-sounding and not-as-familiar-sounding speech. They respond to other Central American speakers who, in kindred style, incorporate a more regional sense of register whenever they seek to claim evolving forms of belonging. Through this act of poetics, they challenge preexisting linguistic boundaries.

Inflecting voseo within the stanza *Si el poeta sos vos que tengo yo que hablarte?* doesn't aim at replicating the poetic gesture of Milanés. It does show, first, respect toward the stature of Milanés both in radical and music circles. The Cuban singer-songwriter pens an ode to Guevara, which respectfully gives a nod to the towering figure of intellectual Miguel Barnet and his own homage to the revolutionary legend. Chinchilla's intention is more likely to resonate with the sonic capacities that revolutionary affect evokes across generations, aligning with both Milanés's and Barnet's as well as her own. Voseo steers revolutionary affect outwards, seeking for other tones and audible rhythms. Laying one over another, voseo transmogrifies tuteo by intensifying impressible responsiveness among diasporic selves. In fact, as we shall see, diasporic selves retain singularity without muting expressivity.

In the poem, the line "I mean it's just a revolution, honey" (5) serves as a tongue-in-cheek cautionary message, challenging notions of revolutionary subjectivity traditionally associated with the Cold War era. Chinchilla could subscribe to the narrative of revolutionary consciousness as a transition from "individuated bourgeois subjects into collective consciousness" (Saldaña Portillo 2003, 70). Instead, she highlights the intricate process of establishing intersubjective connections to broaden the horizons of solidarity within insurgent struggles. Threatening as it might feel, affirmation of each other's similarities and differences, which Lorde talks about, has the potential to reorientate our erotic attention from "a simultaneous looking away" (1984, 59) to "deep participation" in each other's feeling, knowing, and understanding (58). Indeed, it redirects our focus away from self-awareness and toward the shared joy of fighting oppression through mutually enriching witnessing acts. Chapina poetics amplifies an erotic drive among revolutionary babies, emphasizing how they deepen abyssal responsiveness.[11] In her view, they foster solidarity beyond the point where Cold War antisystemic attitudes hit a wall.

Chapter 2 covers at length the coloniality of bodily mattering. It undertakes the exploration of the technologies of impressibility by which the colonial quest in the Americas cast off liminal embodiments as genderless and less-than-nonhuman. Within that context, I suggest that the notion of *sideways selves* illuminates the sociosomatic practices that amplify more-than-human or less-than-human capacities of flesh. Among these practices, we recognize the emergence of nonconforming bodily projects, including migrant Latinx jotería and Argentina's travestis. Sideways selves recombine skills of bodily transition, of its organic, inorganic, and sacred concreteness. Chinchilla also turns to new images of embodied matter beyond those that reference individual unities. Engaging social change and the activist work that it demands, her cha cha emphatically examines affect, eroticism, and perceptual responsiveness, for they support not just the ends of revolution but the revolution of social formation and its embodied matter.

When Chinchilla borrows from various traditions of subversive and popular songwriting, she puts forth an alternative to the linguistic practice of cross-citation. She appeals to the sonographic memory of minoritized Latinx and AfroLatinx lifeways. Voseo and tuteo reach into muscle-memory—tongue, soft palate, roof, and larynx—and into the physiology of cross-cultural competence. They materialize diasporic sonic reenactments. They give birth to soundscapes that merge differing scales of our sensual responsiveness. The revolution of differential consciousness in Chinchilla's poetics begins with a tactile awareness of collective identity, belonging, displacement, and yearning. Her focus on sound encourages us to view poetry as a form of carnal pedagogy. She invites us to engage with the visceral forms of knowing and learning, which modernity separated into mind and body, while reshaping postsecular and dissenting sensibilities.

In *Dissonant Divas*, Deborah Vargas (2012) argues that music has often been the mechanism for minoritized communities to access counterhistorical narrative, self-representation, and cultural empowerment. In addition to reflecting on the cultural politics of minoritarian subjects through audioscapes, Vargas innovates sound studies by turning our attention to a corporeal memory of dissonance, of looking and sounding *odd*. This turn in sound studies, Vargas argues, engages different terrains of knowledge that ensue from visceral scales (2012, 112). When Chinchilla transitions from tuteo to voseo in her tribute to two Cold War revolutionary icons, it goes beyond mere code-switching. She evokes memory cells in an audience that is familiar with the cadence in Milanés's voice, its solemn and heartfelt tone during his tribute to Guevara. These sounds evoke familiarity with the themes of loss and grief for one of the region's greatest rebels, intertwined with a hopeful longing for collective revolutionary actions.

Members in the audience of one of Chinchilla's 2012 performances in

Albuquerque, New Mexico, nodded with little restraint when she quickly punctuated the relevance of Milanés to an audience of postmillennials. While she probably listened to Milanés's rendition in her parents' living room, her gesture veers sideways as it renders his delivery unfamiliar in the ears of new recipients. For many a Central American migrant who fled the bloody Guatemalan conflict, these gestures are deeply visceral. They incite a slightly unhinged recognition of an impassionate but somber form of praise for spirit rebels of generations past.[12]

Like Vargas, Chinchilla invites us to study unusual inhabitations of sound. By magnifying actual transitions of one form of address—tuteo—to another—voseo—Chinchilla signifies more than the mere switch from the most widespread to the more localized dialogical choice for the Latin and Central American diasporas. She enacts a phonetic and dialectical history that extends selfhood across sonic locales.[13] Vargas pursues the concept of sonic imaginary in *Dissonant Divas*. This concept refers to the social space of a "musically sounded/sonic field where people come to understand, relate, and connect to notions of belonging, history, place, and cultural sensibilities" (Vargas 2012, x). Dissonance, in Vargas's view, stands for "giving sound to the odd-looking [or] the strangely registered" (113). Chinchilla's rendition of "Si el poeta eres tú" plays with the strange register of the Central American diaspora. She employs Central American dialect but without reducing it to an arithmetic of linguistic choice or use. It plays with sounds that connect lips and ears with waves of familiarity and proximity. It expands the sonic reach, from the closest-sounding community member to those who may become closer once displacement reconfigures the reach of (un)familiar differences. Speakers from Guatemala may engage in voseo among other diasporic Central Americans to convey that sounds—motions of lips or aspirations in one's throat—reverberate with strangers' kindred registers. Voseo encodes resilience of a familiar and yet odd-sounding linguistic use in its assertion of emerging identities beyond national affiliations.

Chinchilla creates a sonic opening by infusing voseo into *la nueva canción*'s soundscape. Her strategy traces sonic sensibilities among migrant communities as they negotiate the crossroads of assimilation into and in opposition to what I call *genders*. She makes visible the workings of masculinity and its strong hold over revolution and the avant-garde throughout the 1970s. The diasporic practice of voseo aligns with the linguistic patterns of Guatemalan migrants, but particularly among women in both Chinchilla's and a younger generation. Guatemalan women from senior generations, such as those of the Cold War era, may not be as comfortable with this practice. A linguistic study conducted by Pinkerton (1986) suggests that Guatemalan college-educated, cisgender women in the diaspora tend to switch between *ustedeo* and *tuteo*.[14] Apparently, class conventions also influence the way middle-class cisgender women use sound to show respect to one another and to indicate the level of deference they expect from others. Chinchilla crafts her own way of showing deference to elders. She has an almost whimsical approach to voseo. She chooses the song's title to introduce this diasporic form of address. The underlying metaphor of the line "Si el poeta sos vos, qué tengo yo que hablarte?" links struggles for justice and liberation with creativity and poetry. Voseo comes to occupy the diasporic and poetic heart between song, singing, music, and revolutionary habits.

Chinchilla's sonic style invokes, perhaps, a more dispersed sense of the body social. Political consciousness, she leads us to reflect, does not live primarily in the rationalist ideals of the mind, or the intellectual abstractions within revolutionary plots. Instead, she invites us to interrogate post–Cold War habits of the flesh. As the notion of *naguala* does, Chinchilla's sonic artistry demonstrates that revolution begins with the inner workings of psyche and soul. Indeed, she responds to the more curdling, impure, codetermining composition of Latinx, Afro-Latinx, and Latin American counterhegemonic sentiments. While Cold War politics adheres to the dichotomy of Latin American Left versus US-backed intervention in the region, the revolutionary sentiments championed by Chinchilla's generation suggest an expansion of various forms of bodily dissent.

Mostly due to protracted internal conflicts, large-scale immigration from Central America has been prominent in the United States since the 1970s and has, at the same time, diversified with influx from seven different countries (Hamilton and Stoltz Chinchilla 2001). Northern Triangle countries in Central America rank within the top ten immigrant-senders (Gramlich and Scheller 2021). Counterhegemonies in the post–Cold War era react to evolving dynamics that blend the mass displacement of underpaid, informal, feminized labor with economic salvage strategies crafted and executed by supranational organizations in Central America. They leave an imprint on the personal tribulations of new waves of migrants who, such as Roxsana Hernandez or Alejandra Alor Reyes, carry their undocumented and illegible languages into far-reaching, dissident sentiments and soundscapes.

Sonic dissonance and resonance arise from the reconfiguration of patriarchal tenets within an archive of Cold War revolutionary anthems.

Chinchilla joins the dialogue that Milanés initiates with Guevara. Akin to the approach that she fosters with her parents' generation, she moves gingerly, with a humble style of sonic intervention. She enriches the sonic imaginary of belonging, sensibility, and location within the horizon of Latin American and Latinx liberation. When Cold War revolutionary ideals bespoke the future of a new man (*un hombre nuevo*), they envisioned subjects capable of not only rechanneling capitalist desires but also surging above all other forbidden and "malformed deviations" that flesh incubates. Presumed conversion of revolutionary men, from alienation to liberation, would come along with a reengineering of consciousness at the expense of impassionate flesh.[15] Although virtual and somewhat hidden, feared deviations of the flesh haunt the rational persuasion of an emancipated class. In fact, and sometimes with torturous methods, revolutionary cisgender men kept liberation under the hegemony of modernist and primitivist visions of mind/body/spirit. They allow the hegemony of *genders* to proceed with its regulation of habits of flesh.

By contrast, Chinchilla's *Solidarity Baby* gains access to a more expansive base for the visceral fight against social inequality. Solidarity babies encode a feminist-sounding voice where the emerging body of dissidence—the link from inner to outer worlds that naguala enables—relocates revolution to an affective region. If *nueva canción* and *nueva trova* focus their resources on sensible responsiveness among historically marginalized communities, mostly of peasants and underemployed peri-urban dwellers, Chinchilla's sonic pedagogy sings to the hearts and spirits of diasporic configurations. At this sonic twilight, rural and urban sensibilities learn to entangle environment, migration, and belonging. It shouldn't go unnoticed that Chinchilla's revolutionary praxis delves deep into trans-sensorial, even trans-dermal, affective transmission. It incites sonic affinity without excluding a leftist rationality characteristic of the Cold War, or its memorializing of social aspirations in the nueva trova's record. Rather, it transmogrifies the meaning and practice of singing and listening, of finding one's heart swelling with hope, into a sonic device that mines differential consciousness for more-than-rational, more-than-human openings.

Chinchilla's cha cha announces that matter vibrates to the rhythm of sociosomatic entanglements. Solidarity babies actualize uncharted biophysical and sociocultural looping. In a manner akin to hallucinating knowing, they practice solidarity by sharing sonic expressions. Chinchilla's cha cha files challenge revolutionary ideals for relying on colonial legacies. The files' sonic dissonance and resonance create unprecedented and perhaps postrevolutionary subjectivities among formerly colonized populations. Their poetics appeals to visceral sensibilities where hope and love render migration and diaspora experiences into insurgent theories of the flesh. Dissemination of this diasporic erotics demands the assistance of messengers. According to Chinchilla, babies and *honees* attend to this labor of dissemination. Her poetics invites community members to embrace each other politically, highlighting this affective gesture by teaching them to go by the appellatives *baby* or *honee*. Next, I examine this labor within the practice of messenger maneras.

Mensajeras of Solidarity

The art of solidarity, its language, tone, and affect, evolves through *The Cha Cha Files*' opening. As described above, it begins with an archival excavation that Chinchilla undertakes into the living room of her revolutionary parents. As a cultural activist with an established body of work, Chinchilla has before her the possibility of assessing that archive from the standpoint of contemporary visions of social justice. Instead of taking that route, she extends that archive by acting as messenger, or *mensajera*, between generations and across spaces.

Chinchilla equips herself with the tolerance for uncertainty that translation demands (Anzaldúa 1999; Castillo 2014; Chávez 2013). Through parodic and whimsical style, she makes geopolitics into childhood riddles along the lines of "Was Reagan a good guy or a bad guy?" Mischievously, she intertwines acronyms representing intelligence agencies and revolutionary movements, crafting them into lines resembling a coded message with hyphens separating each element. Furthermore, she amusingly incorporates the familiar introduction of alphabet songs for preschoolers into a single line, such as "A-B-CIA-GIC-FMSLN-URNG-UFW-XYZ." It places side by side the looming memory of CIA-backed intervention in Guatemala and leftist insurgency throughout Central America, such as the Frente Sandinista de Liberación Nacional (FMSLN, Sandinista National Liberation Front) from Nicaragua and Unidad Revolucionaria Nacional Guatelmateca (URNG, Guatemalan National Revolutionary Unit). Her genius for geopolitical riddles invokes an internationalism intrinsic to liberation struggles in the continent. Her riddles include the United Farm Workers' history of protesting Manifest Destiny in the United States (L. Pérez 2007; Blackwell 2011). She demonstrates great flexibility pivoting from one to the next context of struggle. Through these practices of translation, she becomes a mensajera, trying out riddles and coding secret messages. Her translations incite emerging forms of carnal responsiveness. At the heart of this pedagogy lies a fierce competence to seed, cultivate, and germinate loving dispositions across generations of solidarity babies.

Locating her childhood within pedagogies of solidarity, Chinchilla offers lessons about "translator techniques" (5). She sees them as an acquired competence for conveying *mensajes* combining diverse understandings of revolution. *Messenger maneras* can be roughly glossed as "the messenger's ways" or, alternatively, as "the ways of a messenger." By associating the task of revolutionary translation with lessons learned during her childhood, Chinchilla distinctly challenges conventional notions of infants' innocence. Dissonance occupies layers of time and space across intergenerational struggles for revolution.

According to Sandra Harding (2018), epistemic or knowledge-based remedies fare poorly before the disorienting clash of multiple realities. That is, I don't think that Chinchilla is keen on demonstrating that children have a unique and singular take on revolution. Rather, she implies that there are worlds, such as the leftist, multigenerational environment of her parents' living room, in which children actively participate in the co-construction of revolutionary goals and methods. In Chinchilla's multiple worlds, children also learn and shape techniques of revolution. In fact, she embodies this clash in her meditations on liberation pedagogies. She begins by humorously acknowledging her generation's modest commitment to revolutionary struggles. She juxtaposes her generation's role with that of her parents' contemporaries, who played a monumental part in denouncing US-backed dictatorships in Latin America. Beneath her seemingly humbling position as a messenger of solidarity lies deep intersubjective transformation, like those exemplified by Lorde's teachings on relational affectivity. With the whimsical tone of "But, what have I ever done" (2014, 5), Chinchilla reveals the plurality of not just revolutions but also ways we shape them, learn about them, and communicate their meanings.

Decolonizing engagements with translation contest dominant practices of meaning-making. As previously explained, noun-centered, toponyms-centered versions of reality create and follow one-way links between reality and language, or context and reference. Humanist legacies suggest that languages have equal referential functions and that descriptive competence is inherent in all languages. By contrast, postcolonial critique and decolonial praxis view colonization as an idiom of generalization, which asserts superiority in truth-making for Westernizing linguistic ideologies over others (Rafael 1988; Price 2012, 2023; Veronelli 2015). Coloniality of expressivity contends with linguistic subordination. It entails not only the misrepresentation of linguistic competence—among both subscribers and targets of colonial power—but also and, perhaps most importantly, denial of expressive sovereignty.

In its Chapina poetics, Chinchilla pursues an erotics of solidarity. She attends to a relational affectivity that feminist coalitional building demands. Attuned to what I have previously called ungendering, she engages unauthorized subjects of revolution. Through this shift, she encourages solidarity babies to betray the mind/body split, focusing on maneras more than on manifestos, more on modes and verbs than on the slogans of liberation. This turn enlivens revolutionary imagination, since it pays attention to "what is not obvious" (2014, 5). Chinchilla understands that maneras preserve contestation and recreation as intrinsic to the arts of social transformation. As mentioned earlier, she compares scales among revolutionary ideals while searching for "my place" (4) within "*a* revolution" (5; emphasis added). She doesn't concede to the pressure of proving who is "more down" (5) or imposing one's "guru" on another (5). Venturing into the realm of the playfully absurd, she claims that her place and quest hold little significance. She feels intimidated by the zealous tone of political manifestos, wherein revolution often highlights future visions without giving equal importance to expanding alternative subjectivities in the present.

Chinchilla's orientation about revolution focuses on an intimate domain of flesh, or what I have been calling *bodily responsiveness*. To her own question about what she has ever done, she answers, "nothing," except for the not so trivial acts of "[surviving] race riots in high school," "[getting] through college when the high school counselor said it couldn't be done," or "[telling] stories on a microphone" (2014, 5). She takes her analysis of scale, between a senior and younger generation, into a tactile metaphor. She reminds us that even the mere possibility of "touching [. . .] a microphone" (5) indicates varying levels of agency.[16] While they may carry little weight for most, small acts such as a high school riot or grabbing a megaphone enact a more granular poiesis. They break through bounded architectures of revolution. With her expressivity and emphasis on maneras, she seeks to provincialize revolutionary truths.

Messenger maneras report truths that might otherwise remain untold. Muting operates not only because the politics of death exterminates dissent, debris, excrement, and trash but also because twenty-first-century notions and methods of liberation continue to draw on colonial translation. The labor of Decolonize Oakland that I mentioned earlier is one example, among many, about the salience of maneras for contemporary solidarity struggles. During the post-bank-bailout in the Bay Area, Decolonize enacted dissemblance by creating visual signs capable of invoking discomfort toward both capitalist extraction *and* settler dispossession. Decolonize resembles Occupy, and yet it also employs this resemblance to infuse, channel, and incite visceral dissemblance. Messenger maneras employ translation techniques that emulate dissemblance. They negotiate more vernacular, and perhaps less bold, idioms of revolution. This approach, which first and foremost communicates humility, is a way of theorizing the relation between conditions of existence and consciousness, on one end, and between consciousness and political activity, on the other. By layering resonances among revolutionary subjectivities from Cold War and post–Cold War periods, Chinchilla captures contradictory configurations. Amplifying dissemblance across resemblance, she aligns her cha cha with solidarity maneras.

Playful self-doubt enables messengers to dwell in liminal domains. They are not so hung up on traditional imaginings of revolution. With lines such as "I used to get the names of dictators and leaders of the people mixed up: Somoza or Sandino? Ríos Montt or Otto René Castillo" (2014, 4), Chinchilla affirms a radical potential of dissemblance. She offers confusion and hunch as cognitive devices along the memory docket of revolutionary praxis. Rather than making absolute statements, Chinchilla explores phonetic similarities between figures like Somo*za* and *Sa*ndino or Ríos Mon*tt* and *Ot*to René Castillo. In doing so, she gingerly invokes emerging dissenting subjectivities—those attuned to nuanced sounds and tones. Chinchilla occupies a place of dissonance that she hasn't found yet but whose materiality—an in-between entangling of dissidence—lies with conjecture and guesswork. In the diasporic voseo style described earlier, she emphasizes how solidarity babies harness the power of creating vibrations, transforming the more-than-worldly significance of revolution into sonic revelations. Sounds, unlike words, ask for a more tenuous literacy labor, less driven by equivalence and more prone to a dispersed way of doing interpretation.

We find yet another example of messenger maneras in Chinchilla's "Solidarity Baby." She recognizes in these maneras potential for "(un)disciplining destiny" (2014, 5). Chinchilla suggests that fostering solidarity demands ongoing renegotiation. Sifting through the mobile record, tangible and intangible, of rebellious "inheritance" (Moraga 2011), she draws inspiration from archives of situated dissidence. For honees, this archival project is part of their culture of love (5). Unlike typical interpretations of rebellion, babies accommodate less confrontational or legible forms of countering dominant power. In fact, tricksterism arises as a conceptual tool that resembles Chinchilla's turn to babies and honees as enactors of social change. Relying on a "long line of resilience" ("Solidarity Baby," 3), Chinchilla dives into many orientations and directions within the trickster figure. Some scholars have rigorously researched this figure alongside first-person narratives of members of subaltern groups (H. Jacobs 1999, 533–682). Anthropologists provide ethnographic evidence of tricksterism within long-standing "weapons of the weak" (Scott 1985; Tuhkanen 2008). Chinchilla's maneras lay claim to a similar low-frequency, or low-intensity, resistance and opposition. This manera, however, resonates more vibrantly with messengers who learn to outwit the oppressor's knowledge. Messenger maneras facilitate a post-oppositional, dispersed, at times ineffable, but always tangible erotic sense of dissent among solidarity mamas, babies, and honees.

The Cha Cha files magnify our understanding and experience of messenger maneras. Switching to voseo, fostering dissemblance across resemblance, and transferring an otherworldly force into what appears trivial, messengers announce a novel economy of solidarity. They illustrate, as sideways selves do, a collective authoring of nonconformity. In the style of body-to-body engagement that *This Bridge Called My Back* theorizes (Moraga and Anzaldúa [1981] 2022), solidarity mamas, babies, and honees underscore that revolution, at a time when the world is literally on fire, demands a differential awareness of the body social and its capabilities. The network where I encountered Chinchilla became my jotería kin. Their pedagogies habituate bodies in alignment with the principled modes of consciousness and emancipation identified by Chela Sandoval (2000, 45) among third-world and US queer and lesbians of color in the late twentieth century.[17] Through diasporic recalibrations, to which messenger maneras attest, solidarity babies recombine third-world feminist synergies into decolonizing methods of healing, expressivity, and bodily responsiveness.

María Josefina Saldaña-Portillo examines revolutionary discourses both in Latin America and the Latinx representational borderlands. Specifically, she argues that normative notions of human subjectivity as well as political consciousness and agency are essential to these discourses within the post–World War II period (2003). Theorists of subaltern and decolonial thinking have named these normative aspects in various ways, among them the legacy of imperial "soul-making" (Spivak 1985), coloniality of knowledge (Mignolo 2012), coloniality of gender (Lugones 2007), epistemicide (de Sousa Santos 2015), and genre of the human (Wynter 2003). In Saldaña-Portillo's view, enlightenment's premises, such as liberty, progress, and prosperity, paradoxically implicate both revolutionary discourses and hegemonic developmentalist policies. Her argument shows that dialogical relations between developmentalism and revolutionary ideologies remain caught within *humanitas*. They are attached to modernizing aspirations of full subjectivity. In other words, human-centered discourses of emancipation *subalternize* the very populations that colonial/modern power historically renders *subaltern*.

Subjects of coloniality lag in evolutionary time, while modernity offers them development as the route for assimilation into capitalist modes of extraction and domination. However, the promise of emancipation, of being uplifted by progress, rehashes the very configuration of full-fledged subjectivity. That is, an aspirational subjectivity fits the sociosomatic project that renders racialized, disabled, and ungendered responsiveness into a zone of stagnation. Destined to death, modes of nonbeing work as an assumption without which developmentalist ideologies could not prompt civilization toward the future.[18] Scholars in the field of postdevelopmentalism criticize the hidden goals of achieving full-fledged subjectivity. For instance, Arturo Escobar (2018) critiques state-led modernization plans, because they presuppose Latin and Central America's lack of technological and political progress compared to first-world nations. Escobar's point goes beyond geopolitical perspectives as he reveals that both neoliberal technocrats and left-leaning groups in Central and Latin America often pursue "excessive development" (2018).

Chinchilla runs into this psychosocial and sociosomatic conundrum as she grows up amid her parents' incessant plotting of revolution during the Cold War period. Narratives of anti-capitalist struggles pressure her to "prove who's more down" (2014, 5). Like some of the population of Central American migrants, diasporic Latinx children and teenagers experience the civilizing features of colonial power, cast as unwanted and chronic interlopers who encroach on public resources. There is angst in this interval or temporal twilight between anti-capitalist and assimilationist ideals of (r)evolution. Chinchilla's solidarity babies carry this pressure to the very edge, turning to an erotics of reciprocity and accountability. She favors continuous engagement with specific locations, positions, and embodiments, less fixated on the universal roots of alienation and more in synch with the sociosomatics of everyday insurgencies.

The Latin American left often neglects the erotics of solidarity that Chinchilla embraces. Her parents' generation relied on abstract and universal notions of subjectivity and liberation (Lugones 2003a, 53–64[19]). The myth of individuation as the source of freedom still influences leftist philosophies, hindering intentional engagement with sociosomatics and, thus, perpetuating colonial violence. Denying the significant role that flesh has in revolutionary struggles leaves the coloniality of gender, as well as the coloniality of transgender, intact, allowing the genre of the human to ongoingly draft progressive ideals of social change into notions of stagnant and ungendering subjectivities. Leftist investment in collective consciousness without a comparable focus on sociosomatics reinforces an individualizing commitment to the genre of the human, to both Gender and *genders* as stepping stones on the way toward full humanity. Solidarity babies instead announce a dissident present through messenger maneras.

In the words of Chinchilla's "Solidarity Baby," one plays one's role in the struggle by fighting "con lo mejor" (with the best) we each have (2014, 5). To honestly assess the best we each have, we must delve into the intricate ways our lives implicate each other. This perspective reshapes our understanding of collective consciousness, shifting from universalizing notions of left-leaning albeit liberal individuality to embodied, situated responsiveness. Messenger maneras appeal to the outer contouring of a liberal subject, unveiling its many layered skins. They may gravitate toward an enigmatic reality of subjectivity, as illustrated in previous chapters through the bodily responsiveness of Salustiana Párraga Arraya and Elena Humana. Or, as exemplified by the diasporic voseo-tuteo style, messenger maneras may infuse cha cha poetics into the language of revolution. These maneras challenge our reliance on univocal, however collective, formations of revolutionary subjectivity. Solidarity babies acquire competence in witnessing, critically listening, and co-performing these dissident erotics of the body social. This competence entails a body-to-body practice of honestly affirming the best in each other.

Unlike Cold War and developmental discourses of social transformation, *The Cha Cha Files* rehearses a twenty-first-century erotics of feminist coalition. It seeks to touch the deep place of knowledge that lies between the manyness of revolutionary subjectivities and imaginings. Chinchilla's solidarity babies, and the more extended network of Afro-Latinx and Latinx cultural activists from the Bay Area, labor at the very edge, on the abyss, of black holes, sewage pipes, and other systems of disposability and precarity. Messenger maneras, voseo-switching, and sonic dissemblance, they all entangle babies, honees, and mamas in the summoning of the polymorphous and enigmatic erotics of (post)posthuman selfhood.

Storytelling and Loving Perception

In her storytelling, Chinchilla gives an insightful account of coalitional erotics. Specifically, she describes lived experiences as they pertain to the phenomenology of loving perception. Her phenomenological account is intertwined with a way of knowing that emerges from the practice of solidarity. I submit that her emphasis on solidarity enhances coalition-building efforts, foregrounding habits of perception among beings whose condition exists on the brink of viability. Additionally, she rejects the idea that the mechanics of the sensorial apparatus solely determine perception. She introduces her readers, instead, to storytelling as a germinative state. I associate this state with the stanza in which she dedicates her rhythmic cha cha to babies who "love the world with eyes that have not yet been born" (4). This stanza draws attention to the material design of perception and the role that solidarity babies play as they develop these loving eyes.

Chinchilla locates loving eyes at the edge of existence. How are we to love the world with eyes that have not yet been born? She links the material regeneration of organs with both lived experience and sociosomatic orientation. She suggests that solidarity babies may learn the ways of perceiving-in-the-present-with-perceiving-yet-to-come. Almost in the vein of agential realism, Chinchilla offers a glyph of bodily responsiveness across multiple timelines and geographies. What is yet to be seen may demand an alternative materiality of seeing. This is how *we* do *loving*, she implies, within a coalitional horizon.

María Lugones introduced the notion of loving, playful world-traveling as a coalition-building competence for feminist transformation in the mid-1980s (Lugones 2003b, 77–100; DiPietro, McWeeny, and Roshanravan 2019, 9–12). Through world traveling, Lugones offers a methodology of loving perception. Those who live in the margins of the social find themselves traveling across worlds out of necessity. World-traveler selves encounter ways of knowing and being that make evident the trappings of the human. Amidst this sense of suffocation, selves experience multiple oppressions as fragmenting. The sociality of resistance, Lugones thinks, sometimes decenters but often strengthens worlds in which nondominant agency may flourish. She favors the language of active subjectivity, since she considers agency to belong within a liberal theory of subject formation.[20] It matters to her that resistances become more enduring and that their theorizing accommodates infrapolitical realms of intention and bodily engagement. Theorizing resistance and its many logics, Lugones pushes back against suffocation, distortion, and fragmentation. Her praxical thinking adumbrates ways of perceiving and engaging the social, with loving eyes, through inhabitations of ourselves that most may find hard to interpret as resistance.

Loving perception seeks out ethical commitments, or a different approach to the relation between self and other, to the relationality that originates with the ways that we learn to sense the world. This perceptual learning enables selves to meet one another face-to-face. Lugones thinks of selves who cross worlds and who, through and within this crossing, learn to dwell in each other's realities, possibilities, and feelings. The world-traveler self sees another's "own sense of herself from within her world" (2003b, 86). Proposed as a practice that begins with the vantage point of women of color who are "outsiders to the mainstream" (77), world-traveling builds on skillful ways of living that are not always willful. Neither individual nor personal freedom is the driving engine of perception, as if the self were ever outside a specific situation. Lugones's framework refutes arrogant perception precisely by unveiling how dependent we are on one another to dispel dehumanization and reduction. World-traveler selves learn to tap into the most post-oppositional aspects of subjectivity. We learn to perceive by remembering and affirming each other's multiplicity. Within this in-between bridge, selves foster perceptual skills across multiple worlds.

Some philosophers, such as Mariana Ortega, are skeptical of Lugones's emphasis on ontological multiplicity. They interpret Lugones's emphasis on multiple worlds as not just ontologically but also phenomenologically problematic. They question whether world-traveler selves could claim any multiple existence if they lacked "existential continuity" (Ortega 2016, 50). Without this continuity, Ortega argues, even selves facing the most contradiction or ambiguity couldn't maintain "a sense of being an 'I'" (50). She draws on a Heideggerian notion of *mineness*, which she develops as "a way of being of the self that emerges from the type of temporality" that allows "the self to project toward the future while being in a particular present situation and being informed by a particular past" (79–80).

Chinchilla's stanza about perceiving with eyes yet to be born vividly captures the type of temporality that Ortega has in mind. However, I argue that the coalition-building erotics emphasized in Chinchilla's poetics resonates more vibrantly with Lugones's concept of multiple selves. Like Chinchilla's interpretation of diasporic styles of sonic multiplicity, I find that multiple selves provide a more faithful account of resistant socialities and their continuous responses to coloniality. In deciphering these responses, I have examined at least three ways of making sense of multiple selves.

Firstly, hallucinating knowing works as a device by which Afro-Latinx, Latinx, and Xicanx selves navigate psychic unrest without the need for existential continuity. Notably, perceptual learning comprises cultural conditioning that greatly shapes whether we experience hallucinations. In response to coloniality, multiple selves hallucinate through dispersed ways of being, rather than tightly held-together senses of self. Secondly, we have explored experiences related to Gender, *genders*, and "genders." For instance, the Cuareca forty experience a colonial encounter through bodily contradictions among nonhuman, beneath-animal, and dekunafied stations. Coloniality upends any temporal continuity among these experiences. Temporal discontinuity is the material mode of existence for beings who embody at once "I" and "non-I," but also many variations of non-I.[21] This phenomenon partially involves what we have termed species stagnation. Lastly, within Andean Spanish–speaking communities, we recognize worlds whose events rely on germination and change rather than on continuity. In those worlds, senses of an "I" are informed by numinous aspects of multiplication. Deities often preside over and even possess practitioners of Afrodiasporic spiritualities in the Caribbean. Horses may lack any memory that they consider "theirs" about possession. Indeed, these practices offer embodied recalibration of knowledge and reality and, more precisely, experience.

Reflecting on what I describe above, I submit that Ortega's version of existential continuity, rooted in the idea of mineness, stands in stark opposition to intercultural and decolonial philosophies. The notion of mineness is purported to provide room for contradiction and ambiguity while maintaining a temporal, discrete continuity. Necessity of temporal continuity tracks back to Enlightenment and secular representations of selfhood. To appreciate resistance at its most infrapolitical sense, intercultural and decolonial philosophies can help us, instead, to perceive worlds with senses yet to be born. It is not farfetched to assume that a metaphysics of discrete objects continues to guide philosophical explications of the self's sensorium. Agential realism and Native and Indigenous philosophies, instead, advance compelling critiques of the Newtonian paradigm and its secular dependence on the metaphysics of discrete objects.

In the context of agential realism, distributed cognition is just one of many neurolinguistic developments that challenge the notion of mineness. According to Peter Garratt (2017), "thinking" disrupts the traditional split between inner and outer psychic realms. Unlike Heidegger's philosophical architecture, contemporary neurobiology presents accounts of thinking that align more closely with notions of multiple and otherworldly selves found among Indigenous and Native philosophies. In theories of distributed cognition, thinking assembles enmeshed objects, among them the mind, which behave as a localized unit and also as a more vague, more dispersed, yet enactive whole. This proposition better resonates with experiences of hallucinating knowing and possession within Afro-Latinx and Latinx spiritual contexts than the notion of mineness does.

As Karen Barad suggests, what Westerners call the self, and its situation across time and space, emerges through specific material configurations. As a configuration, it demands from decolonial philosophers, which Chinchilla suggests, that we learn perceiving-in-the-present-with-perceiving-yet-to-be-born. Decoding critical teachings from Karen Barad's agential realism, Deboleena Roy states that "'we' as we tend to define ourselves as scientists and knowers also may not preexist but rather [. . .] participate in the 'mutual constitution of entangled agencies'" (2018, 74). That is, to paraphrase M. Jacqui Alexander, decolonial philosophy calls us to task as we configure novel ways of being and knowing. Alexander further highlights the importance of distinguishing between living alterity premised in difference and living intersubjectivity premised in relationality and solidarity (2005b, 7–8). It is for the sake of relationality and solidarity that I embrace multiple selves as a faithful methodology for making intercultural and decolonial senses of selves across multiple worlds.

Unprecedented technologies of loving perception arise, according to Evelynn Hammonds (1994), out of the zone of illegibility and misrecognition. Loving perception that is yet to be born, in Chinchilla's poetry, contains untapped resources for thinking about the nonhuman, an unintelligible and distorted sense of selfhood. Chinchilla's attention to the erotics of solidarity is compatible with Lugones's granular undertaking of resistance. The productive genesis of the social that Lugones illustrates with oppressing⇔being oppressed⇔resisting exemplifies entanglements that coproduce illegibility, misrecognition, and opposition to both.[22] Arrogant perceiving to an extent co-constitutes loving perceiving. Indeed, Lugones painstakingly makes sense of the carnal reduction of multiple selves to the zone of nonbeing, but she reminds us that oppression is never a done deal. The zone of nonbeing codetermines and co-constitutes a recalibration of the human. Loving perception gives uptake to polymorphous and cacophonic socialities, which Hammonds, as we had previously examined, calls black holes.

We must wonder whether subjectivities that gravitate toward black holes, and who emerge in response to multiple oppressions, affirm multiple realities as a way of resisting erasure. Hallucinating knowing enacts a type of syncopation, accenting selves who are often weakened by power structures. Perceiving black holes' complexities, as Hammonds suggests, invokes seeing-in-the-present-with-seeing-yet-to-emerge. These practices that acknowledge resistances to multiple oppressions assemble parallel and competing worlds. Selves who sustain their multiplicity create energetic exchanges across many generations.

Elizabeth Spelman provides a provocative interpretation of Lugones's body of work, while focusing on the materialism of world-traveling selves. Spelman underscores the significance of acknowledging the social genesis of nondominant selfhood, even when such selves are often treated as disposable (2019, 31–46). Partaking in the act of making another disappear, or of banishing them from view, ruling groups pretend to avoid responsibility for anyone's viability. Spelman's insight lies with the notion that trash, often considered disposable, does not truly vanish. She argues that trash, in its ability to *talk back*, unveils uncomfortable truths about its own creation (2019, 40). It sheds light on the processes of perception and objectification that reduce selves to disposable entities.

World-traveler selves embody an unfinished, incomplete, not-quite-ever-settled, materiality. They live in the twilight between dehumanizing and sustaining entanglements. Groups that engage in degrading others may become tethered to the relentless task of eliminating what or who refuses to fully vanish or disappear. Spelman expands on the phenomenon of arrogant perception to identify a stubborn disposition among groups who relentlessly ignore the harms that banishment inflicts. Moreover, trash also serves as a reminder that for arrogance to persist, a degree of denial is required among those who engage in banishing others. Denial obstructs the perception of resistance within the realm of trash. When trash talks back, it unveils an alternative reality of mattering. Loving perception incites modes of being duplicity, knowing duplicitously, and experiencing duplicitousness. As in the case of trash, world-traveler selves engage simultaneously with both logics, arrogance and love. From within this condition of co-enactors, not always agonistic toward each other, multiple selves unravel temporal continuity or the lived experience of mineness. In fact, a pluriverse underwrites resistant, oppositional, and post-oppositional inhabitations of the social.

Chinchilla's poetics incisively communicates the many afterlives of (un)-vanishing selves whose world-traveling perception, whose perceiving-in-the-present-with-perceiving-yet-to-come, offers profound feminist wisdom. Curled up on her father's lap, Chinchilla gravitated toward, heard, and felt the "Chapín Spanish booming from his chest" (2014, 3). "For the silent who carry this country on their backs!" she discerns what is not obvious, dares reporting truths untold, and layers laughter amidst tears (5). Chinchilla's Chapina poetics foregrounds intergenerational reciprocity that seeks to restore justice to the memory of those who have been treated as trash. Revising this history traverses many timelines, spanning Guevara's generation to her parents', or from her parents' to her own. The Reagan-backed dictatorships of the 1980s in Guatemala sought to erase, mute, and distort revolutionary subjectivities. Post–Cold War liberation struggles and artmaking unearth nonconforming projects often overshadowed by Enlightenment imaginaries of individual freedom and collective consciousness. As we see next, one of these projects emerges from the abyssal subjectivities and practices of jotería's multiple selves.

Jotas, Joterías, and Harmonies

In "Jota Poetics," Chinchilla illustrates yet another wave of ripples in the mattering of solidarity babies. About jotería, she states that "we are a bless-ed home" whose hospitality warms up with "unexpected guests" (2014, 56). It wouldn't be farfetched to suggest that Chinchilla counts jotería among solidarity babies. She summons the matter of sound and its agency when she states that "broken tongues speak jotas into harmony" (56).[23] She taps into sonic dissonance for her rendition of jotería beyond the strictures of rationalist meaning, which usually fall under the guise of either homogenizing notions of nonconforming sexualities or Westernizing categories of LGBTQIA+ identities.

For the reasons I present below, it makes sense to acknowledge Chinchilla's line about speaking *jotas* into harmony as a decisively odd-sounding occurrence. It is strikingly playful how she weaves two similar sounds with contrasting provenance. She juxtaposes *jota*, which is the noun for the Spanish alphabet letter *j* (/j/), to the sound *aitch*, which describes the English alphabet letter *h*, needed for speakers to utter the word *harmony*. It's important to note that the word *jota* carries a derogatory meaning with queerphobic connotations within Mexican American communities. Often, queer Xicanx and some other Latinx communities reclaim *jota* as a term of belonging and affirmation. Chinchilla invites readers and performance attendants to gleefully halt the usual anglicization of non-English spelling. She would like us to sustain a not only bilingual but also multivocal way of listening. She reduplicates the sonic matter, and the graphic trace, I must add, of the word *jota*. This stylistic choice reflects the complexity of jotas as they navigate and exist within multiple worlds, often in tension with each other. Chinchilla's art embodies the reality of jotas at a place where the logics of two colonizing languages, English and Spanish, contend with speakers of three subalternized languages, Spanish in the United States, and Nahuatl and K'iche' in both Central America and America.[24]

In Spanish, the letter *jota* carries grammatical and phonetic histories fraught with colonial and postcolonial conflicts. Shortly upon the arrival of colonizers, an oral Nahuatl culture developed a robust writing system that was based on an already abundant glyphic and phonetic tradition. Major centers, such as Mexico-Tenochtitlan and Tlatelolco, adopted the Roman alphabet's orthographic conventions in the 1530s, which laid down the foundation for this Nahua writing tradition (Olko and Sullivan 2014). While Nahuatl spread throughout New Spain and became an administrative language that crossed various ethnic regions, Christianization restricted Native autonomy.

Demonyms such as *Mexica* and *K'iche'* were used as emic designations of the first peoples of present-day Mexico and Guatemala. Both demonyms share a startling phonetic feature. The sounds "x" and "ch" present strong graphic and phonetic resemblance. Most English speakers pronounce the demonym "Mexica" (/ˈmeksɪkə/) the same way as they do "Mexico" (/ˈmeksɪkoʊ/). However, those fluent in Nahuatl or K'iche' might prefer the *sh*-like sound (/ʃ/) commonly found in English for words like *fishing* or *ocean*. In such cases, the phonetic notation for *Mexica* is /ˈmeʃɪkə/. Postcolonial Spanish phonetics normalized the Native sound "x" (/ʃ/) found in Mexica by claiming that "x," in precolonial and colonial Castilian, represented the phoneme /j/ (Coester 1925). This attempt to regulate the sound of "x" and make it align with /j/ reflects broader expressive hierarchies. By extension, it normalized the Spanish toponym as *México* (/méjiko/[25] or /méxiko/)[26]. Ironically, despite efforts to domesticate it, the Spanish toponym "México" demands the sound *jota* (/j/) for its pronunciation, even as it retains the visual trace of the Nahuatl "x." For what appears to be the same toponym, colonialism and anticolonial resistance introduced the coexistence of three phonetic and graphic iterations: /ˈmeksikoʊ/, /ˈmeʃiko/, and /méxiko/ or /méjiko/. Among these glyph-like iterations, where does temporal continuity lie?

The trace of Nahuatl in current spellings of *Mexico* and *México* makes for a postcolonial condition characterized by multiplicity. By the time Nahuatl became a written language, Castilian grammar had significantly altered it. The "x" sound in Castilian was at times pronounced /j/ (as in "Quixote"), or /ʒ/ (as in *muger*), or even as a sibilant, /ʃ/ (like in the English word *sharp* or the Portuguese word *dexar*). A sound in English that most closely resembles the contemporary Spanish /j/ is /h/, as in the words *her* or *harmony*. English-speakers would resort to this *aitch* sound (/h/) if they had to pronounce the Spanish word *jota* or words containing it. At the same time, they would anglicize the Spanish *equis* (/x/) sound. Spanish-speakers, instead, would nowadays use the /j/ or /h/ sounds to pronounce the "x" character.[27]

A corollary of the postcolonial condition described above finds expression in the bilingual, or polylingual, toponym *Mexico* or *México*. Speakers who are situated across different geopolitical histories approach this toponym according to contrasting linguistic repositories. Spanish speakers employ the /j/ or /h/ sounds to pronounce the "x" character in México (as in /ˈme.xi.ko/ or /ˈme.hi.ko/). Speakers who are bilingual both in Spanish and Nahuatl may prefer the sibilant /ʃ/ for the same "x" character. In Spanish, the sound /j/ associated with the character *j* erases the Nahuatl-originated sound /ʃ/ associated with the character *x*. This sonic colonial legacy removes a Nahuatl sound from both the Indigenous demonym (*Mexica*) and toponym (*Mexico, México*). A non-Western lineage remains, however, visually embedded under the guise of an "x" character, or what I would rather describe as a glyph.[28] This is the case in both the Spanish and English spellings of the toponyms *México* and *Mexico*, respectively.

Therein lies a double entendre of sorts within postcolonial linguistic multiplicity. Coloniality of expressivity operates on two coexisting fronts. It anglicizes *Mexico* (/ˈmeksɪkoʊ/) while banishing (Spanish) *México* (/ˈme.hi.ko/) from the sonic realm. Yet, anglicized *Mexico* (/ˈmeksɪkoʊ/) and Spanish *México* (/ˈme.hi.ko/) both attempt to erode the sibilant Nahuatl sound that lived in both *Mexica* (/mēʃika/) and *Mexico* (/mēʃiko/). If we considered that K'iche' and Mexica were mostly oral and glyphic systems of expression prior to the conquest, the insurgent role that the graph "x" plays in this double entendre becomes evident. It relocates the "x" graph, which is the trace of a sibilant Nahuatl sound, to the written expression of colonial linguistics for both the Spanish and English toponyms (*México, Mexico*). Despite ongoing colonization, I would like to note, nonwritten languages such as Nahuatl trespass on the expressive form of colonial linguistics.

Across these sonic worlds, institutional and subjective transformations took place. It wasn't until 1815 that the Spanish Academy settled the spelling of Castilian. A paradox threatened this ambitious search for order. On one end, orthography treatises over the span of almost three centuries aimed at unifying an entire subcontinent under Castellano's linguistic force. On the other, Spanish linguists painstakingly debated over the internal (in)coherence of their imperial language. The presence of numerous linguistic roots before the emergence of Castilian did not help their cause (Ticknor [1891] 1965, 11–13; George 2018). *Jota* comes, as Chinchilla reminds us, from a trail of broken tongues. I submit that dissonance and resonance between *x* and *j* enact multi-local and multi-temporal transpositions. Jotería poetics transport repositories of dissonant agencies and, as is the case with the diasporic dissemination of *Mexica* (/ˈme.hi.ka/, /mēʃika/) and *jota*, they enliven realities where solidarity babies outlive sonic legacies of coloniality. I hope to have shown the transmogrifying force of sonic decolonization and the ways that it transfers its energies into key sounds (*x, j*) for Afro-Latinx, Latinx, and jotería studies.

Chinchilla addresses jota poetics as "the threads that weave a bed for you to lay" (2014, 57), proposing that an identity, more than reflecting an injured aspect of subjectivity, or perhaps because it includes an injured aspect of subjectivity, offers an affective and material infrastructure for selfhood. Jotería grows, she says, as "wild roots that can't be cut back" (57). Consider this statement in relation to the double entendre of postcolonial sonic realms that I engaged above. The character "x" grows as a Nahuatl-inspired glyph that colonial expressivity cannot cut back. Certainly, Chinchilla doesn't expect us to take her metaphor literally. Instead, she invites us to focus on the resistance that the growth of roots may encounter and how their movements result in new sprouts, subtly altering the structure and appearance of the root. She employs the metaphor of *wild roots* because they evoke jotería's multiplicity. The composed term *wild roots* can refer to various things: it can refer to edible wild roots like chicory and dandelion, or it can refer to the unruly roots we find in our hair, making it difficult to comb neatly. One might attempt to tame these roots, only to realize that it's a futile effort. Alternatively, one might choose to let one's hair remain untamed, irregular roots and all. This alternative allows one to adapt and embrace more styling options. Regardless of how much one tries to eliminate roots by cutting them off, they tend to multiply from a section or graft of their original structure.

I am inclined to think that jotería resonates with the geophysical irregularities that express an agential poetics of wild roots—spreading, proliferating, adapting, leading, retreating, and sprouting up. Two aspects of the body social among "Central American–Americans" come to the fore in Chinchilla's artful theorizing of bringing jotas, or wild roots, into harmony. Chinchilla capitalizes on dissonance, as in the case of wild roots, to signify jotería and its dual nature of both principled poiesis and intersubjective, excavating project. Dissonance invites excavation of wild roots, such as the sibilant sound that "x" indexes. Through this excavating labor, the decolonial layers of (x)(j)otas emerge. Once again, we could also mention that xotas, jotas, and hotas, a rendering of multiple realities, are underwritten by dispersed otherness rather than mineness.

The statement regarding broken tongues speaking jotas into harmony doesn't imply the need to fix or heal expressivity, nor does it suggest a remedy for the stigma, or wild roots, associated with jotería. Instead, it highlights the principled poiesis of jotería, a performance that encourages bodily, perceptual, cognitive, and affective responses of dissent. Jotería resides in this realm of unruly sonic dissent, where it involves registering what sounds unusual without necessarily revealing any straightforward meanings. Speaking jotería into harmony calls upon interstitial ways of encrypting underground emotions and affects. Most important, however, it instills in us an appreciation for the glyphic and vernacular presence of the Nahuatl "x." This visual trace also summons transitional sounds that fade in and out of the /j/ and /h/ sounds. Ultimately, there can be no *jar-monies* without *x*otas, can there?

Dissonance encourages harmony within jotería worlds. Chinchilla underscores that broken tongues assist in "communing thru generations" (2014, 56). Like trash, dissonance embodies what the sociomaterial order tries to banish from existence. Chinchilla testifies to the eccentric mate-riality of selves who have been banished, such as those that fade in and out of black holes and abyssal geographies. As explained earlier, interlock-ing systems of oppression reduce jotas to waste and trash. The haunt-ing glyph "x" in Mexico wheezes out into sonic and visual afterlives: an *x* being reduced to colonial expression yet not behaving as a conduit of colonial rule. Eerily traversing Central America, Guatemala, and Maya K'iche' lands, jotería poetics cross-dresses as both Spanish and English. This poetics invokes nearness and also-ness, the codetermining mattering of selves, dissembling, passing a glyph for another, a sound for another, and entangling through decolonial sociosomatic reconfigurations. The dynamic of harmonizing jotas and jotas harmonizing doesn't mean that they negate one another.

Messenger maneras draw on the insights gleaned from jotería poetics. They empower solidarity babies to develop skills in transition, translation, and transposition. When mobilized together, these skills enhance responsiveness across generations while providing access to hidden wisdom. Chinchilla's performance art, much like jotería poetics in general, hints at perspectives beyond the colonizing domestication of expressivity. It engages the human because it seeks the (post)posthumanist realms of meaning-making, embodiment, and, as we shall see next, the environment. The following section illustrates a jotería style that underwrites Chinchilla's poetics and its envisioning of the links between the geophysical and sociopolitical epicenters of the Américas.

Volcanic EpiCenters

Chinchilla's messenger maneras manifest networks of dissonant intermediaries. They negotiate the poetics of social justice between past and present, here and there, as well as human and nonhuman. Her artivism comes from a hefty history of collective labor, which she has theorized through the curation of one of the digital iterations of *EpiCentro*. Originally conceived in 2000 by writers Raquel Gutierrez and Marlon Morales, *EpiCentro*'s blog presence defined the project as "an organic literary collective straddling performance, spoken word and testimonial artforms." It was composed of cultural activists of Central American extraction who "write to resurrect memory and inspire action." Gutierrez, of Salvadorian and Mexican descent, and Morales, a Salvadoran American, collaborated with Jessica Grande, Gustavo Guerra Vasquez, and Dalilah Mendez to establish this blog. *EpiCentro* became an influential cultural initiative within the Central American diaspora.

I could bring attention to both the *transfronteriza* and anti-imperial roots of the blog's diasporic identifying practices (Arias 2012; A. Rodríguez 2009). Instead, I want to focus on Chinchilla's artful work as a continuation and recalibration of *EpiCentro*'s. Hers has become over time a complex articulation of the center of America and, simultaneously, of Central America as a social body. Her portrayal is premised not on shared common identities but on the interconnectedness supported by landscapes and bodies. She draws attention to the organic and imagined entanglements that give rise to the epicenter of América. Through her decolonizing poetics, we shall unpack the mattering transitions lying at the heart of the hemisphere.

The etymology of the prefix *epi* designates what lies near to or in the vicinity of another. The preposition *toward* also concerns the semantic field of the prefix. Yet, *toward* emphasizes the relational configurations of mattering, at once inter-active and intra-active, at once location, orientation, and position. Neighboring locales, ecologies, and communities find definition not solely in their intrinsic characteristics but rather in the intricate web of relationships that interweave, and intraweave, their existence. As we learn next, contemporary cultural workers redefine our understanding of Central America and its epicenter by undertaking unprecedented ways of coding ontological, epistemic, and political claims.

Contributing to the collective *EpiCentro*, Chinchilla develops her writing style, referencing cultural, political, and natural configurations at the heart of Central American identities. This epicenter spasms from the bowels of a continent plagued by "bombs and gunfire" (2014, 21), an unbolted fury fueled by colonial and imperial histories—from Spanish colonialism to US interventions, and from ravaging extractivism to environmental racism. The opening lines to her now landmark poem "Central American–American" agitate readers with artful wisdom. They disrupt our understanding of an epicenter, prompting questions about the very nature of being and knowing "Centralamerican American."

Bombs and gunfire are tropes that often vilify the region's populations. The symbolic force of the tropes builds on an infamous volcanic nature that ruling regimes, both colonial and not, employ to rationalize violence against marginalized groups from Central America, especially when these groups defy their subjugation as has been the case, for example, through Indigenous insurrection and *cimarron* uprising. There is a geophysical and chemical architecture to volcanoes. It consists of at least a twofold structure: (1) their skirts have the deepest hem, all the way down to the chambers where magma and its gases accumulate, and (2) their mouths communicate the ongoing motions of tectonic plates, either because the very opening originates with collisions and tears between plates or because lava adopts varying degrees of activity. This dual structure integrates both liquid and gas, and their interaction, with the topographical features of vents and openings. Far removed from magma chambers, volcanic mouths roll lava out, sometimes with exquisite precision, layer upon layer, preserving the internal sutures that support the volcano's bodice. Agentic entanglements of inorganic matter therein ongoingly reconfigure centers, epicenters, and margins.

Chinchilla's focus on volcanoes reminds us of her initial question about the space that "comes with" "Central American–American." Many fault lines run throughout the spine of the continent, known as the American Cordillera, connecting what might otherwise seem disparate and broken. These fault lines bring north and south together, but they remain disjointed. Dangerously hanging on to the fine thread of dormant vibrations, north and south converge in odd synchronicity at the waist of the Américas. I interpret Chinchilla's question about the space, the fault lines, that "comes with" Central America as a geopolitical gesture. It draws a parallel between the volcanic nature of Central America and both past and contemporary descriptions of the region as untamable, unendingly grappling with instability, political distress, and explosive conflict. However, I argue that the geophysical structure of the region cannot solely be understood through these discourses. Similarly, we cannot dissociate pervasive ideas of eruption and intensity surrounding the region from the rebellion of its marginalized groups. By examining both the physical landscape and the sociopolitical dynamics, we gain a deeper understanding of the interconnectedness of Central America's natural and human landscapes. This interconnectedness gains greater relevance, since Chinchilla's poetics spins the journey, against the legacy of species stagnation, toward nonconforming or even decolonizing ways of living and knowing.

The poem "Central American–American" introduces diasporic pluriverses with a visual conundrum:

Central American–American

Centralamerican   American
does that come with a hyphen?
a space?
Central   America
America
América
Las   Américas

Pluriverse has emerged as both practice and horizon in the pursuit of an analytics of problems and an envisioning of solutions that center historically situated approaches to the world and science. It often expands on oppositional and post-oppositional responses to Westernization while crafting resonating ontologies, epistemologies, and political ideologies (Reiter 2018; Connell 2018; Harding 2018). I suggest that the neologism "Central American–American" is a way of naming an ontology, epistemology, and political ideology that arises on behalf of Abya Yala and diasporic jotería migrants. Intervening in this fashion, Chinchilla works on the specificity of Central America while evoking key methods for decolonizing the center of the continent and its many guises. She begins by displaying "Central American–American" as a glyphic trace, demanding a sensorial response. The poem as a visual sign elicits dis-ease, an off-center pivot where we meet "Centralamerican American." It juxtaposes manifestations of strikingly similar forms over a nonlinear sequence.

Chinchilla asks whether "Centralamerican American" comes "with a hyphen" (2014, 21). We may consider whether the hyphen lends clarification force to the compound that the poet creates, or whether it allows diasporic subjects to dwell in-between the dynamic of departure and arrival. The hyphen seeks to tidy up the messy connection between leaving and coming, attempting to smooth out the striated perils of diasporic communities. As a symbol, this punctuation mark lives on as a reminder of what is no longer here. Chinchilla's poetic turn invites me to think of Central America as a hollow presence. It is not surprising that both neo-colonial and left-leaning discourses rely on this notion of the region as boiling hollowness, always nearing eruption. The hyphen is underwritten by the logic of an absence, haunted by enduring traces left behind, simultaneously signifying both pause and drive, a recoiling foreground and an advancing background.

I propose that we delve into the interplay between banishment and return, not only where what goes missing and continues to haunt us intersect but also where they refract. As we have previously discussed regarding sideways selves, hypervisibility and invisibility mutually reinforce each other. This dynamic of banishment and return resembles the logics of intersectionality and refraction. Intersecting lines of power cast Central America as both the geophysical and social site of eruption. Right where this intersection exists, as Chinchilla reminds us, an eruption unlocks the mysteries of the unseen, of what lies under the shroud of ash and shadow. The presence of a hyphen, as in "Central American–American," creates a composite from fragmented halves, each reduced to absolute and discrete units. This intersection locks in an order of incommensurable fragments.

The noun *American* renders time into the aftermath of an eruption. It organizes history in its banishing of a center that cannot hold. As a matter of colonial expansion, *American* subjugates *el epicentro* of Abya Yala's identities. *American* describes a discerning body of biopolitical responsiveness. *Central American* instead presents a chaotic epicenter of devouring wild roots. If hyphens are meant to name a reality by coupling units that typically stand on their own, an emerging intersection behaves to some extent as an arbitrary razing of uneven histories. Without the hyphen, an unnerving tension endures, much more so when Chinchilla allows the graph *Centralamerican American* to haunt the continent with the weight of imbalances and conflicts. Refuting hyphenation displaces the urgency to bring order into the volcanic nature of the region. Through this refusal, *CentralAmerican American* refracts contentious realities into the background, into that in-between space from within which diasporic selves pivot sideways.

The poem first signals the textual epicenter of *Centralamerican*, highlighting that myriad subject positions generate diverging fabulations and narratives about the region. A text, however, can also be understood as an attempt at bringing coherence into a world of chaotic meaning. It assumes that meaning responds to sequential encoding. In contrast to this view, Chinchilla examines nonlinguistic elements that fall off the *Central American–American* text. She calls our attention to mountains, volcanoes, and seismic forces. She engages the entangling entanglements that sustain inorganic and organic ways of mattering. By suggesting that texts, fabulations, and narratives share material status with thermal and geophysical agencies and intensities, Chinchilla provides important lessons about the realities and lived experiences of Centralamerican Americans. She points to Central America as a diasporic epicenter where myths need not domesticate matter, land, or space.

Following the form of migrant patterns, Chinchilla unfolds the remaining stanzas in a cascading effect (see stanza above). Often, protagonists and scholars of migration refer to these movements from one region to another in terms of cascading effects, including economic opportunities, influx waves and flows, and networks or family chains. Since Central America is known for its seismic phenomena, the pattern of cascading interconnections also fits the geophysical narration of the region's matter.[29] The poem links geophysics and socioeconomic matters through the figures of eruptions and cascades. I argue that this stylistic and formatting choice highlights interconnectivity as the key notion in the discussion of hyphenation. The poem prompts reflection on how the hyphen bears a hyperreal effect since it cloaks separation, distance, and void under the sign of tight juxtaposition. Discomfort undergirds the reality of hyphens.

In her monograph on *dominicanidad* and diaspora, Lorgia García Peña highlights that *rayanos* (border dwellers) gain affective and epistemic advantages. She cites the liminal unease expressed by the works of Gloria Anzaldúa about the US-Mexico border, Luis Rafael Sánchez on Puerto Rican transnationalism, and Gustavo Pérez Firmat about "Cuban-American" life in the hyphen. This unease shapes the condition of the "border-immigrant-transnational subject" (García Peña 2016, 4).

Understanding that hyphenation intervenes in the ways that diasporic communities make sense of interconnections confirms the assertions that prior chapters raised about culturally specific, twilight-like responses to colonial prompts.

Chinchilla's use of hyphenation extricates a critique of dichotomous thinking, of the splitting of Central American–American identities and embodiments. Hyphenation designates a space-time of reflection about the truths that nonconforming, fractured, and fragmented identities mobilize (Hames-García 2011). Cultural critique scholars usually focus on hyphenated identities as the by-product of minoritizing colonial and national projects (Pérez Firmat 1994; Flores 2001). I suggest that, without denying the significance of split identities, Chinchilla seeks to query the diasporic body's responsiveness to multiple timelines, including the past and present of decolonization. Her poetics makes room to examine simultaneity of multiple realities in the embodiments of Centralamerican Americans. Multiplicity haunts the presumptive ordering that hyphenation sanctions.

Inquiring into this multiplicity, Chinchilla's poetry engages time, space, identity, embodiment, and political ideology. By *multiplicity*, I refer to what an agential realism describes as contingent relationality, both through inter- and intra-connectedness. Primitivist views of the center of the continent, we may argue, follow a more modernist notion of interconnection, which builds on leveling operations that render connectedness into a process, first, of fragmentation and, second, of subordination. Instead, Chinchilla defies the modernist notion by presenting *EpiCentro* as one of the sociosomatic forms of diasporic pluriverses. At this *EpiCentro*, Salvadoran, Guatemalan, Mexican, and—why not—K'iche', Oaxacan, and Argentinean embodiments ongoingly reach backward/forward from present to past and back. *Centralamerican American* challenges the hyphenating pause, which seeks to neatly tie together species-stagnant Central America and forward-looking America.

The space that unfolds between the title and the first verse offers to our senses an imaging of emptied expansiveness and distant void. This imaging opens into duplicitous hollowness, evoking entangled agencies of black holes that upend their invisibility from the location of a specific *nowhere*. The visual brokenness and spatial dissonance of the first stanza appear as formal elements to our perception. While the poem aligns with the left margin, it also undulates unevenly on the right, a fitting glyph or sensorial marker of a spoken word performance emerging from "the center of America" (Chinchilla 2014, 21). Notably, the central place on the page is not at the geometric center but rather off-center, enacting an eccentric entangling.

Syncopation in music consists of unexpectedly accentuating a note. It emphasizes the offbeat, making for a more lively dynamic. Latin music, such as the cha cha that gives a title to Chinchilla's book, often employs syncopation.[30] The stanzas previously presented rely on pauses and spaces to accentuate waves of sounds and signs, creating breaks in the performer's voice and the readers' or audience's act of listening. Additionally, the visual and sonic waves undertake a process of reduplication. The poem repeats words such as "America" and "Central America" and introduces their full or partial homophones like "América," "Centralamerica," and "Central American–American." Chinchilla's poem engages syncopation, emphasizing the offbeat, "Centralamerica," in unexpected fashion.

The poem's sonic and linguistic space come into being through anadiplosis, linking separate units of discourse by duplicating and reduplicating the last element of the preceding line or word. "Central America" precedes "America," while "América" follows the latter. Halting a visual sequence and filling gaps with echoing sounds materialize the poem's many epicenters. They express, over and through the very matter of the page, the forces that cleave open the first stanza. All elements combined, Chinchilla makes us think of hyphenation as a concrete form of mattering, of assembling vibrations, voices, glyphs, and signs. She invites us to reflect on the hyphen's materiality as it negotiates American and Central American, and their pluriverses of centers and margins.

In the transition from title to first verse, chosen fonts intensify rocking motions that boil between and under *Central American–American* and *Centralamerican American*. The larger font of the title helps enhance the hyphenating operation of *Central American–American*. Size allows this subordinating intersection to hang over the top of the page with greater hierarchy. Visually, however, this scale also transitions from a scripted straight line into a blank space that drifts outwards. Including a hyphen, "Central American–American" lays out the proper orthographic convention that cordons off its own immediate surroundings. An epicenter materializes on the page, and, through the performative resonances of the verses and their spacing, matter and its enigmatic natural force come through, stretching outwards and spinning sideways. This visual aspect of the poetic performance amplifies a pattern of intraconnectivity. It foregrounds the shifting assembling of the American Cordillera as it anchors both carriage and breakage, as well as seismic waves and friction.

Matters That Matter

It is tempting to follow the geophysical rhetoric in Chinchilla's poetry as a blueprint for thinking about Central American diasporic embodiments. We must remember, however, that colonizing narratives and practices remain in the background, shaping an imaginary link between unknown land and nature's force. Colonial chronicles document the arrival of the Spaniards to Yucatán and present-day Guatemala. They assign monstrous forms to the nature of the "center of America," where Chinchilla finds her heart (2014, 21). Blas González was one of the early conquistadores in the Yucatán region. His 1567 *probanza* offers a stark portrayal of the area as both unwelcoming and untamed. He goes on to equate the Indigenous people's perceived "savage" customs with their belligerent nature against the invaders' authoritarian assertion of religious superiority. Concerning the Spaniards' invasion of the Chauaca region, González states: "I had to take care of a lot of work and I had to share a lot of work with others since the land was monstrous and the people belligerent, and there was no water; ultimately, I was one of the first conquerors" (Chamberlain 1948). Tropes of barbaric idleness link the early mission of genocide to the Spanish model of settler colonialism. They hold together the "unbridled degeneracy" of Native populations, which theologians of the time code as species stagnation (1552; Las Casas 2004), and the land's virginal (in)fertility. It is worth noting that González acknowledges the absence of water in Chauaca, but he does not offer any explanation for how the "belligerent" people in the region secured their own sources of sustenance and hydration.

In alignment with this marking of species stagnation, early chronicles describe land as susceptible to turning from virginal to anthropophagous. Far from neatly differentiating between passive Indigeneity and active invaders, colonial chronicles ambivalently deal with Native physicality, behavior, and environment. Colonial discourses depicted Indigeneity as nefariously agentic. They expressed fear of Native people's capacity to spread sin and disease, as well as swallow conquerors. By coupling land and environment with its inhabitants, chroniclers appropriated the present tense. Eventually, as documented by historians such as Nancy Appelbaum, Anne S. Macpherson, and Karin Alejandra Rosemblatt (2003), the Latin American nation-state hacked into colonial classifications that the chroniclers first justified. Histories of colonial situations cannot be reduced to flattening dynamics between invaders and invaded "others" (De Lima Grecco and Schuster 2020). However, chronicles did set the rhetorical stage to domesticate Abya Yala. If Central America emerged as a postcolonial polity of independence, it also entailed the subordination of Indigenous and Afro-diasporic peoples—among them, Garifuna, Kuna, Lenca, Maya, Miskito, Nahuatl, and Rama peoples. Domestication of land went far beyond an othering rhetorics. Rather, it gave birth to an extractivist operation, which at once made attributions regarding organic lives and inorganic resources.

Chinchilla's poem about Central America performs an exquisite job of knitting notions of revolution and insurgency together with volcanoes' activity and seismic friction. Since the colonial record couples land and people's behavior in similar fashion, I contend that Chinchilla's files spread lessons on how to unlearn the colonialist allocation of vital force between human (*bio*) and nonhuman (*zoe*) and between organic lives and inorganic resources. Consider the depiction of the Carib populations of the Lesser Antilles in the fifteenth century. From the very inception of the colonial quest, Columbus and his chronicling create a specific genre of truth-making. He insists on portraying the Caribs as cruel, cannibalistic, and bellicose. His genre relies on transferring the unknowability of the environment, the impossibility of accessing the lay of the land, onto its inhabitants.

Scholars argue that the Caribs were not original to the lesser Antilles and that they likely migrated from the south, specifically the Orinoco Valley (Rouse 1986; Patterson 1991).[31] Historical records describe them as ferocious vagrants whose expansion project included killing their Arawak neighbors and marrying their spouses. Furthermore, in the latter half of the sixteenth century, a mythology arose casting the Amazonian jungle as a hostile and voracious environment, capable of swallowing and keeping captive even the most seasoned explorers (Borchard 2010). In other words, this mythology bifurcates the provenance of the first peoples the colonizers encountered on their way toward unbound expansion. It places the Caribs, and by extension, Central Americans, within the historical context of Amazonian anthropophagy through temporal associations (see also Rouse 1993, 495–496).

Chinchilla responds to the colonizing ways that render Central America a lagging impossibility. She directs our attention to the haunting dormancy of both the geophysical environment and the dwellers it houses. As discussed earlier, volcanic eruptions remit to interconnectedness of systems, to inactivity and motion. Convergence, divergence, and lateral movements are major forms of tectonic activity. They can help us understand the Earth's layers and the constant drifting of its uppermost crust or lithosphere. Seismic behaviors such as volcanoes and earthquakes originate from plates that the continent is yet to settle. Their motions may converge, diverge, or slip sideways. Some of this activity typically remains imperceptible to most, while in other instances it bursts out in lava showers or mountain ranges. Dormant and latent motions build up to the verge of eruption.

Volcanic formation in Guatemala is the result of the Cocos Plate and the Caribbean Plate colliding, with the former pushing down on and at once being pushed beneath the latter. For Chinchilla's jota poetics, the center in *EpiCentro* and in the center of the Américas evokes the "skirts of a volcano con su boca ebullada [with its blistering mouth]" (2014, 57). Does the sensation of a blistering mouth evoke the haunting recurrence of plates colliding in the depths of an underground, often merging seamlessly and yet breaking with unanticipated intensity? Pulsing magma and blistering mouth connect through a shared rhythm of unexpected patterns. As occurs in the music phenomenon known as syncopation, which consists of accenting unusual beats, volcanic realities unfold through irregular and unconventional displacements. This way of mattering at the epicentro, at the very heart of volcanic formations, offers an exceptional account of the centers of América. It hints at the tense coexistence, not always agonistic, between colonial constructs of Central America as cannibalistic and Abya Yala's realities breaking into multiple intensities.

Chinchilla's jotería poetics becomes a rehearsal for subjectivities that dwell in the multiple realities of Abya Yala's epicentro. It gestures toward an ontological framework that lies deep within Indigenous and non-Western philosophies. Her poetics helps us understand a volcano and ourselves as a web of entangling entanglements. Its configuration begins with the emergence of molten magma from a tectonic rift, which, subsequently cooling down, will harden, carving thereby channels for liquid magma to reach the surface. This process occurs at the outer edges of tectonic plates, where various degrees of materiality coexist. These tectonic forces adapt to a multimodal reality characterized by differing degrees of solidification.

It wouldn't be surprising if we read Chinchilla's careful attention to volcanoes as the jotería way of reworking experiences, affects, and ideologies while linking them to both the matter of the center of América and the matters that matter at the Américas' centers. She avails the collective of diasporic Centralamerican Americans with the jotería methods of adaptation, transformation, and reaffirmation among tectonic entanglements but also among the coexisting realities we have come to appreciate in the duplicitous constructs *jotas*, *xotas*, and *hotas*.

By engaging *The Cha Cha Files*, we have arrived at a deeply situated and finely attuned account of nonconforming matter. We examined unusual, off-the-center, syncopated ways of thinking and experiencing the centers of the Américas. From within multiple realities, we encountered damaging operations that remove alternatives to the legacy of the human from the sites of diaspora, revolutionary subjectivity, and jotería poetics. These sites coexist at the duplicitous stage of both matter and matters. The damaging legacy of the human persists today in preemptive attempts at humanizing the matter and matters of Abya Yala into Central America, revolution into progress, and volcanic nature into species stagnation.

In the case of Chinchilla's invocation, *Central American–American* is a mattering process, a sociosomatic response, that sanctions the harm that colonialism authorized. Centralamerican Americans matter, because we engage more than a posthumanist response to the sociosomatic of dehumanization. Indeed, by following the syncopated rhythm of *The Cha Cha Files*, and their dissonant messenger maneras, we contend with the myriad enticements of posthumanization. They reveal that posthumanist intentions can often be as destructive as both humanization and dehumanization.

Jotería poetics offers Chinchilla a standpoint to make sense of the Américas' epicenters. In her *Cha Cha Files*, jotería presents simultaneously as practice and social process. By affirming *Centralamerican American*, her poetics examines and enacts a bodily practice and sociocomatic process of dissent. Jotería as body social, as sociosomatic entanglement of diasporas, enlivens many centers of the Américas. Out of blistering mouths, we acquire "broken tongues [who] speak jotas into harmony" (Chinchilla 2014, 56). Cacophony, voseo, and cha cha inspire an otherworldly humming. At the hyphen of *Central American–American* lives an *x* glyph, such as the one we find in *xotería*, a sonic and visual dissonance of diasporic configurations underwritten by Indigenous systems of knowledge. Dissonance across generations and revolutionary projects summons a novel subjectivity of dissemination, which invites us to engage and cultivate messenger maneras. They sound unprecedented songs of solidarity, listened to and joined by babies and honees who tag, encode, and encrypt the erotics of embodied multiplicities, the pluriverses of flesh beyond the genre of the human, and the mattering of selves through reciprocal interdependencies. At this juncture, we may begin to discern in a dispersed yet collectivist style the germination of sideways selves as we bud with and brood jotería erotics.

Afterword

Beloved Mom and Dad,

I'm writing to you from the year 2024 and from Haudenosaunee territory. Who would have imagined that I would live this long? In my childhood, I would show up by the side of your bed after midnight to ask whether I could cuddle with you. I was afraid that the world would end in the year 2000. I won't tell you about technologies that we now have, because it would overwhelm you, especially you, my never-forgotten Mom, since you made your transition back in the mid-80s. Wherever you are, and if you happen to be together, Dad must have already told you that there is something called the Internet. I know, I know. Isn't it hilarious?

I'm writing to tell you that I've just finished writing a book. It would be a bit arrogant if I said that it's all mine. In fact, it belongs to the knowledge and practice of many communities that sustain my heart and spirit, and with whom we navigate toward social justice and everyday justice. It also belongs, in part, to you.

I won't explain much about how I became a person who bridges social movements and university. You almost thought that I had written one of those novels or science fiction books, or one of those popular science books, didn't you? I write other kinds of books. At least, I'll tell you that I'm a *profesora* of gender studies, women's studies, and anti-racist trans-feminist theories at a university located in the center of the state of New York. I do research, which means that I collaborate with social movements that examine the material and historical causes behind unjust, discriminatory, and dehumanizing realities.

I'm like a weaver, weaving fabrics with theoretical and practical threads that come from various ways of thinking and doing. For example, I turn to philosophical reflections on the experience and practice of communities whenever they affirm realities beyond normative arrangements, specifically, when they point beyond normative sexualities, beyond racializing dynamics that differentiate between superior and inferior beings, and beyond genders, such as male and female, that efficiently fit within that ableist institution we call the family. I also turn to cultural interpretations of what is most specific to those who construct these nonnormative, nonracist, nonsexist, or nonableist realities. Between philosophizing and interpreting, I learn to listen with a lot of ears and senses. These senses are so many that, quite often, it is difficult to label the most specific aspects of these realities. In this letter, you will notice that I use words that perhaps you have not heard before. I sometimes resort to these words because I am trying to avoid labels that are way too loaded for the points that I would like to raise. I use these words to talk about the most specific aspects of these realities. Some of these words are *Latinx people, Afro-Latinx people; travesti communities, jotería, trans people and communities,* or *the LGBTQIA+ community; Native and Indigenous people; Abya Yala* and *Turtle Island;* and *coloniality* and *decoloniality.*

I am picking three of these words to expand on: *travesti, trans,* and *jotería.* They are the most central in the fabrics that I am weaving. Try to take these words as invitations to weave. Then, weaving with me, we will be doing the enmeshing of all these threads into one or a few fabrics. Let's start by understanding that they are not words that define a universe of people all over the planet. On the contrary, when I talk about travesti people, I am almost always referring to communities rooted in the northwest of Argentina, in the city of Buenos Aires, and less frequently in Peru and Bolivia. When I talk about trans people, I sometimes also refer to fellow comrades from Argentina, but many others from the United States. I tend to connect with trans people from the Latinx community and other communities of color in this country. When I refer to jotería, I am mainly located in the United States and, particularly, the southwest of this country.

Travesti people are creators of magnificent bodies. They travel between many territories of desire, eroticism, and identity. In the course of building themselves up, they join networks of collaboration and assistance. They often end up homeless when their families can no longer bear the scandal announced by their bodies. Exiled and in transit, they may become sex workers. Through this work, they develop reading and organizing devices with which they do politics, challenging inequalities between social classes, genders, and racial groups.

Trans or transgender people are doing amazing work against the injustice of bodily binaries. For the ruling ideas about the body even today, this dualistic and hierarchical understanding must be marked. It verifies, absolutely and efficiently, and with utmost certainty, an anatomical function of the family as a reproductive unit. That is, as a social and biological unit whose sole purpose is making babies to perpetuate privileges, particularly those related to property, citizenship, and racial superiority.

It is important to tell you that jotería communities originate in Mexican American neighborhoods. The words *joto* and *jota* were used, and are sometimes still used within these contexts, to insult people who renounce normative sexualities and genders. As a way of interrupting this pattern of harm and shame, jotería started to group together. They learned to reclaim what was once a hurtful slur and turn it into a sign of belonging and caring solidarity. While doing this justice work, they also expand their communities by inviting in other people who, identifying as Latinx or migrants from the Americas, shared with them a sense of nonconforming kinship. I myself have learned to commune, to become community, through hemispheric connections between jotería and Latin American travesti and trans communities.

You may be wondering, "How did you come to learn these difficult words?" You may also be wondering why I pour my heart and put my body into these fabrics. What probably surprises you the most (or not) is that I am calling myself a *profesora* or *profesore* these days and not a *profesor* (a male professor). Dad wouldn't be surprised when learning that I'm still living in the belly of the beast. Mom is probably shocked, to say the least. This letter, however, as I told you, is about the book. I prefer to now tell you about the book. After you read this letter, you may begin to imagine possible answers to the questions that you must be asking yourselves about me.

In this book, I am trying to trace a material way of living, knowing, and living together among those of us who are dispossessed. I'm not talking about the type of dispossession that takes place when a person is written off a will, becoming legally barred from ever receiving any assets that families usually pass from one generation to the next. Rather, I am talking about the harmful way in which both state and society neglect and abandon certain people. They neglect us because we are considered troublemakers, a big problem for social, cultural, and economic norms. I am thinking of the lack of protection that threatens the lives of travesti, transgender, and jotería peoples and of many others who do not follow the script of the heterosexual family and, therefore, do not contribute to the efficient functioning of a racist and ableist society. I am referring to this form of dispossession. It feels like living under the condition of being excluded from the group that we call "humanity."

When I think of being dispossessed, I am thinking of feeling abandoned, forgotten, and even under attack. That is, I am concerned about the many ways in which society and its different institutions, such as family, state, school, and church, continually exile and expel travesti, transgender, and so many others. We do not fit within the heterosexual, racist, and ableist family. We are those people who have become the last ones in line.

I have realized that, just like it happens to travesti, trans, and nonheterosexual and nonbinary people, I grew up within a context of precarity. I also got used to being something like dispossessed. Sometimes, I even had doubts about whether my life was worth living. At school, they shouted horrible things at us and even beat us. At home, they told us that we were the reason for those horrible things and beatings, that we had to change and be more normal and less flashy. In church, they made us feel the target of all jokes and the cause of a fateful future. The state, if we could understand what the state was, remained absent.

Do you remember, Mom, when you found me playing doctor and patient with the neighbor? Do you remember making me promise to you and Dad that I would never partake in touching another boy's body or let any boy touch my own, ever again? You made me kneel in front of the rosary that was hanging on the living room wall, and there you left me praying for an hour, not even seven years old, supposedly repenting for the sins of my flesh. I admit that it was a bit out of place for the neighbor and me to touch each other under our clothes. But, to me, it felt like a game of recognition and affirmation. It wasn't *that* bad. Well, I'm referring to that type of harm that intertwines several social institutions and that, by taking residence in the flesh of our being, condemns us to shame, exile, and abandonment.

Another example would be the shame that you both, Mom and Dad, felt for having abandoned the families you had already formed before meeting each other. You left them to embark on a life and family together. When I grew up, I found out that you filed a birth certificate for me at the smallest and most remote city clerk office you found in the province of Jujuy. You were determined not to disclose, to any of your neighbors in town, that you were living together without a marriage certificate. Do you two realize how family, church, and state are intertwined, and how they collaborate with each other to classify people as dangerous and deviant and, therefore, make them attackable, harmful, and forgettable?

This book deals with that social, cultural, and bodily way of living, knowing, and living together that allows dispossessed communities to affirm our own possibilities. In that affirmation, we include a cornucopia of creations, meditations, ceremonies, remedies, and healings. What matters to us is to build ourselves with a politics of love and eroticism that points beyond the mold of humanity, a mold that seems so normal and essential to most of society. Returning to the example I gave you about the shame you felt for not being married, either by church or by civil ceremony, it is possible to recognize, and I'm sure you did, that all the effort you put into building us as a family went beyond the common mold of normality. Going beyond the normal implies a bunch of actions, very creative ones, to practice new senses of being and making kin. I hope you understand why I am focusing on those creative forces that dispossessed communities generate while hallucinating alternative realities.

The book pays special attention, precisely, to those acts of intellectual, political, and aesthetic creation. I am in awe of people who, facing such magnitude of dispossession, deploy operations and relationships that long for and seek the impossible, that channel energies toward communal healing and care. Throughout the writing, I focus on five practices that manifest these productive and communal energies:

1. Analyzing the situation of vulnerability faced by collectives of sex and gender dissidence, such as travesti and jotería communities. This analysis is called *transversalidad* within Latin American travesti/trans theory, and *weness* or *nostredad* within jotería studies in the United States.

2. Reconfiguring the understanding of bodies and bodily practices when they are constructed by travesti, trans, and jotería collectives. This reconfiguration includes a rather novel model that distinguishes between Gender (with a capitalized G and in singular), *genders* (with lower case, in plural, and in italics), and "genders" (in quotation marks, in lower case, and in plural). The model accounts for different habits of the flesh according to the historical relationship between colonialism, its legacy in the present, and various processes of decolonization of knowledge, doing, and living.

3. Learning to disregard the presuppositions that Gender and *genders* track. By unlearning and unlistening to Gender and *genders*, we gravitate toward the politics of bodies that Indigenous philosophies, practices, and ceremonies sustain and justify. I refer to philosophies among Aymara, Quechua, K'iche', Kuna, Maya, and Nahua

communities, to name just a few. It is a practice that begins to displace the idea that travesti, trans, and jotería collectives only exist as a recent or modern invention or as constructions that seek to overcome their supposed primitive and perverse condition.

4. Discerning the way in which what I am calling "genders" configure carnal politics through hallucinating knowledge and action. In the cultural productions of Latinx, Afro-Latinx, and Xicanx communities, such as literature and plays, hallucinations are used to respond to the abuse and harm that colonialism set off. In this way, the carnal relationship between the current generation and the next proposes alternative worlds—with sensations, emotions, gestures, sounds, and flavors—through which these communities cultivate relationships of kinship, love, and friendship. These relationships emerge as hallucinations—that is, almost like portals to a parallel present that decenters the power of the heterosexual, nationalist, and ableist family. Precedents for these hallucinations can be found in pre-Columbian visual and philosophical arts.

5. Invoking various senses of solidarity that resonate with the poetics of dissonance in jotería communities. Displacements and exiles generate dissonances. For example, there is dissonance among revolutionary projects of different generations. The way that social justice collectives mobilized against dictatorships in the 1970s and 1980s within South and Central America is quite different from how we do solidarity today within Latinx and Afro-Latinx communities in the United States. The poetics of jotería entails affective and bodily activity, an artful doing of care and collaboration. Through this poetics, we foster ways of doing solidarity across time and space.

As I write this letter, I am reminded of the style of communication that nourished our relationship, from your generation to mine. While I teach as part of my job, I also practice humility, which I hope allows me to recognize that you continue to be my teachers. I still carry with me a certain fascination with chemistry that I learned from you both. With you, Mom, I learned about the magic that bleach, salt, and lemon can cast on fabrics and textiles. That's how we refreshed and cleaned tablecloths, dish towels, sheets, and even my clothes. With you, Dad, we played with the effects of acetone, salt, baking soda, and vinegar on the tempera paints I used for my school projects. We taught and learned from each other the art of revealing, through magic, what lies dormant, latent, in a mysterious nature.

Applying those principles of engagement with enigmatic forces, I propose that we learn from some slices, or prints, with which the book illustrates knowledges and practices stemming from travesti, trans, and jotería communities. Printmaking is a visual art that is based on chemical principles that reveal dimensions of reality that are not always evident. Each of the practices I have already described, and with which I organized the book, originates with this revelation work. Its chemistry announces a new physics, one that disputes colonial legacies while affirming sacred worlds of collaboration and reciprocity.

Print One: *Transversalidad* and *Nostredad*

On a map of differences, power patterns exile and hide travestis/trans and jotería communities. In a way, this kind of map neutralizes differences. Tourism in Argentina imagines the center of the country, Buenos Aires, as a great metropolis that includes gay and lesbian communities. Similar power patterns represent the northwest as a reservoir of Indigenous cultures on the brink of extinction. In this imaginary, both the center and northwest of the country lack travesti and trans individuals. This map is about not only cultural regulations but also material structures of expulsion of people, environmental negligence, and dispossession of Indigenous sovereignty and Afro-Argentines. It's like a black hole.

Those of us who understand the physics and chemistry of this geometry of power perceive dispossessed communities even when the state and capital enterprise seek to have them banished. The immigration apparatus in the United States also makes jotería individuals disappear. They arrest and imprison people who are migrating from Central America and treat them as if they were a herd of cattle, as if they were to be contained and then tortured and domesticated. Mind you that I equally disagree with the insidious technologies that subject cattle to torture. Many among jotería migrate because capital and gender norms expel them from their places of origin. From within this abyss, from within black holes, both jotería and travesti communities organize themselves, giving rise to nostredad. As we generate that sense of *we*ness, we attend to the specificities of our dispossession—but also, to the multiple connections we recognize in our condition of dispossession.

Just as you and I worked creating prints that revealed a hidden chemistry and physics among textiles and tempera paints, so too do these communities, as they unveil what could only be perceived from within their standpoints. Fellow travesti comrades Lohana Berkins, Marlene Wayar, Susy Shock, and Florencia Guimaraes account for an orientation that allows them, as Berkins would say, to *transversally* confront a "shithole reality"—the condition of being treated as excrement—and simultaneously pilgrimage among various abysses and drains. Transversalidad is a technology of decipherment and engagement. It recognizes and responds to racist and extractivist capitalism and, at the same time, reconfigures the flesh when its politics emerge from a lateral orientation, from a sideways repositioning.

Less uniform and less normative embodiments underwrite dispossessed communities, thus giving birth to collateral subjectivities. I give a new meaning to the word *collateral*. On one end, I refer to that lateral, or sideways, orientation that addresses those who are beside us and not those who are in front of us. On the other end, I also allude to the cooperation that sustains that orientation. Companionship comes with the prefix *com*, which means "together" or "to share." The notion of cooperation and companionship is associated with togetherness, which we experience while pilgrimaging through social margins. Between cooperation, companionship, and marginal orientation, the term "sideways" emerges. You and I behave as sideways selves.

Sideways selves link in within their specific communities but also with more hemispheric, wider constellations and enclaves. Together with activists and intellectuals Jennicet Gutiérrez and Suyapa Portillo Villeda, we have been linking in a hemispheric nostredad, exploring the aftermath of colonialism and its imposition of dehumanization as a system of discipline and control over all forms of carnal and erotic expression. A collective under the name of AJAAS (Association of Jotería Arts, Activism, and Scholarship) in the United States amplifies the notion of nostredad by developing a political project, a cooperative movement, and a site of identification. In this way, we contribute to practicing eroticism, desire, and embodiment in antisystemic ways.

Print Two: Gender, *genders*, "genders"

This meditation is somewhat complicated but no less important. Dad witnessed the uprising of ethnic and sexual and feminist minorities, but Mom, you missed all of that. How can I explain what I want to say, trying to respect the page's limitations without losing depth? In various parts of the world, people who identify as lesbian, gay, transgender, transsexual, bisexual, and intersex have legal protections against discrimination. For example, today people who do not identify as either male or female can get married. Along with these protections, various social and cultural movements, such as feminisms and gender studies, have developed insightful critiques of the reality of sex and gender. That is, behind these protections against discrimination, which states and societies evidently tolerate today more or less than in years past, various circles of activists and scholars have offered radical examinations of the gender binary, its origins and sinister impacts. As capitalism loves to package everything, it has also learned to package these examinations, making them circulate endlessly as if they were the only, entire, and totalizing truths.

Currently, for example, some of us are fortunate to have access to what is called trans healthcare. This type of care seeks to affirm gender expression for any person. However, in a country such as the United States, access depends on other variables. At least in theory, it exists for some privileged people and within more accepting jurisdictions. If you live in one of those states or countries with laws that ban trans-exclusionary policies in the healthcare system, you can access treatments that affirm gender expression. That is, gender can be conceived as a horizon and not just as biological or sociocultural destiny. Even in the state of New York, where I live, the medical system considers transgender people as suffering from a condition known as "gender dysphoria." With this diagnosis, transgender people are understood as people who live with a mental health condition, whose needs demand redress and treatment. What we have much less of, unfortunately, is access to community knowledge authorizing our own questions, as clients or patients, about the universality of those dominant models that the medical establishment employs to deal with gender and sexuality.

This dominant model centers an individual and its intrinsic attributes. According to clinical knowledge, an individual is either this or that, male or female. The clinic reproduces unequal values, distributing vitality among, on one end, bodies that conform to reproducibility and, on the other, bodies that do not. What I'm telling you next comes from the standpoints of travesti, trans, and jotería communities with whom I collaborate. What often hurts us is that the contemporary medical-legal model favors self-realization over less individualistic and more communal and ancestral ways of making sense of embodiments. As it occurs with the metaphor of the black holes that I described earlier, dispossessed communities lack opportunities to counteract this notion of transgender as a universal sieve. This universal slant connects transgender solely to

transitioning from one gender to another. Other social forms of nonconforming embodiments fall off the abyss into the depth of black holes. We
often get lip service about the notion of transgender being always already
about race, about class, and about ability.

The unusual thing, though, is that all that medical, legal, and academic
knowledge that aligns behind the idea that transgender is a universal
occurrence has not found a way to respond to patterns that colonialism initiated. By *pattern*, I mean a mode of control and regulation. For
instance, conquerors who invaded Abya Yala classified as perversion and
sin any carnal intimacy that was not justified by a supposedly natural
model of kinship, a husband with a penis and a wife with a vagina. They
demonized everything and anything that did not correspond to these
ideas of the Old World. There are colonial documents describing colonial envoys burning Indigenous people alive whenever Native peoples
related to each other through bodily practices that did not coincide with
the habits of the nuclear family. They also document torturous treatment
against African and American Black populations that colonizers and, later,
mixed-race populations enslaved. I just mentioned another one of those
words. This time it is *Abya Yala*, which is borrowed from the Indigenous
Kuna language and which many communities utilize with anti-colonial
goals. Abya Yala relates to the continent that the conquest rechristened
America.

We rarely find social and legal frameworks that allow us to question
the limits of the human, or the cast or prototype of the human, especially
with respect to gender and embodiment. Many of us were never human,
nor do we aspire to be. Therefore, and consequently, we are very cautious
about promoting the idea that bodily transition works as another way of
becoming human or more human.

To explain these divergent practical positions and horizons, insofar as
they relate to the dispossessed communities I have been talking about, I
am putting forward a three-pronged schema. It accounts for bodily practices and their horizons regarding bodily habits. I am thinking of a body
that is neither given nor immutable. It responds because of its responsive
characteristics, at once a product and productive. Do you remember, Dad,
how you used to giggle when you felt out of place at a social gathering? It
was something like a reaction, not only reactive but also proactive. A habit
in your flesh, I believe, that you had learned over time and with which you
weighed and navigated the consequences of exposing your situation, your
condition as a man who grew up in the countryside and who did not have
access to university education or the social manners of the middle class.

Our bodies are, indeed, productive and at once produced. This is what I call the body as impressionable, susceptible to responding and being responded to and corresponded with.

By focusing on those habits of impressibility, I elaborate a schema that explains decades and sometimes centuries of carnal politics. At the heart of the matter is coloniality, a pattern of power that orders social relations based on the imposition of race as a planetary classification of all people. This pattern began with the conquests launched by monarchic powers at the end of the fifteenth century. María Lugones, a mentor and teacher whom I greatly admire, points out that coloniality introduces gender as a metaphysical imposition. Yes, I know, another word that leaves you puzzled. What she means by *metaphysics* are those categories of understanding that make reality meaningful. Think of our lay understanding of fruits and veggies. Typically, you think of them as sweet and savory things that we eat. If you dig a bit deeper, you will notice that most fruits are like the flowers of a plant and that they contain seeds. Veggies, unlike fruits, do not contain seeds and we eat many of their parts, not just the flowery part. To differentiate fruits from veggies, we identify the relations that they have alongside other forms of organic lives, what roles they play, and what processes are involved in what they do or generate. This is how we go about understanding metaphysical categories. Within these categories, we find frameworks that make reality meaningful. We won't try to find seeds in either the stems or flowers of broccoli, because, in fact, they do not behave as fruits. There are, of course, stark differences between fruits and social facts. For now, we'll leave that tangent for the next letter.

Going back to my mentor María and her statement about gender. She argues that colonialism introduced gender as a metaphysical category, which in turn instilled, from then onwards, a binary and biological framework to make sense of people whom colonizers counted and did not count as humans. For María, a colonial account of gender justifies the cognitive needs of capitalism and the nuclear family. Capitalism is an economic system wherein those who own means of production seek to accumulate profits by exploiting the working class. You two and I are part of the working class. We have our labor to make a living. In your case, Mom, your labor went mostly unpaid and unwaged. Within the nuclear family, those positions of hierarchy get reproduced, and benefits ripped, from one generation to the next. Many people who do the work that I do have, in the past, argued that "gender" is a type of pervasive hierarchy across societies and within the nuclear family. María began to think about the historical emergence of this hierarchy and challenged the idea that gender has always been at work as a hierarchy across all time and space. She provided ample evidence about the colonial introduction of gender and, especially, about the ways that racialization efficiently but also contradictorily uses bodily differences to hierarchically distinguish between those who possessed the attributes of gender, male and female, and those who lacked them (enslaved and indentured populations). This distinction determined the humanity and exploitability of peoples. The more controllable through slavery and servitude Native peoples and the peoples from Africa were, the greater their exclusion from the universe of *men* and *women*.

I don't want you to forget that I am building these points to talk about the schema that I have put together as I make sense of habits of the flesh within colonialism's legacy. María cared more about intentions and motivations among peoples who are pushed to treat some as nonpeople within conflicting material histories. In addition to the intentions of those denied gender, I am interested in what two feminist teachers, M. Jacqui Alexander and Laura Elisa Pérez, call the sacred. That is, I am interested in how the mysteries of nature and, above all, of the spiritual world come to reside in our bodies. I am interested in the sacred as a logical implication of María's point about gender being a colonial introduction. If colonialism introduced gender, how did Native and Indigenous peoples of Abya Yala, and Afro-descendants in the Americas, come to frame the body within a reality where everything, both of this world and otherworldly, manifests as inseparable?

Earlier, I suggested that I consider bodies to be both produced and productive. They demand an energetic expenditure or output. If the reproduction of the nuclear family is not the purpose of our bodies, what can we, then, learn from the creative expenditures that go into generating travesti, trans, and jotería embodiments? This mysterious and enigmatic outpouring is what pushed me to elaborate a schema that no longer speaks only of gender but differentiates among Gender, *genders*, and "genders."

By Gender, I understand the bodily behaviors of those who reproduce white and ableist superiority through the nuclear family. This institution is based on principles of hierarchy, asymmetry, confinement, invariability, and uniformity. With the idea of *genders*, I account for bodily behaviors among those who, racialized as not-quite-humans, can approach but never establish themselves as reproducers of the nuclear family. Currently, as I told you earlier, even lesbian, gay, and transgender people can get married and formally access the legality that authorizes the nuclear family. However, in the substantive sense of the nuclear family, lesbian, gay, and transgender communities only assimilate to, especially if they are privileged in terms of race, class, and ability, but never quite fit the cast of the human. Finally, the term "genders" refers to the cluster of bodily behaviors with which dispossessed communities respond to both Gender and *genders* and, simultaneously, establish and recalibrate ways of living, being, and coexisting within principles of reciprocity, symmetry, openness, contingency, and multiplicity. If you are still with me, I appreciate your attention. I really do. I am aware that it will take many sit-downs to go over this letter from beginning to end.

It won't surprise you if I reiterate that, nowadays, many in the transgender community follow bodily patterns of assimilation into the human cast. Travesti, trans, and jotería communities denounce that transgender is becoming a model for revaluing what doctors once turned into monsters. Transgender as a medicolegal category pushes what is monstrous forward and into a human prototype. If in my childhood I was a monster for not fitting into the *genders* order, today I am given a diagnosis to seek treatment. Through treatment, apparently, I am made into less of a monster and more of a human. Yet, as a negatively racialized person, I am often treated as *less than animal*. While I advocate for the provision of gender affirming care, I remain mindful of the ways that clinical knowledge aligns transitioning with Eurcentered and white-supremacist norms.

Print Three: "genders" Repositories

What I call "genders" express, manifest, and recalibrate social forms that embody multiple realities, plural knowledges, and politics of communion and cooperation. Described as "social forms," they give rise to a repository that, even though it is constantly in flux, shows incredible persistence. The extraordinary thing about this persistence is that we can still recognize this repository despite centuries of attacks and distortions. Do you remember the times when Grandma Rosa prepared homemade remedies for us? Camphor to relieve the respiratory tract, sulfur bars to extract winds from bones, lemon to be applied on eczema, kombucha tea for gastrointestinal issues; and could we recall many other remedies! You will laugh when I tell you that now there are transnational companies that bottle kombucha tea in half-liter containers and sell them for $4 each at the grocery store. Do you remember, Dad, when I was nine years old and you became the provider of the kombucha fungus for all the teachers at my school? Imagine if you had sold them a jar of tea with its fungus, over and over again. But precisely, I refer to *that* when I say that the repository betrays the principles of a system of extraction and dispossession. This is the case because this repository, the one that I am talking about, depends on the act of feeling responsible for the well-being of another person. Therefore, I also speak of the persistence of those social forms that shape and give rise to this repository. Community knowledge and practice are not sold. They belong to a community. They are remedies that we receive through networks of care and cooperation. In the peasant world in which you grew up, Dad, community knowledge is respected. It is a way of remaining autonomous, as many Indigenous communities in our country and other parts of the world have done.

A repository, cultivated with and through "genders," has many sources or origins. I am concerned with listening carefully to and bearing witness of that repository, because dispossessed communities concern me (I am also a part of them). Between the periphery of Jujuy and the periphery of the AfroLatinx and Latinx migration in the United States, we come to realize that *germination* is a verb for everything that exists. It behaves like a verb opposing to and yet pointing beyond the social reproduction of inheritance and dispossession. In the book, I follow a sacred constellation wherein Andean Catholicism, Andean Spanish, hallucinating knowing, and jotería poetics flicker with germinating intensities.

Print Four: Unlistening to Gender and *genders*

You know that one of the ways in which coloniality lives on in the present is through racializing and racist education. It is very clear to me that you and I have had, like, a secret pact. You wanted your children to achieve with public education the professional comfort that you never had. It was the most accessible way to humanize ourselves, becoming less Syrian-Lebanese and more Italian-Argentinean, less like Jujuy's mountains and more like the country's flatlands, less rural and more urban. This humanization, in my own experience, had to do with blurring the sins of the flesh, those that did not fit the norms of a heterosexual, whiteness-centered family. I think that we saw a lot of that anxiety about these norms within the local networks that mattered to us. Our secret pact was about belonging to humanity. By longing to belong, we became complicit in denying Indigenous peoples and Black communities, in abandoning those communities to nationalist, urban, and racist projects.

As a family that saw some value in belonging, we found ourselves in a rather challenging position, where it was even more difficult for us to recognize, respect, and contribute to the repository I have been talking about. Jujuy's Carnaval is one of those festivals where we can try out bodily habits that transform colonial legacies. Linked to germination and, specifically, to a germinative act, Carnaval operates in an underground reality. Koya families of the Quebrada and Puna, but also many other people like you and me, who are not Indigenous but who dwell in a quite ambivalent racial border, have irreconcilable doubts about the Catholic Church and catechism. While the central ideas of Catholicism frame the divine as a superior being totally different from a mundane and sinful individual, subterranean spiritualities uphold conviviality and proximity among all that exists. Celebrating Carnaval and offering food to the deities of an Indigenous pantheon, such as the Sun and Earth, keep alive cosmological arrangements that affirm economic, social, and bodily germination. They invoke associative, communal, and reciprocal ways of being, knowing, and living. This invocation often takes on the guise of modified and stretched, even reconfigured, Catholicism. Carnaval reminds us today that *man* and *woman* are not the cornerstone of life reproduction.

Perhaps you do not yet see it the way I am conveying it all. It is not uncommon for us to feel attached to the ideas of *men* and *women* whenever we want to explain the reproduction of life. That is part of the colonial legacy that uses race to make us think about the superiority of privileged groups and the contributions they make to maintain a healthy society. Let me give you another example from my childhood years; I feel that it might help. When you taught me to go to the bathroom by myself, you told me that I had to wash my *poto* (bottom). You used that word to teach me the bodily part involved with doing number two. I spent my childhood listening to "poto this," "poto that," "wash your poto well," "put your poto square in the chair," and so many other formulations about my famous poto.

Once I went to play at a classmate's house and I had to use the bathroom. The bidet wasn't working. So, embarrassed, I called my classmate from inside the bathroom and asked him to ask his mother what I should do to wash my poto. No one understood me. It was a scandal. It took them about five minutes to figure out that I was talking about my rear end. When I got back home, I told you what had happened and, amid laughter, you explained to me that people from Argentina's south usually say the word *poto*, but people from Jujuy not so much. Nowadays, when people say "cola" (butt), I can relate not only to the reality of medical anatomy or what commonly corresponds to standard Spanish, but also to a reality specific to a marginalized culture like that of Argentina's Patagonia. Something similar happens with the designations *man* and *woman* that we use all the time to talk about social reproduction. Realities specific to marginalized ways of being, doing, and living decenter the foundational role that the West gives to Man and Woman for life reproduction.

Spanish is spoken in Jujuy, but many of its inhabitants speak Indigenous languages. Often, we find people who speak primarily an Indigenous language, such as Quechua or Guarani, and Spanish only as a second language. We also find people who are monolingual in Spanish and who, however, grew up in a household where they speak both Spanish and an Indigenous language. This also happens in Central America with speakers of Maya K'iche' or Otomi, among other languages. For these bilingual speakers, a reality of objects, which are defined in essentialist ways, by means of absolute exclusions, does not turn out to be the main reality. This apparently occurs because Indigenous languages *lack* what grammar understands as nouns. Instead of thinking of this aspect of a language as a lack, we could also interpret it as a unique attribute. Abundance of verbs in Indigenous languages suggests that designations such as *man* and *woman* cannot emerge from a static, hierarchical, and binary reality. On the contrary, there is dissonance between colonial and colonized languages. In Andean Spanish, those sideways selves that I mentioned earlier speak of grammatical numbers and genders in a way that confuses people who only speak Spanish. There are some interesting and peculiar examples.

Elena Humana hails from a small village in the Quebrada. She recounts that many years ago men took for granted all the duties that women should perform as wives. When Elena recounts this story, her Spanish becomes ambiguous, almost expressing a reality where "man" and "woman" substitute for one another and where also speaking about a person can mean talking about several. I think about this use of speech as consisting of two traits. One relates to the blurred boundaries between what belongs to the universe of *man* and what belongs to that of *woman*. The other relates to the multiplicity that each of these terms can mean, almost as if she was saying that *man* may convey not only manhood but also its difference or differences. She speaks of "a husband" as the initiator of an activity and, shortly thereafter, refers to "men" instead. She also speaks of "women" as the collective subject of an action that is, glaringly, for all practical purposes, the outcome of a man's behavior. I wouldn't want to go into the kind of details that would require several other letters, but at least I leave you with these concerns with the purpose of establishing that, within "genders," unlistening to Gender and *genders* is much more organic than listening to them.

Print Five: Hallucinating Knowing

For dispossessed communities, hallucinating knowing is a type of cognitive and affective response. They hallucinate as a cultural response to the experience of living in a twilight world. They live within the cast of the human while working against it. The roles of these cultural productions resonate less strongly within the domain of Gender, but more strongly among *genders*. Therefore, these productions lead us to ask whether it would be possible to hallucinate realities where *genders* withdraw into a background while, at the same time, "genders" become more prominent.

Hallucinations are more than physiological responses. They help us address a neurobiology of cultural specificities. Medical knowledge generally speaks to us of capacities that we all have because we are humans. Among these capacities, humans experiment with the mind and its boundaries. Many people have come to believe that hallucinating is a pathology, something that only happens to us if our brains don't work right. But other people, especially those who study cultural aspects in neurobiology, as well as healers and shamans, teach us that we hallucinate to not only expand our consciousness but also navigate conflict and trauma. Hallucinating, under this light, could be healing. Furthermore, in the field of hallucinations, there is sensory plasticity that responds to learned cultural traits. As traits, they relate to individuals due to both a social and communal sense of belonging. I understand that the condition of precariousness in which we find dispossessed communities operates as a call to hallucinate, expanding consciousness between parallel and multiple worlds. We engage hallucinations for their potential to generate unprecedented cognitive and affective relationships through which we may demystify the roots of harm and oppression.

Sideways selves hallucinate and, in doing so, contribute to a cognitive and sensory repository that decenters the prototype of the human. In jotería communities, there are several cultural workers who employ hallucinations. With them, they confront and reconfigure the reasons that authorize the banishment of passions, among them, those that Catholicism demonized. In a society where culture condemns Latina women to the limiting roles of self-sacrificing mothers, prostitutes, or nuns, Cherríe Moraga writes plays where protagonists betray this patriarchal mandate.

One of these protagonists is named Medea and identifies as Chicana (as shorthand, think of Chicana as an identification that Mexican American women cultivate to politicize their minority status within both American and Latino communities). Medea resides in at least three worlds, or three discontinuous times: Phoenix, Aztlán, and the psychiatric hospital. She is Chac-Mool's mother, and the partner of another woman, whose name is Luna and who identifies as Black. Together they are living in Phoenix, in a near future where the United States has become a cluster of separatist states in which each racial minority finally has its own land. Medea is part of the Yaqui community, an Indigenous community. Jasón, Chac-Mool's father, lives in Aztlán, the nation of the Chicano people. Medea also lived there once. You may be wondering why, being Chicana, Medea does not continue to live in Aztlán. They won't let her; that's why. As it happens, in the present, because of her love for Medea, they are treated as dispossessed. Only people without a nation reside in Phoenix.

The dilemma posed by hallucinations is Chac-Mool's return to Aztlán. If he went back to live with Jasón, he would inherit the land that belongs to the father. If Chac-Mool moved to Aztlán, he would abandon Medea and, consequently, the parallel, sovereign, and multiracial life cultivated in Phoenix. Medea does not want the control of Chicano men and husbands to turn Chac-Mool into a member of the nation. She is afraid that Chac-Mool, her own son, will end up reproducing the same norms that exiled Medea and Luna. That's why Medea poisons him.

The story takes place in a hallucinogenic contiguity between Aztlán, Phoenix, and the psychiatric hospital where Medea has been confined. It is hallucinations, through their connections to the Indigenous Nahua world within Abya Yala, that make available to protagonists, but also audiences, a space for the practice and theorization of "genders." Within that space of escape and rupture, as it were, between worlds, the human is disfigured. Hallucinating Latinx folks reimagine trust and credibility. They challenge the ideas that schooling and medicine propagate about "pathological" hallucinations.

You may not have as many suspicions about hallucinations as other city-dwelling people. You taught me to investigate mysteries without being so afraid or trying to find all the answers for things we can't explain. I believe that, as a sideways way of knowing, hallucinations suggest that their object varies from one community to another, especially when we consider the material conditions they face. At the same time, I believe that the object is as important as the hallucinogenic medium itself. Among pre-Columbian philosophers and artists, we find various roles and occupations that express the importance of a hallucinogenic medium. Those who were responsible for painting and chanting the knowledge of the community held highly respected positions. Two of these officials were known as *tlacuilo* and *tlamatinime*. They had the communal task of, on one end, drawing the sign linking mundane and extraordinary domains and, on the other, interpreting it according to changes in context and the passage of time. The multisensory modality of knowing, of constantly germinating everydayness and sacredness, implied therefore learning to wear someone else's skin. This back-and-forth between past and present cultural productions responds to the longing of inhabiting the practical doing of dispossessed communities, making available new lessons about migration from various bodily states to many others. Wearing other selves' skins is not an appropriative act but one of companionship and cooperation. It is a modality of germination of and among sideways selves. That modality also gifts us its poetry.

Print Six: Jotería

Poetry becomes a balm for all dispossessed communities facing atrocities. It offers ideas and practices. It engenders a sensorium to discern creative potential, which we need in the affirmation of our daily insurgencies. Jotería communities invite us to participate in this collective commitment. They do so by drawing our attention to an interpersonal way of fostering political coalition and activist cooperation. Jotería teaches us, as sideways selves, to examine the art of making revolutions. They call us to reflect on our revolutionary practices and on the artful methodologies that jotería brings to material, intellectual, and political struggles.

A unique characteristic of the creative potential of jotería is its poetics. We refer to this poetics in terms of a carnal method. Primarily, this poetics accounts for the deciphering and decoding of the legacy of colonialism. The method infuses dissonance, an eccentric affection and feeling, into our approaches to the realities we encounter at the center of the Américas. Here I am playing a bit with words, and it probably feels like a tongue twister. I do it for a purpose, precisely to infuse a dissonant poetry into our beliefs and practices around the centers of the Américas.

I'm going to tell you two more things that expand on the notion of the black hole, about which I wrote to you before. This letter is getting longish, I know. But you will surely read it bit by bit. I had told you that maps of differences tend to marginalize dispossessed populations and, since we exist in various contexts, there are populations that are dispossessed by and within more than one community. That kind of marginalization is the result of the intersection of what happens between at least two contexts, worlds, or communities. That process of marginalization, of dispossession, is like a fall into the abyss within the black hole. For example, at home, you didn't speak to me as a child that could do without an anatomy that meant biological destiny. At school, something similar happened; there was physical education for either boys or girls, never together. From compounded marginalization, my carnal possibilities were falling into the black hole. I was never at the center of anyone's life, more than as an absence.

The poetics of jotería speaks to us of that synchronicity between absence and trace. The black hole is like a geometry that accounts not only for what is not there but also, if we refine our poetics, for the relationship between what is no longer seen but left a trace, and the ghostly guise that the trace undertakes. Why isn't the travesti community at the center of social transformation, of the decolonization of Argentina or the American continent? Why isn't jotería at the center of the decolonization of the Latino community and the Central American diaspora in the United States? In what ways is that absence linked to colonial legacies, their philosophy of absolutes and nouns, their politics of ableism and disability, and their aesthetics of primitivism and pathologization? The poetics of jotería suggests to us, sometimes with expressions of sound, or visual or tactile expressions, to appreciate the carnal habits that redefine solidarity, what in other words we could call the political work between generations.

Crucial to this poetics is an ecological sense of connection among all that exists. With that affectivity, we investigate the art of translating senses and testimonies pointing to solidarity, not only from mouth to mouth but also across gestures, sighs, looks, and presences that we *transversally* summon. That poetic affectivity demonstrates that it is not necessary to discard everything we receive from the generation before ours. Instead, it makes tangible that germination lies with intensifying the ways in which we message a vernacular, underground, and often imperceptible impressibility of our bodies.

In this print, I'm going to share an example that I think you will enjoy. Several people who migrate from Central America to the Southwest of the United States tend to adopt pronominal forms like *vos* when speaking with other Latinx and Afro-Latinx people. You, because you grew up in Argentina, are accustomed to the use of *vos*. In Central America, its use is most frequently recorded among those who come from bilingual contexts where an

Indigenous language is present. People from Guatemala, especially if they are peasants and Indigenous, such as Maya K'ich'e, tend to chat with other Central Americans, like Hondurans and Salvadorans, alternating between *tú* and *vos*. The sound of *vos*, but above all its associated muscle memories and bodily habits, authorizes a closeness, a transversal sideways method, that invokes a more eccentric sense of speech. In its aesthetic expression, speech pulsates in the center of the Américas. In a way, this poetics makes the trace of Abya Yala more tangible at the Américas' centers.

In this eccentric poetics resides a sensibility of conversion and transmutation. It presents itself as a scaffold for subjectivity. Poet Maya Chinchilla makes me think about Central America, but more importantly, about Central Americans and the role they play in redefining the continent's epicenter. Her poetry critically invokes the imagery that represents Central America as a people-devouring land and as an epicenter of volcanic and destructive action (how ironic, right? Especially when we think about how it was Spaniards who threw Indigenous peoples to be devoured by dogs). That imagery derives from the legacy of colonial chronicles. Today, that imagery is repeated in the conception that international organizations disseminate about the region, which they describe as rife with corruption, violence among gangs, and socioeconomic chaos. When Chinchilla conjures a decolonial sensibility with her poetry, she turns to volcanoes' organic matter. In that matter, she leads us to recognize the mysteries of what lives in a boiling void, which she refers to as "a blistering mouth."

By bringing us to the codes of nature like volcanoes, and their boiling points, Chinchilla demonstrates that revolutionary solidarities of the present can *emphatically render nonnormative* the perception of the world with eyes that have not yet formed—that is, with a type of perception that comes into being only when approaching or anticipating what is imperceptible, like the lives, knowledges, and politics of the communities that dwell within black holes. In other words, it is a perception that we arrive at in sideways fashion, with the company of those who are expanding the present and recalibrating the future.

You used to enjoy dancing, closely together. I remember Saturday evenings, when you would take a shower and then put on your favorite clothes. You wore perfume and cologne. You looked so in love. You had a drink. Dad liked sweet wines, like port that is served for dessert. Mom preferred bitterness in her drinks. Maybe Campari? I watched you from the green armchair. You danced in the dim light and to the rhythm of the record player. Nat King Cole sang "Perfidia" in Spanish, that unforgettable bolero that drove you closer. Cole didn't sound very boleresque, but maybe that was his charm, enmeshing a very metallic "t" every time he sang the word "tú" with a more sinuous and open rhythm to improvisation than that of the bolero. It was beautiful to see rhythm sweeping your bodies away and how, almost in unison, you accentuated those beats that Cole suggested with his interpretation.

Jotería poetics makes us vibrate with that syncopated rhythm, like Cole's almost-bolero that emerges from the underground of jazz. Volcanoes' behaviors in the Central Cordillera materialize transitions, constantly giving shape to the heart of the hemisphere. Those behaviors express mystery and undergroundness stemming from what cannot be seen. We may not see mystery or undergroundness, but we've learned ways of sensing and revealing their presence. They materialize the very matter of the center of the Americas while also materializing matters that matter to the Américas' centers.

I imagine that you two are a bit like that underground presence in my life and, even, in my body. Your ways of living and doing, which I can only now remember, recalibrate, and even hallucinate, impress me. May traces of your absence continue to express the companionship you provide me! Without that loving and fleshy company, I could not exist. Absence leaves traces, which mobilize interdependent ties. Without them there would be no sustaining myself. Without interdependence, no sideways selves emerge, arise, or come forth.

Sideways selves need not be understood. What seems important to me is that you take seriously our ways of living and doing. That's why I decided to write this missive to you. I have taken seriously the lives of both of you, and, in that manner, you continue breathing life into the poetry of my right-here-and-right-now. My commitment lies with jotería poetics, with the transversalidad that generates bonds of nostredad and sideways selves. My commitment is to caring for Andean Catholicism and Andean Spanish, for Mesoamerican Catholicism and Mesoamerican Spanish, for Abya Yala. My hopes seek to deflate Gender and *genders*, to enhance an artful entangling of embodiments with dissonant "genders," and to disfigure Catholicism and other myriad expressions of the genre of the human. Through these disfigurations, I shall continue communing with the sideways selves that transversalidad and nostredad underwrite.

Your indomitable spirits are always in my heart.

José, Checho, PJ, your sideways kin
Syracuse, New York State, planet Earth, Haudenosaunee territory

Acknowledgments

I was once told that making a meal is a communal affair, even when only one person is doing the cooking. I often experience this sense of communality myself, especially when I am trying to replicate a recipe for one of those scrumptious treats that sweetened my childhood. Can I recreate my mom's *buñuelos*? Her recipe calls for *jarabe de caña de azúcar*, the molasses syrup we used to get from nearby Ingenio La Esperanza. Did I learn well from her style of mixing batter, patiently whisking dry ingredients before folding them into wet ones? Did I learn to assist the flour molecules in blending with other ingredients, releasing proteins that lend just enough elasticity to the batter? Did I stay close and hear her whispering secret encouragement to a leavening buñuelos batter? Even in a world where I could easily purchase buñuelos at the grocery store, I gravitate toward realities where relationships materialize the mysterious chemistries of leavening dough. I refuse to see, experience, and understand myself as the sole creator of buñuelos. Laborious hands near and far have touched this batter, my mother's recipe, and the ingredients it calls for.

Sideways Selves embodies this kind of communing, whose provenance lies with comrades, mentors, teachers, friends, relatives, and other kinspeople who have supported me along this journey. I have the fortune of acknowledging and honoring their support, which varies in shape and reach. This support sometimes was of an official kind, provided within institutions of learning. Some other times, it was received in the form of long-standing, untiring mentorship. Often, it entailed the reconceptualization of what it means to become activist co-inspirators, remaining truly intentional about interdependence and reciprocity.

I would like to especially acknowledge the cherished members of familial constellations: Yamile Dip, Hugo DiPietro, Haydée DiPietro

(Tía Nené), Cecilia Sánchez DiPietro, Cristian DiPietro, Agustina Checa, Pachi Sánchez, Santiago Checa, Lidia Patagua, Hugo Alejandro DiPietro, Matías DiPietro, and José Luis Checa.

Among the friends that I made during my childhood or teenage years, I would like to mention those I keep close to my heart: Claudia Mendieta, Carla Angel, María Alejandra Mudry, Karina Nelson, Verónica García Bond, Valeria Bordallo, Fabiana Flores, Sebastián Matthews, Diego Vidal, and Gustavo Conde. With their company, I battled the turmoil of shame and isolation.

School brimmed with curiosity, which I longed for the most. There, I encountered teachers who often delved beneath the surface of things: Bettina Aragón, Marta García, Gladis Herrera, Adoración Martínez Ferri, Trinidad Santa Cruz, and Coca Volpi.

Jujuy National University granted me open and tuition-free admission for my bachelor's degree. During those formative years, I engaged in student-centered mobilization, participated in undergraduate research and mentoring opportunities, and became involved in feminist and union grassroots organizing. I treasure the visions of liberatory knowledge that the following scholars and mentors shared with me: Jorge Accame, Elena Bossi, Alejandra García Vargas, Flora Guzmán, Paula Jure, Gabriela Karasik, Alejandro Kaufman, Liliana Louys, Flora Losada, Ariel Monterrubianesi, Mario Rabey, Marta Rondoletto, Marta Ruiz, and Gabriela Salas. At a time of vulnerability, I counted on the brilliance and solidarity of fellow classmates, such as Rubén Agüero, Patricia Yaber, Juan Müller, and Vivi Arce.

I received a scholarship to attend the graduate program in Society, Gender, and Politics at Facultad Latinoamericana de las Ciencias Sociales (FLACSO, Buenos Aires). I have great respect for this program, where Gloria Bonder mentored me and later offered me my first teaching position in feminist policy studies. Since then, I have cherished this space and its enriching network of colleagues and students. They have witnessed the process of birthing *Sideways Selves*. Among them, I would like to honor Line Bareiro, Micaela Bazzano, Anabella Benedetti, Alexa Cotignola, Blas Fernández, Carolina Gaete, Suyai García Gualda, María Angélica Ginieis, Virginia Guzmán, Paula Luzzi, Ana Rodríguez, Sara Sanz, Verónica Sorbera, María del Carmen Tamargo, Emma Theumer, Paolina Vercoutere Quinche, Lucía Villafañe, and Marlene Wayar.

At Binghamton University, the doctoral program and the center in Philosophy, Interpretation, and Culture (PIC) offered radical ways of inhabiting scholar-activist commitments and longings. Faculty, students, guest speakers, visiting scholars, and staff members at Binghamton listened to, engaged with, and discussed the earliest reflections about sideways selves. For their generosity, I am indebted to many of them. Among them, I would like to acknowledge: Mazi Allen, M. Jacqui Alexander, Wanda Alarcón, Ellen Badger, Alisa Bierria, Mary Pat Brady, Elisa Camiscioli, María Celeri, Vick Chauvey, Manuel Chávez Jr., Carlos Decena, Jeanne Constable, Juanita Diaz-Cotto, Laura Dumond-Kerr, Carmen Ferradás, Josh Franco, Marilyn Gaddis Rose, Nalima Gaonkar, Gladys Gimenez, Suronda Gonzalez, Michael Hames-García, William Haver, Sarah Hoagland, Colette Jung, Nicholas Karkov, Cricket Keating, Jen-Feng Kuo, Hil Malatino, Karen Keefe-Guzikowski, Katharine Krebs, Nelson Maldonado Torres, Ernesto Martinez, Jen McWeeny, Walter Mignolo, Nontsasa Nako, Mariana Ortega, Laura Elisa Pérez, Joshua Price, Anibal Quijano, Chantal Rodais, Shireen Roshanravan, Chela Sandoval, Oktay Sekercisoy, Gabriel Soldatenko, Ovidiu Tichindeleanu, Collen Tims Parks, Gabriela Veronelli, Helena María Viramontes, Catherine Walsh, and Donna Young.

The Department of Ethnic Studies at the University of California, Berkeley, provided me with resources and communities where *Sideways Selves* gained a hemispheric scope. I would like to mention a few of them for their engaged and affirming ways of listening: Paola Bacchetta, Francisca Cázares, Keith Feldman, Ramón Grosfoguel, Celia Herrera Rodriguez, Laura Jimenez-Olvera, Beatriz Manz, David Montejano, Carlos Muñoz Jr., Laura Elisa Pérez, Alex Saragoza, Dewey St. Germaine, and Katharya Um. During this postdoctoral period, I lived in Oakland, where I embraced, and was in turn embraced by, jotería, queer people of color, BIPOC, and decolonial collectives. Among them, I would like to honor Angela Aguilar, Wanda Alarcón, Giuliani Alvarenga, Jorge Aquino, Darren Arquero, Hossein Ayazi, Luz Calvo, Maya Chinchilla, Randy P. Conner, Cindy Cruz, Patricia Flores Yrarrázaval, Marcelo Garzo, Banah Ghadbian, Karla Gomez Pelayo, Jorge Gonzalez, Osa Hidalgo de la Riva, Ariko Ikehara, Cynthia Ledesma, Lois Lorentzen, David Melena-Castro, Edgar Mojica, Fuifuilupe Niumeitolu, Sandra Pacheco, David Preciado, Andrea Preza, Abraham Ramirez, Sara Ramirez, Reina de Aztlán, Yosimar Reyes, Catriona Rueda Esquivel, Moi Santos, Marisol Silva, Santiago Slabodsky, David Hatfield Sparks, Sonia Suárez, Julie Thi Underhill, Kim Tran, Carolyn Vera, and Ashton Wesner.

Sideways Selves has benefited from research and writing grants at various stages of development. I would like to acknowledge the support of the National Scientific and Technical Research Council of Argentina

(CONICET), the Tinker Foundation, the Ross Fellowship for Dissertation Writing (Binghamton University), the Andrew W. Mellon Postdoctoral Fellowship in the Humanities (University of California, Berkeley), and the Townsend Humanities Center Postdoctoral Fellowship (University of California, Berkeley). Gratitude is also owed to several librarians and archivists, specifically at the Syracuse University's Library, the Museo Nacional de Etnografía y Folklore in Sucre, Bolivia, the Archivo Histórico del Obispado de San Salvador de Jujuy, Argentina, and the State of Jujuy Archivo Histórico.

Syracuse University and the College of Arts and Sciences provided generous support for my research and the production of this book. I am particularly grateful for the family leave granted to me during a critical time when I needed to care for my life partner amid health uncertainties. Moreover, the university extended kindness when I decided to undergo gender-affirming surgeries while on the tenure track.

Former and current colleagues at Syracuse have been gracious to me over the years. I am grateful to the following for their support and camaraderie: Lois Agnew, Barbara Appelbaum, Philip Arnold, Chaz Barracks, Crystal Bartolovich, Patrick Berry, Gail Bulman, Dympna Callaghan, Jorge Castillo, Francine D'Amico, Carol Fadda-Conrey, Alejandro García, Myrna García Calderón, Linda Carty, Melissa Chipman, Kathryn Everly, Verena Erlensbusch-Anderson, Marie Garland, Michael Gill, Tula Goenka, Diane Grimes, Marcelle Haddix, Roger Hallas, Gail Hamner, Mariaelena Huambachano, Coran Klaver, Gretchen Lopez, Aaron Luedtke, Ethan Madarieta, Gladys McCormick, Charles Morris III, Laura-Anne Minkoff-Zern, Brice Nordquist, Jackie Orr, Teresita Paniagua, Cristina Pardo Porto, Mario Perez, Heather Law Pezzarossi, Guido Pezzarossi, Gretchen Purser, Rob Pusch, Erin Rand, Romita Ray, Alicia Ríos, William Robert, Karin Ruhlandt, Chie Sakakibara, Sascha Scott, Becky Schewe, Adam Singerman, Scott Manning Stevens, Silvio Torres Saillant, Diane Wiener, and Jamie Winders.

The Democratizing Knowledge (DK) collective, also at Syracuse University, focuses on producing transformative knowledges and collectivities with the purpose of contributing to the growth of inclusive publics in higher education. Since I joined in the year 2017, I have had the distinct pleasure of communing with Himika Bhattacharya, Linda Carty, Hayley Marama Cavino, Dellareese Cofield-Martinez, Carol Fadda-Conrey, Stephanie Fetta, Mary Rose Go, Marcelle Haddix, Paula Johnson, Talina Jones, Aja Martinez, Chandra Talpade Mohanty, Jackie Orr, and Silvio Torres Saillant.

I have become a more attentive thinker pursuing theoreticopractical collaborations in a decolonial vein among different groups and projects. At the Latina Feminism Roundtable hosted by Mariana Ortega, I crossed paths with Linda Martín Alcoff, Mariana Alessandri, Natalie Cisneros, Veronica Isabel Dahlberg, Brittan Davis, Theresa Delgadillo, Carmen Lugo-Lugo, Jacqueline Martinez, Jennifer McWeeny, Cynthia Paccacerqua, Laura Elisa Pérez, Patricia Pedroza Gonzalez, Andrea Pitts, Monique Roelofs, Stephanie Rivera Berruz, Alexander Stehn, Gloria Vaquera, Sujay Vega, Ernesto Rosen Velasquez, Elena Ruíz, Chela Sandoval, Ofelia Schutte, Daphne Taylor Garcia, and Kelli Zaytoun. Alongside Jen McWeeny and Shireen Roshanravan, we coedited *Speaking Face-to-Face: The Visionary Philosophy of María Lugones* (SUNY Press, 2019); with Perry Zurn, Andrea Pitts, and Talia Mae Bettcher, we coedited *Trans Philosophy* (University of Minnesota Press, 2024); at the América Transgénerx Roundtable of the 2019 Latin American Studies Association Annual Meeting, I encountered exuberant interlocution alongside Pilar Cabrera, Jennicet Gutiérrez, Indyra Mendoza Aguilar, Suyapa Portillo Villeda, Pilar Salazar Argueta, Susy Shock, Marlene Wayar, and Nahil Zerón; within the Community, Liberation, Indigenous, and Eco-psychologies specialization of the MA/PhD program in Depth Psychology at Pacifica Graduate Institute, I am learning the art of transdisciplinary translation alongside Susan James, Nuria Ciofalo, Jenny Escobar, Karen Jarratt-Snider, and Chela Sandoval.

Few places have widened my understanding of sideways selves the way both the National Women's Studies Association and the American Studies Association have. My grateful respect to the following colleagues and comrades within this constellation: Lisa Anderson, Marlon Bailey, Maylei Blackwell, Andrea Bolivar, Suzanne Bost, Ginetta Candelario, Norma Elia Cantú, Anna Carastathis, María Celeri, Xiomara Cervantes-Gómez, Elora Chowdhury, Chris Cuomo, Carlos Decena, Francisco Galarte, Lorgia García-Peña, Bernadette Hernandez, Ellie Hernandez, Jillian Hernandez, Cricket Keating, AnaLouise Keating, Lawrence LaFountain-Stokes, Amy Lind, M. Shadee Malaklou, Marisol Negrón, Marcia Ochoa, Richa Nagar, Cole Rizki, Juana Maria Rodriguez, Judy Rodriguez, Chela Sandoval, Felicity Amaya Schaeffer, Amanda Swarr, Sandra Soto, Susan Stryker, Barbara Sutton, Michelle Tellez, Gladys Tzul-Tzul, Deb Vargas, Roberta Villalón, and Kerry White.

The Association for Jotería Arts, Activism, and Scholarship (AJAAS) is the kind of collective whose work quite literally saves lives. This is where I go to do the face-to-face labor of envisioning, activating, and furthering nonconforming ways of living and learning within the broadest Afro-Latinx, Latinx, and Xicanx constellation. It is my hope that *Sideways Selves* honors the love and wisdom that the following AJAAS comrades have shown me: Xaime Aceves Equihua, José M. Aguilar Hernandez, Christian Alejandro Bracho, Marco Cerqueira, Erika Viviana Cespedes, Maya Chinchilla, Marivel Danielson, Jorge Estrada, Olga Estrada, Yovani Flores, Desiré Galvez, Eric-Christopher Garcia, Liliana Gonzalez, Ángel de Jesus González, Sergio A. Gonzalez, Gibrán Papaloyaotl Güido, Cynthia Melendrez, Joanna Núñez, Irina Núñez, Roberto C. Orozco, Daniel Enrique Pérez, Leda Ramos, Sofía Ramírez, Juan Ríos, Jaimé Korima Rodriguez, Omi Salas-SantaCruz, Verónica Sandoval, Manuel Santillana Blanco, Ire'ne Lara Silva, Verónica Solís, Rafael Solorzano, Francisco Soto, Anita Tijerina Revilla, Gerardo Torres, Rita Urquijo-Ruiz, Úmi Vera, Nadia Zepeda, and Lizeth (Liz) Zepeda.

Over the years, colleagues from both near and far have extended invitations to visit their institutions and share my progress on *Sideways Selves*. It has been humbling to engage in so many soul-making dialogues. Among them, I would like to acknowledge the following: Paola Bacchetta (Women's, Gender, and Sexuality Studies, UC-Berkeley), Dina Bopp (Gender Studies, Universität Basel), Talia Mae Bettcher (Cal State Los Angeles), Loren Canon (Philosophy, Humboldt State University), Debra Castillo (Cornell University), Breno Cypriano (Universidade Federal de Minas Gerais), Penelope Deutscher and José Medina (Philosophy, Northwestern University), Melina Gaona (Universidad Nacional de Quilmes), Luis Alberto Herrera Montero (Philosophy, Universidad de Cuenca, CLACSO), M. Shadee Malaklou (The bell hooks Center, Berea College), Hil Malatino (Rock Ethics Institute, Pennsylvania State University), Juliana Martinez and Perry Zurn (Arts and Sciences, American University), Anna Moltchanova (Carleton College), Laura Elisa Pérez (Latinx Research Center, UC-Berkeley), Andrea Pitts and Perry Zurn (Trans Philosophy Project), Santiago Slabodsky (Religion, Hofstra University), Lynn Stephen and Rocío Zambrana (Latin American Studies and Philosophy, University of Oregon), Deb Vargas, Kyla Schuller, and Carlos Decena (Women's, Gender, and Sexuality Studies, Latino and Caribbean Studies, Rutgers University), GradCon22 collective (SUNY Stony Brook), Graduate Students at the California College of the Arts Graduate Visual and Critical Studies Program, Guepardxs Collective (Jujuy National University), and the LGBTQ Studies Programs both at Colgate University and Cornell University.

I have found solid and inspiring support among former and current colleagues at Syracuse University's Department of Women's and Gender Studies, Himika Bhattacharya, Eunjung Kim, Rebecca Lambert, Vivian May, Danika Medak-Saltzman, Sarah Miraglia, Jaynelle Nixon, Dana Olwan, Gwendolyn Pough, Minnie Bruce Pratt, Robin Riley, Chandra Talpade Mohanty, and Jiwoon Yulee. Especially, I acknowledge the feedback on my writing that I received from Dr. Eunjung Kim, and the advice and guidance that I received from my departmental mentor, Dr. Gwendolyn Pough. Staff members in the department and the College of Arts and Sciences provided administrative and technical support while I completed this manuscript. Among them, I would like to acknowledge Luke Connelly, Susann DeMocker-Shedd, Alice Loomis, Cassidy Perreault, and Stacy Webb.

The following individuals, who remain a source of boundless strength, are part of a community of undergraduate and graduate students that I met in the women's and gender studies classroom: Cody Benbow, Farrell Brenner, Karisa Bridgelal, Sophie Clinton, Jersey Cosantino, Katie Cross, Janet Flores, Natalie Gallagher, Abel Gómez, Valerye Hidalgo-Martinez, Laura Jaffee, Lorena Kanzki, Keish Kim, Meaghan Krazinski, Crystal Letona, Atiya McGhee, Angie Mederos Coronel, Angie Mejia, Hannah-Abigail Mosier, Jestina Ortega, Urmi Parekh, Katie Pataki, Seth Quam, Amy Quichiz, Ionah Scully, Brandon Tamez, Angelina Vargas, and Haoran Zeng.

Friendship entails mutual respect and affirmation, revealing deep interdependency between lives. I honor the labor and care of many whose friendships have nourished my sense of sideways selfhood. They are Rubén Agüero, Eddy Alvarez Jr., Bettina Aragón, Micaela Bazzano, Mabel Belucci, Gloria Bonder, Pilar Cabrera, William Calvo-Quiros, Sandra Cardoso, Melina Cid Conde, Joseph Cordaro, Claudia Dagum, Maria Ester David, Joe Galante, Constanza Guzmán, Peter Fazo, Michael Hames-García, Lourdes Ibarra, Ana Paula Jaramillo, Paula Jure, Jen-Feng Kuo, Claudia Laudano, Liliana Louys, Leonor Lugones, Paula Luzzi, Hil Malatino, Ernesto Martinez, Claudia Mendieta, Ariel Monterrubianesi, Bubu Montes, Juan Müller, Mariana Ortega, Andrea Pitts, Shireen Roshanravan, Mariana Sanchez de Bustamante, Vicky Scaro, Omi Salas Santa-Cruz, Maya Strohmeier, John Strohmeier, Emma Theumer, Ramiro Tizón, Agustina Veronelli, Gabriela Veronelli, Silvana Veronelli, Marlene Wayar, Lori Wieder, Maris Wieder, and Patricia Yaber.

I appreciate the healthcare that I have received from Elizabeth Asiago-Reddy, Don Pascual Yaxon, Pablo Salamea, and Jennifer Schumacher.

I would like to acknowledge Dr. Cynthia Willett, Dr. Jackie Orr, and

Dr. Carlos Ulises Decena, who made invaluable recommendations to early versions of some of the book's chapters.

I found outstanding mentorship in the generous praxis of Dr. M. Jacqui Alexander.

Dr. Himika Bhattacharya guided me with honesty, care, and gentle discipline through the tenure review process. I extend my deepest gratitude for her unwavering support in her role of departmental chair.

I am also appreciative of the careful work of the editorial team at the University of Texas Press, including Kerry Webb, Laura Gauggel, and Christina Vargas. Thank you to the copyeditor, who chooses to remain anonymous, to Natalie Sowa for the cover design, to Six Red Marbles for typesetting the manuscript, and to Douglas Easton for compiling the book's index. Deepest gratitude to Kerry Webb for believing in *Sideways Selves* and for patiently encouraging me throughout the last stretch. Additionally, I am grateful to Nicole Guidotti-Hernandez and Lorgia García-Peña for including *Sideways Selves* in the "Latinx: The Future Is Now" series.

Laura Elisa Pérez and Joshua Price have mentored me with brilliance, humility, and swag. I am deeply thankful for the generosity they extended to me during a near-death experience.

Ceci Sánchez DiPietro has been the one constant witness. I deeply appreciate her.

The late María Lugones taught me the art of wearing each other's skins. I honor her indomitable sense of possibility.

Bisel was a canine ambassador and spiritual guide who taught me interspecies love. His delightful presence saw me through grad school and the initial phase of this book.

Inti is another canine companion, who offers a mirror in which I experience the daily gift of mutual care.

Brian enacts loving life-partnering with me. We ongoingly rehearse deep intimacy and togetherness. In a lasting embrace, we have seen valleys and mountains. To him, I extend the most profound respect.

Notes

Introduction

1. The travesti and trans community in Argentina includes gender nonconforming individuals who face systemic discrimination and marginalization.
Through bodily practices, they modify and recalibrate their identities across
social institutions. Since the mid to late 1990s, transgender sex workers have
rooted their political and socioeconomic struggles in the self-identification
"travesti," a term used by community members for approximately forty years.
As discussed later, political consciousness and activism within this community have challenged homophobia, queerphobia, transphobia, and the sociocultural roots of dispossession and precarity. In the 2010s, the community
increasingly embraced the term *trans*, and currently identifies as "travesti/
trans." Rather than indicating a rigid division, the slash represents an ongoing negotiation that reflects how generations and geopolitical conflicts shape
bodily projects and identities. This book honors the formulation "travesti/
trans." It is critical to notice that while the term *trans* is also inclusive of trans
men and trans masculinities, the more visible history of that travesti/trans
movement aligns with feminine embodiments and identities, or what this
book later explains as *femininities* and "femininities."

Chapter 1. Sideways Selves, *Realidades Atravesadas*

1. LGBT is an acronym for Lesbian, Gay, Bisexual, Travesti, Transgender, and
Transsexual. In Latin America, some community organizations add the category Intersex or Queer (Cuir) to this arch. There is tension within this con-
stituency. *Travesti* is the autonym or endonym used by travestis (Sívori 2005).
I translated all original statements from Spanish into English, attending to
class, ethnic, and regional variations.
2. In their original Spanish, these categories of identification are gay, lesbi-
ana, *transgénero*, *transexual*, intersex, pansexual, and asexual. This nomencla-
ture continues to sprout novel identifiers as both individuals and collectives

struggle to make visible nuanced iterations of belonging and marginalization. The term *cuir* emerges in the second decade of this millennium, pointing to the geopolitical boundary between north and south. Leticia Sabsay (2014) understands that the terms *queer* and *cuir* coexist in tense negotiations about identity and field formation. Negotiations about subjectivity refer to individual and collective identification, while those about cultural and political formation refer to theoretical and sociological categories. Undoubtedly, *cuir* gives rise to context-specific cultural and political critiques and practices. Subjectivities that relate to these critiques and praxes adopt the term *cuir* to claim transnational kinship in queer world-making. Simultaneously, they affirm cross-cultural competence to navigate global kinship. See also Falconí (2014) and Sabsay (2014).

3. I follow an impure account of Latina/o/x/e and Xicana/o/x identities and subjectivities. Specifically in reference to Xicana/o/x, I appreciate the critical take of journalist Rubén Salazar. Back in 1970, Salazar wrote in the *Los Angeles Times*, "a Chicano is a Mexican-American with a non-Anglo image of himself." He conveys that the term's origins are neither demographic nor solely identity-related. Statements such as Salazar's emerge from the politicization of the double condition, as both conquered and immigrant, of the great majority of members of the Mexican American community (see also C. Muñoz 2007). Chicana/o/x intellectuals and activists, such as Ana Castillo (2014), Michael Hames-García (2006), Cherríe Moraga (2011), and Horacio N. Roque Ramírez (2003), examine heterogeneity and resistance to normativity within varied projects of Chicanismo/a and Chicano nationalism. I join others who use "x" in Xicana/o/x to highlight both the Nahuatl spelling of the "ch" and the links among Native peoples in the diaspora (Castillo 2014; Moraga 2011). When I choose to use the gender duality "Chicana and Chicano," I am quoting the works of others or a different period.

4. Nicolas Shumway (1991, 134–135, 164–165) examines this discursive boundary within Argentina's intelligentsia in the second half of the nineteenth century. The pampas were considered the reservoir of undisciplined gauchos, their unlabored lands, and ignorance. They were pitted against the man from the interior (Indigenous, from the mountains) and its "primitive [*barbaric*]" condition.

5. See also chapter 4 on the relation between hallucinating knowing and liminal experiences.

6. By *white-stream feminism*, I refer to what Paola Bacchetta explains as an amnesic habit among feminists regarding racialization and colonialism (Bacchetta, Jivraj, and Bakshi 2020).

7. Caste is an Indian institution of depersonification and humiliation based on the stratification of social status, occupation, and, often, religious affiliation. Anticaste feminists, such as Shailaja Paik Palik (2021) and Jebaroja Singh (2018), examine the experiences of women who belong to "scheduled castes," also known as "Untouchables." By centering these experiences, they demonstrate the "double oppression" of Dalit women within the caste system, as both Untouchable and female.

8. Lugones (2005) insightfully engages Gloria Anzaldúa's understanding of intimate terrorism and the Coatlicue state. This dialogue offers a carnal

model of metamorphosis as active subjectivity, an entangling of stasis and germination.

9. In *On Making Sense*, Ernesto Martínez describes an equitable narrative responsibility for queer experience and identity in his analysis of queer of color narratives. This narrative style shifts the site of queer enunciation, relocating the articulation of queerness from a queer subject to their siblings, friends, parents, and neighbors (2013, 112–136). I recognize in Susy Shock's performances a kindred style of shifting trans enunciation from proper transgender subjects to the network of relationships among multiply marginalized and nonnormative subjectivities.

10. See Laqueur (1992) on the Galenic unisex body vis-à-vis the two-sex body model.

11. Mary Pat Brady (2002) underscores the articulation of social relations and their inherent spatial form.

12. For the scholarship centered on queer and trans spatiality in the United States, see Bailey and Shabazz (2014), Alvarez (2016), D'Emilio (1992), Halberstam (2005), Herring (2011), and Mumford (1997). In what concerns the Latin and Latina/o/x Americas, the scholarship is scarce. Neither Murray (1995) nor Balderston and Guy (1997) filled that void. Perlongher (1999) and Rapisardi and Modarelli (2001) should be noted for their spatial approach. Thanks to Lynda Johnston for recommending the work of Grupo de Estudos Territoriais (GETE) in Brazil.

13. See Ministerio de Turismo y Deporte, "Movimiento turístico récord en todo el país. Con el impulso del programa PreViaje," March 4, 2022, https://www.argentina.gob.ar/noticias/movimiento-turistico-record-en-todo-el-pais.

14. Lugar Gay is located in the San Telmo neighborhood, which many consider the prime, if not the very first, example of gentrification in CABA. See their webpage at http://www.lugargay.com.ar/english/index.php.

15. Bayardo and Lacarrieu (1998) study gentrification in the city of Buenos Aires's Palermo, La Boca, and San Telmo quarters.

16. Mariana Vieira Cherro (2011, 352) concurs by stating that the presence of travestis in media—TV shows, theatre, and magazines—does not translate into "reflexivity about being travesti and much less about the homophobia [*sic*] found in Argentine society." I think the passage should refer to transphobia. She has in mind Flor de la V, who has been a pop-culture darling since the latter half of the 2000s.

17. See also Cecconi (2009) about the post-2001 role that tango and tango venues have played in the gentrification process of some of CABA's neighborhoods such as San Telmo, Montserrat, Balvanera, and a few of the streets in Palermo and Villa Crespo (63).

18. Jujuy's Indigenous population represents 10.1 percent of the state's total, while the city of Buenos Aires's remains comparatively low at 2.1 percent (INDEC 2022). Kollas are the largest Indigenous ethnic group in Jujuy. According to Instituto Nacional de Asuntos Indígenas, roughly 50,000 of the country's Kolla population live in the northwestern states of Jujuy and Salta (www.desarrollo.gob.ar), sharing a broader Andean worldview with Aymara and Quechua peoples of the highlands (Occhipinti 2002).

19. For the 2021 Carnaval season, the state of Jujuy records an unprecedented number of visitors.

20. *Quincena* is the two-week period that the tourism industry employs to gauge occupancy and revenue. The summer vacation period consists of four quincena slots. See "Turismo: Jujuy superó el récord que había logrado en el verano del 2020," January 18, 2022, https://www.sinlimites.com.ar/provinciales /item/6726-turismo-jujuy-supero-el-record-que-habia-logrado-en-el -verano-del-2020.

21. The *NYT* ignores the rise of the Frente de Liberación Homosexual in the seventies and its ties to socialism (Perlongher 1999; Rapisardi and Modarelli 2001).

22. Guano (2003) reads contemporary racial relations in Argentina through a class lens.

23. Peaking at the turn of the nineteenth century, eugenics encompasses positivist disciplines invested in explaining sexual difference as Darwinian types of racial development and deviancy.

24. According to Miranda (2018, 35), this period is characterized by foregrounding heterosexual coupling, "the indissolubility of a marital bond with the potential to produce eugenically fit individuals; the reinforcement of gender roles, and within that context, the promotion of increasing birth rates along with the simultaneous prohibition of contraception" (translation is mine).

25. "The race" refers to "Roman civilization" in this sentence. It is worth noticing that the scholarship on the Anglo iteration of eugenics highlights the crucial role that sterilization plays in brutally enforcing the purity of race and biotype.

26. Under the umbrella of "Black genocide," there exists a broad spectrum of perspectives, ranging from descriptions of exclusion to depictions of outright extermination. On Black exclusion, see Claudia Briones (2002); on Black genocide, see Emilio Corbière (2000); on Black discursive genocide, see Alejandro Solomianski (2003).

27. I would like to qualify Edwards's assertion that Argentina sidelines *mestizaje* since it imagines itself as a white rather than a mixed-identity country (2020, 1–2). While I concur with the notion that the country imagines itself as white, mestizaje anchors different degrees of both racist and anti-racist sentiment. In the confines of the nation, mestizaje served racially mixed communities to negotiate belonging with neighboring minorities and visiting nonnationals. Such is the case of the northwestern states of Jujuy and Salta, where mestizos navigate the racial state in ways that resemble the mixed-race population of cities like Santa Cruz in Bolivia.

28. The African population was disappeared from the imaginary of the nation in favor of Black mixtures such as Zambos and Mulatos.

29. Groundbreaking historical monographs, such as Andrews's (1980, 217) and Edwards's (2020), draw attention to paradoxical dynamics that sanctioned miscegenation as socially accepted against a backdrop of anti-Black sentiment.

30. Consider that Argentina's population was approximately 4.4 million in 1898. The country's area is 2,740,000 square feet.

31. Salessi states that Karl Heinrichs Ulrichs first used the term *uranist* in 1862 when referring to Urania, Greek mythology's muse among "men who love other men" (1995, 225). However, Salessi's vast study demonstrates that early eugenics discourse freely uses the term to also include, in this classification, the "dangerous immoral behavior" of cisgender women (303). Eugenicist rationality pulls into the category "feminine uranists" behavior and practice as diverse as political activism, preference for anarchic views, or a capricious nature. As it concerns "invert," the medicolegal experts and school administrators of the time anchor this classification to the existence of a "culture of men who had sex with men, men who dressed as women and who cohabitated with the 1900s *guapos* (knives men in the tango environment)" (184). "Third sex" encompasses cisgender women who reject traditional mother and wife roles. More specifically, it represents women whose independence takes them away from a position of subordination under men, because of either changing work conditions, shifting values, or displacement (210).
32. Sexual panic points to narratives of fear and anxiety delineating boundaries between good and evil as they relate to a sexual community of certain sexual practice(s) (Patton 2005; Rubin 2002). On the permutation of these cultural operations into fascist nationalism in 1970s Argentina, see Rizki (2020).
33. *Lunfardo* is a slang term developed by criminals in the late nineteenth century. It was created to remain unintelligible before policemen and prison guards, combining the Italian dialect Lombardo, which immigrants brought to the port of Buenos Aires, with elements from Quechua and African languages and gaucho speech.
34. Also known as Comuna 14, Palermo was founded in the late sixteenth century, but its famous green areas (*los bosques*) were developed after 1852. Being close to the port, it grew with waves of immigration from mainly Spain and Italy but also Armenia, Lebanon, and Poland.
35. Travestis have worked in coalition with street vendors and an organization of female sexual workers (AMMAR, Asociación de Mujeres Meretrices de Argentina en Acción por Nuestros Derechos).
36. Alisa Bierria (2014) describes, for example, the compound violence and erasure faced by Janice Wells, a Black schoolteacher in rural Georgia. In 2010, Wells made a call to the police to report a prowler in her vicinity. Upon responding to her call, Officer Tim Murphy, who is white, erroneously categorized Wells as a victim of domestic violence. Unfortunately, Murphy failed to attentively listen to Wells's account of the incident that had prompted her call. Instead, he pressed Wells to reveal the identity of a houseguest who had departed prior to the officer's arrival. Wells, however, declined to disclose the guest's name. This led Murphy to call for backup, and Officer Ryan Smith, also white, arrived at the scene. In a distressing turn of events, Officer Smith swiftly employed a taser on Wells, causing her to collapse on the ground as she begged to be left alone. Bierria contends that law enforcement relies on a "historically constituted, socially reinforced, and institutionally authorized archive [that] acts as a silent resource used by other agents to discern what black women's actions 'really mean'" (2014, 133).
37. See my discussion of snuff in chapter 2. See also C. Riley Snorton and Jin Haritaworn (2013).

38. Ley de Salud Sexual y Procreación Responsable [Responsible Reproduction and Sexual Health] (Bill 25.673/2002), Argentina, Congreso de la Nación, 2002 Session. [https://www.argentina.gob.ar/normativa/nacional/ley-25673-79831/texto], Programa Nacional de Educación Sexual Integral [National Program of Integral Sex Education] (Bill 26.150/2006), Argentina, Congreso de la Nación, 2006 Session.

39. Nicolas Zuberman, "Marlene Wayar: 'Soy un gerundio: No sé qué soy, sí que estoy siendo travesti.'" *Tiempo Argentino*, September 20, 2018. Accessed November 3, 2022. https://www.tiempoar.com.ar/informacion-general/marlene-wayar-soy-un-gerundio-no-se-que-soy-si-que-estoy-siendo-travesti/.

40. Marce Butierrez and Patricio Simonetto (2020) spearhead formidable historical work on the links between travesti sex work, criminalization, and social exclusion in the last quarter of the twentieth century.

41. As far as ethnographies are concerned, the more substantive accounts of the interweaving of racialization, Indigeneity, and sexuality are Decena (2011, 2023), Stephen (2002), and Prieur (1998). Other ethnographies unfortunately lack an understanding of the coproduction of race and sexuality, among them, Sívori (2005), Fernandez (2004), and Núñez Noriega (1999).

42. OutRight Action International (OutRight) is an LGBTIQ human rights nongovernmental organization that addresses human rights violations and abuses against lesbian, gay, bisexual, transgender, and intersex people. Formerly known as the International Gay and Lesbian Human Rights Commission, it designated Lohana Berkins as the recipient of its Felipa de Souza Award. The award recognizes outstanding leadership in the fight for LGBTQ+ human rights. Felipa de Souza (1556, Portugal–1600, Brazil) was a woman who met her demise due to the onslaught of the Catholic Inquisition during the Brazilian colonial period. She was accused of sodomy because she had romantic relationships with other women.

43. Philosopher Enrique Dussel (2006) has framed an ethics of transcultural communication under the notion of transversality. Unlike his approach, which focuses on avant-garde intellectuals, my interpretation bears witness of *transversalidad* among racialized travestis who excel as intellectuals in their own right.

44. All translations are mine unless stated otherwise. The original in Spanish states, "En la construcción de esa autoafirmación se pierde algo muy importante para mí, que es la transversalidad de lo que yo soy. Yo hoy, decirte a vos [que puedo] pararme frente a la gente y decir 'soy travesti' y, a lo sumo, me darán un aplauso. Porque ya no sorprende a nadie ser travesti. Entendés? Ahora, si yo a eso. Si empiezo a hablar de la tranversalidad de lo que es ser travesti; entonces, las travestis somos pobres. [. . .] No tenemos acceso a la educación[,] [. . .] a la salud[,] [. . .] a la vivienda[,] [. . .] o a un trabajo digno; nos matan. Digo, esa transversalidad y a esa tranversalidad la confronto, la discuto, la disputo con piqueteros, piqueteras. [. . .] Sino me pongo junto, que se levanten las banderas de los derechos humanos de treinta mil desaparecidos, de los cuales muchos eran lesbianas, maricones y travestis. Me entendés?"

45. For instance, there was the decade-long dispute that travestis waged against powerful factions within the gay and lesbian movement. The dispute stems

from the latter's advocacy in support of transforming the Pride parade into entertainment (fieldwork notes, June 2003).

46. "Picketers" (*piqueteros*) refers to a collective identity within Argentina, shaped in the second half of the 1990s. They protested the spike of unemployment rates under neoliberal regulations. Their strategy was to block highways for weeks at a time by setting up pickets and demanding employment programs and public services (Dinerstein 2010).

47. In the case of travestis, criminalization is attached to their labor. For a critique of neoliberalism and its sexual politics, see Duggan (2003, xx) and Sabsay (2011, 32).

48. The government of Néstor Kirchner first supports the creation of this cooperative in 2008. Since then, the cooperative has explored opportunities to satisfy demands from outside buyers, launch a self-sustaining clothing brand, and fight the threat of shutdown with the rise to power of the right-leaning party PRO in 2016.

49. Alma Fernandez, "Amor Travesti, Motor de la Cooperativa Textil Nadia Echazú," *Agencia Presentes*, March 31, 2021. Accessed November 4, 2023. https://agenciapresentes.org/2021/03/31/el-amor-travesti-motor-de-la-cooperativa-textil-nadia-echazu/.

50. Interviews with Lohana Berkins (Asociación de Lucha por la Identidad Travesti-Transexual, ALITT), Mónica León (Hotel Gondolín), and members of the Area Queer de la Universidad de Buenos Aires. See also one of Berkins's published speeches (Fernandez, D'Uva, and Viturro 2002).

51. Section 81 of Buenos Aires's city code sanctions sexual solicitation. Based on an analysis by former city councilor Diana Maffía, the city filed 7,470 cases for alleged violations of section 81 in a single year. The Prosecutor's Office in CABA released a report citing 5,427 cases for alleged violations of section 81 for the year 2011, among which a whopping 99.2 percent were initiated by the police force.

52. According to the *Diccionario de la lengua española* (2020), a gaucho was a "mestizo who, in the 18th and 19th centuries, inhabited Argentina, Uruguay, and Rio Grande do Sul in Brazil, and was a migratory horseman, and adept in cattle work." Pisano (2018) states that there is continuity surrounding the cultural production of gaucho characters between the colonial and post-1810 period in Argentina. Specifically, gauchesca literature accumulates themes and plots where marriage constitutes the main milestone for gaucho subjectivity. For a group whose social standing is defined by migration, getting married served at least two goals: affirmation of the self within the project of the nation, and of the group's contribution to settling the nation's territory. Both objectives function as pathways toward the eventual whitening of the flatland settlers in Argentina, with the goal of shaping them into the nucleus of Rioplatense culture during the transitional period spanning the late eighteenth to early nineteenth centuries.

53. See also Delaney (1996).

54. For another compelling critique of Kulick's findings, see "Espaço Interdito" (Silva 2013, 148–149).

55. The vignette *Clemente* was published from March 1973 through December 2012. His creator, Caloi, passed in May 2012 but left stories to be published posthumously through the end of that year.

56. See also Sterling (2010) and Moreno Figueroa and Saldívar Tanaka (2015).

57. See also Ocoró Loango (2011).
58. According to Julia Broguet (2016, 203), "to be *negra* or *negro* in Argentina, often referred to as 'de alma' (meaning 'from the bottom of one's soul,' as some add to clarify that they are not referring to 'Black race'), implies a series of aesthetic, moral, and erotic characteristics that can be relatively independent of one's skin color (Blázquez 2008)." In other words, even without being recognized as phenotypically Black, one can be identified (and occasionally self-identify) as a "negro del alma" for engaging in "Black things."
59. For an expansive sociohistorical analysis of the Gender Identity bill in Argentina, see Theumer (2020).
60. The binary male/female option was later expanded to include the designation *X* by Executive Order 476/2021. Executive Order accessed November 10, 2023, https://www.boletinoficial.gob.ar/detalleAviso/primera/247092/20210721.
61. The Open Society Foundation, Pitzer College, Syracuse University, and a GoFundMe campaign provided the funds to cover expenses associated with travel, lodging, visa processing, and per diem for the following six activists and intellectuals: Pilar Salazar Argueta (journalist, activist, Guatemala), Jennicet Gutiérrez (activist, Familia:TQLM, United States), Indyra Mendoza Aguilar (lawyer, Cattrachas, Honduras), Susy Shock (activist, performer, author, Argentina), Marlene Wayar (activist, performer, author, Argentina), and Nahil Zerón (historian, activist, Cattrachas, Honduras). Both Portillo Villeda and Mendoza Aguilar identified as cisgender and nonheterosexual. It is important to note that Dr. Lynn Stephen, at the time the President of LASA, enthusiastically supported the roundtable.
62. Gentili passed away unexpectedly on February 6, 2024.
63. This project seeks to create evidence to lobby state agents through the campaign Indemnización Travesti/Trans Ya (Reparation for Trans/Travesti Communities Now). The first phase of this project launched in September 2022, consisting of eight two-hour virtual meetings over two months with the participation of the following trans- and travesti-identified activists: Ivanna Aguilera, Victoria Antola, Libertad Aranguez, Feda Baeza, Sofía Díaz, PJ DiPietro, Quimey Ramos, Miss Romi, Cole Rizki, Victoria Stefano, Szabine Vollenweider, and Marlene Wayar. Rocío Pichon-Rivière, a cisgender woman ally, also contributed to this space.
64. Pilar Cabrera is the creator and host of the YouTube channel Activismo Travesti.
65. *Copla* is a poetic and musical genre that combines Indigenous and Spanish contributions to popular culture (Páez et al. 2021). While it originates from a diverse heritage, it is often noted for aligning with the tonal structure found in Andean music.
66. Hate-based and prejudice-based crimes against people who identify as LGBTQA+ or gender dissidents are an index of the gap between formal and substantive citizenship. Data on violence based on gender expression and identity paint a bleak picture. *El prejuicio no conoce fronteras* report (Colombia Diversa 2019) shows the number of violent deaths among the LGBTQ+ population of ten Latin American countries over the 2014–2019 period. This dossier reports 1,300 violent deaths, indicating that countries such as Colombia and Mexico, whose legal provisions for LGBT+ rights are relatively

comprehensive, registered 75 percent of those deaths. Honduras followed, with a distant 13 percent, but, in its case, the legislation runs against LGBT+ protections, since the country excludes same-sex couples from marriage and adoption, LGBT+ people from military service, and trans people from access to health.

67. See, for example, Isa Noyola of Familia: Trans Queer Liberation Movement (TQLM) in "Isa Noyola at the Supreme Court – Masterpiece," Transgender Law Center, 3:02, December 5, 2017, https://youtu.be/YPWidNZNSFU. See also de la Garza (2019).

68. According to Amnesty International, the Protection of Life and the Family Bill (Ley 5272) is a serious threat to human rights and families in Guatemala. Although the president, Alejandro Giammattei, voiced its disagreement with the bill, the fact that the national congress passed it on March 8, 2022, sends a clear message about the strength of the country's religious right. The bill seeks to amend the penal code to criminalize miscarriages and impose prison sentences on anyone who "promotes or facilitates access to abortion." It would expressly proscribe same-sex marriage, as well as sex education and training on diversity and gender equality in schools, and outlaw the criminal prosecution of individuals or groups who discriminate against others based on their sexual orientation. Giammattei vetoed and archived the bill in March of 2022.

69. Omi Salas-SantaCruz provides an expansive critique of trans legibility and its archive. Their work on jotería as "decolonial praxis" performs the epistemic shift that I am trying to convey (2023, 79–81).

70. But see Contreras (2009, 183), who argues otherwise.

71. I shared this story briefly with one of my introductory women's and gender studies courses at Syracuse University. A student's response provided a poignant critique, highlighting my ongoing negotiation of the legacy of cisgender privilege from my upbringing, despite my current commitment to anti-racist and trans feminism. The student, who identifies as a cisgender queer woman with Mohawk ancestry, suggested that I could pay more attention to the fact that my sister's ownership of the convenience store is a noteworthy accomplishment.

72. See chapter 4, "Hallucinating Knowing."

Chapter 2. The Coloniality of Transgender

1. Feminist critiques of gender as a universalizing method of inquiry stage the contradictions between an Othering construction, which is both cultural and ideological, and the material, real, and concrete experiences of collective subjectification. Post-structuralist, post-colonial, and decolonial debates examine gender as a concept, critiquing its universalizing force by advancing complex accounts of local histories, social and collective forms of resistant agency, and cross-cultural continuities and variations. Sometimes these critiques are friendly to each other, as is the case of the works of Chandra Talpade Mohanty (1984, 2003), Oyèrónkẹ́ Oyěwùmí (1997), and Gloria Wekker (2006). Sometimes they are not, as is the case of the positions of Alcoff (2005) and Lugones (2020).

2. But consider more recent developments in trans philosophy and, specifically, metaphysics. See, for example, Dembroff (2018) and Zurn et al. (2024).
3. See Karera (2019).
4. This is María Lugones's contribution to theorizing multiple oppressions. See DiPietro, McWeeny, and Roshanravan (2019).
5. On social kinds and philosophical analysis, see Haslanger (2006).
6. As I will show shortly, chromosomal distinction is always already sociosomatic.
7. Feminisms are committed to the business of examining whose expectations these are.
8. It is my understanding that Haslanger is referring to distinctions between egg-bearing and sperm-bearing human animals. Typically, human animals present with XX and XY chromosomes, respectively. The gender function of such distinction may align with contexts that either stabilize or disrupt that function. The objective reality of XX does not change, as she would have it, but its function does, due to the interaction of systemic oppression and context. The first-order ascription occurs at the level of *distinction*, while second-order at the level of *difference*. Perry Zurn (personal communication) suggested to me that there is a carceral logic in Haslanger's model as it pertains to the prominence of first-order ascription. I concur because this prominence traps what I call sociosomatic looping within the colonial/modern gender system. See also DiPietro (2024).
9. In his study of the galenic unisex body, Laqueur (1992) argues that sex remains an epiphenomenon of gender hierarchies, for Western societies, until at least the sixteenth century.
10. This statement resembles Charlotte Witt's notion of unification essentialism or "uniessentialism" (2011).
11. Ethnohistories document multiple gender systems. Lugones works with a schematic approach through which she examines the introduction of racial classification over the long sixteenth century to extract human differences and distinctions out of colonized bodies. Gender dimorphism and sexualization have an axial role in coloniality's extractive mode.
12. See An Act Relating to Abortion, including Abortions after Detection of an Unborn Child's Heartbeat; Authorizing a Private Civil Right of Action, Tex. S.B. 8, 87th Leg. (2021–2022), available at https://capitol.texas.gov/tlodocs/87R/billtext/pdf/SB00008F.pdf.
13. It is not far-fetched to anticipate a near future when reproductive and cloning technologies will at least partially replace the gestational sac. In such cases, whose last menstruation would S.B. 8 refer to? Zygotes are in fact placed in the gestational sac of people who do not provide eggs for in vitro fertilization. How to determine, in such cases, the carrier's last menstruation with respect to S.B. 8's construction of pregnancy?
14. New York Reproductive Health Act, S.B. S240, available at https://legislation.nysenate.gov/pdf/bills/2019/S240.
15. I am aware that the category "intersex" is often imposed upon people who do not identify as such. For accounts of "intersex" as a diagnostic imposition, see Swarr (2023).
16. See, for example, Schultz et al. (2009), 534–536.

17. It matters that I show the way that second-order ascription (normative coherence) bears on first-order ascription (normative assignation or assessment). Ultimately, I am aware that the political salience of these bills is that they typically (though not always) target self-identified cisgender women more than anybody else. I mean to show that even an incendiary bill such as S.B. 8 can mobilize metaphysical ascriptions that other social groups, or actors, would effectively and effervescently mobilize with feminist ends. I thank Rowan Bell for their invitation to engage this kind of metaphysical reflection on gender.

18. I don't mean to flatten the political valence of the subject "woman" as intrinsic to sexual and reproductive rights struggles. However, I do mean to point out that "woman" is a narrow category for anti-racist, intersectional, and transnational feminist struggles, including sexual- and reproductive rights struggles. I am not jumping from an ontological to a political analysis. I am claiming that they inform and implicate each other across epistemology and ontology.

19. Linda Martín Alcoff responds to Haslanger's realism with a more concrete and politically relevant perspective on the metaphysics of sex (2005). Her approach recognizes the importance of lived experiences and discourse in the material world. Alcoff engages directly with cisgender women's experiences, blending phenomenology and hermeneutics to explore how social subjects embody and interpret their world (95). She highlights the generative force of discourses, that subjectivity is a social kind, and that, to a significant extent, discourse creates social things manifesting subjectivity. Note, however, that I wouldn't arrive at the same metaphysics of sex that Martín Alcoff offers (2005).

20. On scopic regime, see Jay (1988). My reading of *snuff* differs from Valencia and Falcón's (2021). They are focused on emotions, feelings, and grievances as forms of consent, which in their view, media elicits from individuals whose prejudices align with an "axiology inherited by racism, misogyny, and 'Compulsory heterosexuality'" (36).

21. On the Situationists, see McDonough (2009).

22. For a situationist thinker such as Henri Lefebvre, symmetry/asymmetry is a property of social space. It also relates to the matter of an energetic body whose outpouring at once follows and counters symmetries. Sex worker and solicitor both cruise streets. Yet, they each differentiate each other through positions and practices.

23. CONASIDA (National Commission for the Fight against AIDS) does not have a web presence that I could find, other than a Facebook page. The last activity recorded on this page dates to the month of June in the year 2022. The National Secretary of Health is the last state agency to issue a report that mentions CONASIDA. This 2023 report audits all expenditures on the fight against HIV/AIDS for the 2021 period.

24. See also DiPietro, McWeeny, and Roshanravan (2019) and Gramling and Dutta (2016).

25. Chapter 4 examines Xicana, AfroLatinx, and Latinx narratives where nonhuman accounts of thinking explicate resistant responsiveness against the coloniality of transgender.

26. Materialist theories such as distributed cognition have profound consequences for philosophical arguments about consciousness and multiplicity among historically marginalized social groups. For instance, Mariana Ortega, a leading voice in feminist phenomenology, turns to the notion of "mineness" to explicate existential continuity for Latina selves (2016, 80). Far from furnishing a detailed critique of Ortega's theorization of multiplicitous selves, I opt to engage an agential realist account of sideways selves that clearly rejects the notion of mineness. Sideways selves and their bodily projects refute even the most benign forms of atomism, which purportedly existential mineness supports. See also chapter 5 in this book.

27. See also Karina Ochoa Muñoz (2018).

28. While Hortense Spillers introduces the notion of "ungendering" in her essay "Mama's Baby, Papa's Maybe" (1987), I seek to expand the often overlooked ontological commitment that the term demands with respect to time. If ungendering can only be conceived as a process undoing what is already there, the bodily projects of sideways selves entail multiple ontologies, including, among them, a retroactive yet enduring present, a future perfect, and an imperfect ongoing past.

29. In 2014, *Time* magazine's cover features actress and trans activist Laverne Cox under the heading "The Transgender Tipping Point." The headline aims to normalize trans visibility but doesn't acknowledge Cox's racial identity, possibly due to her being African American, or assuming that racial visibility predates the current political climate. Consequently, it separates trans from racial identities.

30. I am referring to context-specific yet interrelated fields, products, research labs, marketing strategies, and even therapy groups. See, for instance, Hil Malatino's rigorous account of biohacking gender (2017).

31. A notorious slippage can be found in Hayward and Weinstein's (2015) account of the prepositional figuration of trans* across geopolitical domains. While their position beautifully conveys the "expressive force" of the "asterisk" (embedded in *trans**) as it sticks to specific materializations, they provide a limiting example of what this expressive force entails. As they cite (197–198) Marcia Ochoa's magnificent ethnography about "the Venezuelan *loca*," Hayward and Weinstein emphasize the ontological salience of the asterisk in *trans** as "it sticks" to *loca-lizations* (this is Ochoa's wording). Hayward and Weinstein's inquiry overlooks whether *locas*, encompassing bodily projects, sociality, and politics, *relocates trans** from a prepositional to a postpositional standpoint, from an English-sounding context to cacophony, or from "equal to one" to an equal-to-none specificity.

32. See the latest research on the marbled crayfish, who in the last thirty years went from sexual to asexual reproduction, and to cloning (Pennizi 2018).

33. I don't imply that the distinction between egg-bearing and sperm-bearing infrastructures could change in one's lifetime. However, the case of the marbled crayfish calls our attention to the potential of variation at the biomolecular and genetic levels.

34. These critiques range from brazenly transphobic positions (Raymond 1979) to nuanced accounts of the intersection of biotechnology, self-determination,

and normativity (Stone 1992), and from engagements with cyborgs (Haraway 1991) to dystopian monstrosity (Lewis 2017, 114).

35. Among posthumanist materialisms that perpetuate hybrid universalism, I find Butler's (1993), Halberstam's (2018), and Braidotti's (2002, 2013). By contrast, Cynthia Willett's (2014) and Karen Barad's (2007, 2014) foreground intercultural, decolonial features.

36. See also Karera (2019).

37. "Foulest vice" follows the semantic of "contagion." Ochoa (2016) draws connections among three different colonial versions of this attack.

38. See the engraving at http://activehistory.ca/wp-content/uploads/2014/04/Image-2.jpg.

39. On deterritorialization, reterritorialization, the molar, and the molecular, see Merriman (2019).

40. Anality does not relate to psychoanalysis.

41. Notice that *same-sex* poorly glosses the bodily projects of Chumash and other communities both in Abya Yala and Turtle Island. Both denominations are political in nature and signal an ongoing cross-border resistance. They seek to decenter the settler-colonial state throughout the continent. See Bergman et al. (2020).

42. Heterogeneity is paramount in this account of bodily impressibility. For what the record shows, the Cuareca forty engage anal practices across social hierarchies. The brother of the community's chief is among the practitioners of anal sex. We cannot state with certainty that anal sex constitutes a route for nonconformity. We can, however, recognize the vital, physiological, and social asymmetries that it assembles.

43. See also Dutta and Roy (2014) and Snorton (2017).

44. But also see Schuller (2018), who finds that in nineteenth-century America, civilizing habits refined the nervous system and, thusly, turned their impressibility into acquired quality.

45. It is worth noticing the resonance between three locales and their politics of rehabilitation: Kim's undertaking in South Korean and mine, through a different approach, in both Argentina and the United States.

46. Since transgender sits in the periphery of the light side, its bodily responsiveness remains closer to *genders* and not Gender. Hence, (lowercase plural) masculinities and femininities.

47. See the analysis advanced by C. Riley Snorton (2017, 59–64) about Peter Sewally, alias Mary Jones, who was dubbed "The Man-Monster" by New York's print media in the early nineteenth century.

48. The exclusion was finally eliminated in 2014. The policy originated in 1948; see Women's Armed Services Integration Act of 1948, 62 Stat. 365, Public Law 625, accessed November 4, 2022, https://govtrackus.s3.amazonaws.com/legislink/pdf/stat/62/STATUTE-62-Pg356a.pdf.

49. Mallory, Brown, and Conron (2019) document the perils of conversion therapy for LGBT youth.

50. There are anxieties about the regimentation of transgender variations. On transnormativity under the formula "I was born this way," see Bettcher (2012) and Valentine (2007).

51. On monstrosity within Foucault's scholarship, see Malatino (2019, 47–48).
52. Foucault describes monstrosity as an othering variation of the human (1997, 51–52).
53. See also Bacchetta (1999).
54. My proposal expands María Lugones's approach (2007) by following more closely the molar and molecular scales of coloniality.
55. In Sandy Stone's (1992) counter to Janice Raymond's transphobia (1979), artificial intelligence gives uptake to the twenty-first-century incarnation of trans-monstrosity. It opens lines of flight such as cyborg corporality (Haraway 1991, 150).
56. Trans activist Jennicet Gutiérrez taught me the motto "My existence means resistance."
57. The Colima hollow sculptures include clay figurines of dogs and their anthropomorphic variations (Burrison 2017, 258). Native Mesoamerican peoples placed faunal and sacrificial offerings in their graves (de la Garza 1997; Burrison 2017). When canine remains were interred with the dead, they symbolized the afterlife of both Kuna and non-Kuna animals.
58. Xolotl is the twin brother of Quetzacoatl within the Mexica pantheon. They are the children of the world's original pair and oppose each other (de la Garza 1997, 126). While Quetzacoatl represents the morning star and the wisest being, Xolotl represents the evening star and the fall into the netherworld (Burrison 2017, 258). The word *xoloitzcuintli* ("hairless dog," in Spanish) needs the sound *xolo*. The connection between dogs and the netherworld becomes evident.
59. The Mexica considered twins to be anomalies (de la Garza 1997, 127). The term *axolotl*, which designates a water animal, provides further evidence that *xolo* underscores something extraordinary.
60. Casabindo peoples are a pre-Hispanic Indigenous group located in the central plateau of the state of Jujuy. Their presence in the area dates to the Late Regional Development Period (ca. 1250–1430 AD). According to anthroponymy studies, the last name Patagua belongs to a group that, although influenced by the arrival of the Inka population in the fourteenth century, does not share ethnic roots with either Aymara or Quechua peoples.
61. See Price (2023).
62. I gingerly engage with ethnographic studies of Indigenous peoples, considering, as Linda Tuhiwai Smith (2012, 16–17) argues, that non-Indigenous researchers must question practices that weaken and deny Indigenous sovereignty and autonomy.
63. See also a complex account of Lakota relational ontology in Posthumus (2022).
64. Personhood within Kuna and Aymara cosmologies does not match Western accounts of individuals. For the Aymara's, see Arnold and Yapita (2007, 59).
65. *Kuna-animal* is a neologism that troubles equivalence between human and Kuna personhood.
66. I am drawn to Cynthia Willett's compelling thesis on interspecies ethics (2014). Drawing on concepts of affective attunement and contextual egalitarianism among species, Willett argues that animal play shapes "ethical capacities and communicative technologies" (81).

67. The neologism *dekunafication* highlights the geopolitical and ontological distance between *human people* and Kuna personhood. The Kuna people, also referred to as the Guna or Cuna, are an Indigenous community mainly found in the Gulf of Panamá and the San Blas Islands in Panamá, along with regions in Colombia. Matrilineality is a significant feature of their political organization.

68. See Alexander (2005b), Keating (2012), and L. Pérez (2019) for posthumanist readings of Anzaldúa's oeuvre.

69. In her earliest writing, Anzaldúa relied on stereotypes about Indigenous women (Keating 2012, 57; Contreras 2009, 183; Ramirez 2007, 142). However, AnaLouise Keating suggests that we may (1) praise Anzaldúa's attention to Indigenous worlds within border cultures, for which *mexicanidad* and *tejanidad* often signified amnesia about an ancestral past; (2) criticize her sometimes "monolithic [. . .] representations of Native women" (57); and (3) recognize her work along Indigenous and Native communities to confront her own ignorance.

70. It should be clear by now that I move away from Hil Malatino's call for a "coalition of monsters" (2019, 204). Out of the respect and affection that I have for Malatino's labor, I shall journey with him to an abyss beyond *and before* monstrous formations.

71. The Aymara's theory of numerals features ontological relations exceeding Western dialectics. Singular personal pronouns—*naya, jupa*, and *juma*—enact cosmological principles of opposing complementarity that cannot be reduced to the dynamic thesis/antithesis (Miranda Luizaga and Del Carpio Natcheff 2000). Through triadic relations of creativity, the number one (pronoun *naya*, singular) contains germinating stasis as plurisingularity. *Many-one* turn into *many-many* (pronouns *juma* and *jupa*) through self-reflection and inversions, but without antagonisms. See also the magnificent account of "cosmolectics" coined by Gloria Chacón in her work about Maya and Zapotec literatures (2018).

72. For contrasting philosophical views on Anzaldúa's pluralism, see Ortega (2016) and Paccacerqua (2016).

Chapter 3. Stressing Verbs, De-stressing Nouns

1. See Lugones (2007); Oyěwùmí (1997); Arvin, Tuck, and Morrill (2013); but also Segato (2015), Paredes (2010), and Paredes and Guzmán (2014).

2. The Movimiento al Socialismo (Movement for Socialism) is a Bolivian left-wing political party led by Evo Morales, which was founded in 1998. It evolved out of the Aymara-led movement to defend the interests of coca growers.

3. I prefer the "greater than" sign (>) to convey that the counterparts stand together yet are linked by a dichotomous and hierarchical logic.

4. While textual and ethnographic research on Mesoamerican Catholicism informs this chapter, the cross-cultural specificities demand a more robust undertaking. Comparative analysis brings the following texts in dialogue among many others: Marcos (2006, 2009); Boone, Burkhart, and Tavárez (2017); Aguilera (2009); Scheper Hughes (2016); and Christensen (2010).

5. Copla-singing refers to a type of Andean music that many in Jujuy recognize as part of Kolla ancestral cultural and religious practices. Typically accompanied by a *caja* (drum), locals improvise short songs, "often as witty and slightly suggestive repartees" (Occhipinti 2002, 320).

6. González-Wippler's (1995) understanding of syncretism allows for the combination of specific religious systems and a more generalized crisscrossing, fusing, and intertwining of disparate cultural elements. Instead of thinking about syncretism as a defining feature of exotic and disappearing cultures, González-Wippler reminds us that a feature of the vitality and endurance of religious systems is precisely their disposition toward change, proliferation, and mixing.

7. Eunjung Kim's (2017) words about curative violence, a paradigm linked to supremacist and ableist ideologies, serve as contrast.

8. In Jujuy, the Andean Catholic calendar combines agricultural and liturgical calendars, blending pre-Hispanic and Christian festivities. June celebrates the Sun (Inti Raimi), August focuses on fecundity and Pachamama's gifts. December to early January includes Christmas, while January to late February centers on Carnaval, Lent, and Resurrection. Ritual participants offer cuartos (gifts), typically sheep's or goat's meat, accompanied by music from instruments like the *erke* (cornet) and drum or performances by *sikuris* and *saya* dancers (Ontiveros 2003, 161). *Siku* is a wind instrument, and *saya* is a music and dance genre in this region.

9. Dual complementarity is a principle of social organization. It consists of the division of political authority between two polities. Anthropology in the south-central Andes identifies a system of vertical integration predating the arrival of Spaniards. This system provides a material basis for dual complementarity. Moieties secure resources from their counterparts, which are located in an environmentally contrasting agricultural region. See Zuidema (1989, 1990) and Murra (1975).

10. *Gastar* (to spend) works as in "cama," the Quechua term that conveys the existence of a power to reestablish the order of the cosmos. Regina Harrison (1993) describes the sacred role that spending plays among Quechua speakers as they foster reciprocity between mundane beings and Andean deities. *Cama*, in her view, refers to "[a way of transferring] energy allowing something to come into existence" for the well-being of the commons (174).

11. Linguists consider Andean Spanish a dialectical continuum that cuts across the Andean Cordillera. Historical and social variables must be considered to understand its formation. See Lang 1990.

12. My interpretation, in this case, is connected to the framework that refracts the lens of social analysis when the center is no longer occupied by dominant subjectivities. See the introduction to Hull, Scott, and Smith's *All the Women Are White, All the Blacks Are Men, But Some of Us Are Brave* (1982).

13. In physics, refraction is the change in direction of a wave passing from one medium to another (air to water, for example) or resulting from a gradual change in the medium (evaporation, for example). Light, sound, and water waves, among others, experience refraction. I use refraction as an epistemic metaphor to analyze the work that any aspect of social formation, such as gender, performs when it travels from one sociohistorical medium to another.

Gender belongs to the sociohistorical medium of coloniality. An approach such as Salustiana's about her life story underscores the directional change of an analytics across different media, from Gender, to *genders*, to "genders."

14. In the 1980s, post-structuralist thinkers established a systematic deconstruction of binaries. They argue that cultural logics exceed the often underexamined rift between constructivist and essentialist views about social phenomena, from those that most consider ostensibly social, such as taste, to those that few could consider artificial, such as sexed difference (Fuss 1989; Sedgwick 1990). Simultaneously, the logical implications of post-structuralist positions raised skepticism toward identity and its politics. They ultimately undermined the epistemic authority of historically marginalized groups. Specifically, they cast doubt on the imaginings and narratives that marginalized groups create based on appeals to their reflections on identity as a project of strong objectivity. For a viewpoint contrasting mine, see Puar (2012).

15. According to Ferdinand de Saussure, semiotics entails identifying the units of a system of meaning. Relations between signs produce meaning through two main axes, one that concerns the combination of units or signs—which relies on a syntagmatic axis—and another that concerns the association of units or signs—which relies on a paradigmatic axis. While syntagmatic combinations follow an additive logic (this-*and*-that), associative combinations follow an either/or logic (this-*or*-that). In standard Spanish grammar, the sign *el* (article masc. sing.) can be combined with any noun on the syntagmatic axis, as long as the speaker applies proper rules to select a happy unit from those available on the paradigmatic axis. All nouns are available, but they should accommodate the gender and number of the first unit in the syntagmatic axis. Applied to the statement before us, the universe of available nouns must meet both masculine gender and singular number.

16. Spanish uses reflexive pronouns when the subject and direct object of the reflexive verb is the same. For example, "I name myself."

17. I acknowledge that the concern with self-delusion could also apply to my interpretation of Salustiana's use of language.

18. In 2001, Argentina faced a severe economic crisis marked by a massive debt default, high unemployment, social unrest, and widespread protests. It led to the collapse of the Alianza Party's government.

19. The Virgen del Socavón represents the contemporary negotiation of Bolivian identities within the context of Carnaval. Her iconography weaves together pre-Hispanic and colonial elements, but most important, it entails the sovereign affirmation of Oruro's Indigenous past and present. She is associated with the working class of miners and their need for protection in the mine shafts (Lecount 1999, 234–235; Kaliman 1999).

20. Historiography on the formation of ruling elites in Jujuy and Salta in northwestern Argentina remains limited, with most studies focusing on the marriage market in the pampas region, and the immigration-driven changes in the late nineteenth to early twentieth centuries (Mazzeo and Perelman 2016). In the late eighteenth century, Spanish-identified individuals accounted for just 5 percent of Jujuy's white population, with 75 percent of them residing in the state capital and holding political power and wealth (Paz 1997). The

mestizo population made up 19 percent of the province's registered residents, while Indigenous people constituted a significant 57 percent. Despite diverse demographics, the ruling authority was concentrated in Spanish-sounding family names, with a notable forty of them dominating. An analysis of nuptials reveals that Spanish families primarily married within their own group (Paz 1997). Twenty-seven of these last names remain influential in today's financial and political landscape in San Salvador de Jujuy.

21. Leandro Losada (2012) surveys the Argentine marriage market in the forty-year period between 1900 and 1940. His study shows the slow yet defining shift of the traditional origins of Argentine culture and national values, from families associated with dominant power to the ranks of the middle classes.

22. For the most delightful account of *servinakuy*, see Millones and Pratt (1990). This pre-Hispanic social form is still alive among Aymara and Quechua peoples, and it consists of "common law" unions or trials of long-term cohabitation between men and women. I come from an area in northwestern Argentina where the institutions of "amichamiento" and "concubinato" are widespread.

23. Race is a fiction. Thus, phenotype does not express an underlying biological reality or condition. Race is the by-product of racial formation (See Omi and Winant 2014; Quijano 1991).

24. Catholicism wasn't the sole social institution associated with colonial expansion. Puritanism played an equal role in colonial expansion, as emphasized by Dugre: "The success of early modern colonial ventures like Massachusetts hinged not only on the internal balance of church and colony government but also on regional geopolitics [. . .]. Puritan efforts to devise an intercolonial confederation offer insight into some of the ways early English colonists worked to turn disparate polities of varying origin and legitimacy into functional commonwealths" (2018, 387).

25. Aztecs attacked the cultural memory of vanquished groups as they did when they burnt Toltec *amoxtli* (Brotherson 1997). Cristóbal Vaca de Castro, who governed Peru from 1541 until 1544, had great difficulty determining the lineage of Inkas. According to Jiménez de la Espada (1892), few *quipus* or *quipucamayocs* (*quipu* weavers or keepers) still existed. Apparently, Huáscar Atahuallpa "had ordered his captains to kill all the quipucamayocs they could find and burn their quipus" (Yeakel 1983, 45).

26. See Dussel (1994).

27. On seminal logic as critique of causality within Western thinking, see Kusch (2010, 130–132).

28. Note that I intervene in the English language to emphasize activity in the gerund, which works as noun.

29. See also Rivera Cusicanqui (2013) for a nonlinear understanding of history among Aymara and Indigenous peoples of Bolivia.

30. Dative case has the basic role of distinguishing the recipient of something given, transferred; accusative case has the basic role of marking a direct object; and genitive case the basic role of marking a noun or noun phrase that is added to another noun or noun phrase. See Matthews (2014).

31. The English speaker may find such a transliteration awkward-sounding.
32. It goes without saying that linguistic expression within Andean Spanish is a much stronger proponent of self-identification through flexible, nonbinary gender pronouns.
33. Michael Horswell (2005) and Tom Zuidema (1990) identify nontraditional gender subjectivities within the Andean *ayllus'* kinship system. While not delving into the metaphysical coloniality of gender, they describe communal roles primarily determined by kinship rather than gender or anatomy, with *ipa* serving as one prominent signifier. Typically translated as "aunt" on the father's side, an ipa's responsibilities extend throughout the community. Their evidence highlights how kinship shapes bodies through accountability and reciprocity, demonstrating that it's not solely women's bodies that fit these kin positions. Instead, kinship and embodiment coproduce complex sociosomatic connections, resulting in diverse styles of being that evolve, mutate, and endure over time.
34. By positivity, I mean the type of relation that defines existents without reference to what they exclude. For instance, in the colonial/modern gender system, Woman is defined by reference to what Man excludes. It lacks positivity as an existent.
35. Intersectional studies seek to make sense of oppressive social formation in the tense relation between distortion and illegibility. Perhaps it is the agentic aspect of oppression and resistance to oppression that shapes the lack of intelligibility that these studies underscore (Crenshaw 1991; Carastathis 2016; May 2015).
36. It should be noted that Halberstam's work examines butch variation as combining performative and nonperformative features. Halberstam's work is, indeed, a counter to key limitations in Butler's proposal. Both Butler and Halberstam, however, converge in their additive understanding of race and racialization (See DiPietro 2016b; Roen 2006).
37. While I specifically examine Andean Spanish and its use of clitics, available scholarship on Central American and Mesoamerican Spanish provides key elements upon which to extend my hypothesis about loísmo and its gender-de-stressing effect. See Heinze (2005), García (2006), and Hernández Méndez and Palacios Alcaine (2015).
38. Furthermore, as Cynthia Willett suggests, the trend to single out nonhuman animal life forms as radically foreign in ethical and erotic domains makes Butler's edifice even more ontologically problematic (2014, 77–78, 179n36).
39. See also McCall (2005).

Chapter 4. Hallucinating Knowing

1. I follow an impure understanding of Latinx and Xicanx subjectivity (Lugones 2003b, 121–150; Rueda Esquibel 2003, 296). This network consists of cultural activists from diverse socioeconomic and geographical backgrounds, from cis and trans communities, including Chicanas, Mexicanas, Tejanas, Nuevomexicanas, Chapinas, Oaxaqueñas, Salvadoreans, Dominicans, Cubans, Puerto Ricans, and many more. They expand Chicana and Latina

standpoints (Arredondo et al. 2003, 2–3). I join others who use "x" in *Xicana* to highlight both the Nahuatl spelling of the "ch" and the links among Native peoples in the diaspora (Castillo 2014; Moraga 2011). I use *Chicana* and *Chicano* to signal that I am quoting the works of others or a different period.

2. Even Fray Bartolomé de las Casas, known as an early critic of colonialism, tied his advocacy for Indians to anti-Black sentiment. He initially suggested replacing Indian labor with African slaves, assuming Africans were hardier workers.

3. Michel Foucault's theory of biopower (1980) centers on a political power that manages populations, focusing on their productive capacities as a species rather than as individuals. Before the emergence of Western democratic nation-states in the seventeenth and eighteenth centuries, Foucault identifies two earlier forms of power rationality—concerned with divine and princely authority. With the advent of modern democracies, a new state rationality emerged, aiming to (1) learn about humans as a species and identify their biological secrets and (2) increase humans' capacity for self-discipline and productivity. Biopower, according to Foucault, is interested in the health of people in statistical rather than existential terms.

4. Following the scholarship of Nancy Hartsock (2004) and Sandra Harding (2004), I understand that social facts shape the position of all subjects and that, as such, they occupy a perspective along the lines of both dominant *and* nondominant positions. Meanwhile, a standpoint comes into being through conscious reflection to transform oppressive structures. Those who are located at the margins of power structures are better situated yet not necessarily bound to acquire a critical standpoint. See also Lugones (2003c) and Collins (1990).

5. Cultural studies scholars such as Juana María Rodriguez (2014) engage the materiality of film celluloid while developing a theory of loss. She argues that film offers a gesture remitting to irreparable loss, a body whose withering or own finality only exists as protracted absence (178–179). My medium is not film but rather the very sensorium where absence prompts a hallucinating response. In fact, hallucinations may assist sideways selves to navigate the dynamics between trace and loss.

6. According to Bill Ashcroft, "the child became important to the discourse of empire because the invention of childhood *itself* in European society was coterminous with the invention of that other notion of supreme importance to imperialism: race" (2001, 37; italics in the original). See also Martin Bloomer (2006) for a discussion of the historical link between humanism in the sixteenth century and the invention and education of children as prototypes of *man*.

7. Amalia Mesa-Bains (1999) and Laura Pérez (2007) theorize aesthetic strategies of minoritized Chicana/o cultural production, such as *rasquache* and *domesticana rasquache*. Although perceived as tacky, "insane," and ragged by the mainstream, rasquache affirms delegitimized Chicana/o culture. Imbued by a barrio or "underdog" sensibility, rasquache enacts an attitudinal disposition (Ybarra-Frausto 1991a, 1991b) that includes making beauty with what is available, such as strikingly disparate colors, waste, or cheap objects.

8. Aztlán refers to both the US Southwest and the mythical place of origin of Aztec peoples, ancestors of Xicanx communities.

9. The 1964 translation of Kant's work on mental "disorders" refers to "artificial insanity," whereas the 1974 translation opts for the phrase "artificially induced dementia."

10. In philosophical debates, Cartesian dualism explains what I call mind/body split. Fear of sensorial capabilities resonates with Kant's account of derangement.

11. This doesn't deny that they are equally yet differentially fused in the production of *women*.

12. See also a more robust engagement with the symbolism of both Malinche and Virgin of Guadalupe in Lozano-Díaz ([2002] 2021) and Gil and Vazquez (1996).

13. Colonizing desire was present from the onset of Spanish rule over Abya Yala. Its legacy shows resonance with the situation of Ana Paula's travesti bodily project in twenty-first-century Jujuy.

14. Chicano speech sanctions colonizing violence by using the epithet *chingada* to describe activity that prompts ill feelings. Its force derives from the notion that, by lying with Cortés (*chingar* in Nahuatl), Malintzin consents to be "fucked over" (Alarcón 1989, 61). *Malinche* or *malinchista* is anyone transgressing perceived group interests.

15. See also Lugones on Latina Lesbian as an oxymoron (2003a).

16. Brady (2002, 170) refers to the notion of *temporal geography* that Moraga develops as an analytic of queer Brownness in *Waiting in the Wings* (1997).

17. For instance, on matters such as spatialization and Chicana identity, Soto draws on the persuasive argument of Deena González (1997) about Moraga's essentializing rhetoric. However, Soto ignores the insightful counterpoints that Brady (2002) provides about Moraga's oeuvre within this debate.

18. I believe that Soto has in mind Michel Foucault's rendering of the power of the sword as prohibition. In this account, power must be ostensibly deployed for all its threatening might. By refusing, blocking, and canceling certain practices, juridical power recontours the social and places unlawful practitioners within a geography of unthinkability.

19. See also Lugones's treatment of *estar siendo* Chicana in her introduction to the translation of Rodolfo Kusch's *Indigenous and Popular Thinking in América* (2010).

20. The conceptualization of the entire play gathers elements of ritual performance, including the cave-like focal points where most of the action takes place. I don't consider the Cihuateteo performance as a primitivist reenactment designed to bring back Native and Indigenous lives into existence.

21. Arvin, Tuck, and Morrill (2013) argue that settler colonialism is a gendered process with lasting impacts on social relations, including kinship structures. They see heteropatriarchy and heteropaternalism working in tandem to harden Native and Indigenous social arrangements around bloodlines. Bonita Lawrence (2003) examines federal legislation, in both Canada and the United States, that defines Native and Indigenous women out of existence. For instance, Indigenous women in Canada are pressured to choose certain Native men for marriage or risk being excluded from becoming "part of the destiny of her own nation(s)" (5).

22. There are contrasting views regarding the ways that colonial power organizes, furthers, expands on, or introduces patriarchal arrangements. Julieta Paredes (2010) and Rita Segato (2015) view patriarchy as a pre-Hispanic social hierarchy whose magnitude increased with the introduction of race as social classification. María Lugones, instead, states that racial classification introduced a new gender system or that gender operates as a metaphysical imposition.

23. See also Emma Pérez (1999).

24. Richard Rodríguez (2009) studies the reproduction and disruption of a Chicana/o hegemonic patriarchal, nuclear, and heteronormative family across popular culture texts.

25. *Hounsis* and "horses" are key roles that women practitioners play in Vodoun and Santeria rites within Afro-Latinx diasporas (A.-M. Lara 2006; Sánchez-Carretero 2005). *Tlacuilo* and *tlamatinime* were painters and wise people who advanced philosophical and spiritual inquiry among Aztecs (Pérez 2007, 13 and 22).

26. In the 1980s, cisgender women represented 65 percent of Mexican healers (Marcos 2006). Healers self-identify as "shamans" in the Mexican states of Morelo and Chiapas (Marcos 2006, xviii).

27. On Afro-diasporic religiosities, see also Roberto Strongman, (2019).

28. Consider the encounter between Inka Atahualpa and Fernando Pizarro in 1532. It exemplifies colonial perceptual suppression. Atahualpa asked Castilian emissaries for evidence of the authority of their religious beliefs. In Cajamarca, Atahualpa dismissed the power of the Bible when it failed to "speak to [him]" even after he "held it close to his ears" (Poma de Ayala 1980, 2:357). Atahualpa inhabits a realm where he perceives nonworldly matters through hearing, sight, and possibly even scent.

29. Crucial is the neurocognitive research that makes room for the historical plasticity of perceptual experience and learning. Some tests show that the centrality of sight in Western modernity narrows the potential for cross-modal perception (O'Callaghan 2008, 325).

30. Neurocognitive experiments often use basic models, tracking responses to one or two sensory stimuli, with varying numbers and sequences. Anthropological theories of the mind, however, align with my approach to "cross-modal perception." See also Serino et al. (2007) for more on multisensory peripersonal space.

31. The Humanities Center at Syracuse University hosted the twenty-day residency of Maestra Cherríe Moraga as the Distinguished Watson Visiting Professor in 2017. Among several other activities engaging arts, scholarship, and activism, Moraga directed the first reading of the play at the Syracuse Stage. The support of colleagues Myrna García-Calderón, Chandra Mohanty, and Vivian May (HC director) made this residency possible.

32. According to Moraga, artist Ricardo Bracho contributes to writing the character Malinche for this play (pers. comm. 2017).

33. I am also referring to the dynamic between foreground and background that I documented in chapter 3 between (1) Salustiana Párraga Arraya and Elena Humana and (2) my mother, Yamile, and aunt, Haydée.

34. See Dussel (1994) for evidence of the cross-cultural misunderstanding between Nahua peoples and Spaniards.
35. Among his literary influences, Reyes counts James Baldwin, John Updike, Henry Miller, Manuel Muñoz, and Cherríe Moraga (pers. comm., April 13, 2013).
36. As part of an autoethnographic project, I met with Reyes, along with drag performer Reina de Aztlán, over a two-year period. We were working on reconstructing the intersections between the slam circuit in the San Francisco Bay Area and his personal journey as an art activist.
37. Unless otherwise noted, I use quotation marks in this section to signal fragments of my interviews with Reyes or quotes from "TRE (My Revolutionary)" (Reyes 2009).
38. See Armando García (2015).
39. For the video performance, see Reyes (2011). Archived in 2022.
40. Brooms underscore the availability of migrant women's labor, particularly Mexican American and Central American, for the domestic service sector in the United States. The feminist association between witches and brooms pulls this instrument away from the domestic domain of gender subordination.
41. Mia Mingus (2011) differentiates disability justice from accessibility, emphasizing a shift from individual independence (personal access) to collective and interdependent transformation. The latter contests a system of ableism that favors nondisabled individuals. Throughout this chapter, I've primarily depicted capabilities as they typically exist in human animal bodies. However, I acknowledge that hallucinations and sensory cross-references suggest atypical physiological and neurodivergent potentials. I engage with these reflections in the context of transformation, encompassing critiques of ableism and contributions to disability justice.

Chapter 5. *Jotería* Poetics

1. Cherniavsky (2014, 290) characterizes Decolonize Oakland by emphasizing critical contradictions in its public self-fashioning. In her view, Decolonize claimed forms of representation that, on one end, no longer fit into the grammar of public dispute vis-à-vis the nation-state and, on the other, adopted organizational structures that align with Occupy's self-fashioning. These contradictions confirmed, for her, a broader argument about the reconfiguration of representational grammars and the rise of the specular constitution of contemporary politics' subjects as drifters who "live off the grid" (283), whose capacity for self-constitution lies in the realm of virtuality rather than actual existence (296). Cherniavsky interpreted the structure of both Occupy and Decolonize as sharing much more in common than the latter would admit: specifically, their embrace of autonomy, open-endedness, and the significance of process over final answers.
2. Luz Calvo's presentation at the 2012 AJAAS meeting in New Mexico about their participation in Decolonize Oakland was pivotal for my understanding of its goals and the process through which it came into being. The poster

created by Dignidad Rebelde for Indigenous Peoples' Day can be accessed at https://www.facebook.com/DignidadRebeldeArt/photos/a.103388351846 /10150330503056847/?type=3&theater.

3. Frank Owaga Plaza is later renamed Oscar Grant by Occupy protesters. Oscar Grant was a twenty-two-year-old African American civilian who was murdered by BART police officer Johannes Mehserle on New Year's Eve 2009.

4. On the diasporic connections between Cuban danzón and cha-cha-chá, see Malcomson (2011). On the Indigenous agency underlying the history of musical instruments, such as the marimba, in Guatemala, and the process of their reclamation as Chapina aesthetic, see Monsanto (1982).

5. See Roshanravan (2014) and the Santa Cruz Feminist of Color Collective (2014).

6. In "Chapina 2.0"(2014), Chinchilla talks of the documentary *When the Mountains Tremble* (1983), which the Nobel Prize–winner Menchú narrated. Chinchilla includes in her article a photograph featuring Menchú and Chinchilla's mother on the Maya K'ich'e leader's visit to Los Angeles. Norma Stoltz Chinchilla is shown onstage while she interprets live for Menchú.

7. Otto René Castillo (1934–1967) was a writer, poet, and revolutionary from Guatemala who had an active role in peasant revolutions. He went into exile in 1954 but returned to Guatemala in 1966, where he was ultimately captured, tortured, and burned alive. Ediciones Vanguardia published his influential *Vamos patria a caminar*. Pablo Milanés (1943–2022) gained notoriety as part of the *nueva trova* music movement that emerged in Cuba after Fidel Castro's revolutionary rise to power. Trova nova combines folk music with politically inspired lyrics.

8. The poem's line, written in Chinchilla's Spanish register, doesn't distinguish between *que* as relative pronoun and *qué* as question word. The latter corresponds to the meaning that the poem's line intends. The original lyric penned by Pablo Milanés records this line as follows, "Si el poeta eres tú, qué tengo yo que hablarte." See https://www.letras.com/pablo-Milanés/227158/.

9. Voseo consists of using *vos* instead of *tú* when addressing the second-person singular and its verbal forms. This is a regional use widespread in the Río de la Plata and Central America, particularly in El Salvador, Guatemala, Honduras, and Nicaragua.

10. For example, "you feel" is rendered *tú sientes* in Mexican Spanish and in most other South American countries' Spanish, but *vos sentís* in many speech situations within the Spanish language spoken in Guatemala, other Central American countries, and South American countries such as Argentina, Chile, Uruguay, and Colombia.

11. Throughout the chapter, Chinchilla widens our communal sense of jotería by evoking intergenerational technologies of oppositional consciousness and praxis. The term *babies* is part of this praxis. Drawing on this term, she conveys the power of regeneration for revolutionary struggles.

12. Since 2011, I have followed Chinchilla's Facebook page. While living in the same town, we hung out together. I attended at least ten of her spoken word performances and screenings over a three-year period. After I moved to Syracuse, Chinchilla and I met occasionally at AJAAS biannual conferences. She also came to the Syracuse University's campus as a guest speaker

of the department of women's and gender studies. We sometimes text each other. I have met her mother, Norma Stoltz Chinchilla, as well as some of her romantic partners.

13. On October 8, 2019, Chinchilla posts a comment on the social network Facebook, precisely about the topic of voseo and the intimate acoustic that it brings into the public sphere. Chinchilla recalls a woman at a gas station who was wearing a T-shirt that says "también marcho por vos," which the artist loosely translates as "I also march for you." She recommends that her facebook friends read "vos" as an "intimate you form [. . .] common in Central America and some South American countries."

14. *Ustedeo* refers "to the use of the second person singular pronoun of formality usted" among Spanish speakers throughout Latin America (Rincón 2006, 15).

15. The theory of *hombres nuevos* was first generated by the legendary Ernesto "Che" Guevara (1967) who, outlining the psychosocial characteristics of moral and brave warriors for socialist transformation, envisioned society as a whole becoming a giant school (Holst 2009). At this school, a new orientation in consciousness would emerge out of the synthesis of ideas and relations of prior societal structures. Guevara was the first to represent the authentic new man, with his bravery, intellect, and connection to the welfare of the masses. Nowhere was this more prominent than in his international incursions. Several authors explore the treatment of homosexuality in postrevolutionary Cuba and its conflicts with the concept of the new man. By examining this theme, they delve into the complex interplay between individual liberties and ideals of communist revolution. Specifically, they highlight how homosexuality functioned as a point of contention, shaping the delayed incorporation of bodily autonomy into a broader narrative of societal transformation during the postrevolutionary era (Quiroga 1997).

16. In *Pilgrimages/Peregrinajes* (2003b), María Lugones painstakingly accounts for subterranean and hidden idioms of agency against multiple oppressions. With great attention to both the microphysics of space and the need for a more enduring sociality of resistance, she introduces the notion of active subjectivity. Unlike a modern sense of agency, which relies on individuation as the site and source of autonomy, Lugones sees in active subjectivity a more fruitful rendering of the ways that larger, permeable, even impressible selves provide backing for resistant intentions. For another account of agency as socially authored, see Bierria (2014).

17. See also L. Pérez (2010).

18. Michael Hames-García arrives at a similar critique in their provocative discussion about whether modern sexual identities are desirable. While engaging LGBTQ organizations in the Global South, Hames-García states that organizations that work within postcolonial contexts "understand the important connections between anti-colonial struggles and true sexual freedom—freedom as personal fulfilment and communal connection rather than merely the license to do what you want, when, where, how, and with whomever you want" (2011, 109).

19. Contra Ortega (2016) and Zaytoun (2022).

20. While Lugones provides enriching views on subject formation, specifically theorizing resistant intentionality beyond Euroamerican notions of individual

interaction, her language at times relies on the divide between activity and inactivity. Does the language of active subjectivity imply that passive subjectivity has no place in our understanding of resistance? Her coinage also foregrounds motility as having a crucial role in subjects' responses to multiple oppressions. A major revision of active subjectivity, however, can be found in her "From within Germinative Stasis: Creating Active Subjectivity, Resistant Agency" (2005).

21. In my view, decolonial subjectivity points to more than a dialectics such as I/non-I or being/nonbeing. Lugones's understanding of oppressing⇔being oppressed⇔resisting speaks to more than a dialectics.

22. See also "From within Germinative Stasis: Creating Active Subjectivity, Resistant Agency" (2005) and "Toward a Decolonial Feminism" (2010).

23. When engaged as an intercultural practice, jotería makes possible a rather deep degree of impressibility. It entangles with flesh beyond Eurocentered equivalences, such as queer or gay, or any of the acronyms in the LGBTQIA+ umbrella (See Hames-Garcia 2014).

24. I am aware that there is great linguistic heterogeneity among Indigenous peoples and nations in Central America and the Caribbean. Among these languages, I would like to mention the following: Garifuna, K'iche', Lenca, Mam, Miskito, Pocomam, Q'eqchi', Rama, Paya, and Xinca.

25. Royal Spanish Academy's phonetic system.

26. International Phonetic Alphabet (IPA).

27. Even though the "h" is typically silent in Spanish, it often affects the pronunciation of adjacent vowels by causing them to be aspirated, especially in certain dialects or speech patterns. It results in a breezy intonation that resembles, not surprisingly, a softened "j" sound.

28. Following Laura Elisa Pérez (2007, 27–28), I understand glyphs to be part of a pre-Columbian and yet contemporaneous practice of sign-making that points beyond itself, "to significations that are spiritually and politically interdependent and simultaneous, and that hold ancient but relevant alternative knowledges" (27). Specifically, Pérez draws this understanding from studying Nahua glyph-makers and glyph-readers, who, apparently, were known as *tlacuilo* and *tlamatinime*. She connects contemporary Chicana artists, writers, and cultural performers to the practice of tlacuilo and tlamatinime, who mediate the presence of the spirit-world into persisting ways of fostering interdependence and well-being among all that exists.

29. See Ana Patricia Rodríguez's *Dividing the Isthmus* (2009, 145–151) for a powerful account of the earthquake trope and its multiple relations to Central American literature.

30. I appreciate the work of Micaela J. Díaz-Sánchez on syncopation as a scholar and practitioner of Chicana and Mexican feminist performances. I attended one of Díaz-Sánchez's presentations at the 2024 AJAAS National Conference at Plaza de la Raza, Los Angeles.

31. Torres-Saillant (2012) reminds us of the importance of recognizing and respecting the specificity of the Caribbean for its political, cultural, intellectual, and social autonomy. I don't seek to conflate the Antilles with Latin or Central America either.

References

Agamben, Giorgio. 1998. *Homo Sacer: Sovereign Power and Bare Life*. Stanford: Stanford University Press.

Aguilera, Miguel. 2009. "Mesoamerican Communicating Objects: Mayan Worldviews before, during, and after Spanish Contact." In *Maya Worldviews at Conquest*, edited by Timothy Pugh and Leslie G. Cecil, 160–182. Boulder: University of Colorado Press.

Ahenakew, Cash. 2016. "Grafting Indigenous Ways of Knowing onto Non-Indigenous Ways of Being: The (Underestimated) Challenges of a Decolonial Imagination." *International Review of Qualitative Research* 9 (3): 323–340.

Alaimo, Stacy, and Susan J. Hekman, eds. 2008. *Material Feminisms*. Bloomington: Indiana University Press.

Alarcón, Norma. 1989. "Traddutora, Traditora: A Paradigmatic Figure of Chicana Feminism." *Cultural Critique*, no. 13, 57–87.

Alcoff, Linda Martín. 2005. *Visible Identities: Race, Gender, and the Self*. Oxford: Oxford University Press.

Alexander, M. Jacqui. 2005a. "Making the Invisible Tangible." In *Pedagogies of Crossing*, 287–332.

Alexander, M. Jacqui. 2005b. *Pedagogies of Crossing: Meditations of Feminism, Sexual Politics, Memory and the Sacred*. Durham: Duke University Press.

Alvarez, Eddy Francisco, Jr. 2014. "Jotería Pedagogy, SWAPA, and Sandovalian Approaches to Liberation." *Aztlán: A Journal of Chicano Studies* 39 (1): 215–227.

Alvarez, Eddy Francisco, Jr. 2016. "Finding Sequins in the Rubble: Stitching Together an Archive of Trans Latina Los Angeles." *Transgender Studies Quarterly* 3 (3–4): 618–627.

Anderson, Robert. 1996. "The Quilombo of Palmares: A New Overview of a Maroon State in Seventeenth-Century Brazil." *Journal of Latin American Studies* 28 (3): 545–566.

Andrews, George Reid. 1980. *The Afro-Argentines of Buenos Aires, 1800–1900*. Madison: University of Wisconsin Press.

Angelo, Dante. 2014. "Assembling Ritual, the Burden of the Everyday: An Exercise in Relational Ontology in Quebrada de Humahuaca, Argentina." *World Archaeology* 46 (2): 270–287.

Antoniucci, Melina. 2016. "El acceso a la salud de las personas trans: El caso del CADS de la ciudad de Mar del Plata." Bachelor's thesis, Universidad de Mar del Plata.

Anzaldúa, Gloria. 1999. *Borderlands / La Frontera*. 2nd edition. San Francisco: Aunt Lute Books.

Anzaldúa, Gloria E. 2002. "now let us shift…the path of conocimiento…inner work, public acts." In *This Bridge We Call Home: Radical Visions of Transformation*, edited by Gloria E. Anzaldúa and AnaLouise Keating, 540–578. New York: Routledge.

Anzaldúa, Gloria. 2009. *The Gloria Anzaldúa Reader*. Edited by AnaLouise Keating. Durham: Duke University Press.

Anzaldúa, Gloria, and AnaLouise Keating, eds. 2002. *This Bridge We Call Home: Radical Visions for Transformation*. New York: Routledge.

Appelbaum, Nancy P., Anne S. Macpherson, and Karin Alejandra Rosemblatt. 2003. "Racial Nations." In *Race and Nation in Modern Latin America*, edited by Nancy P. Appelbaum, Anne S. Macpherson, and Karin Alejandra Rosemblatt, 1–31. Chapel Hill: University of North Carolina Press.

Arabzadeh, Ehsan, Colin W. G. Clifford, and Justin A Harris. 2008. "Vision Merges with Touch in a Purely Tactile Discrimination." *Psychological Science* 19 (7): 635–641.

Arguedas, José María, and Francisco de Ávila. 1966. *Dioses y hombres de Huarochirí; Narración quechua recogida por Francisco de Ávila*. Lima: Museo Nacional de Historia y el Instituto de Estudios Peruanos. Originally published in 1598(?).

Arias, Arturo. 2012. "*EpiCentro*: The Emergence of a New Central American–American Literature." *Comparative Literature* 64 (3): 300–315.

Arnold, Denise Y. 1988. "Matrilineal Practice in a Patrilineal Setting: Rituals and Metaphors of Kinship in an Andean Ayllu." PhD diss., University College London (University of London).

Arnold, Denise. 2006. *The Metamorphosis of Heads: Textual Struggles, Education, and Land in the Andes*. Pittsburgh: University of Pittsburgh Press.

Arnold, Denise, and Juan Yapita. 2007. "Ensayo sobre los orígenes del textil andino: Cómo la gente se ha convertido en tela." In *Hilos sueltos: Los Andes desde el textil*, edited by D. Arnold, J. Yapita, and E. Espejo Ayca, 49–80. La Paz: Plural e ILCA.

Arredondo, Gabriela F., Aída Hurtado, Norma Klahn, Olga Nájera-Ramírez, and Patricia Navella, eds. 2003. *Chicana Feminisms: A Critical Reader*. Durham: Duke University Press.

Arvin, Maile, Eve Tuck, and Angie Morrill. 2013. "Decolonizing Feminism: Challenging Connections between Settler Colonialism and Heteropatriarchy." *Feminist Formations* 25, no. 1 (Spring): 8–34.

Ashcroft, Bill. 2001. *On Post-colonial Futures: Transformations of a Colonial Culture*. London: Continuum.

Ásta, Ásta. 2018. *Categories We Live By: The Construction of Sex, Gender, Race, and Other Social Categories*. Oxford: Oxford University Press.

Bacchetta, Paola. 1999. "When the (Hindu) Nation Exiles Its Queers." *Social Text*, no. 61, 141–166.

Bacchetta, Paola, and Jin Haritaworn. 2011. "Queer Times, Queer Assemblages." *Antipode* 33 (5): 874–889.

Bacchetta, Paola, Fatima El-Tayeb, and Jin Haritaworn. 2018. "Queers of Colour and (De)colonial Spaces in Europe 1." In *Global Raciality: Empire, PostColoniality, DeColoniality*, edited by Paola Bacchetta, Sunaina Maira, and Howard Winant, 158–170. New York: Routledge.

Bacchetta, Paola, Suhraiya Jivraj, and Sandeep Bakshi. 2020. "Decolonial Sexualities: Paola Bacchetta in Conversation with Suhraiya Jivraj and Sandeep Bakshi." *Interventions* 22, no. 4: 574–585.

Baez, Josefina. 2012. *Levente no. Yolayorkdominicanyork*. New York: I Om Be Press.

Baez, Josefina. 2017. *Dominicanish: With Photographs by Giovanni Savino*. New York: I Om Be Press.

Bailey, Marlon, and Rashad Shabazz. 2014. "Editorial: Gender and Sexual Geographies of Blackness: Anti-Black Heterotopias (Part 1)." *Gender, Place and Culture: A Journal of Feminist Geography* 21 (3): 316–321.

Balderston, Daniel, and Donna Guy, eds. 1997. *Sex and Sexuality in Latin America: An Interdisciplinary Reader*. New York: New York University Press.

Banner, Olivia. 2010. "Sing Now, O Muse, of the Recessive Mutation: Interrogating the Genetic Discourse of Sex Variation with Jeffrey Eugenides' Middlesex." *Signs* 35 (4): 843–867.

Barad, Karen. 2007. *Meeting the Universe Halfway: Quantum Physics and the Entanglement of Matter and Meaning*. Durham: Duke University Press.

Barad, Karen. 2014. "Diffracting Diffraction: Cutting Together-Apart." *Parallax* 20 (3): 168–187.

Barkan, Elazar, and Marie-Denise Shelton. 1998. *Borders, Exiles, Diasporas*. Palo Alto: Stanford University Press.

Barrett, Robert J. 2004. "Kurt Schneider in Borneo: Do First Rank Symptoms Apply to the Iban?" *Cambridge Studies in Medical Anthropology*, no. 11, 87–109.

Barrionuevo, Alexei. 2007. "In Macho Argentina, a New Beacon for Gay Tourists." *New York Times*, December 3.

Bayardo, Rubén, and Mónica Lacarrieu, eds. 1998. *La Dinámica Global/Local*. Buenos Aires: Ediciones Ciccus / La Crujía.

Beccalossi, Chiara. 2017. "Italian Sexology, Nicola Pende's Biotypology and Hormone Treatments in the 1920s." *Histoire, médecine et santé*, no. 12, 73–97.

Bergero, Adriana. 2008. *Intersecting Tango*. Pittsburgh: University of Pittsburgh Press.

Bergman, Carla, Magalí Rabasa, Ariella Patchen, and Seyma Özdemir. 2020. "Turtle Island (North America)." In *Pandemic Solidarity: Mutual Aid during the Covid-19 Crisis*, edited by Marina Sitrin and Colectiva Sembrar, 183–230. London: Pluto Press.

Berkins, Lohana, and Josefina Fernandez. 2006. *La Gesta del Nombre Propio*. Buenos Aires: Editorial Madres de Plaza de Mayo.

Bettcher, T. M. 2012. "Full-Frontal Morality: The Naked Truth about Gender." *Hypatia* 27 (2): 319–337.

Bhattacharya, Himika. 2017. *Narrating Love and Violence: Women Contesting Caste, Tribe, and State in Lahaul, India*. New Brunswick: Rutgers University Press.

Bidaseca, Karina. 2018a. "Desbordes: Estéticas descoloniales y etnografías feministas post-heroicas." In *Epistemologías del sur—Epistemologias do sul*, edited by Maria Paula Meneses and Karina Bidaseca, 165–182. CLACSO.

Bidaseca, Karina. 2018b. *Territories of Dispossession: Latin American Women and the Search for Social Justice*. London: Pluto Press.

Bierria, Alisa. 2014. "Missing in Action: Violence, Power, and Discerning Agency." *Hypatia* 29 (1): 129–145.

Blackwell, Maylei. 2011. *¡Chicana Power! Contested Histories of Feminism in the Chicano Movement*. Austin: University of Texas Press.

Blázquez, Gustavo. 2008. "Negros de alma: Raza y procesos de subjetivación juveniles en torno a los bailes de cuarteto (Córdoba, Argentina)." *Estudios en antropología social* 1 (1): 7–34.

Bloomer, W. Martin. 2006. "The Technology of Child Production: Eugenics and Eulogics in the *De Liberis Educandis*." *Arethusa* 39 (1): 71–99.

Boone, Elizabeth Hill, Louise M. Burkhart, and David Tavárez. 2017. *Painted Words: Nahua Catholicism, Politics, and Memory in the Atzaqualco Pictorial Catechism*. Vol. 39 of *Studies in Pre-Columbian Art and Archaeology*. Washington DC: Dumbarton Oaks Research Library and Collection.

Borchard, Kimberly. 2010. "Death in El Dorado: The Anthropophagous Jungle in One Account of Lope de Aguirre's Revolt." *Hispanófila*, no. 160, 43–59.

Bossi, Elena. 1998. *Seres mágicos que habitan en la Argentina*. San Salvador de Jujuy: Talleres Gráficos de la Universidad Nacional de Jujuy.

Bouysse-Cassagne, Thérèse. 1978. "L'Espace Aymara: Urco et Uma." *Annales: Histoire, sciences sociales* 33 (5–6): 1057–1080.

Brady, Mary Pat. 2002. *Extinct Lands, Temporal Geographies: Chicana Literature and the Urgency of Space*. Durham: Duke University Press.

Brady, Mary Pat. 2022. *Scales of Captivity*. Durham: Duke University Press.

Braidotti, Rosi. 2002. *Metamorphoses: Toward a Materialist Theory of Becoming*. Cambridge: Polity.

Braidotti, Rosi. 2006. *Transpositions: On Nomadic Ethics*. Cambridge: Polity.

Braidotti, Rosi. 2013. *The Posthuman*. Malden: Polity Press.

Braidotti, Rosi. 2020. "Nomadic Theory." In *Posthumanism in Art and Science: A Reader*, edited by Susan McHugh and Giovanni Aloi, 40–42. New York: Columbia University Press.

Briones, Claudia. 1998. "(Meta)cultura del estado-nación y estado de la (meta) cultura: Repensando las identidades indígenas y antropológicas en tiempos de postestatalidad." *Serie Antropología*, no. 244, 1–54.

Briones, Claudia. 2002. "Mestizaje y blanqueamiento como coordenadas de aboriginalidad y nación en Argentina." *Runa*, no. 23, 61–88.

Broguet, Julia. 2016. "'Black Is Somewhere…': Spatial-Racial Order and Afro-Uruguayan Candombe in Barrio Refinería (Rosario, Argentina)." *Revista Colombiana de Antropología* 52 (1): 197–222.

Brooks, Joanna. 2005. "The Early American Public Sphere and the Emergence of a Black Print Counterpublic." *William and Mary Quarterly* 62 (1): 67–92.

Brotherson, G. 1997. "La América indígena en su literatura: Los libros del cuarto mundo." México: Fondo de Cultura Económica.

Browne, Kath, Catherine Jean Nash, and Sally Hines. 2010. "Introduction: Toward Trans Geographies." *Gender, Place, and Culture: A Journal of Feminist Geography* 17 (5): 573–577.

Bruchac, Margaret. 2018. *Savage Kin: Indigenous Informants and American Anthropologists.* Tucson: University of Arizona Press.

Bunge, Carlos Octavio. 1932. *La novela de la sangre.* La Tradición Argentina 19. Buenos Aires: Biblioteca.

Burman, Anders. 2011. "Chachawarmi: Silence and Rival Voices on Decolonisation and Gender Politics in Andean Bolivia." *Journal of Latin American Studies* 43 (1): 65–91.

Burrison, John. 2017. *Global Clay: Themes in World Ceramic Traditions.* Bloomington: Indiana University Press.

Butierrez, Marce, and Patricio Simonetto. 2020. "Las embajadoras de Travestilandia." *Moléculas Malucas,* October 28. https://www.moleculasmalucas.com/post/las-embajadoras-de-travestilandia.

Butler, Judith. 1990. *Gender Trouble: Feminism and the Subversion of Identity.* New York: Routledge.

Butler, Judith. 1993. *Bodies That Matter: On the Discursive Limits of Sex.* New York: Routledge.

Butler, Judith. 2004. *Undoing Gender.* New York: Routledge.

Cabeza de Baca, Tomás, Aurelio José Figueredo, Heitor Fernandes, and Vanessa Smith-Castro. 2020. "Exchanging Fluids: The Sociocultural Implications of Microbial, Cultural, and Ethnic Admixture in Latin America." *Politics and the Life Sciences* 39 (1): 56–86.

Cajete, Gregory. 2000. *Native Science: Natural Laws of Interdependence.* Santa Fe: Clear Light Publishing.

Caloi. 2013. *Todo Clemente.* Vol. 6. Buenos Aires: Clarín.

Calvo-Quirós, William A. 2014. "The Aesthetics of Healing and Love: An Epistemic Genealogy of Jota/o Aesthetic Traditions." *Aztlan: A Journal of Chicano Studies 39* (1): 181–194.

Cantú, Lionel, Jr. 2009. *The Sexuality of Migration: Border Crossings and Mexican Immigrant Men,* edited by Nancy Naples and Salvador Vidal Ortiz. New York: New York University Press.

Carastathis, Anna. 2016. *Intersectionality: Origins, Contestations, Horizons.* Lincoln: University of Nebraska Press.

Carneiro, Sueli. 2005. "Ennegrecer el feminismo." *Nouvelles questions féministes* 24 (2): 21–26.

Carrasco, Davíd. 2011. *The Aztecs: A Very Short Introduction.* Oxford: Oxford University Press.

Castillo, Ana. [1993] 2005. *So Far from God.* New York: W. W. Norton & Company.

Castillo, Ana. 2014. *Massacre of the Dreamers: Essays on Xicanisma.* Updated and expanded ed. Albuquerque: University of New Mexico Press.

Castro, Donald S. 2001. *The Afro-Argentine in Argentine Culture: El Negro del Acordeón.* Edwin Mellen Press.

Cecconi, Sofía. 2009. "Territorios del tango en Buenos Aires: Aportes para una historia de sus formas de inscripción." *Iberoamericana: Nueva época* 9 (33): 49–68.

Cereceda, Verónica. 1986. "The Semiology of Andean Textiles: The Talegas of Isluga." In *Anthropological History of Andean Polities*, edited by John V. Murra, Nathan Wachtel, and Jacques Revel, 149–173. La Paz: Hisbol.

Chacón, Gloria Elizabeth. 2018. *Indigenous Cosmolectics: Kab'awil and the Making of Maya and Zapotec Literatures*. Chapel Hill: University of North Carolina Press.

Chamberlain, Robert. 1948. "Probanza de Méritos y Servicios of Blas González, Conquistador of Yucatán." *Hispanic American Historical Review* 28 (4): 526–536.

Chávez, Karma R. 2013. *Queer Migration Politics: Activist Rhetoric and Coalitional Possibilities*. Urbana: University of Illinois Press.

Chávez, Karma R. 2021. *The Borders of AIDS: Race, Quarantine, and Resistance*. Seattle: University of Washington Press.

Chen, Mel Y. 2012. *Animacies: Biopolitics, Racial Mattering, and Queer Affect*. Durham: Duke University Press.

Cherniavsky, Eva. 2014. "'Refugees from This Native Dreamland": Life Narratives of Occupy Wall Street." *Biography* 37 (1): 279–299.

Chiang, Howard, ed. 2012. *Transgender China*. New York: Palgrave Macmillan.

Chinchilla, Maya. 2014. *The Cha Cha Files: A Chapina Poética*. Oakland: Kórima Press.

Chiu, Leo P. W. 1989. "Differential Diagnosis and Management of Hallucinations." *Journal of the Hong Kong Medical Association* 41 s(3): 292–297.

Christensen, Mark Z. 2010. "The Tales of Two Cultures: Ecclesiastical Texts and Nahua and Maya Catholicisms." *The Americas* 66 (3): 353–377.

Cid Uribe, Miriam Elizabeth, and Macarena Céspedes Morales. 2008. "Rasgos de simplificación en el habla rural de dos localidades de Chile: Descripción fonotáctica y discursiva." *Literatura y lingüística*, no. 19, 197–210.

Coester, Albert. 1928. *The Literary History of Spanish America*. New York: Macmillan.

Cohen, Cathy J. 2001. "Punks, Bulldaggers, and Welfare Queens: The Radical Potential of Queer Politics?" In *Sexual Identities, Queer Politics*, edited by Mark Blasius, 200–227. Princeton, NJ: Princeton University Press.

Collins, Patricia Hill. 1990. *Black Feminist Thought: Knowledge, Consciousness, and the Politics of Empowerment*. Boston: Unwin Hyman.

Collins, Patricia Hill. 2004. *Black Sexual Politics: African Americans, Gender, and the New Racism*. New York: Routledge.

Colombia Diversa. 2019. *El prejuicio no conoce fronteras: Homicidios de lesbianas, gay, bisexuales, trans en países de América Latina y el Caribe 2014–2019*. https://sinviolenci a.lgbt/el-prejuicio-no-conoce-fronteras/.

Combahee River Collective. 2018. "Combahee River Collective Statement." In *Feminist Manifestos: A Global Documentary Reader*, edited by Penny A. Weiss and Megan Brueske, 269–277. New York: New York University Press.

Connell, Raewyn. 2018. "Meeting at the Edge of Fear: Theory on a World Scale." In *Constructing the Pluriverse: The Geopolitics of Knowledge*, edited by Bernd Reiter, 9–38. Durham: Duke University Press.

Conner, Randy P., David Hatfield Sparks, and Mariya Sparks. 1997. *Cassell's Encyclopedia of Queer Myth, Symbol, and Spirit: Gay, Lesbian, Bisexual, and Transgender Lore*. London: Cassell.

Contreras, Sheila M. 2009. *Blood Lines: Myth, Indigenism, and Chicana/o Literature*. Austin: University of Texas Press.

Corbière, Emilio J. 2000. "Lucas Fernández: Precursor del socialismo en la Argentina." Paper presented at Primeras jornadas de historia de las izquierdas, Centro de Documentación e Investigación de la Cultura de Izquierdas en la Argentina, Buenos Aires, *December 8–9, 2000.*

Crenshaw, Kimberlé. 1991. "Mapping the Margins: Intersectionality, Identity Politics, and Violence against Women of Color." *Stanford Law Review* 43 (6): 1241–1299.

Cumes, Aura Estela. 2012. "Mujeres indígenas patriarcado y colonialismo: Un desafío a la segregación comprensiva de las formas de dominio." *Anuario de Hojas de WARMI*, no. 17, 1–16.

Curiel, Ochy. 2007. "La crítica poscolonial desde las prácticas políticas del feminismo antirracista." In *Colonialidad y biopolítica en América Latina*, 92–101. Revista NOMADAS 26. Bogotá: Universidad Central.

Dalton, David S. 2022. "Eugenics and Doubly Marginalized Mexican and Chicana Women." In *Healthcare in Latin America: History, Society, Culture*, edited by David S. Dalton and Douglas J. Weatherford, 130–139. Gainesville: University Press of Florida.

Damrosch, David. 1991. "The Aesthetics of Conquest: Aztec Poetry before and after Cortés." *Representations* 33 (Winter): 101–120.

de Beauvoir, Simone. 2011. *The Second Sex.* Translated by Constance Borde and Sheila Malovany-Chevallier. New York: Vintage Books.

Decena, Carlos Ulises. 2011. *Tacit Subjects: Belonging and Same-Sex Desire among Dominican Immigrant Men.* Durham: Duke University Press.

Decena, Carlos Ulises. 2016. "Multiplying Archives." *Small Axe: A Caribbean Journal of Criticism* 20 (3): 179–188.

Decena, Carlos Ulises. 2023. *Circuits of the Sacred: A Faggotology in the Black Latinx Caribbean.* Durham: Duke University Press.

de Granda, Germán. 1993. "Quechua y español en el Noroeste Argentino: Una precisión y dos interrogantes." *Lexis* 17 (2): 259–274.

de la Cadena, Marisol. 2000. *Indigenous Mestizos: The Politics of Race and Culture in Cuzco, Peru, 1919–1991.* Durham: Duke University Press.

de la Garza, Antonio Tomas. 2019. "A Eulogy for Roxsana Hernández: Tracing the Relationship between Border Rhetoric and Queer Debility." *QED: A Journal in GLBTQ Worldmaking* 6 (3): 94–99.

de la Garza, Mercedes. 1997. "El perro como símbolo religioso entre los mayas y los nahuas." *Estudios de cultura Nahuatl*, no. 27, 111–133.

Delaney, Jeane. 1996. "Making Sense of Modernity: Changing Attitudes toward the Immigrant and the Gaucho in Turn-of-the-Century Argentina." *Comparative Studies in Society and History* 38 (3): 434–459.

Delgadillo, Theresa. 2011. *Spiritual Mestizaje: Religion, Gender, Race, and Nation in Contemporary Chicana Narrative.* Durham: Duke University Press.

de Lima Grecco, Gabriela, and Sven Schuster. 2020. "Decolonizing Global History? A Latin American Perspective." *Journal of World History* 31 (2): 425–446.

Dembroff, Robin. 2018. "Real Talk on the Metaphysics of Gender." *Philosophical Topics* 46 (2): 21–50.

D'Emilio, John. 1992. *Making Trouble: Essays on Gay History, Politics, and the University.* New York: Routledge.

Department of Defense. 1996. *Instruction 1332.38: Physical Disability Evaluation.* https://palmcenterlegacy.org/wp-content/uploads/2019/03/DoD_Number _1332.38.pdf.

de Souza Santos, Boaventura. 2015. *Epistemologies of the South: Justice Against Epistemicide.* New York: Routledge.

Dinerstein, Ana Cecilia. 2010. "Autonomy in Latin America: Between Resistance and Integration; Echoes from the Piqueteros Experience." *Community Development Journal* 45 (3): 356–366.

DiPietro, PJ. 2016a. "Decolonizing Travesti Space in Buenos Aires: Race, Sexuality, and Sideways Relationality." *Gender, Place, and Culture* 23 (5): 677–693.

DiPietro, PJ. 2016b. "Of Huachafería, Así, and M'e Mati: Decolonizing Transing Methodologies." *TSQ: Transgender Studies Quarterly* 2 (4): 67–76.

DiPietro, PJ. 2020. "Hallucinating Knowing: (Extra)ordinary Consciousness, More-Than-Human Perception, and Other Decolonizing Remedios within Latina and Xicana Feminist Theories." In *Theories of the Flesh: Latinx and Latin American Feminisms, Transformation, and Resistance*, edited by Andrea Pitts, Mariana Ortega, and José Medina, 220–236. Oxford: Oxford University Press.

DiPietro, PJ. 2024. "'I Look Too Good Not to Be Seen': Multiple Meaning Realism and Sociosomatics." In Zurn et al., 99–120.

DiPietro, Pedro, Jennifer McWeeny, and Shireen Roshanravan. 2019. *Speaking Face-to-face: The Visionary Philosophy of María Lugones.* Albany: State University of New York Press.

Domingues, José. 1995. *Sociological Theory and Collective Subjectivity.* London: Palgrave Macmillan.

Dotson, Kristie. 2014. "How Is This Paper Philosophy?" *Comparative Philosophy* 5 (1): 3–29.

D'Souza, Paschal, and Sanjay K. Rathi. 2015. "Shampoo and Conditioners: What a Dermatologist Should Know?" *Indian Journal of Dermatology* 60 (3): 248.

Duggan, Lisa. 2003. *The Twilight of Equality? Neoliberalism, Cultural Politics, and the Attack on Democracy.* Boston: Beacon Press.

Dugre, Neal T. 2018. "Repairing the Breach: Puritan Expansion, Commonwealth Formation, and the Origins of the United Colonies of New England, 1630–1643." *New England Quarterly* 91 (3): 382–417.

Dussel, Enrique. 1994. "A Nahuatl Interpretation of the Conquest: From the 'Parousia' of the Gods to the 'Invasion.'" *Latin American Identity and Constructions of Difference*, no. 10, 104.

Dussel, Enrique. 2006. "Transmodernity and Interculturality." *Poligrafi* 2 (41–42): 5–40.

Dutta, Aniruddha, and Raina Roy. 2014. "Decolonizing Transgender in India: Some Reflections." *Transgender Studies Quarterly* 1 (3): 320–337.

Duviols, Pierre. 1979. "Un symbolisme de l'occupation, de l'aménagement et de l'exploitation de l'espace: Le monolithe 'Huanca' et sa fonction dans les Andes préhispaniques." *L'homme*, no. 19, 7–31.

Edwards, Erika Denise. 2020. *Hiding in Plain Sight: Black Women, the Law, and the Making of a White Argentine Republic.* Tuscaloosa: University of Alabama Press.

Escobar, Arturo. 2018. "Farewell to Development," interview, Great Transition Initiative. Accessed on September 17, 2024. http://greattransition.org/publication/farewell-to-development.

Espinosa Miñoso, Yuderkys. 2009. "Etnocentrismo y colonialidad en los feminismos latinoamericanos." *Revista venezolana de estudios de la mujer* 14 (33): 37–54.

Estrada, Gabriel S. 2003. "An Aztec Two-Spirit Cosmology: Re-sounding Nahuatl Masculinities, Elders, Femininities, and Youth." *Frontiers: A Journal of Women Studies* 24 (2): 10–14.

Falconí Trávez, Diego. 2014. "La leyenda negra marica: Una crítica comparatista desde la teoría queer hispana." In *Resentir lo "queer" en América Latina: Diálogos desde con el sur*, edited by Diego Falconí Trávez, Santiago Castellanos, and María Amelia Viteri, 81–116. Barcelona: Egales.

Fanon, Frantz. 2008. *Black Skin, White Masks.* New York: Grove Press.

Felski, Rita. 1989. *Beyond Feminist Aesthetics: Feminist Literature and Social Change.* Cambridge: Harvard University Press.

Ferguson, Roderick. 2004. *Aberrations in Black: Toward a Queer of Color Critique.* Minneapolis: University of Minnesota Press.

Fernandez, Josefina. 2004. *Cuerpos desobedientes: Travestismo e identidad de género.* Buenos Aires: Edhasa.

Fernandez, Josefina, Mónica D'Uva, and Paula Viturro, eds. 2002. *Cuerpos Ineludibles.* Buenos Aires: Ediciones Ají de Pollo.

Flores, Juan. 2001. "Life Off the Hyphen: Latino Literature and Nuyorican Traditions." In *Mambo Montage: The Latinization of New York City*, edited by Agustín Lao Montes and Arlene Dávila, 185–206. New York: Columbia University Press.

Fortis, Paolo. 2010. "The Birth of Design: A Kuna Theory of Body and Personhood." *Journal of the Royal Anthropological Institute* 16 (3): 480–495.

Foucault, Michel. 1980. *The History of Sexuality: An Introduction, Volume I.* Translated by Robert Hurley. New York: Vintage.

Foucault, Michel. 1997. "The Abnormals." In *Ethics: Subjectivity and Truth*, edited by Paul Rabinow, 51–57. New York: New Press.

Foucault, Michel. 2002. *The Birth of the Clinic.* London: Routledge.

Fraser, Nancy. 1997. *Justice Interruptus: Critical Reflections on the Postsocialist Condition.* New York: Routledge.

Friedman, Elisabeth Jay. 2017. *Interpreting the Internet: Feminist and Queer Counterpublics in Latin America.* Oakland: University of California Press.

Fuerst, James W. 2018. *New World Postcolonial: The Political Thought of Inca Garcilaso de la Vega.* Pittsburgh: University of Pittsburgh Press.

Fuss, Diana. 1989. *Essentially Speaking: Feminism, Nature and Difference.* New York: Routledge.

Galarte, Francisco J. 2021. *Brown Trans Figurations: Rethinking Race, Gender, and Sexuality in Chicanx/Latinx Studies.* Austin: University of Texas Press.

Gannon, Shane. 2011. "Exclusion as Language and the Language of Exclusion: Tracing Regimes of Gender through Linguistic Representations of the 'Eunuch.'" *Journal of the History of Sexuality* 20 (1): 1–27.

García, Ana Isabel. 2006. "Contacto de lenguas en Guatemala: Cambios en el sistema pronominal átono del español por contacto con la lengua maya tzutujil." *Tópicos del Seminario* 15 (enero–junio): 11–71.

García, Armando. 2015. "The Illegalities of Brownness." *Social Text* 33 (2): 99–120.

García Peña, Lorgia. 2016. *The Borders of Dominicanidad: Race, Nation, and Archives of Contradiction*. Durham: Duke University Press.

Garcia-Rojas, Claudia. 2017. "(Un)disciplined Futures: Women of Color Feminism as a Disruptive to White Affect Studies." *Journal of Lesbian Studies* 21 (3): 254–271.

Gargallo Celentani, Francesca. 2014. *Feminismos desde Abya Yala. Ideas y Proposiciones de las Mujeres de los Pueblos en Nuestra América*. Ciudad de México. Editorial Corte y Confección.

Garratt, Peter. 2017. "On Entanglings: Disciplines, Materiality and Distributed Cognition." In *Minding Borders: Resilient Divisions in Literature, the Body and the Academy*, edited by N. Gardini, A. X. Jacobs, B. Morgan, M. Omri, and M. Reynolds, 150–168. Oxford: Legenda.

George, Christopher. 2018. "The Role of Castilian in George Ticknor's Spain." *Journal of Romance Studies* 18 (3): 421–437.

Giddens, Anthony. 1991. *Modernity and Self-Identity: Self and Society in the Late Modern Age*. Palo Alto: Stanford University Press.

Gil, Rosa Maria, and Carmen Inoa Vasquez. 1996. *The Maria Paradox*. New York: Putnam.

Gill, Sam D. 1981. *Sacred Words: A Study of Navajo Religion and Prayer*. Westport: Greenwood Press.

Giménez Folqués, David. 2017. "Influencia quechua en el español andino en cuentos y leyendas populares de la Argentina." *Revista Caracol*, no. 13, 296–324.

Gonzales, Patrisia. 2012. *Red Medicine: Traditional Indigenous Rites of Birthing and Healing*. Tucson: University of Arizona Press.

González, Deena. 1997. "Chicana Identity Matters." *Aztlán: A Journal of Chicano Studies* 22 (2): 123–138.

González-Wippler, Migene. 1995. "Santería: Its Dynamics and Multiple Roots." In *Enigmatic Powers: Syncretism with African and Indigenous Peoples' Religions among Latinos*, edited by Anthony M. Stevens-Arroyo and Andres I. Pérez y Mena, 99–111. Decatur: Association for Hispanic Theological Education.

Gott, Richard. 2007. "Latin America as a White Settler Society." *Bulletin of Latin American Research* 26 (2): 269–289.

Gramlich, John, and Alissa Scheller. 2021. "What's Happening at the U.S.-Mexico Border in 7 Charts." Pew Research Center. https://www.pewresearch.org/fact-tank/2021/10/19/whats-happening-at-the-u-s-mexico-border-in-7-charts/.

Gramling, David, and Aniruddha Dutta. 2016. "Translating Transgender." *TSQ: Transgender Studies Quarterly* 3 (3–4): 333–345.

Grinberg, Silvia. 2017. "Vivir y estudiar en las villas del sur global: Modulaciones gerenciales de las biopolíticas de la vida urbana." *Educar em Revista*, no. 66, 57–76.

Grosz, Elizabeth. 1994. *Volatile Bodies: Toward a Corporeal Feminism*. Bloomington: Indiana University Press.

Grosz, Elizabeth. 2011. *Becoming Undone: Darwinian Reflections on Life, Politics, and Art*. Durham: Duke University Press.

Gruzinski, Serge. 1992. *The Aztecs: Rise and Fall of An Empire*. New York: Harry N. Abrams.

Gruzinski, Serge. 1995. "Images and Cultural Mestizaje in Colonial Mexico." *Poetics Today*, no. 16, 53–77.

Guano, Eleonora. 2003. "A Color for the Modern Nation: The Discourse on Race, Class, and Education in the Porteño Middle Class." *Journal of Latin American Anthropology* 8 (1): 148–171.

Guevara, Ernesto. 1967. *Man and Socialism in Cuba*. Havana: Guairas Book Institute.

Guidotti-Hernández, Nicole M. 2011. *Unspeakable Violence. Remapping US and Mexican National Imaginaries*. Durham: Duke University Press.

Guimaraes, Florencia. 2021. "Necropolíticas: Basta de travesticidios." In *Géneros y sociedad: Aportes desde el conurbano*, edited by Gustavo Naón and María Fernanda Vazquez, 50–57. Lomas de Zamora: Universidad Nacional de Lomas de Zamora.

Gutiérrez, Jennicet, and Suyapa Portillo [Portillo Villeda]. 2018. "Trans(Formation) of a Movement: Roxsana Hernández, an Immigrant Transgender Woman from Honduras, Died in ICE Detention Earlier This Year. LGBTI Activists Refuse to Let Her Death Be in Vain." *NACLA Report on the Americas* 50 (4): 392–394.

Guyot, Sylvain. 2011. "The Instrumentalization of Participatory Management in Protected Areas: The Ethnicization of Participation in the Kolla-Atacameña Region of the Central Andes of Argentina and Chile." *Journal of Latin American Geography* 10 (2): 9–36.

Gužauskytė, Evelina. 2014. *Christopher Columbus's Naming in the 'Diarios' of the Four Voyages (1492–1504): A Discourse of Negotiation*. Toronto: University of Toronto Press.

Halberstam, Jack. 2018. *Trans: A Quick and Quirky Account of Gender Variability*. Berkeley: University of California Press.

Halberstam, Jack. 2019. *Female Masculinity*. Durham: Duke University Press.

Halberstam, Judith. 2005. *In a Queer Time and Place: Transgender Bodies, Subcultural Selves*. New York: New York University Press.

Hames-García, Michael. 2006. "What's At Stake in 'Gay' Identities?" In *Identity Politics Reconsidered*, edited by Linda Alcoff, Michael Hames-García, Satya Mohanty, and Paula M. L. Moya, 78–95. New York: Palgrave Macmillan US.

Hames-García, Michael. 2011. *Identity Complex: Making the Case for Multiplicity*. Minneapolis: University of Minnesota Press.

Hames-García, Michael. 2014. "Jotería Studies, or the Political Is Personal." *Aztlán: A Journal of Chicano Studies* 39 (1): 135–142.

Hames-García, Michael, and Ernesto Martinez, eds. 2011. *Gay Latino Studies: A Critical Reader*. Durham: Duke University Press.

Hamilton, Nora, and Norma Stoltz Chinchilla. 2001. *Seeking Community in a Global City: Guatemalans and Salvadorans in Los Angeles*. Philadelphia: Temple University Press.

Hammonds, Evelynn. 1994. "Black (W)holes and the Geometry of Black Female Sexuality." *Differences* 6 (2–3): 127–145.

Hammonds, Evelynn Maxine. 2004. "Power and Politics in Feminism's History— and Future." *Journal of Women's History* 16 (2): 36–39.

Haraway, Donna. 1988. "Situated Knowledges: The Science Question in Feminism and the Privilege of Partial Perspective." *Feminist Studies* 14, no. 3: 575–599.

Haraway, Donna. 1991. *Simians, Cyborgs, and Women: The Reinvention of Nature.* New York: Routledge.

Haraway, Donna. 2008. *When Species Meet.* Minneapolis: University of Minnesota Press.

Harding, Sandra G., ed. 2004. *The Feminist Standpoint Theory Reader: Intellectual and Political Controversies.* New York: Routledge.

Harding, Sandra. 2018. "One Planet, Many Sciences." In *Constructing the Pluriverse: The Geopolitics of Knowledge*, edited by Bernd Reiter, 39–62. Durham: Duke University Press.

Harding, Sandra. 2019. "State of the Field: Latin American Decolonial Philosophies of Science." *Studies in History and Philosophy of Science*, no. 78, 48–63 (part A).

Haritaworn, Jin, Adi Kuntsman, and Silvia Posocco, eds. 2014. *Queer Necropolitics.* New York: Routledge.

Harris, Olivia. 1978. "Complementarity and Conflict: An Andean View of Women and Men," in *Sex and Age as Principles of Social Differentiation*, edited by Jean LaFontaine, 21–40. London: Academic Press.

Harrison, Regina. 1993. "Confesando el pecado en los Andes: Del siglo XVI hacia nuestros días." *Revista de crítica literaria latinoamericana* 19 (37): 169–184.

Hartley, George. 2010. "'Matriz sin tumba': The Trash Goddess and the Healing Matrix of Gloria Anzaldúa's Reclaimed Womb." *MELUS: Multi-Ethnic Literature of the US* 35 (3): 41–61.

Hartsock, Nancy C. M. 2004. "The Feminist Standpoint: Developing the Ground for a Specifically Feminist Historical Materialism." In *The Feminist Standpoint Theory Reader: Intellectual and Political Controversies*, edited by Sandra G. Harding, 35–54. New York: Routledge.

Haslanger, Sally. 2000. "Feminism in Metaphysics: Negotiating the Natural." In *The Cambridge Companion to Feminism in Philosophy*, edited by Miranda Fricker and Jennifer Hornsby, 107–126. Cambridge: Cambridge University Press.

Haslanger, Sally. 2006. "What Good Are Our Intuitions: Philosophical Analysis and Social Kinds." In *Proceedings of the Aristotelian Society*, no. 80, 89–118.

Haslanger, Sally. 2012. *Resisting Reality: Social Construction and Social Critique.* Oxford: Oxford University Press.

Hayward, Eva. 2008. "Lessons from a Starfish." In *Queering the Non/human*, edited by Myra J. Hird, 249–263. New York: Routledge.

Hayward, Eva, and Jami Weinstein. 2015. "Introduction: Tranimalities in the Age of Trans* Life." *Transgender Studies Quarterly* 2 (2): 195–208.

Healy, Claire. 2006. "Review Essay Afro-Argentine Historiography." *Atlantic Studies* 3 (1): 111–120.

Heinze, Ivonne L. 2005. "Kaqchikel and Spanish Language Contact: The Case of Bilingual Mayan Children." PhD diss., University of Kansas.

Heisler Weiser, Anja. 2021. "Cosmos against Nature in the Class Struggle of Proletarian Trans Women." In *Transgender Marxism*, edited by Jules Joann Gleeson and Elle O'Rourke, 230–258. London: Pluto Press.

Henderson, Jason. 2013. *Street Fight: The Politics of Mobility in San Francisco.* Amherst: University of Massachusetts Press.

Hernández Méndez, Edith, and Azucena Palacios Alcaine. 2015. "El sistema pronominal átono en la variedad de español en contacto con Maya Yucateco." *Círculo de lingüística aplicada a la comunicación (CLAC)*, no. 61, 36–78.

Herring, Scott. 2010. *Another Country: Queer Anti-urbanism*. New York: New York University Press.

Hoagland, Sarah. 2004. "Walking Together Illegitimately." *Off Our Backs: The Feminist Newsjournal* 34 (7–8): 38–47.

Hoffmann John. 2016. "Kant's Aesthetic Categories: Race in the 'Critique of Judgment.'" *Diacritics* 44 (2): 54–81.

Holst, John. 2009. "The Pedagogy of Ernesto Che Guevara." *International Journal of Lifelong Education* 28(2): 149–173.

Horswell, Michael. 2005. *Decolonizing the Sodomite: Queer Tropes of Sexuality in Colonial Andean Culture*. Austin: University of Texas Press.

Hull, Akasha Gloria, Patricia Bell-Scott, and Barbara Smith, eds. 1982. *All the Women Are White, All the Blacks Are Men, But Some of Us Are Brave: Black Women's Studies*. Old Westbury: Feminist Press.

Humphrey, Paul R. 2019. *Santería, Vodou and Resistance in Caribbean Literature: Daughters of the Spirits*. Cambridge: Legenda / Modern Humanities Research Association.

Ibáñez Cerda, Sergio, Israel Martínez Corripio, and Armando Mora-Bustos. 2017. "Some Grammatical Characteristics of the Spanish Spoken by Lacandón and Mazahua Bilinguals." In *Language Contact and Change in Mesoamerica and Beyond*, edited by Karen Dakin, Claudia Parodi, and Natalie Operstein, 126–155. Amsterdam: John Benjamins.

INDEC (Instituto Nacional de Estadísticas y Censos). 2012. *Censo Nacional de Población, Hogares y Viviendas 2010*. Buenos Aires.

INDEC (Instituto Nacional de Estadísticas y Censos). 2024. *Censo Nacional de Población, Hogares y Viviendas 2022. Población indígena o descendiente de pueblos indígenas u originarios*.

Indiana, Rita. 2019. *Tentacle*. Translated by Achy Obejas. New York: And Other Stories.

Instituto Nacional de Asuntos Indígenas. Información Estadística. www.desarrollo.gob.ar.

Irni, Susana. 2016. "Steroid Provocations: On the Materiality of Politics in the History of Sex Hormones." *Signs* 41 (3): 507–529.

Isoke, Zenzele. 2018. "Black Ethnography, Black (Female) Aesthetics: Thinking/Writing/Saying/Sounding Black Political Life." *Theory and Event* 21 (1): 148–168.

Jackson, Neil. 2016. "Introduction: Shot, Cut and Slaughtered." In *Snuff: Real Death and Screen Media*, edited by Neil Jackson, Shaun Kimber, Johnny Walker, and Thomas Joseph Watson, 1–19. London: Bloomsbury Publishing.

Jacobs, Harriet (Linda Brent). 1999. "Incidents in the Life of a Slave Girl 1861." In *I Was Born a Slave: An Anthology of Classic Slave Narratives; 1849–1866*, edited by Yuval Taylor, 533–681. Chicago: Lawrence Hill.

Jacobs, Sue Ellen, Wesley Thomas, and Sabine Lang, eds. 1997. *Two-Spirit People: Native American Gender Identity, Sexuality, and Spirituality*. Urbana: University of Illinois Press.

Jay, Martin. 1988. "Scopic Regimes of Modernity." In *Vision and Visuality*, edited by Hal Foster, 3–27. New York: New Press.

Jiménez de la Espada. 1892. *Primeros Descubrimientos del País de la Canela*. Madrid: El progreso editorial.

Johnson, Eithne, and Eric Schaefer. 1993. "Soft Core / Hard Gore: Snuff as a Crisis in Meaning." *Journal of Film and Video 42 (2–3)*: 40–59.

Johnson, E. Patrick, and Mae G. Henderson, eds. 2005. *Black Queer Studies: A Critical Anthology*. Durham: Duke University Press.

Johnson Reagon, Bernice. 1983. "Coalition Politics. Turning the Century." In *Homegirls: A Black Feminist Anthology*, edited by Barbara Smith, 357–68. New York: Kitchen Table Women of Color Press.

Jones, Leah. 2020. "#NotAgainSU: A Case Study of the Counterpublic, Public, and Reactionary Circulation of a Racial Justice Hashtag in the Public Sphere." PhD diss., University of Central Florida.

Jones, Russell T., Christina Kephart, Audra Langley, Mary N. Parker, Uma Shenoy, and Cheri Weeks. 2001. "Cultural and Ethnic Diversity Issues in Clinical Child Psychology." In *Handbook of Clinical Child Psychology*, edited by Eugene Walker and Michael C. Roberts, 955–973. New York: Wiley.

Kaliman, Ricardo J. 1999. "Identidades heterogéneas: Aciertos e ilusiones del conocimiento local." *Revista de crítica literaria latinoamericana*, no. 50, 113–119.

Kant, Immanuel. 1964. *The Classification of Mental Disorders*. Doylestown, PA: Doylestown Foundation.

Karasik, Gabriela. 2000. "Tras la genealogía del diablo: Discusiones sobre la nación y el estado en la frontera Argentino-Boliviana." In *Fronteras, naciones e identidades: La periferia como centro*, edited by Alejandro Grimson, 152–184. Buenos Aires: Ediciones CICCUS-LA CRUJÍA.

Karera, Axelle. 2019. "Blackness and the Pitfalls of Anthropocene Ethics." *Critical Philosophy of Race* 7 (1): 32–56.

Keating, AnaLouise. 2009. *The Gloria Anzaldúa Reader*. Durham: Duke University Press.

Keating, AnaLouise. 2012. "Speculative Realism, Visionary Pragmatism, and Poet-Shamanic Aesthetics in Gloria Anzaldúa—and Beyond." Women's Studies Quarterly 40 (3–4): 53–71.

Kelley, Robin. 1992. "An Archeology of Resistance." *American Quarterly* 44 (2): 292–298.

Kelly, Evadne, Seika Boye, and Carla Rice. 2021. "Projecting Eugenics and Performing Knowledges." In *Narrative Art and the Politics of Health*, edited by Neil Brooks and Sarah Blanchette, 37–62. Cambridge: Cambridge University Press.

Kim, Eunjung. 2015. "Unbecoming Human: An Ethics of Objects." *GLQ: A Journal of Lesbian and Gay Studies* 21 (2–3): 295–320.

Kim, Eunjung. 2017. *Curative Violence: Rehabilitating Disability, Gender, and Sexuality in Modern Korea*. Durham: Duke University Press.

Kingsbury, John M. 1992. "Christopher Columbus as a Botanist." *Arnoldia* 52 (2): 11–28.

Knight, Alan. 2022. *Bandits and Liberals, Rebels and Saints: Latin America since Independence*. Lincoln: University of Nebraska Press.

Kulick, Don. 1998. *Travesti: Sex, Gender, and Culture among Brazilian Transgendered Prostitutes*. Chicago: University of Chicago Press.

Kusch, Rodolfo. 2010. *Indigenous and Popular Thinking in América*, translated by Maria Lugones and Joshua Martin Price. Durham: Duke University Press.

La Fountain–Stokes, Lawrence. 2014. "Epistemología de la loca: Localizando a la transloca en la transdiáspora." In *Resentir lo "queer" en América Latina: Diálogos desde con el sur*, edited by Diego Falconí Trávez, Santiago Castellanos y María Amelia Viteri, 133–146. Barcelona: Egales.

Lane, Kevin. 2009. "Engineered Highlands: The Social Organization of Water in the Ancient North-Central Andes (AD 1000–1480)." *World Archaeology* 41 (1): 169–190.

Lang, Mervyn F. 1990. *Spanish Word Formation: Productive Derivational Morphology in the Modern Lexis*. London: Routledge.

Laqueur, Thomas. 1992. *Making Sex: Body and Gender from the Greeks to Freud*. Cambridge: Harvard University Press.

Lara, Ana-Maurine. 2006. *Erzulie's Skirt*. Washington, DC: RedBone Press.

Lara, Irene. 2005. "Bruja Positionalities: Toward a Chicana/Latina Spiritual Activism." *Chicana/Latina Studies* 4 (2): 10–45.

de Las Casas, Bartolomé. 2004. *A Short Account of the Destruction of the Indies*. New York: Penguin.

Lawrence, Bonita. 2003. "Gender, Race, and the Regulation of Native Identity in Canada and the United States: An Overview." *Hypatia* 18 (2): 3–31.

Leander, Birgitta. 1991. *In Xochitl In Cuicatl: Flor y canto; La Poesía de los Aztecas*. Mexico, DF: Instituto Nacional Indigenista.

Lecount, Cynthia. 1999. "Carnival in Bolivia: Devils Dancing for the Virgin." *Western Folklore* 58 (3–4): 231–252.

Lefebvre, Henri. 1991. *The Production of Space*. Malden: Blackwell.

Lewis, Abram J. 2017. "Trans Animisms." *Angelaki: Journal of Theoretical Humanities* 22 (2): 205–215.

Linthicum, Kate. 2013. "In Buenos Aires, Tango Queer Lets the Dancers Switch Roles." *Los Angeles Times*, October 4.

Lloyd, Genevieve. 1984. *The Man of Reason*. Minneapolis: University of Minnesota Press.

Lockhart, James. 2001. *Nahuatl as Written: Lessons in Older Written Nahuatl, with Copious Examples and Texts*. Stanford: Stanford University Press.

López de Gómara, Francisco. 1943. *Historia de la Conquista de México*. México: Editorial Pedro Robredo.

Lorde, Audre. 1982. *Zami: A New Spelling of My Name—A Biomythography*. Watertown: Persephone Press.

Lorde, Audre. 1984. *Sister Outsider*. New York: Random House.

Losada, Leandro. 2012. "El mercado matrimonial de las familias tradicionales argentinas, 1900–1940: Algunas dimensiones y tendencias." *Secuencia*, no. 82, 127–151.

Lozano-Díaz, Nora O. 2021. "Ignored Virgin or Unaware Women: A Mexican-American Protestant Reflection on the Virgin of Guadalupe." In *A Reader in Latina Feminist Theology: Religion and Justice*, edited by María Pilar Aquino, Daisy L. Machado, and Jeanette Rodríguez, 204–216. Austin: University of Texas Press.

Lugones, María. 2000. "Multiculturalism and Publicity: On María Pía Lara's Moral Structures." *Hypatia* 15 (3): 175–181.

Lugones, María. 2003a. "El Pasar Discontinuo de la Cachapera/Tortillera del Barrio a la Barra al Movimiento: The Discontinuous Passing of the Cachapera/Tortillera from the Barrio to the Bar to the Movement." In *Pilgrimages/Peregrinajes: Theorizing Coalition against Multiple Oppressions*. Lanham: Rowman & Littlefield.

Lugones, María. 2003b. *Pilgrimages/Peregrinajes: Theorizing Coalition against Multiple Oppressions*. Lanham: Rowman & Littlefield.

Lugones, María. 2003c. "Playfulness, 'World'-Traveling, and Loving Perception." In *Pilgrimages/Peregrinajes: Theorizing Coalition against Multiple Oppressions*, 77–100. Lanham: Rowman & Littlefield.

Lugones, María. 2005. "From within Germinative Stasis: Creating Active Subjectivity, Resistant Agency." In *EntreMundos/AmongWorlds: New Perspectives on Gloria E. Anzaldúa*, edited by AnaLouise Keating, 85–99. New York: Palgrave Macmillan US.

Lugones, María. 2007. "Heterosexualism and the Colonial/Modern Gender System." *Hypatia* 22 (1): 186–209.

Lugones, María. 2010. "Toward a Decolonial Feminism." *Hypatia* 25 (4): 742–759.

Lugones, María. 2020. "Gender and Universality in Colonial Methodology." *Critical Philosophy of Race* 8 (1–2): 25–47.

Lugones, María C., and Elizabeth V. Spelman. 2018. "Have We Got a Theory for You! Feminist Theory, Cultural Imperialism and the Demand for 'the Woman's Voice.'" In *Feminism and Philosophy: Essential Readings in Theory, Reinterpretation, and Application*, edited by Nancy Tuana and Rosemarie Putnam Tong, 494–507. New York: Routledge.

Luhrmann, Tanya M. 2011. "Hallucinations and Sensory Overrides." *Annual Review of Anthropology*, no. 40, 71–85.

Luna, Kausha. 2018. "Caravan of Central American Illegal Aliens Heads to the U.S." *Center for Immigration Studies Blog*, March 30, 2018. https://cis.org/Luna/Caravan-Central-American-Illegal-Aliens-Heads-US.

Luongo, Michael. 2004. "What's New, Buenos Aires?" In *Out Traveler*, Winter 2004. https://www.outtraveler.com/features/2004/10/13/winter-2004-whats-new-buenos-aires

Lussagnet, Suzanne. 1948. "Civilisations précolombiennes en territoire argentin." *Annales: Histoire, sciences sociales* 3 (4): 510–518.

MacLean, Hope. 2001. "Sacred Colors and Shamanic Vision among the Huichol Indians of Mexico." *Journal of Anthropological Research* 57 (3): 305–323.

MacLean, Hope. 2012. *The Shaman's Mirror: Visionary Art of the Huichol*. Austin: University of Texas Press.

Maffie, James. 2014. *Aztec Philosophy: Understanding a World in Motion*. Boulder: University Press of Colorado.

Malatino, Hilary. 2019. *Queer Embodiment: Monstrosity, Medical Violence, and Intersex Experience*. Lincoln: University of Nebraska Press.

Malcomson, Hettie. 2011. "The 'Routes' and 'Roots' of Danzón: a Critique of the History of a Genre." *Popular Music* 30 (2): 263–278.

Maldonado-Torres, Nelson. 2008. *Against War: Views from the Underside of Modernity*. Durham: Duke University Press.

Mallory, Christy, Taylor N. T. Brown, and Kerith J. Conron. 2019. "Conversion Therapy and LGBT Youth—Update." Williams Institute, School of Law, UCLA. https://williamsinstitute.law.ucla.edu/publications/conversion -therapy-and-lgbt-youth/.

Mansbridge, Jane. 1996. "Using Power / Fighting Power: The Polity." *PS: Political Science and Politics* 29, no. 4: 472–476.

Marcos, Sylvia. 2006. *Taken from the Lips: Gender and Eros in Mesoamerican Religions*. Leiden: Brill.

Marcos, Sylvia. 2009. "Mesoamerican Women's Indigenous Spirituality: Decolonizing Religious Beliefs." *Journal of Feminist Studies in Religion* 25 (2): 25–45.

Marker, M. 2004. "Theories and Disciplines as Sites of Struggle: The Reproduction of Colonial Dominance through the Controlling of Knowledge in the Academy." *Canadian Journal of Native Education* 28 (1–2): 102–110.

Martin, Biddy, and Chandra Talpade Mohanty. 1986. "Feminist Politics: What's Home Got to Do with It?" In *Feminist Studies / Critical Studies*, edited by Teresa de Lauretis, 191–212. London: Palgrave Macmillan UK.

Martínez, Ernesto Javier. 2013. *On Making Sense: Queer Race Narratives of Intelligibility*. Stanford: Stanford University Press.

Martínez, Juliana, and Salvador Vidal-Ortiz. 2021. "Travar el Saber: Travesti-Centred Knowledge-Making and Education." *Bulletin of Latin American Research* 40 (5): 665–678.

Martyr, Peter D. 1912. *De Orbe Novo: The Eight Decades of Peter Martyr D'Anghera*. New York: GP Putnam's Sons.

Matthews, Peter Hugoe. 2014. *The Concise Oxford Dictionary of Linguistics*. Oxford: Oxford University Press.

Maturana, Humberto R., and Francisco J. Varela. 1980. *Autopoiesis and Cognition: The Realization of the Living*. Dordrecht: D. Reidel Publishing Company.

May, Vivian. 2015. *Pursuing Intersectionality, Unsettling Dominant Imaginaries*. New York: Routledge.

Mazzeo, Victoria, and Pablo Perelman. 2016. "Un siglo de contrastes en el comportamiento de la nupcialidad en la Ciudad de Buenos Aires." *Revista latinoamericana de población* 10 (19): 83–106.

Mbembe, Achille. 2003. "Necropolitics." *Public Culture* 15 (1): 11–40.

Mbembe, Achille. 2019. *Necropolitics*. Translated by Steve Corcoran. Durham: Duke University Press.

McCall, Leslie. 2005. "The Complexity of Intersectionality." *Signs: Journal of Women in Culture and Society* 30 (3): 1771–1800.

McDonough, Tom, ed. 2009. *The Situationists and the City: A Reader*. London: Verso Books.

McFadden, Johnjoe, and Jim Al-Khalili. 2018. "The Origins of Quantum Biology." *Proceedings of the Royal Society. Mathematical, Physical, and Engineering Sciences A* 474, no. 2213: 20180674.

McKittrick, Katherine, ed. 2015. *Sylvia Wynter: On Being Human as Praxis*. Durham: Duke University Press.

Merma-Molina, Gladys. 2007. "Contacto lingüístico entre el español y el quechua: Un enfoque cognitivo-pragmático de las transferencias morfosintácticas en el español andino peruano." PhD diss., Universidad de Alicante.

Merriman, Peter. 2019. "Molar and Molecular Mobilities: The Politics of Perceptible and Imperceptible Movements." *Environment and Planning D: Society and Space* 37 (1): 65–82.

Mesa-Bains, Amalia. 1999. "'Domesticana': The Sensibility of Chicana Rasquache." *Aztlán: A Journal of Chicano Studies* 24 (2): 155–167.

Mignolo, Walter. 1995. *The Darker Side of the Renaissance: Territoriality and Literacy*. Ann Arbor: University of Michigan Press.

Mignolo, Walter. 2012. *Local Histories / Global Designs: Coloniality, Subaltern Knowledges, and Border Thinking*. Princeton, NJ: Princeton University Press.

Mignolo, Walter, and Madina Tlostanova. 2006. "Theorizing from the Borders: Shifting to Geo- and Body-Politics of Knowledge." *European Journal of Social Theory* 9 (2): 205–221.

Millones, Luis, and Mary Louise Pratt. 1990. *Amor Brujo: Images and culture of love in the Andes*. Syracuse: Syracuse University Press.

Mingus, Mia. 2011. "Changing the Framework: Disability Justice." Blog post, February 12, 2011. https://leavingevidence.wordpress.com/2011/02/12/changing-the-framework-disability-justice/.

Ministerio de Educación y Deportes de la Nación (MEDN). 2016. *Guaraníes, chanés y tapietes del norte argentino: Construyendo el 'ñande reko' para el futuro*. Ciudad Autónoma de Buenos Aires: Ministerio de Educación y Deportes de la Nación.

Miranda, Deborah. 2002. "Dildos, Hummingbirds, and Driving Her Crazy: Searching for American Indian Women's Love Poetry and Erotics." *Frontiers* 23 (2): 135–149.

Miranda, Deborah A. 2010. "Extermination of the Joyas: Gendercide in Spanish California." *GLQ: A Journal of Lesbian and Gay Studies* 16 (1–2): 253–284.

Miranda, Marisa A. 2018. "La eugenesia tardía en Argentina y su estereotipo de familia, segunda mitad del siglo XX." Supplement, *História, ciências, saúde—Manguinhos* 25, no. S1: 33–50.

Miranda, Marisa Adriana. 2020. *¡Madre y patria!* Buenos Aires: Teseo.

Miranda Luizaga, Jorge, and Viviana Del Carpio Natcheff. 2000. "El 'en sí' y el 'para sí' y el 'porque sí' de la filosofía andina." In *Aportes al diálogo sobre cultura y filosofía andina*, edited by Viviana del Carpio Natcheff and Jorge Miranda-Luizaga, 1–48. La Paz: Publicaciones Siwa Consejo Del Saber Qulla, Goethe Institut.

Mohanty, Chandra Talpade. 1984. "Under Western Eyes: Feminist Scholarship and Colonial Discourses." *Boundary 2* 12 (3): 333–358.

Mohanty, Chandra Talpade. 2003. "'Under Western Eyes' Revisited: Feminist Solidarity through Anticapitalist Struggles." *Signs: Journal of Women in Culture and Society* 28 (2): 499–535.

Mollett, Sharlene. 2006. "Race and Natural Resource Conflicts in Honduras." *Latin American Research Review* 41 (1): 76–101.

Monkevicius, Paola C. 2013. "May the Afro be a Part of the Argentinean Nation: State Resignifications of Black Memories." *Tabula Rasa*, no. 19, 227–243.

Monsanto, C. 1982. "Guatemala a través de su marimba." *Latin American Music Review* 3 (1): 60–72.

Montesinos, Fernando. 1882. *Memorias Antiguas Historiales y Políticas del Perú*. Edited by Marcos Jiménez de la Espada. Madrid: Imprenta de Manuel Hernández.

Moraga, Cherríe L. 2011. *A Xicana Codex of Changing Consciousness: Writings, 2000–2010*. Durham: Duke University Press.

Moraga, Cherríe. 1983. "A Long Line of Vendidas." In *Loving in the War Years: Lo que Nunca Pasó por Sus Labios*, 90–144. Boston: South End Press.

Moraga, Cherríe. 1983. *Loving in the War Years: Lo que Nunca Pasó por Sus Labios*. Boston: South End Press.

Moraga, Cherríe. [1995] 2001. *The Hungry Woman*. New York: West End Press.

Moraga, Cherríe. 1996. "Heroes and Saints." In *Contemporary Plays by Women of Color*, edited by Kathy Perkins and Roberta Uno, 332–378. London: Routledge.

Moraga, Cherríe. 1997. *Waiting in The Wings: Portrait of A Queer Motherhood*. Ithaca, NY: Firebrand Books.

Moraga, Cherríe. 2011. *A Xicana Codex of Changing Consciousness: Writings, 2000–2010*. Durham: Duke University Press.

Moraga, Cherríe. 2015. "The Mathematics of Love." Unpublished manuscript.

Moraga, Cherríe, and Gloria Anzaldúa, eds. [1981] 2022. *This Bridge Called My Back: Writings by Radical Women of Color*. Albany: State University of New York Press.

Moreno Figueroa, Mónica G., and Emiko Saldívar Tanaka. 2015. "Comics, Dolls, and the Disavowal of Racism: Learning from Mexican Mestizaje." In *Creolizing Europe: Legacies and Transformations*, edited by Encarnación Gutiérrez Rodríguez and Shirley Anne Tate, 175–201. Liverpool: Liverpool University Press.

Morrow, Colette. 1997. "Queering Chicano/a Narratives: Lesbian as Healer, Saint and Warrior in Ana Castillo's 'So Far from God.'" *Journal of the Midwest Modern Language Association* 30 (1–2): 63–80.

Mortimer-Sandilands, Catriona, and Bruce Erickson. 2010. *Queer Ecologies: Sex, Nature, Politics, Desire*. Bloomington: Indiana University Press.

Mosbergen, Dominique. 2018. "Transgender Asylum-Seeker Who Died in ICE Custody Was Beaten, Autopsy Shows." *Huffpost*, November 27, 2018. https://www.huffpost.com/entry/roxsana-hernandez-transgender-asylum-seeker-autopsy_n_5bfd0f20e4b03b230fa66995.

Mumford, Kevin. 1997. *Interzones: Black/White Sex Districts in Chicago and New York in the Early Twentieth Century*. New York: Columbia University Press.

Muñoz, Carlos. 2007. *Youth, Identity, Power: The Chicano Movement*. London: Verso Books.

Muñoz, José Esteban. 1999. *Disidentifications: Queers of Color and the Performance of Politics*. Minneapolis: University of Minnesota Press.

Muñoz, Karina Ochoa. 2014. "El debate sobre las y los amerindios: Entre el discurso de la bestialización, la feminización y la racialización." *El cotidiano*, no. 184, 13–22.

Murra, John V. 1975. *Formaciones económicas y políticas del mundo andino*. Cuzco: Instituto de Estudios Peruanos.

Murray, Stephen O. 1995. *Latin American Male Homosexualities*. Albuquerque: University of New Mexico Press.

New York State. "Gender Expression Non-discrimination Act (GENDA)," Senate Bill S1047, 2019. https://legislation.nysenate.gov/pdf/bills/2019/S1047 (Accessed November 6, 2022).

Nguyen, David Luc. 2007. "No Need for Crying in Argentina." *The Advocate Online*, October 29. https://www.advocate.com/travel/2007/10/30/no-need -crying-argentina.

Noll, Richard. 1983. "Shamanism and Schizophrenia: A State-Specific Approach to the 'Schizophrenia Metaphor' of Shamanic States." *American Ethnologist* 10 (3): 443–459.

Núñez Noriega, Guillermo. 1999. *Sexo entre varones: Poder y resistencia en el campo sexual.* Mexico City: Editorial Plaza y Valdez.

O'Callaghan, Casey. 2008. "Seeing What You Hear: Cross-Modal Illusions and Perception." *Philosophical Issues* 18 (1): 316–338.

Occhipinti, Laurie. 2002. "Being Kolla: Indigenous Identity In Northwestern Argentina." *Canadian Journal of Latin American and Caribbean Studies* 27 (54): 319–345.

Occhipinti, Laurie. 2003. "Claiming a Place: Land and Identity in Two Communities in Northwestern Argentina." *Journal of Latin American Anthropology* 8 (3): 155–174.

Ochoa, Marcia. 2016. "Los Huecos Negros: Cannibalism, Sodomy and the Failure of Modernity in Tierra Firme." *Genders* 1 (1). https://www.colorado.edu /genders/2016/05/19/los-huecos-negros-cannibalism-sodomy-and-failure -modernity-tierra-firme.

Ocoró Loango, Anny. 2011. "La emergencia del negro en los actos escolares del 25 de mayo en la Argentina: Del negro heroico al decorativo y estereotipado." *Pedagogía y Saberes*, no. 34 (January-June): 33–50.

Ocoró Loango, Anny. 2015. "Los afrodescendientes en Argentina: La irrupción de un nuevo actor en la agenda política y educativa del país." *Revista Colombiana de Educación*, no. 69, 17–157.

Offord, Catherine. 2019. "Quantum Biology May Help Solve Some of Life's Greatest Mysteries." *The Scientist*, June 1. https://www.the-scientist.com/features /quantum-biology-may-help-solve-some-of-lifes-greatest-mysteries-65873.

Olko, Justyna, and John Sullivan. 2014. "Toward a Comprehensive Model for Nahuatl Language Research and Revitalization." *Proceedings of the Annual Meeting of the Berkeley Linguistics Society*, no. 40, 369–397.

Omi, Michael, and Howard Winant. 2014. *Racial Formation in the United States.* New York: Routledge.

Ontiveros, Asunción (Yulquila). 2003. "Pobreza y abundancia en la cultura Kolla: Representaciones y valores; El caso de 'La cuadrilla de cajas y copleros del 1800' (La Banda, Humahuaca, Jujuy)." Senior thesis, Universidad Nacional de Jujuy.

Ortega, Mariana. 2001. "'New Mestizas,' '"World" Travelers,' and 'Dasein': Phenomenology and the Multi-voiced, Multi-cultural Self." *Hypatia* 16 (3): 1–29.

Ortega, Mariana. 2016. *In-Between: Latina Feminist Phenomenology, Multiplicity, and the Self.* Albany: State University of New York Press.

Oyěwùmí, Oyèrónkẹ́. 1997. *The Invention of Women: Making an African Sense of Western Gender Discourses.* Minneapolis: University of Minnesota Press.

Paccacerqua, Cynthia M. 2016. "Gloria Anzaldúa's Affective Logic of Volverse Una." *Hypatia* 31 (2): 334–351.

Páez, María Cecilia, Alejandro Martínez, Francisco Eduardo Riegler, and Catalina Martínez Zabala. 2021. "Memoria y resistencia en los relatos de la copla del Valle Calchaquí (Salta, Argentina): Concepciones acerca de la naturaleza." *Runa* 42 (1): 265–282.

Paik, Shailaja. 2021. "Dalit Feminist Thought." In *Routledge Handbook of Gender in South Asia*, 55–69. New York: Routledge.

Paredes, Julieta. 2010. *Hilando fino: Desde el feminismo comunitario*. La Paz: Comunidad Mujeres Creando Comunidad.

Paredes, Julieta, and Adriana Guzmán. 2014. *El tejido de la rebeldía: ¿Qué es el feminismo comunitario?* La Paz: Comunidad Mujeres Creando Comunidad.

Patterson, Thomas C. 1991. "Early Colonial Encounters and Identities in the Caribbean: A Review of Some Recent Works and Their Implications." *Dialectical Anthropology* 16 (1): 1–13.

Patton, Cindy. 2005. "Outlaw Territory: Criminality, Neighborhoods, and the Edward Savitz Case." *Sexuality Research and Social Policy* 2 (2): 63–75.

Paz, Gustave. 1997. "Familia, linaje y red de parientes: La elite de Jujuy a fines del siglo XVIII." *Andes: Antropología e Historia*, no. 8, 145–174.

Pellarolo, Sirela. 2008. "Queering Tango: Glitches in the Hetero-national Matrix of a Liminal Cultural Production." *Theatre Journal* 60 (3): 409–431.

Pennizi, Elizabeth. "An Aquarium Accident May Have Given This Crayfish the DNA to Take Over the World." *Science*, February 5, 2018. https://www.science.org/content/article/aquarium-accident-may-have-given-crayfish-dna-take-over-world

Pérez, Emma. 1999. *The Decolonial Imaginary: Writing Chicanas into History*. Bloomington: Indiana University Press.

Pérez, Gail. 2002. "Ana Castillo as *Santera*: Reconstructing Popular Religion Praxis." In *A Reader in Latina Feminist Theology: Religion and Justice*, edited by María Pilar Aquino, Daisy L. Machado, and Jeanette Rodríguez, 53–79. Austin: University of Texas Press.

Pérez, Laura E. 1999. "El Desorden, Nationalism, and Chicana/o Aesthetics." In *Between Woman and Nation: Nationalisms, Transnational Feminisms, and the State*, edited by Caren Kaplan, Norma Alarcón, and Minoo Moallem, 19–46. Durham: Duke University Press.

Pérez, Laura E. 2007. *Chicana Art: The Politics of Spiritual and Aesthetic Altarities*. Durham: Duke University Press.

Pérez, Laura E. 2010. "Enrique Dussel's *Ética de la liberación*, US Women of Color Decolonizing Practices, and Coalitional Politics amidst Difference." *Qui Parle: Critical Humanities and Social Sciences* 18 (2): 121–146.

Pérez, Laura E. 2019. *Eros Ideologies: Writings on Art, Spirituality, and the Decolonial*. Durham: Duke University Press.

Pérez Firmat, Gustavo. 1994. *Life on the Hyphen: The Cuban-American Way*. Austin: The University of Texas.

Pérez Marín, Yarí. 2020. *Marvels of Medicine: Literature and Scientific Enquiry in Early Colonial Spanish America*. Liverpool: Liverpool University Press.

Perlongher, Néstor. 1999. *El negocio del deseo*. Buenos Aires: Paidós.

Pierce, Joseph M. 2019. *Argentine Intimacies: Queer Kinship in an Age of Splendor, 1890–1910*. Albany: State University of New York Press.

Pinkerton, Anne. 1986. "Observations on the Tú/Vos Option in Guatemalan Ladino Spanish." *Hispania* 69 (3): 690–698.

Pisano, Juan Ignacio. 2018. "'Fictions of People' and Gauchesca during the Decade of 1810: Cielitos, Voz y Uso." *Literatura Lingüística*, no. 38, 127–147.

Pitts, Andrea J. 2016. "Gloria E. Anzaldúa's Autohistoria-Teoría as an Epistemology of Self-Knowledge/Ignorance." *Hypatia* 31 (2): 352–369.

Platt, Tristan. 1980. "Espejos y maíz: El concepto de yanantin entre los macha de Bolivia." In *Parentesco y matrimonio en los Andes*, edited by Enrique Mayer and Ralph Bolton, 139–182. Lima: Pontificia Universidad Católica del Perú.

Podjajcer, Adil, and Yanina Mennelli. 2009. "'La mamita y pachamama' en las performances de carnaval y la fiesta de nuestra señora de la candelaria en Puno y en Humahuaca." *Cuadernos de la Facultad de Humanidades y Ciencias Sociales, Universidad Nacional de Jujuy*, no. 36, 67–90.

Poma de Ayala, Felipe Guamán, and Franklin Pease. 1980. *Nueva corónica y buen gobierno*. Vol. 2. Caracas: Fundación Biblioteca Ayacucho.

Poosson, Sylvain B. 2004. "'Entre Tango y Payada': The Expression of Blacks in 19th Century Argentina." *Confluencia, Revista Hispánica de Cultura y Literatura* 20 (1): 87–99.

Popolo, Fabiana Del. 2017. *Los pueblos indígenas en América (Abya Yala): Desafíos para la igualdad en la diversidad*. Santiago de Chile: Comisión Económica para América Latina y el Caribe (CEPAL).

Posthumus, David. 2022. *All My Relatives: Exploring Lakota Ontology, Belief, and Ritual*. Lincoln: University of Nebraska Press.

Price, Joshua Martin. 2012. *Structural Violence: Hidden Brutality in the Lives of Women*. Albany: State University of New York Press.

Price, Joshua Martin. 2015. *Prison and Social Death*. New Brunswick: Rutgers University Press.

Price, Joshua. 2023. *Translation and Epistemicide: The Racialization of Languages in the Americas*. Tucson: University of Arizona Press.

Prieur, Annick. 1998. *Mema's House: On Transvestites, Queens, and Machos*. Chicago: University of Chicago Press.

Puar, Jasbir. 2007. *Terrorist Assemblages: Homonationalism in Queer Times*. Durham: Duke University Press.

Puar, Jasbir. 2012. "'I Would Rather Be a Cyborg than a Goddess': Becoming-Intersectional in Assemblage Theory." *philoSOPHIA: A Journal of TransContinental Feminism* 2 (1): 49–66.

Pukacz, Ariel. 2022. *Snuff*. Buenos Aires: La Conjura.

Quijano, Aníbal. 1991. "Colonialidad y racionalidad/modernidad." *Perú indígena*, no. 29, 11–29.

Quijano, Aníbal. 2000. "Coloniality of Power, Eurocentrism and Latin America." *Nepantla: Views from the South* 1 (3): 533–580.

Quiñones, Francisco. 2019. "Homenaje a Lohana Berkins: La revolución de la sabia comandanta de las mariposas." *APU Agencia Paco Urondo*, February 8. https://www.agenciapacourondo.com.ar/opinion/homenaje-lohana-berkins-la-revolucion-de-la-sabia-comandanta-de-las-mariposas.

Quiroga, José. 1997. "Homosexualities in the Tropic of Revolution." In *Sex and Sexuality in Latin America*, edited by Daniel Balderston and Donna Guy, 133–151. New York: New York University Press.

Radcliffe, Sarah A. 2019. "Pachamama, Subaltern Geographies, and Decolonial Projects in Andean Ecuador." In *Subaltern Geographies*, edited by Tariq Jazeel and Stephen Legg, 159–178. Athens: University of Georgia.

Rafael, Vicente L. 1993. *Contracting Colonialism: Translation and Christian Conversion in Tagalog Society under Early Spanish Rule*. Durham: Duke University Press,

Ramirez, Horacio N. Roque. 2003. "'That's My Place!': Negotiating Racial, Sexual, and Gender Politics in San Francisco's Gay Latino Alliance, 1975–1983." *Journal of the History of Sexuality* 12 (2): 224–258.

Ramirez, Renya K. 2007. *Native Hubs: Culture, Community, and Belonging in Silicon Valley and Beyond*. Durham: Duke University Press.

Rapisardi, Flavio, and Alejandro Modarelli. 2001. *Fiestas, baños y exilios: Los gays porteños en la última dictadura*. Buenos Aires: Editorial Sudamericana.

Raymond, Janice G. 1979. *The Transsexual Empire: The Making of the She-Male*. Boston: Beacon Press.

Reiter, Bernd, ed. 2018. *Constructing the Pluriverse: The Geopolitics of Knowledge*. Durham: Duke University Press.

Retes, Eduardo. 2020. "VIH-Sida: La Epidemia Olvidada en Honduras." *Innovare: Revista de ciencia y tecnología* 9 (1): 60–61.

Revilla, Anita, and José Santillana. 2014. "Jotería Identity and Consciousness." *Aztlán: A Journal of Chicano Studies* 39 (1): 167–180.

Revuelta, Facundo. 2022. "Hotel Gondolín." In *Queer Spaces: An Atlas of LGBTQ+ Places and Stories*, edited by Adam Nathaniel Furman and Joshua Mardell, 28–29. London: Riba Publishing.

Reyes, Yosimar. 2011. "TRE (My Revolutionary)." YouTube video, https://youtu.be/lq03sppYpGY?si=JB7eiNx6pwz3u8tm.

Rincón, Luz-Mary. 2006. "'Usted,' the Prononominal Address of Familiarity in an Urban Community." *Hispanic Journal* 27 (1): 11–22.

Rivera Cusicanqui, Silvia. 2004. "II. Reclaiming the Nation." *NACLA Report on the Americas* 38 (3): 19–23.

Rivera Cusicanqui, Silvia. 2013. "Ch'ixinakax utxiwa: A Reflection on the Practices and Discourses of Decolonization." *South Atlantic Quarterly* 111 (1): 95–109.

Rizki, Cole. 2020. "'No State Apparatus Goes to Bed Genocidal Then Wakes Up Democratic.' Fascist Ideology and Transgender Politics in Post-dictatorship Argentina." *Radical History Review*, no. 138: 82–107.

Rodríguez, Ana Patricia. 2009. *Dividing the Isthmus: Central American Transnational Histories, Literatures, and Cultures*. Austin: University of Texas Press.

Rodriguez, Joseph A. 1999. "Rapid Transit and Community Power: West Oakland Residents Confront BART." *Antipode* 31 (2): 212–228.

Rodríguez, Juana María. 2014. *Sexual Futures, Queer Gestures, and other Latina Longings*. New York: New York University Press.

Rodríguez, Richard T. 2009. *Next of Kin: The Family in Chicano/a Cultural Politics*. Durham: Duke University Press.

Roen, Katrina. 2006. "Transgender Theory and Embodiment: The Risk of Racial Marginalization." In *The Transgender Studies Reader*, edited by Susan Stryker and Stephen Whittle, 656–665. New York: Routledge.

Romberg, Raquel. 2012. "Sensing the Spirits: The Healing Dramas and Poetics of Brujeria Rituals." *Anthropologica* 54 (2): 211–225.

Roshanravan, Shireen. 2014. "Motivating Coalition: Women of Color and Epistemic Disobedience." *Hypatia* 29 (1): 41–58.

Rouse, Irving. 1986. *Migrations in Prehistory: Inferring Population Movement from Cultural Remains.* New Haven: Yale University Press.

Rouse, Irving. 1993. Review of *Cannibal Encounters: Europeans and Island Caribs, 1492–1763*, by Philip P. Boucher. *Hispanic American Historical Review* 73 (3): 495–496.

Roy, Deboleena. 2018. *Molecular Feminisms: Biology, Becomings, and Life in the Lab.* Seattle: University of Washington Press.

Rubin, Gayle. 2002. "Studying Sexual Subcultures: The Ethnography of Gay Communities in Urban North America." In *Out In Theory: The Emergence of Lesbian and Gay Anthropology*, edited by Elen Lewin and William Leap, 17–68. Urbana: University of Illinois Press.

Rueda Esquibel, Catrióna. 2003. "Velvet Malinche." In *Velvet Barrios: Popular Culture and Chicana/o Sexualities*, edited by Alicia Gaspar de Alba, 295–307. New York: Springer.

Sabsay, Leticia. 2011. *Fronteras sexuales: Espacio urbano, cuerpos y ciudadanía.* Buenos Aires: Paidós.

Sabsay, Leticia. 2014. "Políticas queer, ciudadanías sexuales y descolonización." In *Resentir lo "queer" en América Latina: Diálogos desde-con el sur*, edited by Diego Falconí Trávez, Santiago Castellanos, and María Amelia Viteri, 45–59. Barcelona: Egales.

Saintenoy, T. 2013. "Sur le chemin d'Apurímac: Essai sur la représentation géographique du territoire dans la culture Inca." *L'Homme revue française d'anthropologie*, no. 205, 7–33.

Salas-SantaCruz, Omi. 2023. "Nonbinary Epistemologies: Refusing Colonial Amnesia and Erasure of Jotería and Trans* Latinidades." *WSQ: Women's Studies Quarterly* 51 (3–4): 78–93.

Salazar, Ruben. "Who Is a Chicano? And What Is It the Chicanos Want?" *Los Angeles Times*, February 6, 1970. https://www.latimes.com/california/story/1970–02–06/who-is-a-chicano-and-what-is-it-the-chicanos-want.

Saldaña-Portillo, María Josefina. 2003. *The Revolutionary Imagination in the Americas and the Age of Development.* Durham: Duke University Press.

Salessi, Jorge. 1995. *Médicos, Maleantes y Maricas.* Rosario: Beatriz Viterbo Editora.

Sánchez-Carretero, Cristina. 2005. "Santos y Misterios as Channels of Communication in the Diaspora: Afro-Dominican Religious Practices Abroad." *Journal of American Folklore* 118 (469): 308–326.

Sandoval, Chela. 2018. "'Translation as Trans-Interpretation': Notes on Transforming the Book *Methodology of the Oppressed* into *Metodología de la emancipación.*" *Chicana/Latina Studies* 17 (2): 26–32.

Sandoval, Chela. 2000. *Methodology of the Oppressed.* Minneapolis: University of Minnesota Press.

Sandoval, Chela. 2002. "Dissident Globalizations, Emancipatory Methods, Social-Erotics." In *Queer Globalizations: Citizenship and the Afterlife of*

Colonialism, edited by Arnaldo Cruz-Malavé and Martin F. Manalansan, 20–32. New York University Press.

Santa Cruz Feminist of Color Collective. 2014. "Building on 'the Edge of Each Other's Battles': A Feminist of Color Multidimensional Lens." *Hypatia* 29 (1): 41–58.

Santos Perez, Craig. 2022. *Navigating Chamoru Poetry: Indigeneity, Aesthetics, and Decolonization*. Tucson: University of Arizona Press.

Sarmiento, Domingo F. 2004. *Facundo: Civilization and Barbarism*. Berkeley: University of California Press.

Schaedel, Richard P. 1988. "Andean World View: Hierarchy or Reciprocity, Regulation or Control?" *Current Anthropology* 29 (5): 768–775.

Schaefer, Agnes Gereben, Radha Iyengar Plumb, Srikanth Kadiyala, Jennifer Kavanagh, Charles C. Engel, Kayla M. Williams, and Amii M. Kress. 2016. *Assessing the Implications of Allowing Transgender Personnel to Serve Openly*. Santa Monica: RAND Corporation. https://www.rand.org/pubs/research_reports/RR1530.html.

Scheper Hughes, Jennifer. 2016. "Cradling the Sacred: Image, Ritual, and Affect in Mexican and Mesoamerican Material Religion." *History of Religions* 56 (1): 55–107.

Schneider, Arnd. 2004. "Rooting Hybridity: Globalisation and the Challenges of Mestizaje and Crisol de Razas for Contemporary Artists in Ecuador and Argentina." *Indiana*, no. 21, 95–112.

Schueller, Malini. 2005. "Analogy and (White) Feminist Theory: Thinking Race and the Color of the Cyborg Body." *Signs* 31 (1): 63–92.

Schuller, Kyla. 2018. *The Biopolitics of Feeling: Race, Sex, and Science in the Nineteenth Century*. Durham: Duke University Press.

Schultz, Brett A. H., Soldrea Roberts, Allison Rodgers, and Khalid Ataya. 2009. "Pregnancy in True Hermaphrodites and All Male Offspring to Date." *Obstetrics and Gynecology* 113 (2): 534–536 (part 2).

Scott, James C. 1985. *Weapons of the Weak: Everyday Forms of Peasant Resistance*. New Haven: Yale University Press.

Scott, James C. 1990. *Domination and the Arts of Resistance: Hidden Transcripts*. New Haven: Yale University Press.

Sealey, Kris F. 2020. *Creolizing the Nation*. Evanston: Northwestern University Press.

Sedgwick, Eve Kosofsky. 2008. *Epistemology of the Closet*. Berkeley: University of California Press.

Segato, Rita Laura. 2015. *La crítica de la colonialidad en ocho ensayos: Y una antropología por demanda*. Buenos Aires: Prometeo Libros.

Serano, Julia. 2007. *Whipping Girl: A Transsexual Woman on Sexism and the Scapegoating of Femininity*. Berkeley: Seal Press.

Serino, Andrea, Micaela Bassolino, Alessandro Farné, and Elisabetta Ládava. 2007. "Extended Multisensory Space in Blind Cane Users." *Psychological Science* 18 (7): 642–648.

Severi, Carlo. 1987. "The Invisible Path: Ritual Representation of Suffering in Cuna Traditional Thought." *RES: Anthropology and Aesthetics*, no. 14, 66–85.

Shock, Susy. 2011. *Poemario Trans Pirado*. Ciudad Autónoma de Buenos Aires, Argentina: Nuevos Tiempos.

Shumway, Nicolas. 1991. *The Invention of Argentina.* Berkeley: University of California Press.

Sigal, Pete, ed. 2003. *Infamous Desire: Male Homosexuality in Colonial Latin America.* Chicago: University of Chicago Press.

Silva, Joseli Maria. 2013. "Espaço Interdito e a Experiência Urbana Travesti." In *Geografias Malditas: Corpos, sexualidades e espaços,* edited by Joseli Maria Silva, Marcio Jose Ornat, and Alides Baptista Chimin Junior, 143–182. Ponta Grossa: Todapalavra Editora.

Silva, Joseli Maria, and Marcio Jose Ornat. 2014. "Intersectionality and Transnational Mobility between Brazil and Spain in Travesti Prostitution Networks." *Gender, Place, and Culture: A Journal of Feminist Geography* 21 (4): 1073–1088. http://dx.doi.org/10.1080/0966369X.2014.939148.

Silverblatt, Irene. 1983. "The Evolution of Witchcraft and the Meaning of Healing in Colonial Andean Society." *Culture, Medicine and Psychiatry* 7 (4): 413–427.

Silverblatt, Irene. 1987. *Moon, Sun, and Witches: Gender Ideologies and Class in Inca and Colonial Peru.* Princeton, NJ: Princeton University Press.

Singh, Jebaroja. 2018. *Spotted Goddesses: Dalit Women's Agency—Narratives on Caste and Gender Violence.* Zürich and Berlin: LIT Verlag Münster.

Sívori, Horacio. 2005. *Locas, chongos, y gays.* Buenos Aires: Antropofagia.

Slabodsky, Santiago. 2010. "Emmanuel Levinas's Geopolitics: Overlooked Conversations between Rabbinical and Third World Decolonialisms." *Journal of Jewish Thought and Philosophy* 18 (2): 147–165.

Smietniansky, Silvina. 2013. *Ritual, tiempo y poder: Una aproximación antropológica a las instituciones del gobierno colonial (Gobernación de Tucumán, siglos XVII y XVIII).* Rosario: Prohistoria.

Smith, Andrea. 2011. "Queer Theory and Native Studies: The Heteronormativity of Settler Colonialism." In *Queer Indigenous Studies,* edited by Qwo-Li Driskill, Chris Finley, Brian Joseph Gilley, and Scott Lauria Morgensen, 43–65. Tucson: University of Arizona Press.

Smith, David L. 2016. "Paradoxes of Dehumanization." *Social Theory and Practice* 42 (2): 416–443.

Smith, Linda Tuhiwai. 2012. *Decolonizing Methodologies: Research and Indigenous Peoples.* London: Zed Books.

Smithers, Gregory. 2014. "Cherokee 'Two Spirits': Gender, Ritual, and Spirituality in the Native South." *Early American Studies* 12 (3): 626–651.

Snorton, C. Riley. 2017. *Black on Both Sides: A Racial History of Trans Identity.* Minneapolis: University of Minnesota Press.

Snorton, C. Riley, and Jin Haritaworn. 2023. "Trans Necropolitics: A Transnational Reflection on Violence, Death, and the Trans of Color Afterlife." In *The Transgender Studies Reader Remix,* edited by Susan Stryker and Dylan McCarthy Blackston, 305–316. New York: Routledge.

Solá, Juan. 2016. *La Chaco.* Buenos Aires: Hojas del Sur.

Solomianski, Alejandro. 2003. *Identidades secretas: La negritud argentina.* Rosario: Beatriz Viterbo.

Sorenson, Travis. 2010. "Voseo to Tuteo Accommodation among Two Salvadoran Communities in the United States." PhD diss., Texas A&M University.

Soto, Sandra K. 2010. *Reading Chican@ Like a Queer: The De-mastery of Desire.* Austin: University of Texas Press.

Spelman, Elizabeth. 2019. "Trash Talks Back." In *Speaking Face-to-Face: The Visionary Philosophy of María Lugones,* edited by Pedro DiPietro, Jennifer McWeeny, and Shireen Roshanravan, 31–46. Albany: State University of New York Press.

Spillers, Hortense J. 1987. "Mama's Baby, Papa's Maybe: An American Grammar Book." *Diacritics* 17 (2): 64–81.

Spivak, Gayatri Chakravorty. 1985. "Three Women's Texts and a Critique of Imperialism." *Critical Inquiry* 12 (1): 243–261.

Stanish, Charles. 1989. "Household Archaeology: Testing Models of Zonal Complementarity in the South Central Andes." *American Anthropologist* 91 (1): 7–24.

Stepan, Nancy. 1991. *The Hour of Eugenics: Race, Gender, and Nation in Latin America.* Ithaca: Cornell University Press.

Stephen, Lynn. 2002. "Gender, Sexuality, and Same-Sex Desire in Latin America." *Latin American Perspectives* 29 (2): 41–59.

Sterling, M. D. 2010. *Babylon East: Performing Dancehall, Roots Reggae, and Rastafari in Japan.* Durham, NC: Duke University Press.

Stoler, Ann Laura. 2001. "Tense and Tender Ties: The Politics of Comparison in North American History and (Post)colonial Studies." *Journal of American History* 88 (3): 829–865.

Stone, Sandy. (1992). "The Empire Strikes Back: A Posttranssexual Manifesto." *Camera Obscura* 10 (2): 150–176.

Strongman, Roberto. 2019. *Queering Black Atlantic Religions: Transcorporeality in Candomblé, Santería, and Vodou.* Durham: Duke University Press.

Stryker, Susan. 2008. *Transgender History: The Roots of Today's Revolution.* Berkeley: Seal Press.

Stryker, Susan, Paisley Currah, and Lisa Jean Moore. 2008. "Trans-, Trans, or Transgender? The Stakes for Women's Studies." WSQ: *Women's Studies Quarterly* 36 (3–4): 11–22.

Sutton, Barbara. 2008. "Contesting Racism: Democratic Citizenship, Human Rights, and Anti-racist Politics in Argentina." *Latin American Perspectives* 35 (6): 106–121.

Sutton, Barbara. 2010. *Bodies in Crisis: Culture, Violence, and Women's Resistance in Neoliberal Argentina.* New Brunswick: Rutgers University Press.

Swarr, Amanda. 2023. *Envisioning African Intersex: Challenging Colonial and Racist Legacies in South African Medicine.* Durham: Duke University Press.

Talcott, Molly, and Dana Collins. 2012. "Building a Complex and Emancipatory Unity: Documenting Decolonial Feminist Interventions within the Occupy Movement." *Feminist Studies* 38 (2): 485–506.

Tauil, Juan. 2009. "Bizarra Noche y Día: Entrevista a Susy Shock." *Soy,* January 9.

Taussig, Michael T. 2010. *The Devil and Commodity Fetishism in South America.* Chapel Hill: University of North Carolina Press.

Taylor, Liza. 2022. "Coalition from the Inside Out: Struggling toward Coalitional Identity and Developing a Coalitional Consciousness with Lorde, Anzaldúa, Sandoval, and Pratt," in *Feminism in Coalition: Thinking with US Women of Color Feminism,* 106–149. Durham: Duke University Press.

Theumer, Emma. 2020. "The Self-Perceived Gender Identity." *Interventions* 22 (4): 498–513.

Thyrhaug, E., Tempelaar, R., Alcocer, M. J. P., et al. 2018. "Identification and Characterization of Diverse Coherences in the Fenna–Matthews–Olson Complex." *Nature Chemistry*, no. 10, 780–786.

Ticknor, George. [1891] 1965. *History of Spanish Literature*. 3 vols. 6th ed. New York: Gordian.

Torres-Saillant, Silvio. 2012. "El anti-haitianismo como ideología occidental." *Cuadernos Inter.c.a.Mbio sobre Centroamérica y El Caribe* 9 (10): 15–48.

Tricola, J Mackenzie. 2011. "The Voseo in Comunication Media, Cinema and Literature in Guatemala." Master's thesis, Colorado State University.

Tucker, Joshua. 2011. "Permitted Indians and Popular Music in Contemporary Peru: The Poetics and Politics of Indigenous Performativity." *Ethnomusicology* 55 (3): 387–413.

Tuhkanen, Mikko. 2008. "Queer Guerrillas: On Richard Wright's and Frantz Fanon's Dissembling Revolutionaries." *Mississippi Quarterly* 61 (4): 615–642.

Tzul Tzul, Gladys. 2018. "Rebuilding Communal Life: Ixil Women and the Desire for Life in Guatemala." *NACLA Report on the Americas* 50 (4): 404–407.

Valdés, Gonzalo Fernández de Oviedo. 1959. *Historia general y natural de las Indias*. Madrid: Ediciones Atlas.

Valencia, Sayak, and Liliana Falcón. 2021. "From Gore Capitalism to Snuff Politics: Necropolitics in the USA-Mexican Border." In *Necropower in North America: The Legal Spatialization of Disposability and Lucrative Death*, edited by Ariadna Estévez, 35–59. Cham: Springer Nature Switzerland AG.

Valentine, D. 2007. *Imagining Transgender: An Ethnography of a Category*. Durham: Duke University Press.

Van Gorder, Bryan. 2014. "Do Cry For Me Argentina." *Out Traveler Online*, January 3. https://www.advocate.com/pride/2014/01/03/do-cry-me-argentina.

Vargas, Deborah R. 2012. *Dissonant Divas in Chicana Music: The Limits of La Onda*. Minneapolis: University of Minnesota Press.

Vargas, Pablo, and David Aruquipa Pérez, eds. 2013. *Reflexiones sobre diversidades sexuales y de género en comunidades indígenas de Bolivia*. La Paz: Diakonia.

Velásquez Runk, Jeremy. 2009. "Social and River Networks for the Trees: Wounaan's Riverine Rhizomic Cosmos and Arboreal Conservation." *American Anthropologist* 111 (4): 456–467.

Veronelli, Gabriela A. 2015. "The Coloniality of Language: Race, Expressivity, Power, and the Darker Side of Modernity." *Wagadu: A Journal of Transnational Women's and Gender Studies*, no. 13, 108–134.

Vieira Cherro, Mariana. 2011. "Que se enteren: Cuerpo y sexualidad en el zoom social; Sobre XXY." *Revista Estudios Feministas* 19 (2): 647–656.

Viveros Vigoya, Mara. 2016. "La interseccionalidad: Una aproximación situada a la dominación." *Debate Feminista*, no. 52, 1–17.

Vizenor, Gerald. 2009. *Natural Liberty: Natural Reason and Cultural Survivance*. Lincoln: University of Nebraska Press.

von Vacano, Diego. 2012. "Las Casas and the Birth of Race." *History of Political Thought* 33 (3): 401–426.

Wagley, Charles. 1965. "On the Concept of Social Race in the Americas." In *Contemporary Cultures and Societies of Latin America*, edited by Dwight Heath, 531–545. New York: Random House.

Walsh, Catherine E. 2022. *Rising Up, Living On: Re-existences, Sowings, and Decolonial Cracks*. Durham: Duke University Press.

Ward, Jane, and Beth Schneider. 2009. "The Reaches of Heteronormativity: An Introduction." *Gender and Society* 23 (4): 433–439.

Warner, Michael. 2005. *Publics and Counterpublics*. Brooklyn: Zone Books.

Wayar, Marlene. 2012. "¿Qué pasó con la T?" *Página 12*. Accessed March 11, 2022. https://www.pagina12.com.ar/diario/suplementos/soy/1–2436–2012–05–11.html.

Wayar, Marlene. 2018a. "Soy un gerundio: No sé qué soy, sí que estoy siendo travesti." *Tiempo Argentino*, September 20. https://www.tiempoar.com.ar/informacion-general/marlene-wayar-soy-un-gerundio-no-se-que-soy-si-que-estoy-siendo-travesti/.

Wayar, Marlene. 2018b. *Travesti: Una teoría lo suficientemente buena*. Buenos Aires: Editorial Muchas Nueces.

Weheliye, Alexander Ghedi. 2014. *Habeas Viscus: Racializing Assemblages, Biopolitics, and Black Feminist Theories of the Human*. Durham: Duke University Press.

Wekker, Gloria. 2006. *The Politics of Passion: Women's Sexual Culture in the Afro-Surinamese Diaspora*. New York, NY: Columbia University Press.

White, George, Jr. 2012. "'I Am Teaching Some of the Boys': Chaplain Robert Boston Dokes and Army Testing of Black Soldiers in World War II." *Journal of Negro Education* 81 (3): 200–217.

Wiesner-Hanks, M. 2012. "Sexual Identity and Other Aspects of 'Modern' Sexuality: New Chronologies, Same Old Problem?" In *After the History of Sexuality: German Genealogies with and beyond Foucault*, edited by S. Spector, H. Puff, and D. Herzog, 31–42. New York: Berghahn Books.

Willett, Cynthia. 2014. *Interspecies Ethics*. New York: Columbia University Press.

Witt, Charlotte. 2011. *The Metaphysics of Gender*. Oxford: Oxford University Press.

Wittig, Monique. 1992. *The Straight Mind, and Other Essays*. Boston: Beacon Press.

Wynter, Sylvia. 2003. "Unsettling the Coloniality of Being/Power/Truth/Freedom: Toward the Human, after Man, Its Overrepresentation—an Argument." *CR: The New Centennial Review* 3 (3): 257–337.

Wynter, Sylvia. 2006. "On How We Mistook the Map for the Territory, and Reimprisoned Ourselves in Our Unbearable Wrongness of Being, of Desêtre: Black Studies toward the Human Project." In *A Companion to African-American Studies*, edited by Jane Anna Gordon and Lewis Gordon, 107–118. Malden, MA: Wiley-Blackwell.

Yarbro-Bejarano, Yvonne. 2001. *The Wounded Heart: Writing on Cherríe Moraga*. Austin: University of Texas Press.

Ybarra-Frausto, Tomás. 1991a. "Rasquachismo: A Chicano Sensibility." In *Chicano Art: Resistance and Affirmation, 1965–1985*, edited by Richard Griswold del Castillo, Teresa McKenna, and Yvonne Yarbro-Bejarano, 155–162. Los Angeles: Wight Art Gallery and University of California Press.

Ybarra-Frausto, Tomás. 1991b. "The Chicano Movement / The Movement of Chicano Art." In *Exhibiting Cultures: The Poetics and Politics of Museum Display*, edited by Ivan Karp and Steven Lavine, 128–150. Washington, DC: Smithsonian Institution.

Yeakel, John A. 1983. "The Accountant-Historians of the Incas." *Accounting Historians Journal* 10 (2): 39–51.

Zambrana, Rocío. 2021. *Colonial Debts: The Case of Puerto Rico*. Durham: Duke University Press.

Zamora, Margarita. 1993. *Reading Columbus*. Berkeley: University of California Press.

Zaytoun, Kelli D. 2015. "'Now Let Us Shift' the Subject: Tracing the Path and Posthumanist Implications of La Naguala / The Shapeshifter in the Works of Gloria Anzaldúa." *MELUS: Multi-ethnic Literature of the United States* 40 (4): 69–88.

Zaytoun, Kelli D. 2016. "Resistance as Shapeshifter: A Posthumanist Reading of Subjectivity and Death in the Fiction of Gloria Anzaldúa and Clarice Lispector." *Contemporary Women's Writing* 10 (3): 394–416.

Zaytoun, Kelli D. 2022. *Shapeshifting Subjects: Gloria Anzaldúa's Naguala and Border Arte*. Chicago: University of Illinois Press.

Zuidema, R. Tom. 1989. "The Moieties of Cuzco." In *The Attraction of Opposites: Thought and Society in the Dualistic Mode*, edited by David Maybury Lewis and Uri Almagor, 255–275. Ann Arbor: University of Michigan Press.

Zuidema, R. Tom. 1990. *Inca Civilization in Cuzco*. Austin: University of Texas Press.

Zurn, Perry, Andrea Pitts, Talia Mae Bettcher, and PJ DiPietro. 2024. *Trans Philosophy*. Minneapolis: University of Minnesota Press.

Index